Northern Baltimore County
Maryland
Pioneers

The Land and Their Descendants

The Weisburg Inn

Wayne Carroll McGinnis

HERITAGE BOOKS
2008

HERITAGE BOOKS
AN IMPRINT OF HERITAGE BOOKS, INC.

Books, CDs, and more—Worldwide

For our listing of thousands of titles see our website
at
www.HeritageBooks.com

Published 2008 by
HERITAGE BOOKS, INC.
Publishing Division
100 Railroad Ave. #104
Westminster, Maryland 21157

Copyright © 2006 Wayne Carroll McGinnis

All rights reserved. No part of this book may be reproduced or transmitted in any form or by any means, electronic or mechanical, including photocopying, recording or by any information storage and retrieval system without written permission from the author, except for the inclusion of brief quotations in a review.

International Standard Book Numbers
Paperbound: 978-0-7884-4277-3
Clothbound: 978-0-7884-7466-8

Table of Contents

Introduction 1
Wiseburg Inn 2
Fifth, Sixth, Seventh and Tenth Districts 3
Early History and Political Subdivisions 4
Early Families Along the Chesapeak Bay 5
Seventh District 7
Early Roads 11
 Communties Covered- Shane to Hereford 12
John Almony - James Almony Home on White Hall Road 24
Outline Descendant Tree of John Almony 25
John Almony Farm 28
Joseph Sutton, Robert Kirkwood, Jacob Daily 29
Outline Descendant Tree of Joseph Sutton 31
Outline Descendant Tree of William Kirkwood 33
Outline Descendant Tree of Jacob Dailey 35
Benjamin Shipley, Thomas Meredith 36
Outline Descendant Tree of Benjamin Shipley 37
Outline Descendant Tree of Thomas Meredith 38
Outline Descendant Tree of Arthur Shane 39
Talbott Hall -arial view 40
Ezekiel Slade, Slade- McGinnis Home Graystone Road 41
Outline Descendant Tree of Ezekiel Slade 42
Outline Descendant Tree of John Wilson 44
Joshua Anderson 46
Outline Descendant Tree of Joshua Anderson 47
Outline Descendant Tree of John Bell 49
Outline Descendant Tree of Josias Grover 51
Josias Grover - John Bell farm 52
Thomas Rutledge, Edward Bond, Samuel Bond, Isaac Sampson, John Krout 53
Outline Descendant Tree of Thomas Rutledge 55
Outline Descendant Tree of Edward Bond 57
Outline Descendant Tree of Luke Gorsuch Ensor 58
Edward Bond Land 60
Outline Descendant Tree of Samuel James Bond 61
Outline Descendant Tree of George Bond 63
Outline Descendant Tree of Isaac Sampson 65
Outline Descendant Tree of John Michael Krout 66
David Gorsuch, Thomas Pearce, Francis Sparks Ezekiel Bosley 69
New Market Families House Survey 70
Outline Descendant Tree of David Gorsuch 71
Outline Descendant Tree of Thomas Pearce 73
Outline Descendant Tree of Ezekiel Bosley 77
Outline Descendant Tree of Aquilla McDonald 79
Outline Descendant Tree of Josiah Sparks 81
Outline Descendant Tree of Adam Miller Hendrix 83
Outline Descendant Tree of Shadrach Green 85
Outline Descendant Tree of Blois Wright 88
Outline Descendant Tree of Edward Matthews 91
1850 Residents 93
John Lawson, Thomas Hunt, Samuel Morris, Vincent Standiford 94
Outline Descendant Tree of Thomas Hunt 95
Outline Descendant Tree of John Samuel Morris 97
Outline Descendant Tree of Vincent Standiford 98
Outline Descendant Tree of Jesse Pocock 100

Outline Descendant Tree of Thomas Wilson	102
James Calder, Hugh Cameron, Daniel Walker	103
Calder Farm - Parkton	104
Outline Descendant Tree of Capt James Calder	105
Outline Descendant Tree of Hugh Cameron	106
Outline Descendant Tree of Daniel Walker	108
Christian Stabler, John Rosier, James Tracey, Walter Perdue, Luke Ensor	109
Outline Descendant Tree of Christian Stabler	110
Outline Descendant Tree of Isaac Turnbaugh	112
Outline Descendant Tree of John Rosier	113
Outline Descendant Tree of James H. Tracey	115
Outline Descendant Tree of Luke Ensor	117
Outline Descendant Tree of Walter Perdue	118
Robert Gillis, Isaac Bull, Adam Burns, Robert Nelson, William Pearce	120
White Hall Milk Producers and White Hall Baseball Team	121
Outline Descendant Tree of Isaac Bull	122
Outline Descendant Tree of Adam Burns	123
Outline Descendant Tree of Robert Gillis	124
Outline Descendant Tree of Robert Nelson	125
Outline Descendant Tree of William Pearce	127
Descendants of Early Families in White Hall Area	132
Joseph Norris, Edward Parrish, William Johnson, Abraham Royston, McClung	133
Outline Descendant Tree of Joseph Norris	134
Outline Descendant Tree of George Chalk Norris	136
Outline Descendant Tree of Edward Parrish	137
Outline Descendant Tree of Abraham (Riston) Royston	139
Outline Descendant Tree of Robert McClung	140
McClung Descendants 1917 Gettysburg	143
Thomas Ayres, George Elliott, John Garrett, George Lytle	144
Outline Descendant Tree of Thomas Ayres	145
Outline Descendant Tree of George Elliott	147
Outline Descendant Tree of John Garrett	152
Outline Descendant Tree of Daniel Shaw	153
Outline Descendant Tree of George Lytle	154
Hutchins, Shepperd, Wyle, McComas	157
Outline Descendant Tree of William Carlin	158
Outline Descendant Tree of William Curtis	159
Outline Descendant Tree of Lt Richard Hutchins	161
Outline Descendant Tree of Josiah Shepperd	163
Outline Descendant Tree of Luke Wyle	164
Jonathon Plowman, Moses Collett, Gist Vaughn, William Hunter	166
Outline Descendant Tree of Jonathon Plowman	167
Outline Descendant Tree of Gist Vaughn	168
Outline Descendant Tree of Moses Collett	169
Outline Descendant Tree of William Hunter	170
Hereford Farm House- John Merryman, John Foster, John Mays, John Miller	171
Outline Descendant Tree of John Merryman	172
Outline Descendant Tree of John Foster	175
Outline Descendant Tree of John Mays	177
Outline Descendant Tree of Nehemiah Hicks	179
Outline Descendant Tree of John Miller	181
Resources	182
McGinnis Family and Talbott Hall Home Site	186
1927 Photo of Tydings M. McGinnis Family	187
Outline Descendant Tree of Tydings Miller McGinnis	188
Conclusion	189
Index	190

INTRODUCTION

This Pioneers project is an effort to identify the original settlers of the Seventh Election District area and follow their descendants for three generations. The area covered is roughly from the Harford County line on the Old York Road, to Maryland Line, west on Freeland Road (just west of the Railroad), south to Parkton, following the river to White Hall, over to Hereford and then back to the Harford County Line on Troyer Road. Many of the first pioneers were of English descent, born in the Tenth District, which lies just south of the Seventh District and had family members still living in that area. Succeeding generations became increasingly interrelated through marriage, due to the limited transportation and lack of contact with outside influences. These relationships explain how the many properties were divided and passed from one generation to the next. There will be some extension into neighboring areas as the concentric rings of family always extend outward.

An effort was made to collect as many family histories as possible for this project, but there is never enough time to cover everyone in this area. There will be some unintentional errors, which will be missed by the people helping with this project. Often we see differences in dates and spelling of the same names from one family Bible to another and census information often varies from one decade to the next. We hope this project will stimulate interest in family histories and we invite additions and corrections to be included in any follow-up editions. I am sure there is much more information to be discovered, currently held by many descendants, that would be of interest to readers. I encourage those interested in sharing their information, to contact the contributing researchers.

Many local people interested in family history contributed to this effort. Margaret Almony Cameron has collected family history that extends to the first John Almony, his descendants and many other pioneer ancestors from Parkton, White Hall, Shane and Maryland Line. Anna Lee Kirkwood Smith of Harford County, who helped with some of my early data, has also spent a lifetime researching the area and is descendant from many original families. John Homer Pearce of My Lady's Manor, now deceased, was a tireless researcher who willing shared his findings with others. Evelyn Best, now deceased, of White Hall Road, was a John Moore descendant, who collected history of the White Hall area. Dale Bond, of Michigan, has made numerous trips to Maryland to research the Bond, Gorsuch, Krout, Sampson and Rutledge families that lived around Maryland Line. Jerry Martin has done a tremendous amount of research on Northern Baltimore County with a strong focus on the Fifth and Sixth District areas. Many researchers have worked on family history in these areas and shared freely with their time and findings over the years. The amount of time and expense that has gone into these efforts could not even be estimated. We owe them a tremendous debt for their contributions. The help of George Horvath of the "Old Map Shop" and Robert Wilkinson who have used their mapping expertise to display the original grants on a map of the district has been especially valuable.
I also owe a special thanks to my wife, Harriet, and family for allowing me time to work on this project.

Wayne C. McGinnis 2005

WISEBURG INN

THE WEISBURG INN

The Wiseburg Inn was the center of political, social and traveler's accommodations for the Seventh district in the nineteenth century. The Inn was located along the turnpike between Towson, Maryland and York, Pennsylvania. General Lafayette was reported to have been a guest here at a dance in his honor, during his grand tour of the new nation. The community of Wiseburg was named after John Wise or Weis from the German spelling. He was an early settler who also started the Paper Mill in White Hall. The Hunter family operated a tavern here for many years. Pleasant Hunter was a Sheriff, County Council member and Delegate to the Maryland General Assembly.

The original log kitchen, built before 1800, is located in the back of the house while stables to house the horses is located across the road. Marion Runkles has owned the house for many years and carefully restored much of the original Inn.

Baltimore County Pioneers- 7th District

FIFTH, SIXTH, SEVENTH AND TENTH DISTRICTS

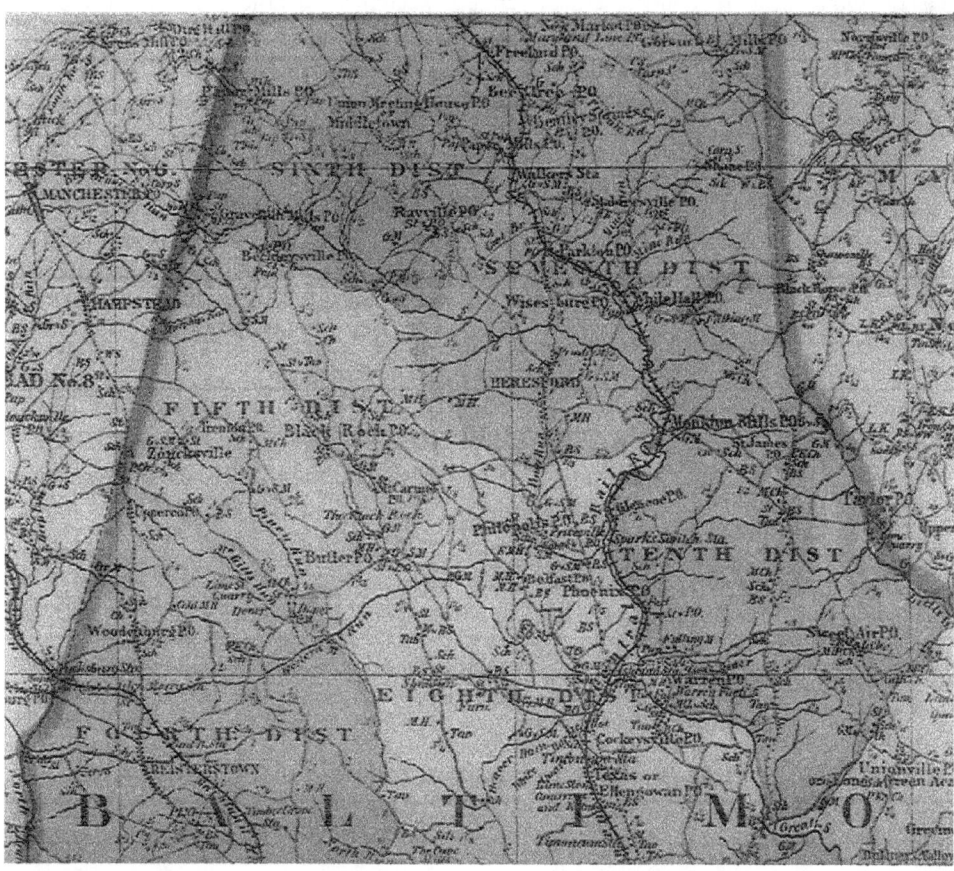

Early map shows various communities in Northern Baltimore County, including post offices, mills, schools, churches, water courses, main roads, blacksmith shops and other shops.

EARLY HISTORY AND POLITICAL SUBDIVISIONS

Maryland's settlement began at St. Clement's in Southern Maryland, when a group of new settlers arrived from England in 1634. The early expansion concentrated in Southern Maryland along the many navigable waterways and gradually spread northward. New immigrants often received grants of land for each person they brought to the new colony. Early arriving families, such as the Dorsey, Shipley and Richardson families, accumulated large tracts of land along the Severn River in Northern Anne Arundel County. They later sold parcels to new arrivals and bought additional lands further inland. While families from Calvert and St. Mary's generally moved westward toward the Prince George's and Montgomery County area, others in Anne Arundel County moved north toward the area around the Gunpowder Falls. In 1661, John Taylor received a 250-acre grant called Taylor's Mount, which was located between Bird River and Gunpowder Falls. Col. Thomas Richardson owned an 800-acre tract called "Richardson's Outlet" bounded by the Gunpowder Falls and the Philadelphia Road in 1686.

A flood of new arrivals soon followed the first settlers from England and the land along the shores was quickly filled. Tobacco and wood products undoubtedly were export items. Officials soon recognized a need to divide the land into subdivisions.

These political subdivisions of the County were described in "Hundreds". This was equivalent to one hundred families living in an area. Spesutia, Gunpowder and Patapsco were the first subdivisions. By 1774 the county contained seventeen Hundreds. By the 1790's new roads and a growing population had necessitated new divisions. The Constable was the chief officer in the old Hundreds and now new officials were needed to administer civil affairs. In 1798 Baltimore County was divided into seven election districts outside the city. Commissioners were appointed to establish boundaries and set polling places. The northern most area was the fifth district. By 1850 the area was the second district and changed again in 1860 to the seventh district. These changes can cause some confusion in searching the census during this period.

Map of Hundreds

Baltimore County Hundreds 1783

EARLY FAMILIES NEAR THE CHESAPEAKE BAY

We find the names Bond, Bosley, Buck, Bull, Cole, Collett, Ensor, Elliott, Foster, Gorsuch, Hunt, Matthews, Mays, Meredith, Merryman, Parrish, Pearce, Richardson, Rockhold, Rutledge, Slade, Standiford, Sampson, Wright and others among the early English landowners along the shore. Descendants of these families gradually moved north and west, away from the shore in each succeeding generation as they searched for more land for their growing numbers. Many of these original families came from Somerset County in Southwestern England. Towns along England's western coast carried on an early tobacco trade with Virginia and Maryland.

In the 1600s, Baltimore County consisted of a vast stretch of land covering what is now Baltimore City, Baltimore, Harford and Cecil Counties as well as parts of Carroll, Anne Arundel, Howard and Kent Counties. Formal boundaries were first mentioned when Cecil County was formed out of Baltimore County in 1674. Howard followed in 1726 and Harford in 1773. Baltimore City completed its separation in 1854. Land records after this time are found in Towson, while earlier records are in Baltimore or Annapolis.

The families that first settled along the bay and its tributaries moved in a northwesterly direction in succeeding generations to acquire land in the Gunpowder Upper, the Middle River Upper and later to Mine Run and North Hundreds. New land was acquired for speculation or for younger family members and often changed owners several times before actual settlement. Many land owners continued to live in Anne Arundel County after purchasing land in Baltimore County.

In 1652 the white settlers signed a treaty with the Susquehannough Indians, but violence was still reported up to about 1662. In 1663, the Seneca Indians, began a campaign against the white settlers and the Susquehannough Indians. As a result of these hostilities, the settlers asked for additional protection from the authorities. Initially, forts were erected in the lower part of the county at fifteen-mile intervals to protect the settlers from Indian attacks. Rangers were assigned to man these forts to help prevent conflict between the various tribes and settlers. Col. Thomas Richardson was a Chief Ranger near the Gunpowder River for a period of time. The Susuehannough, Seneca and later Shawnee tribes were active in the county until the late 1600's.

A vast area near the Pennsylvania line, was known as the "Barrens". The name resulted from a practice by the Susuehannough tribe to burn areas of the forest. The new growth attracted game and thus improved hunting in these areas. When settlers first saw the area, they thought the land must be poor or barren because of the lack of trees. The York Road was laid out following a Susquehanna Indian trail leading from the bay to northern Indian settlements and was thus known as the Susquehanna Trail until recently. Conflicts with the Shawnee, Delaware and Susquehannough tribes continued to about 1700 when settlers began moving further north. By 1715, hundreds of thousands of acres of land were unpatented and still available.

King Charles 1 of England, Lord Baltimore and his heirs, were given all the land in the colony with power to dispose of the land in any manner they deemed fit. Early land grants were made under Lord Baltimore's supervision, but later were administered by the Western Land Office. While the land described as a "grant from the King of England" was true, the grants were not that difficult to receive. In order to obtain a land grant, the settler paid the purchase price and received a warrant that directed a surveyor to survey a certain number of acres that had not been cultivated or developed. After establishing the boundaries, a certificate of survey was needed to have a patent issued. Since additional fees were required at each step, and the warrants prevented others from claiming the land described, many delayed the final step to receive a patent. The two dates shown on some maps indicated the survey and final patent dates. The earlier leases issued, were titles to the land although not a fee simple ownership. Quitrents were yearly taxes or rents that had to be paid to Lord Baltimore. R.Carlton Seitz, in his book of 'Maps of Land Patents', describes this process in greater detail.

Lord Baltimore retained many tracts of land for his own use. The most famous land grant was My Lady's Manor, a grant of 10,000 acres from Charles Calvert, the third Lord Baltimore to his fourth wife Margaret Carlton. At her death, the land went to Charlotte Brerewood, her step-granddaughter. She in turn, assigned it to her father-in-law, Thomas Brerewood. Thomas divided the estate into smaller farms and rented them to farmers. Charlotte Town, named after Charlotte Brerewood, later became Monkton. Some of these leases were for one hundred years or three lives. Long-term leases are still used in England, Scotland and Ireland today.

Strong ties exist between the "Manor" area of the Tenth District and the Seventh Election District located just to the north. Many families that established first in the Tenth Election District, or Mine Run Hundred, were often the first purchasers of land in the newly opened seventh.

Several families that later settled in the Sparks and Fifth District areas, first owned land in Back River Lower and Patapsco Lower which would be in Baltimore City today. Darby Ensor held land east of Jones Falls, John Cole owned "Cole Harbor", Teague Tracey owned "Tracey's Park" in Towson, and William Pearce owned "Molly's Industry", where the old Hutzler's store stood. Mordecai Price also bought land in Towson.

In 1773 and again in 1783 after the close of the Revolutionary War, a census was recorded of those living in Baltimore County. Mine Run Hundred covered those living in the current Tenth and Seventh Districts. This census listed the head of the family and any servants or slaves. The first census taken after the close of the Revolutionary War was in 1783. A Federal Census was taken each decade after 1790. Between 1790 and 1840, only the head of household was named and age groups were used to count children and woman. In 1850, the entire household was listed along with their ages. Information about place of birth, relationship to head of house, occupation and education were added in succeeding years. In 1798, a "Particular Assessment List" was compiled, giving dimensions of dwellings, outbuildings, and land as of the first of October in that year. References were often made as to what other persons were next to the property. A book by George J. Horvath, titled 'The Particular Assessment List for Baltimore and Carroll Counties' contains this information.

SEVENTH DISTRICT

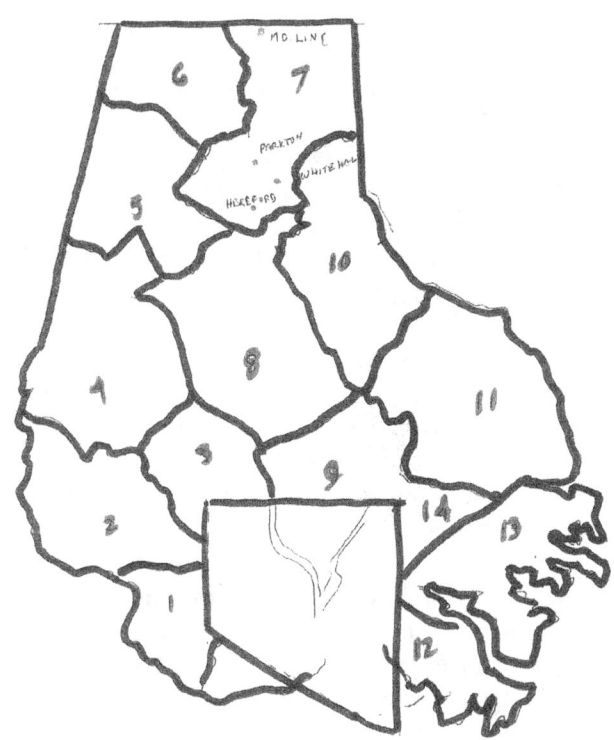

John Norris leased several parcels of land in the Vernon- Stablersville area as early as 1743. John Almony held leases along present day Garrett Road in 1750 and James Calder first leased land near present day Parkton in the same year. These early leases were obtained from the King of England or his representative. After 1782, all crown lands were confiscated and put under the direction of the Western Reserve Land Office for the State of Maryland. Public auctions were held at various sites to sell the land to the highest bidder. Persons holding earlier leases, had to bid against others to retain the land they lived on and had farmed for many years. One document, referring to a court case between Edward Johnson and John Norris, stated that leases holders were given some consideration but did not specify how this was done. Wealthy citizens, such as Doctor Johnson of Baltimore and Jonathan Plowman, were able to buy large tracts of land at these sales. A committee to evaluate Baltimore County confiscated proprietary reserve lands was appointed to appraise the lands held in the reserve. These members set a value on the different properties, which they later patented along both the "York" and "Old York Road". We do not know how these members were selected, but most became owners of the best farms.

The situation was much different in the more settled areas. In 1785, on My Lady's Manor, an auction was held at Slade's Tavern to sell the lands owned by Thomas Brerewood. Since these lands were considered British property, current leaseholders were required to buy their lands or lose them. Officers from the war were in a better position to bid on the land because they had received extra pay for their war service. These monies allowed them to be able to buy additional land, which they could then resell back to the leaseholders for a profit.

By 1800, most of the parcels of the "Reserve Lands" were surveyed and patented. James Calder, a surveyor, accumulated over 3,000 acres above Parkton along the present York Road. In 1792, Doctor Edward Johnson, of Baltimore, purchased a large block of land covering 2560 acres called "Mount Joy". This tract covered much of the land around the Gunpowder watershed between Parkton and Monkton. His heir, Jonathan Plowman, began selling off smaller parcels to later settlers. "Curfman Stradt", covering 857 acres, was located next to the Calder tract. John Almony patented "Nottinghamshire" covering 800 acres, Joshua Anderson's 829 acres "Anderson's Retreat and David Gorsuch's 689 acre "Goshen" were large properties in the eastern part of the district. Sutton's delight covered 685 acres near Shane next to Thomas's Folly of 628 acres for Thomas Meredith. Thomas Gist Jr. purchased a large 560-acre tract called "Deer Park Completed" in 1787. Jesse Jarrett, from Harford County, had purchased 427 acres of Jarrett's Intention in 1793. Further out Middletown Road, Elisha Dorsey purchased "Dorsey's Plains Reserved" covering 655 acres. In the Norrisville area the Norris family patented "Salisbury Plains" covering over 2,000 acres.

The early settlements were small, maybe clearing ten acres to make room for a garden, hay field, small orchard and pasture for a cow and horses. The buildings usually consisted of a one or two room log house, a spring house, meat house and small barn. The 1798 tax assessment describes the dimensions of the buildings, the acres of the property, the nearest landowners and the value of the holdings. Water powered grist mills were built along the many streams to grind the wheat into flour and some to saw boards for new buildings. In the White Hall area, the Wiley Mill was later known as Hunter Mill and the Stabler family ran a mill in the meadow below the Stablersville Road. Steven Gorsuch had a mill in Gorsuch Mills and Roser's Mill in Parkton operated well into the 1900's. Cameron Mill was of course located just west of Parkton on Dairy Road and the Fosters had a mill on the Little Gunpowder near Hereford. Supplies, that were not made or grown locally, were undoubtedly bought from the more settled areas. Farmers would take their products from the farm by wagon and trade them for other supplies needed.

Major roads, often following earlier Indian trails, were improved by widening and farmers helped maintain them by using field stones to fill holes. The Old York Road, from Towson, passed through the Manor area and crossed into Pennsylvania at Wiley's Station. This road was surveyed in about 1807. Markers were established along the route and taverns and watercourses were identified. Slade's Tavern and Blue Rocks Tavern at Shawsville were along this route. The "New" York Road followed the Susquehanna Trail, which was laid out and improved with bridges by a Turnpike Company. Tolls were charged and tollgates were placed along the road. The Wiseburg Inn became a center for political activity in the Seventh District. Maryland Line, then called New Market, had a tollhouse and hotel also.

Religious services were started in the farm homes. Soon the residents contributed money and labor to build small churches in each community. The first families either educated their own children or hired teachers to work with families in the neighborhood. The children were taught reading, writing, and memorizing multiplication tables so as to carry on basic accounting skills. Not every one was allowed the privilege of a formal education as we can see by the number of landowners or their wives who signed documents with a mark. Sometimes, children of wealthier families were sent to boarding schools for the winter. The Milton Academy, in Sparks, was a famous such school. By 1850, small one-room log buildings were built in the various communities and the County paid teachers for these students. The teachers were usually from the farm families and often did not have an advanced education as we would expect today. Tests were given prospective teachers to qualify them for the work. The students would walk to these schools and usually only attended in the winter when the farm work was lightened.

Local officials administered civil affairs, such as settling disputes and recording deeds. These officials were often respected farmers. We find familiar names like Joseph Sutton, William Anderson, Benjamin Sutton, Jesse Pocock, John Garrett, James Turner, Mordecai Parrish, Thomas Kauffman, Henry Wiers, Thomas Rutledge, William Johnson and others carrying out these duties.

Turnpikes became a reality in 1804 with the incorporation of private turnpike companies. The York Turnpike Company employed contractors to widen the existing road and build bridges. Tollgates were built at intervals to collect revenue to repay investors. Farmer William Ensor paid $95 in tolls one year to use a mile and half part of the road to go to the Parkton station on the railroad. A toll gate was in place toward the north end of New Market also.

The North Central Railroad was built in the 1830's along the Little Gunpowder River heading north through White Hall, Parkton, Freeland and on to York. This improvement in transportation had the biggest effect on life in the Seventh District. Travel time to Baltimore was reduced to hours instead of days and farm products could now move more easily to ready customers in the more populated areas. They needed oats, hay and straw for their horses, as well as wood, leather, meat and vegetables. Supplies brought from Baltimore included candles, sugar, molasses, cloth and hardware. White Hall had facilities to handle livestock to ship to slaughterhouses in Baltimore and to receive lime and machinery from distant places. There was a mill to grind flour and grind feed. Parkton had a hotel, bank, school, store, churches and a farm supply center. Small stores were opened either in houses or taverns in each community to supply the farm families. Blacksmiths, shoe makers, tanners, butchers, doctors, teachers and carpenters soon opened for business. Often, the children of the farm families filled these new professions. The pioneers originally had performed these tasks with help from family and neighbors. As more land was cleared and the size of the families increased, many of these tasked were increasingly performed by full time specialist.

During the 1700's, settlement was also moving west from Philadelphia and New Castle along the Maryland- Pennsylvania border. While William Penn held title to lands to the North of Maryland, the land located along this border was much in dispute until settled with a survey by

Mason and Dixon in 1763. German and Scotch-Irish descendants were among this group. The Scotch-Irish families settled in Northern Harford County and Eastern York County with the Germans settling in the area of Shrewsbury and South-Western York County. The Armacost, Fowble, Hoffman, Wilhelm, Shaffer, Rosier, Stabler, Wise, Whitcraft and Wineholt families were among those originating from Germany. Burns, Cameron, Wiley, Ayres, Shaw, McDonald, Harris, Morris, Nelson, Shepperd, Wilson, Gemmill, Jordan, Kirkwood, McGinnis and Bell families are among the descendants of the Scotch-Irish. .

On the "Manor" we find names of future Seventh District residents such as Anderson, Bond, Elliott, Pearce, Shaw, Slade, Standiford, Sampson, Nelson, Rutledge, Hunt, Sparks, Perdue, Pocock and Wiley.

At the close of the Revolutionary War in 1783, vast areas in the northern part of Baltimore County were unsettled. A few scattered leases, by John Almony, John Norris and James Calder, were held, with some as early as 1740. Most of the lands located in the present sixth and seventh election districts were held in the "reserve" and were the most northern and last parts of the county to be surveyed and settled. Settlement that started in the early 1650s along the shores of the Chesapeake Bay, had finally reached the Pennsylvania boarder. Mine Run Hundred covered the present Seventh and Tenth Election districts.

EARLY ROADS LEADING TO PENNSYLVANIA

There were several "York Roads" in the nineteenth century. The "Old' York Road, (now Route 439), originally was a road leading to York, Pennsylvania from Harford County. The Seventh District section runs from the "Susquehanna Trail" at New Market, (Maryland Line), to Blue Rocks, (Shawsville) in Harford County formerly owned by the Gilbert family. Next, the road went to Black Horse and through the tenth district on to Towson. John Almony, Abraham Slade, Edward Bond, Joshua Anderson, Joseph Sutton and Thomas Meredith held large tracts of land along this road. Succeeding generations, divided these large holdings into smaller farms to support the growing families.

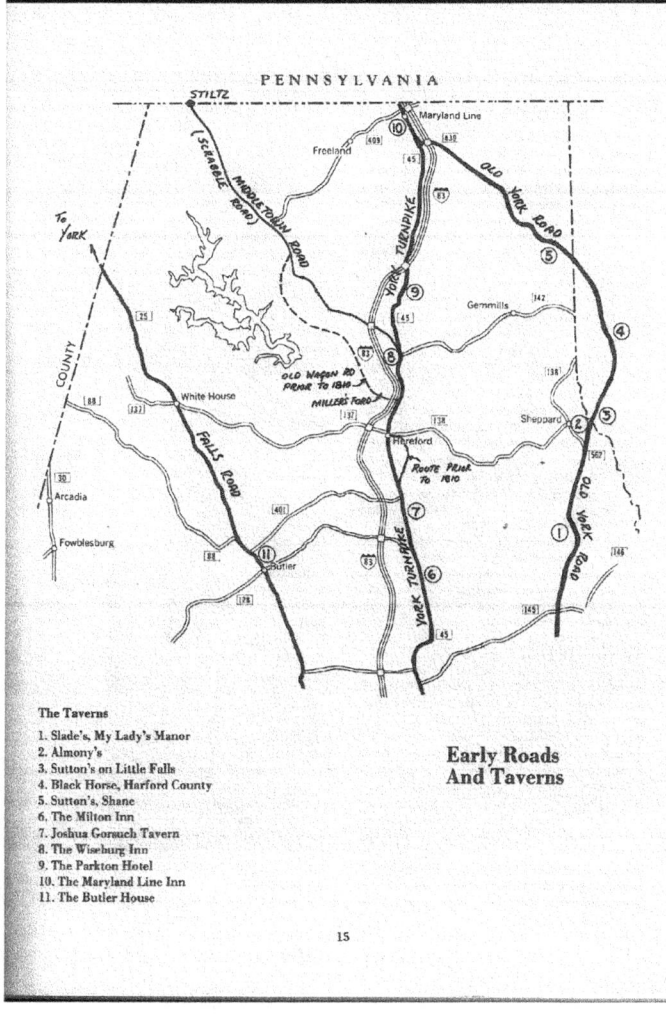

Drawing from Andy Clemens

COMMUNITIES COVERED

Shane

The community of **Shane** was named after Arthur Shane, who operated the store and post office on the corner of the Old York Road and Graystone Road. The original tavern at this location, was operated by the Joseph Sutton family. The Sutton family owned a 685 acre tract known as "Sutton's Delight", which included the town and land to the East. Local tradition maintains that George Washington stayed here before his well known breakfast at Slade's Tavern on the Manor. Early documents record that he traveled ten miles before breakfast and the distance would place him at Sutton's. A cannon ball, used to toss as a game, was reported to have been lost and found on the Birmingham property years later.

Various store keepers operated a general store on this location including James McCullough and his son Clyde, in the 1950's.

Early settlers in the area were: John Almony, Luther Birmingham, Jacob Dailey, Robert Kirkwood, Arthur Shane, Benjamin Shipley, Abraham Slade, Joseph Sutton, John Rutledge

Photo from Margaret Cameron

Home of **Arthur Shane** located at the corner of Openshaw Road and the Old York Road. Destroyed by fire in 2008

West Liberty

West Liberty, located two miles north of Shane, was the site of a church called Meredith's Meeting House over 225 years ago. A store and blacksmith shop were located at the intersection of West Liberty and Meredith Roads. The area was also called "Trump" at one time after a store owner named Samuel Van Trump. Part of the original Anderson lands next to the store, was later owned by John Trout. The remaining Joshua Anderson property, was split into five farms upon the death of William Anderson in 1853. Joshua was an officer in the Revolutionary War and born on the family farm near Monkton. Gibson Road was named after the family that later owned one of these farms.

Joshua Anderson, John Bell, Thomas Meredith, Josiah Grover and Luke Ensor, all lived in the area. Reuben and Robert McCullough owned farms between West Liberty and Shane.

Photo from Ron Koller

M. Geneva Almony McCullough, Isabelle Mc Cullough, Clarence McCullough, Reuban Grant McCullough (about 1914)

Maryland Line (New Market)

Maryland Line was originally called **New Market**, but due to an existing town in Frederick County of the same name, the government changed the name of the post office to Maryland Line. Since the Pennsylvania line was just north of town, the town name soon changed also. Located on the old Susquehanna Trail which was improved by the turnpike in 1810, the town had a toll gate, a post office, two churches, a blacksmith shop, a school, a lodge hall, stores, a canning house and two hotels. Local residents included a veterinarian, judge, medical Doctor and a dentist. Dr. Ephriam Bell, a member of the Maryland Legislature, and Judge Thomas Gorsuch Rutledge were perhaps the most famous inhabitants. Dr. Bell's house, located on the corner of Old Harris Mill Road and the new York Road, was built in 1804.

Before the Civil War, there was considerable underground railroad activity in the area. Some local residents collected large rewards after capturing runaway slaves advertised in the Baltimore newspapers.

Early settlers included: Edward Bond, Moses Freeland, Gosnell, Adam Hendrix, Thomas Hunt, Lawson, John Krout, Richard McDonald, Jesse Pocock, Thomas Rutledge, Isaac Sampson, Vincent Standiford, Josiah Sparks. Located so close to the Pennsylvania line, many of the families either lived at one time or had close relatives in York County, Pennsylvania. Joshua Lowe was a land owner in both Baltimore County and York County.

The Maryland Line Hotel, circa 1906

Freeland- Bentley Springs

Freeland was named after John Freeland who bought land from an earlier settler, Samuel Morris. After the building of the North Central Railroad, a station was located there in addition to the presence of a post office, general store and hotel. Samuel Morris, John Free and the Gemmill families were early residents. Samuel Morris' descendant, Clyde Morris, operates a museum and camp grounds just west of the old North Central Railroad crossing

Baltimore County Pioneers- 7th District

Gorsuch Mills

The **Gorsuch** family has a rich history and many ties to the Glencoe area below Hereford. Stephen Gorsuch established a mill on Deer Creek in the early 1800's. The Gorsuch Mill was located at a cross roads located between West Liberty and Stewartstown, Pennsylvania. A general store, church and blacksmith shop were located there also. Many of the surrounding families moved to Ohio during the 1800's. The mill was bought by the Winemiller family who operated the mill well into the 1900's. David Wiley operated mills on Deer Creek below the Gorsuch mill.

Early settlers were: George Bond, Joseph Bosley, Stephen and David Gorsuch and William Pearce.

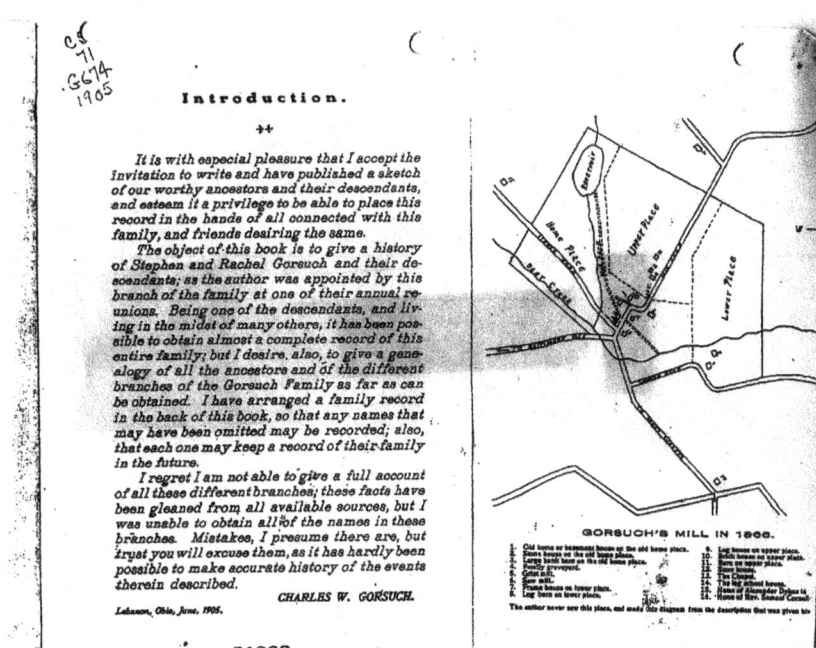

Parkton

Parkton was founded on land owned by Scottish born surveyor, Captain James Calder. Calder surveyed much of the early leases before the Revolutionary War. After the war, he was appointed County Surveyor for the new land office. Calder patented several thousand acres and was undoubtedly the largest land owner in the northern part of Baltimore County. The town received the name Parkton from Davis B. Parke who married James Calder's daughter, Margaret Calder. After the development of the turnpike and later the North Central Railroad, the town contained a bank, hotel, railroad station, two toll gates, a tavern, three churches, stores, an undertaker, a blacksmith and a water powered mill. Captain Calder's daughters and sons-in laws, Thomas Little, Michael Withers and James Turner retained much of the Calder lands after his death. James Calder and his wife are buried under the Parke Memorial Church which was founded by his descendants. Lynn Jones, descendant of Captain Calder, still lives on her family's farm just north of Parkton.

Captain James Calder, Hugh Cameron, and John Walker were all early land owners near Parkton.

Early View of Parkton

Parkton Railroad Station

Stablersville

Stablersville was named after the Christian Stabler family which bought the farm about 1805 from George Chalk Norris. The Stablers were originally from Germany and settled in York County, Pennsylvania. After locating in Baltimore County, the family built a water powered mill, the Stablers Methodist Church, Stabler's Cemetery, a general store and a post office.
Christian Stabler and John Rosier, also from York County, along with Baltimore County natives Jonathan Plowman, James Tracey and William Perdue all lived near the mill. The mill was still identified on the 1877 map. Several members of the Stabler family moved to Ohio in the 1800's. The farm was eventually sold to the Edward Grant Turnbaugh family who where active in the dairy business. Lois Hale, a descendant, was vice principal at the Seventh District School.

A Stabler Farm on Stablersville Road

Vernon

The community of **Vernon**, just North of White Hall, had a store, school, Vernon United Methodist Church and a funeral home. Names over the years were; Mt. Vernon, Moore's Crossroads and Gemmill's.
Early Settlers were: Robert Gillis, Dr. James Moore, John and Edward Norris, James Carlin, William Johnson, George Elliott, John Garrett, Adam McClung, Robert Nelson, Edward Parrish, Abraham Royston, Jane Wilson and Thomas Ayres.

First National Bank of White Hall

White Hall

White Hall was an important station on the North Central Railroad. There were livestock loading pens, a siding for the handling of coal, fertilizer, lime and other agriculture products, a bank, hotel, three stores, a church, school, farm supply company, paper mill, grist mill and blacksmiths. This town was a major center for the agricultural activity in the surrounding area. The origin of the name has been a subject of speculation over the years. The existence of a White Hall in England could be one answer. A white community hall, located in the area behind the Lytle house, was also the traditional Origin the name. The White Hall Fair was held for many years in the field above the town. Local farmers exhibited livestock, produce and local bands performed for the spectators. Dr. Milner Bortner was active with the fair following his discharge from World War 1. There were two early mills along the Gunpowder and one was converted by William Wise to produce paper. The other was located where the Wiseburg Road crosses the river to meet the Graystone Road. The White Hall Grain Milling & Supply Company was in operation between 1903-1910 and was then bought by Thomas Hunter. The White Hall Farmers Association and White Hall Milk Shippers were very active in the town.

Early Settlers were: Adam Burns, Isaac Bull, Moses Collett, William Hunter, George Lytle, Gist Vaughn, Henry Weir, John Wise.

White Hall Station looking South

Wiseburg

John Weise, from Germany, founded tis community at the intersection of the Wisburg Road and the York turnpike. The large brick tavern and inn was built about 1810 and served as a community center for almost a centry. A toll gate was located here and stables were across the road to house the horses and wagons. Pleasant Hunter, owned and ran the Inn for many years. He was a Sherriff, Councilman and Delegate to the General Assembly. The Wiseburg Methodist Church is located one half mile east of the intersection along with a cemetary.
Early settlers were John Miller and William Bull, who owned large properties near by.

Hereford, England

Hereford... *Historic capital of the JJYe Valley*

Hereford Cathedral overlooks the medieval Wye Bridge

Hereford

Hereford was named after the English town of Hereford, in Herefordshire, home of the Merryman family. Herefordshire is located in the west of England along the Wye River.. The Farming landscape of the South Midlands merges into rugged, untamed mid-Wales. Within the County, we find the Wye Valley; a dozen other beautiful river valleys; the Malvern Hills; the half-English, half-Welsh Black Mountains; Mortimer Forest and Woolhope Hills. The land is rich with history going back to the Dark Ages. After the Norman conquest, William Fitz Osbern, one of William the Conqueror's closest associates, was appointed Earl of Hereford.

John Merryman patented the land including the present day Hereford, with a lease as early as 1725. "Hereford Reserve" patented in 1787, totaled 1038 acres, with another 151 acres east of York Road.

Benjamin Merryman held several partials East of the York road, one of 818 acres called "Merryman's Enclosure Rectified", was patented in 1785. "Laural Hill" covered 223 acres. The Merryman burial ground lies just North of the main buildings on the farm just South of Hereford.

John Foster held a large area East of Hereford. Foster also leased 1,439 acres of Foster's Hunting Ground in 1773. "Solomon's Chance" covered 588 acres and Foster's Ramble was 571 acres. The old Foster burying ground lies off Maple hurst Lane, East of Hereford.

John Mays was also of English descent and was among the early settlers in Baltimore County. His descendants were prominent in the history of the town.

Hereford, located on the York Turnpike, was a major intersection with the roads leading West to Carroll County and East to Harford county. In addition to a post office, the town had two lodge halls, a dentist, a butcher, hotels, an undertaker and a newspaper.

The **Hereford High School**, built in 1953, is located just north of town. This school replaced the Sparks High School built in 1909 to serve the northern part of Baltimore County.

JOHN ALMONY

John Almony, a native of England, patented "Nottinghamshire" which covered 722 acres along the Old York and Garrett Roads. He held earlier leases dating to 1750 on smaller parcels within this larger patent. Upon John's death in 1797, the land was divided among his sons while the daughters were given silver. Succeeding generations bought additional farms around the original tract and the Almony family became one of the largest landholders in the 1800's. Lewis Ensor and Malcolm Wiley, who married Almony sisters, owned two of these Almony farms near the Harford County line. The Almony children married with children of the surrounding families such as Ayres, Dunnick, Meredith, Sutton, Bell and Shane. Elizabeth Almony married Thomas Ayres, William Almony married Dorcas Dunnick, Captain James Almony married Mary Sutton and Benjamin Almony married Ruth Sutton.

James Almony served as a Captain in the 41st Regiment of the Maryland Militia in the War of 1812. Thomas Ayres, husband of Elizabeth Almony, was a soldier in the Revolution, enlisting December 17, 1776 and served until 1783. He fought in the battle of Germantown and Brandywine, where he was wounded. Thomas was a Private in the Maryland Line, under Col. William Richardson.

After the death of James Almony in 1855 and his wife in 1859, the property was divided to his five sons, Harrison, Grandison, Jefferson, James and John. The Almony family graveyard is located on a farm on Garrett Road.

James Thomas Almony Home on White Hall Road

Descendants of John Almony

1 John Almony b: 1730 in England d: Aug 1797 in Maryland, Buried Almony Cm.
. +Elizabeth Waddham b: Abt. 1734 m: 06 Feb 1753 d: 1770 in Maryland
...... 2 Elizabeth Almony b: 1756 in Baltimore, Co., Maryland d: 04 Aug 1856 in Harford Co.,Maryland
.... +Thomas Ayres b: 1751 in Scotland m: 11 Jan 1779 d: 13 Mar 1836 in Maryland
.... 3 Nancy Ann Ayres b: 24 May 1780 in Maryland d: Bef. 1870
.... +William Rampley b: Abt. 1778 m: 23 Jan 1802 in Balt,Co. d: Mar 1841
.... 3 Dorcas Ayres b: 28 Dec 1782
.... +Jacob Bradenbaugh b: in Harford Co., Maryland
.... 3 John Ayres b: 04 Dec 1784 d: 10 Mar 1852 in Maryland
.... +Amelia Hitchcock b: 04 Dec 1788 d: 03 May 1862 in Maryland
.... *2nd Wife of John Ayres:
.... +Rachel Dunnuck b: 24 Jun 1793 in Baltimore Co.
.... 3 Elizabeth Ayres b: 19 Aug 1787 d: 08 Mar 1876 in Maryland
.... 3 Joshua Ayres b: 13 May 1790
.... 3 James Ayres b: 07 Jun 1793 d: 21 Dec 1816 in Stubenville Ohio
.... 3 Susanna Ayres b: 07 Feb 1796 d: 03 Mar 1860 in Stubanville Ohio
.... +Nicholas Hutchins b: 1791 m: 31 Jul 1816 d: 1876
.... 3 Mary Ayres b: 30 Jan 1799 d: 29 Jan 1800
.... 3 [2] Thomas Jefferson Ayres b: 15 Apr 1801 in Baltimore, Co., Maryland d: 16 Nov 1886 in Harford Co.,Maryland
.... +[1] Elizabeth Almony b: 18 Apr 1803 in Baltimore, Co., Maryland d: 25 Oct 1886 in Maryland
...... 2 Ann Almony b: 1760 in Maryland
.... +John Johnston b: Jan 1731/32 in Scotland d: 15 Mar 1838 in Steubenville, Ohio
.... 3 Abraham Johnson b: Abt. 1782
.... 3 William Johnson b: 16 Apr 1782 d: 29 Jun 1848
.... +Rosanna Todd b: 22 Feb 1798 m: 22 Feb 1814 d: 03 Jan 1887 in Stubanville Ohio
.... 3 Thomas Johnson b: Abt. 1784
.... +Mary Adams
.... 3 John Johnson b: Abt. 1786
.... +Elizabeth Lee
.... 3 Isaac Johnson b: Abt. 1788
.... 3 Nehemiah Johnson b: Abt. 1790
.... +Mary Bickerstaff
.... 3 Richard Johnson b: Abt. 1792
.... +Dorthy Cable
.... 3 Elizabeth Johnson b: Abt. 1794
.... +Edward Devine
.... 3 Rachel Johnson b: Abt. 1796
.... +Ruell Powell
...... 2 Rachel Almony b: Abt. 1763 in Maryland
.... +Thomas W Ayres b: Abt. 1760
.... 3 Thomas W Ayres b: Abt. 1792
.... +Susan Sharp
.... 3 Mary Ayres b: 06 Jan 1793 d: 03 Oct 1845
.... +Samuel Ady b: 24 Oct 1790 d: 08 Mar 1840
.... 3 Elizabeth Ayres b: 09 Mar 1798
.... 3 Matilda Ayres b: 08 Jun 1801
.... +John Patton
...... 2 John Almony b: 26 Mar 1764 in Maryland d: 1832 in Maryland
.... +Mary Ann McCord b: Abt. 1766 m: 17 May 1827
.... 3 Benjamin Almony b: 01 Jan 1798 in Maryland d: 28 Jun 1884 in White Hall, Maryland
.... +Elizabeth Slade b: 25 Jan 1804 in Maryland m: 17 May 1827 d: 19 Sep 1859 in White Hall, Maryland
.... 3 James Almony b: 10 Jul 1801
.... 3 [1] Elizabeth Almony b: 18 Apr 1803 in Baltimore, Co., Maryland d: 25 Oct 1886 in Maryland
.... +[2] Thomas Jefferson Ayres b: 15 Apr 1801 in Baltimore, Co., Maryland d: 16 Nov 1886 in Harford Co.,Maryland
*2nd Wife of John Almony:

. +Elizabeth Warhorn m: Abt. 1766
*3rd Wife of John Almony:
. +Mary Watson b: Abt. 1740 m: 06 Feb 1770 in ST John's, Parrish d: in Maryland
...... 2 Sarah Almony b: Abt. 1775
...... 2 William Almony b: 1776 in Baltimore Co. d: 04 Mar 1852 in Baltimore Co.
.... +Dorcas Dunnuck b: 1782 in Baltimore Co. m: 14 Mar 1815 d: 11 Jan 1871 in Baltimore Co.
.... 3 [4] Dorcas Ann Almony b: Abt. 1804
.... +[3] Abraham Almony b: Abt. 1802 in Maryland m: 31 Jan 1851
.... 3 Henry Dunnuck Almony b: 1806 in Maryland d: 30 Jun 1860 in Baltimore Co.
.... +Ann Elizabeth Bell b: 03 Dec 1809 in Shane, Baltimore Co., Md. m: 21 Feb 1833 d: 30 Jun 1876 in Baltimore Co.
...... 2 Capt James Almony b: 1779 in Baltimore Co. d: 21 Sep 1855 in White Hall, Maryland
.... +Mary Sutton b: 06 Jul 1790 in Shane, Baltimore Co. m: 12 Nov 1813 d: 19 Dec 1859 in White Hall, Maryland
.... 3 William Harrison Almony b: Apr 1814 in Baltimore Co. d: 09 Aug 1892 in Maryland
.... +Elizabeth Ayres b: 24 Feb 1827 in Maryland m: 31 Dec 1859 d: 04 Feb 1880 in Maryland
.... 3 Grandison Almony b: 19 Dec 1815 in Baltimore County d: 08 Dec 1856 in Maryland
.... +Rachel Ann Pearce b: 19 Aug 1821 in MLM m: 03 Jan 1843 d: 04 Nov 1884 in West Liberty
.... 3 Elizabeth Ann Almony b: 1819 in Baltimore Co. d: 05 Feb 1893 in Harford Co., Maryland
.... +Jacob Bradenbaugh b: 20 Sep 1812 in Harford Co., Maryland d: 23 Sep 1849 in Harford Co., Maryland
.... 3 Jefferson S. Almony b: 28 Jan 1820 in White Hall, Md. d: Aft. 1880 in Don Moore farm
.... +Ann Whitaker Almony b: 1828 in White Hall, Md. m: 20 Jan 1849 in Maryland d: Aft. 1880 in White Hall, Md.
.... 3 Harriet Almony b: 17 Mar 1824 in White Hall, Maryland d: 05 Aug 1894 in White Hall, Maryland
.... +William Sterling b: 24 Mar 1824 in Baltimore d: 11 Jul 1881 in Bethel
.... 3 Col James Almony b: 04 Jul 1829 in Baltimore Co. d: 04 Aug 1893 in Baltimore Co.
.... +Sarah Almony b: 31 Dec 1833 d: 30 Apr 1858 in Baltimore County, Maryland
.... *2nd Wife of Col James Almony:
.... +Juliet Elizabeth Anderson b: 15 May 1839 in 7th District, Baltimore Co. m: Abt. 1860 d: 16 Mar 1913 in Baltimore Co.
.... 3 John Almony b: 02 Apr 1832 in White Hall, Md. d: 19 Dec 1919 in Troyer RD (Smiths)
.... +Annie E Barton b: 28 Dec 1838 d: 12 Apr 1873 in Vernon UM
.... 3 Mary Jane Almony b: 08 Nov 1836 in Baltimore Co. d: 09 Mar 1920 in White Hall, Maryland
...... 2 Elijah Almony b: 1781 d: 1856
...... 2 Abraham Almony b: Jul 1783 in Baltimore Co. d: 29 May 1871 in Norrisville
.... +Cathrine Ann Gardner m: 28 Mar 1810 d: 1836
.... 3 Ann Almony b: in Maryland
.... 3 Jane Almony b: in Maryland
.... +John Montgomery
.... 3 [3] Abraham Almony b: Abt. 1802 in Maryland
.... +[4] Dorcas Ann Almony b: Abt. 1804 m: 31 Jan 1851
.... 3 Mary Ann Almony b: 12 Feb 1811 in Maryland d: 06 Apr 1896 in Norrisville
.... 3 John S. Almony b: 12 Jan 1812 in Maryland d: 21 Sep 1889
.... +Tracey B. Unknown b: 1821 d: 1874
.... *2nd Wife of John S. Almony:
.... +Sarah Lloyd
.... 3 Jarrett Almony b: 15 Sep 1817 in Maryland d: 01 Dec 1861
.... +Mary A Burk b: 22 Sep 1821 d: 02 Jul 1884
.... 3 Benjamin Almony b: 10 Dec 1824 in Maryland d: 28 Mar 1919 in Norrisville
.... +Jennett Gemmill b: 02 Jan 1822 in Harford Co m: 12 Apr 1854 in Bel Air d: 09 Mar 1895 in Norrisville
.... 3 Elizabeth Almony b: 1828 in Maryland d: 1914 in Norrisville
.... +Henry Manifold Strawbridge b: 12 May 1831 in Baltimore co. m: 01 Jan 1851 d: 26 Mar 1904 in Norrisville
...... *2nd Wife of Abraham Almony:
.... +Mary Unknown Tompkins m: Abt. 1850
...... 2 Benjamin Almony b: 1785 in Mine Run Hundred d: 21 Jun 1834 in White Hall, Maryland
.... +Sarah Jackson m: 02 Nov 1811
...... *2nd Wife of Benjamin Almony:
.... +Ruth Sutton b: 1797 in Baltimore Co. m: 02 Feb 1816 d: 22 Feb 1839 in White Hall, Maryland
.... 3 James Almony b: 1814 in Maryland d: Bef. 1860 in Maryland
.... +Rebecca Ann b: 1815 in Pa d: 20 Dec 1850 in White Hall, Maryland
.... *2nd Wife of James Almony:

.... +Elizabeth
.... 3 Benjamin Franklin Almony b: 1818 in White Hall, Maryland
.... +Mary Klinefelter b: Abt. 1820
.... 3 Ruth Almony b: Abt. 1819 in White Hall, Maryland
.... 3 Agustus Caesar Almony b: 12 Oct 1820 in White Hall, Maryland d: 22 Apr 1881 in Md. Line
.... +Elizabeth Ellen Sampson b: 08 Jul 1832 in Maryland d: 18 Dec 1886 in Md Line
.... 3 William Almony b: 1826 in White Hall, Maryland
.... 3 Mordecai Azariah Almony b: 1830 in White Hall, Md. d: 02 Oct 1902 in Baltimore,
.... +Mary E Warner b: Abt. 1832 d: Abt. 1913

John Almony Farm

Farm is located on the Old York Road along the Baltimore - Harford County line. The Original House Shown to Right of Main House. The Lewis Ensor family were the last Almony descendants to own the farm.

Joseph Sutton

Joseph Sutton owned 680 acres called "Sutton's Delight" around the present community of Shane, between West Liberty, Openshaw, Graystone and Old York Roads. The Sutton Family owned land near the Manor on Old York Road in Harford County below Black Horse. The families of Wiley, Dunnick, Shipley, Sterling, Almony, Ayres and Kirkwood are all names connected to the Suttons. Sarah Sutton married Vincent Wiley, Catherine married John Dunnick and Thomas Sutton married Mary Ann Shipley. Granddaughter Dorcas Dunnick married William Almony, Thomas Dunnick married Eleanor Gorsuch and Mary Dorcas Sutton married William Kirkwood. "Sutton's Delight" was broken up by deeds dated 14 September 1803. It was deeded to Joseph's four grandsons: Mordecai, Joseph, Christopher and John. Mordecai's sister Ann married John R. Shipley while John and Christopher's sister Ann married Robert Henry Sterling. William Kirkwood obtained the land between Graystone and Burke roads. The Kirkwood and then Whitcraft families operated the farms until Eldon Slade, a descendant of Ezekiel Slade, bought the farm on Graystone Road. The Kirkwood's operated a wagon and carriage factory at the corner of Kirkwood Shop and Old York Roads. This is now a part of Brown's Auto Parts. A small log schoolhouse called Kirkwood School, was located on the corner of Old York and Burke Road. The structure was apparently also used as a store at one time. The Shane School, located at the crest of the hill in Shane, replaced this school in 1891. Tydings McGinnis bought and remodeled this building into a home in 1931, when he and his wife Amanda McClung McGinnis, retired from their farm on Graystone Road. The Seventh District Elementary School, located on the York Road between Maryland Line and Parkton replaced the many smaller one and two room schools in the area. Thomas Sutton operated a tavern at the corner of Graystone Road and the Old York Road, and historians believe this was where George Washington stayed on a trip through the area. The Tavern was located just above the old general store on the corner of Graystone Road and the Old York Road. Later, around 1860, the tavern and store were sold to Arthur Shane and the name of the village was changed to Shane. The Shane Post Office operated from this site also.

Robert Kirkwood

Robert Kirkwood was born in Donegal, Ireland and came to America in 1731. Robert and his son served in the Militia during the revolution in 1776. The Kirkwood family has long been identified with Harford County in the Shawsville area. The two Kirkwood farms on Graystone Road were a part of the original Sutton land. The Kirkwood family built wagons on the property that now operates as Brown's used auto parts. Kirkwood Shop Road takes the name of this family.

Jacob Dailey

Jacob Daily owned the farm next to the Almony land. Descendants of Jacob, settled in the Middletown Road area. The Sterling family built the existing brick home in the early 1800's. This farm was the last farm in the area to be developed before the new Resource Conservation Zones took effect in Baltimore County. Under the new zoning, only one house per fifty acres could be built. This zoning change prevented any further drastic breakup of the community. The farm was sold for a development called Walnut Springs in about 1980. Jacob was involved with the evaluation of confiscated reserve lands in 1782.

Descendants of Joseph Sutton

1 Joseph Sutton b: 09 Jul 1724 in Mine Run Hundred, Balt.Co. Md. d: 03 Jun 1810 in Baltimore Co.
. +Ruth Adams b: 1726 m: 01 May 1748 d: in Baltimore Co.
...... 2 Sarah Sutton b: 28 Jul 1749 in Baltimore Co. d: 24 Jan 1789
.... +Vincent Wiley b: Abt. 1763 m: 02 Jan 1769 in St. John's
.... 3 Thomas Sutton Wiley b: 31 Aug 1783 in Maryland
.... 3 William Wiley b: 20 Oct 1785 in Maryland
.... 3 John Stephenson Wiley b: 05 Jun 1789 in Maryland
.... 3 [2] Sarah Wyle b: Abt. 1776 in Maryland
.... +[1] John W Dunnuck b: Abt. 1780 in Baltimore Co.
...... 2 Cathrine Sutton b: 1752 in Baltimore Co. d: 16 Jan 1836 in Baltimore Co.
.... +John Dunnuck b: 1747 in Baltimore Co. m: 01 Dec 1771 d: 17 Jun 1819 in Baltimore Co.
.... 3 Joseph Dunnuck b: 1777 in Baltimore Co. d: 11 Apr 1836 in West Liberty
.... 3 Ruth Dunnuck b: 1779 in Baltimore Co.
.... +Alexander Gordon
.... 3 [1] John W Dunnuck b: Abt. 1780 in Baltimore Co.
.... +[2] Sarah Wyle b: Abt. 1776 in Maryland
.... 3 Sarah Dunnuck b: Abt. 1781 in Baltimore Co.
.... +Andrew Wyle b: 1771 d: 21 Sep 1822 in Maryland
.... 3 Dorcas Dunnuck b: 1782 in Baltimore Co. d: 11 Jan 1871 in Baltimore Co.
.... +William Almony b: 1776 in Baltimore Co. m: 14 Mar 1815 d: 04 Mar 1852 in Baltimore Co.
.... 3 Joshua Dunnuck b: Abt. 1783 in Baltimore Co.
.... 3 Kiturah Dunnuck b: Abt. 1784 in Baltimore Co.
.... +George Koffett
.... 3 Thomas Dunnuck b: 25 Aug 1787 in 7th District, Baltimore Co., Md. d: in Ill.
.... +Eleanor Gorsuch b: 17 Dec 1787 in Gorsuch Mills d: Sep 1825 in Ill.
.... 3 Rachel Dunnuck b: 24 Jun 1793 in Baltimore Co.
.... +John Ayres b: 04 Dec 1784 d: 10 Mar 1852 in Maryland
.... 3 Cathrine Dunnuck b: 25 Nov 1796 in Baltimore Co.
.... +John Gott m: 14 May 1815
.... 3 Elizabeth Dunnick b: 1805 in 7TH District, Balt Co d: 07 Nov 1838
.... +Josiah Slade b: 15 Dec 1795 in Talbott Hall d: 06 Jan 1832
...... 2 Henry Adams Sutton b: Abt. 1754 in Mine Run Hundred d: 02 Oct 1801 in Maryland
.... +Mary Unknown
.... 3 Mordecia Sutton b: 1779 in St James p 73 d: 02 Oct 1865 in P.g. co.
.... +Nancy
.... 3 Joseph Sutton b: Abt. 1782
.... 3 Elizabeth Sutton b: 21 Oct 1787
.... 3 William Sutton b: 19 Aug 1792 in bapt 17nov 1792 St. James
.... 3 Ruth Sutton b: 09 Oct 1795
.... 3 Ann Sutton b: 09 Sep 1798
.... +John R. Shipley b: 1793
...... 2 Joseph Sutton b: Abt. 1760 in Baltimore Co.
.... +Mary
.... 3 Christopher Sutton b: Abt. 1798
.... 3 John Sutton b: Abt. 1799
.... 3 Ann Sutton b: 01 Mar 1800 in 7TH DIST d: 30 Mar 1845
.... +Robert Henry Sterling b: 20 Apr 1800 in Balt Co m: 1823 d: 30 Sep 1875
...... 2 Thomas Sutton b: Abt. 1765 in Shane, Baltimore Co., Md. d: May 1845 in Shane, Md.
.... +Mary Ann Shipley b: 26 Apr 1779 in Gist, Balt Co m: 19 Jun 1799 d: 04 Jul 1852 in Maryland
.... 3 Benjamin Sutton b: 19 Feb 1800 in Shane, MD. d: 02 Feb 1845 in Maryland
.... +Lorenza Ayres b: Abt. 1810 m: 09 Feb 1830 in Hickory, Harford Co., Md. d: Abt. 1842 in Maryland
.... *2nd Wife of Benjamin Sutton:
.... +Mary Ann Almony b: Abt. 1800 m: 02 Feb 1845
.... 3 Joseph Sutton b: 22 Apr 1802 d: 1802
.... 3 Nicholas Sutton b: 13 Jun 1803 in Shane, MD. d: 06 Mar 1872 in Zanesville, Ohio

.... +Mary Ann Doran b: Abt. 1806 m: 09 Jan 1827 in St. Ignatius, Hickory, Md
.... 3 Thomas Sutton b: 09 Dec 1804 in Shane, Balt. Co. d: 28 Dec 1884
.... +Rebecca Leddy m: Abt. 1825
.... *2nd Wife of Thomas Sutton:
.... +Hennrietta Butler m: 22 Nov 1844
.... 3 Mary Dorcas Sutton b: 20 Apr 1807 in Shane, Baltimore Co., Md. d: 16 Jan 1873 in Baltimore County
.... +William Kirkwood b: 24 Aug 1801 in Shane, Baltimore Co., Md. m: 25 Nov 1830 d: 12 Aug 1884 in Baltimore Co.

Descendants of William Kirkwood

1 William Kirkwood b: 20 Apr 1760 in Deer Creek d: 28 Sep 1829
. +Jennett Hope b: 27 Oct 1770 d: 10 Mar 1820
...... 2 Sally Kirkwood b: 30 Sep 1790 d: 04 Jul 1816
...... 2 Jennett Kirkwood b: 18 Jul 1792 d: 31 Mar 1816
...... 2 Jane Kirkwood b: 03 Jan 1795 d: in Guinston
.... +Archibald Purdy Thompson b: 1787 d: 1859 in Guinston
.... 3 Joseph Thompson b: Abt. 1819
.... +Jane ADAMS
.... 3 William Thompson b: 1819
.... +Sarah Gemmill b: Abt. 1814
.... 3 Sarah Anderson Thompson b: Abt. 1821
.... 3 Robert A Thompson b: Abt. 1823
.... +Elizabeth Grove b: Abt. 1825
.... 3 Margaret Thompson b: Abt. 1825
.... +Josiah CAMPBELL
.... 3 Elizabeth Thompson b: Abt. 1825
.... +Alexander Gordon Grove b: 1823 d: 1907
.... 3 Archibald Purdy Jr Thompson b: 24 Jul 1825 in HOPEWELL d: 21 Mar 1898
.... +Mary Grove b: 18 Oct 1825 d: 10 Dec 1912
.... 3 Hannah Thompson b: Abt. 1827
.... +John Grove b: Abt. 1825
.... 3 James Thompson b: Abt. 1829 d: 1864 in COLD HARBOR VA
...... 2 Robert Kirkwood b: 13 Jan 1797 d: 12 Dec 1829
...... 2 Richard Hope Kirkwood b: 24 May 1799 d: 17 Feb 1887
.... +Margaret Cairnes b: 11 Sep 1806 m: 17 Oct 1826 d: 19 Aug 1879
.... 3 William Kirkwood b: 05 Dec 1827 d: 23 Jul 1863
.... 3 Jane Kirkwood b: 28 Feb 1829 d: 26 Oct 1882
.... 3 Rebecca Kirkwood b: 16 Jun 1831 d: 17 Jun 1886
.... +Thomas Green b: 1825 d: 1893
.... 3 Sarah Ann Kirkwood b: 28 Jan 1833 in Shane, Maryland d: 30 Apr 1922
.... +John Westley Anderson b: 17 Jan 1837 in 7th District, Baltimore Co. m: 30 Nov 1859 d: 17 Mar 1899
.... 3 Hannah Kirkwood b: 26 Feb 1835 d: 16 Sep 1905
.... 3 George Cairnes Kirkwood b: 14 Aug 1836 d: 22 Sep 1876 in Shane
.... +Isabelle Rebecca Cairnes b: 03 Dec 1841 m: 28 Feb 1859
.... 3 Robert Kirkwood b: 1839
.... +Mary Elizabeth Robinson b: 25 Jul 1844 d: 25 Jan 1903
.... 3 John Henderson Kirkwood b: 24 Sep 1841 d: 23 Jun 1863 in Civil War
.... 3 James Hope Kirkwood b: 12 May 1845 d: 19 Jun 1916
.... +Hannah Alice Davis
.... 3 Isaac Thomas Kirkwood b: 03 Dec 1848 d: 07 May 1885
...... 2 William Kirkwood b: 24 Aug 1801 in Shane, Baltimore Co., Md. d: 12 Aug 1884 in Baltimore Co.
.... +Mary Dorcas Sutton b: 20 Apr 1807 in Shane, Baltimore Co., Md. m: 25 Nov 1830 d: 16 Jan 1873 in Baltimore County
.... 3 Dorcas Kirkwood b: 1827
.... 3 Robert Kirkwood b: 24 Dec 1832 d: 15 Apr 1871
.... 3 William Kirkwood b: 03 Dec 1835 d: 04 Jul 1904 in Baltimore Co.
.... +Mary Sophronia Anderson b: 14 Sep 1841 in 7th District, Baltimore Co. d: 19 Feb 1907 in Baltimore Co.
.... 3 Joseph Kirkwood b: 13 Nov 1837 d: 30 Mar 1928
.... +Elizabeth Ann Stritehoff b: 14 Feb 1835 d: 19 Mar 1910
.... 3 Benjamin Kirkwood b: 07 Nov 1840 d: 15 Jun 1888
.... 3 Mary Jane Kirkwood b: 14 Apr 1843 d: 03 Nov 1868
.... 3 Hannah Kirkwood b: 09 Feb 1845
.... 3 Sarah E Kirkwood b: 02 Apr 1847 d: 13 Apr 1847
.... 3 Thomas S Kirkwood b: 05 May 1884 d: 11 Aug 1884
.... 3 Archibald T Kirkwood b: 19 Sep 1889 d: 18 Jan 1864 in Civil War
...... 2 James Kirkwood b: 14 Oct 1803 d: 24 Nov 1877

...... 2 Hannah Kirkwood b: 14 Nov 1806 d: 30 Nov 1877
...... 2 John Henderson Kirkwood b: 22 Mar 1809 in Harford County d: 15 Sep 1881 in 7th District, Baltimore County
.... +Rebecca Cairnes b: 06 Aug 1811 m: 23 Dec 1836 d: 02 Mar 1876
...... *2nd Wife of John Henderson Kirkwood:
.... +Hannah Gorsuch Meredith b: 15 Nov 1830 m: 05 Oct 1876 d: 21 Dec 1903 in 7th District, Baltimore County

Descendants of Jacob Dailey

1 Jacob Dailey b: Abt. 1750 in Baltimore County d: 1815
. +Martha Unknown b: Abt. 1755 d: Aft. 1840
...... 2 John Dailey b: Abt. 1782 d: in Ohio
...... 2 Keziah Dailey b: Abt. 1784
.... +William Hare
...... 2 Christopher Dailey b: Abt. 1785 d: in 7th district
...... 2 Miriam Dailey b: Abt. 1785 d: Abt. 1814
.... +[1] James McCullough b: 10 Feb 1783 m: Abt. 1806 d: 16 Feb 1864
.... 3 William McCullough b: 1808
.... +Nancy Gore b: Abt. 1810
.... 4 Mary McCullough b: 1839
.... 4 Tufair McCullough b: 1842
.... 4 James H. McCullough b: 1839
.... 4 Thomas McCullough b: 1844
.... 4 Vincent McCullough b: 1846
.... 4 Anne McCullough b: 1849
.... 4 William McCullough b: 1852
.... 4 Jane McCullough b: 1858
.... 3 Dorcas McCullough b: 1812
.... +Mordecai Alban
.... 3 Lysander McCullough b: 11 Sep 1814 d: Aug 1906
.... +Eleanor Ann Hoshall b: 01 Jun 1817 m: 04 Jun 1840 d: 15 Feb 1894
.... 4 Sallie McCullough b: 1841
.... 4 William McCullough b: 1843
.... 4 Martha McCullough b: 1845
.... 4 Maria McCullough b: 1847
.... 4 Clara McCullough b: 1850
.... 4 Franklin McCullough b: 1853
.... 4 Nellie McCullough b: 1857
.... 4 Martha McCullough b: 1860
...... 2 Sarah Dailey b: Abt. 1785
.... +[1] James McCullough b: 10 Feb 1783 m: 23 Mar 1814 d: 16 Feb 1864
.... 3 Susan McCullough b: 1820
.... 3 Sarah McCullough b: Abt. 1824
.... +Unknown McComas b: Abt. 1820
.... 3 James W. McCullough b: 1828
.... +Elizabeth Unknown b: 1828
.... 4 Charles McCullough b: Abt. 1855
.... 4 George McCullough b: Abt. 1857
.... 4 Clara McCullough b: Abt. 1859
.... 3 Mary Ann McCullough b: Abt. 1822
...... 2 Ruth Dailey b: Abt. 1786
.... +Thomas Hutchins b: Abt. 1782 d: 1808
...... 2 Jacob Dailey b: Abt. 1787 d: Bef. 1815
.... +Mary Unknown
.... 3 Elizabeth Dailey
.... +Unknown Johnson
.... 3 Thomas Dailey
.... 3 Jacob Dailey
.... 3 Martha Dailey
...... 2 Thomas Dailey b: Abt. 1788 d: 1821
.... +Elizabeth Unknown
...... 2 Jesse Dailey b: Abt. 1789
.... +Susan Tracey b: 16 Jun 1817
...... 2 Jehu Dailey b: Abt. 1790 d: in Ohio

Thomas Meredith

"Thomas Folly", surveyed in 1786 by **Thomas Meredith** covered 628 acres. Thomas was a Private in Capt. Dean's company in July 18, 1776. The farm was located between West Liberty Road, Kirkwood Shop and Openshaw Road. In his will probated in 1825, daughters Ruth and Elizabeth received the land North of the road leading to Gorsuch's Mill and the land south of the road went to the other children. Micajah received "Thomas' Folly. Thomas Meredith also owned land near Monkton. The Meredith Family started the first church at West Liberty, known as Meredith's Meeting House and was instrumental in the building of West Liberty Church. The Meredith and Gorsuch families were closely related. Thomas Meredith's daughter Nancy Ann married Charles Gorsuch and Samuel Meredith married Belinda Gorsuch. Micajah Meredith's daughter Margaret married Henry Wesley Garrett and James Samuel married Laura Wilson. Hannah Meredith Kirkwood's daughter Gertrude married John Henry Birmingham. Samuel Whitfield Meredith's daughter Ella married William Evans Anderson and Anna Meredith married Samuel Oscar Almony. Samuel Whitfield Meredith was the grandfather of Mrs.Charles Pearce Shepperd of Graystone Road. Donald Eugene Pearce, a former Baltimore County School Board Chairman, was also a descendant of Samuel Meredith.

Benjamin Shipley

Benjamin Shipley surveyed "Shipley's Adventure" containing 235 acres in 1786. The Shipley family originally owned large holdings in Anne Arundel County before coming to Baltimore County. The Shipley land, near Shane, adjoined the Meredith, Sutton and Almony property. Benjamin's daughter, Mary Ann, married neighbor, Thomas Sutton. Benjamin married Mary Ann Almony as his second wife. Mary Dorcas Sutton married William Kirkwood. The Kirkwood family divided off two farms located on the Graystone Road. One is owned by Eldon Slade, a descendant of Ezekiel Slade. Ann Sutton married Robert Henry Sterling and Marie Theresa Shipley married their son, John Sterling. The Sterling families were wealthy merchants from Baltimore. The Sterling farm, originally patented by Jacob Daily, is now the "Walnut Spring" development. Drew and Joan Norman operate a large organic vegetable farm on part of the old Shipley farm. Drew is also a descendant of the Birmingham and Meredith families. The Igor Svec family owns the adjoining farm, which was also a part of the original "Shipley's Adventure".

Descendants of Benjamin Shipley

```
1 Benjamin Shipley  b: Abt. 1750
.  +Elizabeth Unknown
...... 2 Mary Ann Shipley  b: 26 Apr 1779 in Gist, Balt Co  d: 04 Jul 1852 in Maryland
.......... +Thomas Sutton  b: Abt. 1765 in Shane, Baltimore Co., Md.  m: 19 Jun 1799  d: May 1845 in Shane, Md.
............. 3 Benjamin Sutton  b: 19 Feb 1800 in Shane, MD.  d: 02 Feb 1845 in Maryland
................. +Lorenza Ayres  b: Abt. 1810  m: 09 Feb 1830 in Hickory, Harford Co., Md.  d: Abt. 1842 in Maryland
..................... 4 Mary E. Sutton  b: 04 Nov 1830
..................... 4 Rachel Ann Sutton  b: 26 Mar 1831
..................... 4 Maria Sutton  b: 06 Oct 1833
..................... 4 Virginia H. Sutton  b: 15 Mar 1836
..................... 4 Thomas Sutton  b: 07 Oct 1837
............. *2nd Wife of Benjamin Sutton:
................. +Mary Ann Almony  b: Abt. 1800  m: 02 Feb 1845
............. 3 Joseph Sutton  b: 22 Apr 1802  d: 1802
............. 3 Nicholas Sutton  b: 13 Jun 1803 in Shane, MD.  d: 06 Mar 1872 in Zanesville, Ohio
................. +Mary Ann Doran  b: Abt. 1806  m: 09 Jan 1827 in St. Ignatius, Hickory, Md
..................... 4 Joseph Sutton  b: 27 Oct 1827 in Shane, Baltimore Co., Md.  d: 25 Aug 1901 in Zanesville, Ohio
......................... +Anastaqsia Mattingly  m: 16 Jul 1855 in Sumit Co. Pa.  d: 08 May 1897
..................... 4 John Bennet Sutton  b: 15 Nov 1829 in Shane, Baltimore Co., Maryland  d: 12 Feb 1900
......................... +Lucy Kathrine Garretty  m: 27 Apr 1865 in Golden, Jeff Co. Co.
..................... 4 Thomas L. Sutton  b: 15 Nov 1831 in Shane, Balt. Co.  d: in OMAHA, NEB
......................... +Sarah H. Weaver  m: 12 Mar 1862 in Chester, Del., Pa.
..................... 4 Nicholas Sutton  b: 27 Apr 1833 in Shane, Balt. Co.  d: 08 Mar 1872
..................... 4 Francis Joshua Sutton  b: 03 Mar 1835 in Shane, Balt. Co.
..................... 4 Mary Ann Sutton  b: 26 Apr 1836 in Shane, Baltimore Co., Maryland  d: 1851
..................... 4 Marianna B. Sutton  b: 26 Apr 1837 in Shane, Balt. Co.  d: 18 Sep 1867
..................... 4 Benjamin Doran Sutton  b: 01 Feb 1841 in Shane, Balt. Co.
..................... 4 James Alfred Sutton  b: 21 Jul 1842 in Shane, Balt. Co.  d: 02 Jun 1870
..................... 4 Lawrence I. Sutton  b: 1844
..................... 4 John Liquori Sutton  b: 1846
............. 3 Thomas Sutton  b: 09 Dec 1804 in Shane, Balt. Co.  d: 28 Dec 1884
................. +Rebecca Leddy  m: Abt. 1825
............. *2nd Wife of Thomas Sutton:
................. +Hennrietta Butler  m: 22 Nov 1844
............. 3 Mary Dorcas Sutton  b: 20 Apr 1807 in Shane, Baltimore Co., Md.  d: 16 Jan 1873 in Baltimore County
................. +William Kirkwood  b: 24 Aug 1801 in Shane, Baltimore Co., Md.  m: 25 Nov 1830  d: 12 Aug 1884 in Baltimore Co.
..................... 4 Dorcas Kirkwood  b: 1827
..................... 4 Robert Kirkwood  b: 24 Dec 1832  d: 15 Apr 1871
..................... 4 William Kirkwood  b: 03 Dec 1835  d: 04 Jul 1904 in Baltimore Co.
......................... +Mary Sophronia Anderson  b: 14 Sep 1841 in 7th District, Baltimore Co.  d: 19 Feb 1907 in Baltimore Co.
..................... 4 Joseph Kirkwood  b: 13 Nov 1837  d: 30 Mar 1928
......................... +Elizabeth Ann Stritehoff  b: 14 Feb 1835  d: 19 Mar 1910
..................... 4 Benjamin Kirkwood  b: 07 Nov 1840  d: 15 Jun 1888
..................... 4 Mary Jane Kirkwood  b: 14 Apr 1843  d: 03 Nov 1868
..................... 4 Hannah Kirkwood  b: 09 Feb 1845
..................... 4 Sarah E Kirkwood  b: 02 Apr 1847  d: 13 Apr 1847
..................... 4 Thomas S Kirkwood  b: 05 May 1884  d: 11 Aug 1884
..................... 4 Archibald T Kirkwood  b: 19 Sep 1889  d: 18 Jan 1864 in Civil War
```

Descendants of Thomas Meredith

1 Thomas Meredith b: 1756 d: 12 Apr 1840
. +Sarah Tipton b: Jan 1775 d: 24 Mar 1850
...... 2 Elizabeth Meredith b: 08 Dec 1788
...... 2 Nancy Ann Meredith b: 21 Dec 1790 in 7th District, Baltimore Co., Md. d: Feb 1873 in Blackhorse, Harford Co.,
.... +Charles Gorsuch b: 18 Jun 1780 in Charlesborough, Fork, Md. m: 05 Feb 1809 d: 16 Aug 1873 in Blackhorse, Harford Co.
.... 3 Wesley M Gorsuch b: 12 Feb 1810 d: 1897 in Ohio
.... +Susanna Jane Rogers b: Abt. 1812
.... 3 William Gorsuch b: 06 May 1811 d: 1870 in Fork
.... +Caroline M. Wilson b: Abt. 1814
.... 3 Samuel Gorsuch b: 19 May 1813 d: 1814
.... 3 Susannah Gorsuch b: 27 Nov 1814 d: 02 May 1886 in Blackhorse, Harford Co.,
.... +Archibald Henderson b: 1803 in Blackhorse, Harford Co. d: Bef. 1860
.... 3 Luther Meredith Gorsuch b: 13 Aug 1817 in Blackhorse, Harford Co., d: 09 Apr 1894 in Blackhorse,
.... +Sarah Ellen Henderson b: 27 Aug 1825 in Harford Co d: 03 Apr 1892 in Blackhorse,
.... 3 Sarah Ann Gorsuch b: 22 Jul 1819 in Blackhorse, Harford Co., d: 1905 in Indinia
.... +William Gorsuch b: 10 Jul 1813 in Gorsuch Mills d: 18 May 1867 in Indiana
.... 3 REV Thomas Gorsuch b: 23 Jun 1821 in Fork d: 11 May 1911 in Parkville
.... +Annie T. Gatch
.... 3 Nicholas Gorsuch b: 11 Oct 1823 d: 1901
.... +Sarah Unknown b: Abt. 1825
.... 3 Joseph Gorsuch b: 11 Sep 1825
.... +Ruthanna Fussell
.... 3 Eleanor Gorsuch b: 11 May 1829 in Fallston d: 19 Aug 1865 in Upper Cross Roads
.... +Thomas Walker b: 09 Feb 1817 in Harford Co, m: 03 Feb 1852 d: 15 Feb 1894 in Harford Co, Md., Fallston
.... 3 Mary Elizabeth Gorsuch b: 25 Aug 1832 d: 1905 in New Market
.... +James Reed
...... 2 Susannah Meredith b: 19 Jan 1793 d: 03 May 1852
...... 2 Eleanor Nellie Meredith b: 17 Oct 1794 d: 06 Oct 1875 in West Liberty Cm.
.... +Micajaha Meredith b: Abt. 1792 m: 16 Dec 1815 d: 23 Oct 1822 in West Liberty Cm.
...... 2 Samuel Meredith b: 28 Apr 1796 in West Liberty d: 05 Jun 1884 in West Liberty
.... +Belinda Gorsuch b: 1795 in Charlesborough, Fork, Md. m: 17 Feb 1818 d: 04 Aug 1889 in West Liberty
.... 3 Thomas Coke Meredith b: 09 Dec 1818 d: 19 Jul 1901
.... +Mary A. Fullerton b: 1824 m: 17 Dec 1844
.... 3 Charles Gorsuch Meredith b: 05 May 1820 d: 16 Jul 1854
.... +Sarah Eliza Simmons b: Abt. 1822 m: 04 Dec 1849
.... 3 Mary Ann Meredith b: 26 Dec 1822 d: 11 Oct 1822
.... 3 Macajah Meredith b: 05 Nov 1824 d: 15 Aug 1873 in West Liberty
.... +Mary Elizabeth Garrison b: 23 Jan 1827 m: 30 Dec 1852 d: 26 Nov 1901
.... 3 Sarah Jane Meredith b: 04 Jun 1828 d: 25 Apr 1893
.... +Robert Elliott b: 14 Apr 1821
.... 3 Hannah Gorsuch Meredith b: 15 Nov 1830 d: 21 Dec 1903 in 7th District, Baltimore County
.... +Unknown
.... *2nd Husband of Hannah Gorsuch Meredith:
.... +John Henderson Kirkwood b: 22 Mar 1809 in Harford County m: 05 Oct 1876 d: 15 Sep 1881 in 7th District, Baltimore County
.... 3 Susan Tipton Meredith b: 28 Jul 1833 d: 01 Mar 1919
.... +Rev Thomas Henderson b: Abt. 1832
.... 3 Samuel Whitfield Meredith b: 06 Jun 1837 d: 18 Dec 1916
.... +Clarenda L. Treadway b: 04 Apr 1842 m: 21 Dec 1865 d: 14 Feb 1922

Descendants of Arthur Shane

1 Arthur Shane b: 07 Jan 1816 d: 19 Oct 1876 in Shane, Md.
. +Margaret E Pearce b: 14 Mar 1822 in Clynmalira, Monkton, Md. m: 15 Feb 1849 d: 28 Feb 1884 in Shane, Md.
...... 2 Mary Susan Shane b: 21 Mar 1850 d: 07 Mar 1872
.... +[1] John Thomas Almony b: 28 Jun 1849 in West Liberty m: Abt. 1872 d: 29 Mar 1899
.... 3 Daughter Almony
...... 2 Annie Elizabeth Shane b: 17 Feb 1852 d: 08 Feb 1917 in West Liberty
.... +[1] John Thomas Almony b: 28 Jun 1849 in West Liberty m: Abt. 1873 d: 29 Mar 1899
.... 3 Stanley Pearce Almony b: 17 Dec 1874 d: 29 Jul 1935
.... +May Phillips
.... *2nd Wife of Stanley Pearce Almony:
.... +Bettie Almony b: 16 Mar 1879 d: 08 Dec 1918
.... 4 Ella M. Almony b: 05 Apr 1905
.... 4 Benjamin P. Almony b: 01 Jul 1907 d: 22 Feb 1908
.... 4 James Walter Almony b: 24 Nov 1908 d: 04 Apr 1912
.... 4 Dorothy Almony b: 07 Aug 1911 in GARRETT RD, White Hall
.... +Malcolm Fields Wiley b: 24 Feb 1909 m: 23 Jan 1931
.... 4 A. Lucille Almony b: 03 Oct 1914 in White Hall, Maryland d: 17 Jun 1987 in White Hall, Maryland
.... +John Lewis Ensor b: 1910 in Texas, Maryland d: 27 Oct 1991 in White Hall, Maryland
.... 3 Amor Davis Almony b: 05 Oct 1877 d: 19 Mar 1944 in New York
.... +Cathrine Elizabeth Elwood b: Apr 1882 d: 06 Jan 1917
.... 4 Amor Almony b: Abt. 1910
.... 4 Cathrine Almony b: Abt. 1912
.... *2nd Wife of Amor Davis Almony:
.... +Margaret Elwood
.... 3 Grover Cleveland Almony b: 31 Aug 1883 d: 02 Feb 1930
.... +Bessie Lillian Williams b: 03 Mar 1885 d: 24 Aug 1968
.... 4 Cathrine Almony b: Abt. 1905
.... 4 Pearce Almony b: Abt. 1907
.... 4 Virginia Almony b: Abt. 1908
.... 3 Ella Leota Almony b: 30 Apr 1889 d: Jul 1981
.... +Walter Kunkel
.... 3 Lida Adele Almony b: 07 Jul 1894 in White Hall, Maryland d: 05 Oct 1967 in White Hall, Maryland
.... +Harrison Ross Almony b: 05 Feb 1887 in White Hall, Maryland m: 10 Feb 1916 d: 06 Jun 1949 in White Hall, Maryland
.... 4 Ruth Ella Almony b: 26 Oct 1919 in White Hall, Maryland d: in Reisterstown
.... +William Edward Dixon b: 22 Jul 1919 m: 03 Apr 1942 d: 16 Jan 1976
.... 4 Anna Margaret Almony b: 13 Feb 1925 in White Hall
.... +Stuart John Cameron b: 30 Jul 1916 in Parkton d: 09 Feb 1981 in White Hall, Maryland,
...... 2 William F. Shane b: 21 Nov 1853 d: 1909 in West Liberty
.... +Elizabeth Jane McCann b: 1855 d: 1940
...... 2 Emma Jane Shane b: 25 Nov 1858 d: 08 Oct 1852
...... 2 Ella Dorcas Shane b: 29 Apr 1867 d: 10 Jul 1943
.... +Clinton R. Kirkwood b: 21 Dec 1869 d: 18 Jun 1945 in Shane

TALBOTT HALL

View of Talbott Hall looking East toward West Liberty

Talbott Hall originally contained 450 acres when it was surveyed and returned to the Land Office in December 1786 for John Talbott. On September 11, 1795, John Talbott transferred the certificate to Ezekiel Slade who in turn transferred the certificate to John Slade on September 17, 1796. A patent was issued at this time.

Dimensions of the original log house, spring house and meat house were described in the 1798 tax assessments. The stone addition was added in 1811 by Abraham Slade. In the early 1800's, Abraham Slade enlarged his holdings to over a thousand acres, stretching from Downs Road to Garrett Road. The farm was eventually divided among Abraham's four sons, Thomas, Josiah, John and Abraham. Thomas died in 1871 without legal heirs and the farm was finally ordered sold at public auction in 1881. A group headed by Morris McGinnis, who owned a farm east of Shane, bought the farm. Morris ran a saw mill on the property and soon bought out his partners in 1885. He replaced the old log part of the house and extended the house to the present front view in 1890. A wood single roof was replaced by slate from the Delta slate quarries. The old stone barn was replaced by a larger bank barn in 1889. The farm now contains buildings built in three different centuries.

EZEKIEL SLADE

John Talbot surveyed "Talbott Hall" in 1786 covering 450 acres. The certificate was transferred to **Ezekiel Slade** who patented the property in 1796. Ezekiel Slade and sons Abraham, John, William, Thomas and Josiah were all well established on the "Manor". Ezekiel Slade's family owned extensive lands there including Slade's Tavern and "Verdant Valley". The Talbott Hall land was inherited by John and transferred to John's brother Abraham in a trade for land on the "Manor". "Talbott Hall" covered land between the present Ensor Road, Graystone and Stablersville Roads. Abraham Slade moved to the Graystone Road land and eventually owned over 1000 acres located between Downs road and Garrett road. Christopher Slade married Delilah Creighton, John Slade married Mary Perdue, Abraham Slade married Elizabeth Pearce, Josiah Slade married Elizabeth Dunnick, Ann Slade married William Perdue, Thomas Slade married Charlotte Owings Morris and Elizabeth Slade married Benjamin Almony. These marriages tied the Slade family with most of the surrounding landowners. Christopher Slade produced fifteen children and spread the Slade influence over still more families. Delilah Creighton Slade's mother, Mary McClung and the McGinnis family are both descended from Robert McClung who lived on Shepperd Road in Monkton. Morris McGinnis bought the farm at public auction in 1881 and moved from a smaller farm nearby. Morris was born in Lancaster County, Pennsylvania and was the grandson of a Revolutionary soldier, Samuel McGinness. Morris's son Tydings McGinnis bought the adjoining farm from Milton Slade in 1930. John Tydings McGinnis then bought the farm, which is now owned by his son John Wallace McGinnis.

Slade- McGinnis Fieldstone Home built in 1811

Drawing by Nancy Marshall

Descendants of Ezekiel Slade

1 Ezekiel Slade b: 1723 in AA CO, MD d: 20 Aug 1802 in Verdant Valley, MLM
. +Ann Whitaker b: Abt. 1725 in Harford Co, MD m: 07 Jan 1754 in St. John's, Joppa, MD d: 1802
...... 2 Josias Slade b: 12 Oct 1754 in Verdant Valley, Harf Co d: 02 Sep 1802
.... +Elizabeth Anderson b: Abt. 1755 in Maryland d: Dec 1859
.... 3 William Slade b: Abt. 1780
.... 3 Levi Anderson Slade b: 09 Apr 1798 in Monkton d: 27 Oct 1859 in Phoenix, MD
.... +Elizabeth Ann Fuller b: 03 Aug 1806 in MLM m: 17 Mar 1826 in St James d: 05 Oct 1886 in Phoenix, Md.
...... 2 William Slade b: 1755 in Verdant Valley, Harford Co d: 30 May 1826 in Slade's Last SHT, Jarrettsville
.... +Priscilla McComas b: Abt. 1756 m: Abt. 1782
.... 3 Stephen Slade b: 1782 in Harford County d: 29 Mar 1846 in Harford County
.... +Elizabeth Jane St. Clair b: Abt. 1795 m: Jul 1818
.... 3 Ezekiel Slade b: Abt. 1785 in Harford County d: 1853 in Baltimore County
.... +Ann Vogan b: 1779 d: 1863
.... 3 Abraham Slade b: 1787 d: 1860
.... +Rosanna Tipton b: 10 Sep 1790 d: 02 May 1873
.... 3 James Whitaker Slade b: 25 Jul 1793 in Harford County d: 06 May 1849 in Harford County
.... +Hannah McComas b: 1796 in Harford County m: 11 Dec 1813 d: 19 Nov 1877 in Harford County
...... 2 Thomas Slade b: 1756 in Verdant Valley, Harford Co d: 17 Oct 1838 in MLM, LOT99
.... +Rachel Mutchner b: 1763 in LOT 43 m: 18 Dec 1784 d: 25 Sep 1825 in MLM 99 100
.... 3 Ann Slade b: Abt. 1786 d: 1867
.... +Arron Carlin
.... 3 Bazeleel Slade b: 09 Jun 1787 in MLM LOT99 100 d: 13 Mar 1855 in Weisburg
.... +Margaret Birmingham b: 1795 m: 11 Mar 1826 d: 1868
.... 3 Micajah Slade b: 25 Dec 1788 in Maryland d: 22 Aug 1870 in Monroe, Ohio
.... +Temperance Elliott b: 28 Feb 1801 in Baltimore Co. d: 1863 in Butler Co., Ohio, Mound Cm.
.... *2nd Wife of Micajah Slade:
.... +Temperence Tipton b: 28 Feb 1801 in Maryland d: in Butler Co. ,Ohio
.... 3 Caroline Slade b: Abt. 1790 d: 18 Apr 1871
.... 3 Susanna Slade b: Abt. 1792
.... 3 Isaac Whitaker Slade b: 18 Apr 1792
.... +Sarah Lesourd b: 18 Oct 1798 d: 1821
.... 3 Rachel Slade b: 1794 in MLM 99 100 d: 23 Jun 1846
.... +Joseph Pearce b: 1787 in Pearce's Mill, Recordville m: 07 Jan 1816 d: 18 Sep 1857 in Baltimore County
.... 3 Ezekiel Slade b: 10 Jul 1795 in MLM 99 100 d: 09 May 1890 in Salisbury Plains, Norrisville, Md.
.... +Mary Ann Payne b: 10 Nov 1797 d: 03 Aug 1890 in Salisbury Plains
.... 3 Eliza Slade b: 1800 d: 01 Jan 1858
.... 3 Thomas Jefferson Slade b: 1802 in MLM LOT 99 100 d: 03 Apr 1843
.... +Mary Creighton Sterrett b: 1819 m: 07 Dec 1840 in St James d: 1853
...... 2 Ann Slade b: Abt. 1757 d: 1802
.... +Jacob Bull b: 10 Mar 1758 in Harford /Co. m: 12 Jan 1785 d: in North Carolina
.... 3 Jacob Bull b: 23 Jan 1786 d: 02 Apr 1825
...... 2 Ezekiel Slade b: Abt. 1758 in Baltimore , Co., Md. d: 1807 in Harrison CO, Ky.
.... +Sarah
...... *2nd Wife of Ezekiel Slade:
.... +Mary Hodgskin m: 28 Jan 1783
.... 3 James Slade b: 1787 d: 1850 in Madison Co., MS
.... +Susan Margaret Cooper m: 29 Jun 1833 in Hinds Co., MS.
.... 3 William Slade b: 1790 in Maryland d: 1863 in Harrison Co. Ky.
.... +Melvina Clements
.... 3 Ezekiel Slade b: 1793
.... 3 John Slade b: 01 Apr 1795
.... 3 Samuel Slade b: 1796
.... 3 Nancy Slade b: Abt. 1797
.... 3 Andrew Slade b: Abt. 1798
.... 3 Lemuel Slade b: 03 Sep 1800

...... 2 Abraham Slade b: 28 Dec 1763 in Verdant Valley, MLM d: 25 Jul 1847 in Talbott Hall, White Hall, MD
.... +Ann Mutchner b: 03 Feb 1768 in Pa m: 06 Dec 1788 d: 30 Jul 1851 in Talbott Hall
.... 3 Christopher Slade b: 1788 in Talbott Hall Mt. Joy, Shane, MD d: 10 Dec 1858 in White Hall RD, Vernon, MD
.... +Delilah Creighton b: 1790 in White Hall RD, Vernon, MD m: Abt. 1816 d: 07 May 1846 in White Hall RD, Vernon, MD
.... 3 John Slade b: Abt. 1790 in Talbott Hall d: 1853
.... +Mary Perdue b: 02 Mar 1795 in Balt Co m: Abt. 1820 d: in Balt Co
.... 3 Abraham Slade b: 25 Jan 1791 in Talbott Hall d: 16 Dec 1857 in Graystone Road
.... +Elizabeth Pearce b: 09 Feb 1795 in Gorsuch Mills d: 08 Aug 1868 in Gorsuch Mills
.... 3 Josiah Slade b: 15 Dec 1795 in Talbott Hall d: 06 Jan 1832
.... +Elizabeth Dunnick b: 1805 in 7TH District, Balt Co d: 07 Nov 1838
.... 3 Ann Slade b: 11 Nov 1797 in Talbott Hall d: 24 Mar 1877 in Parkton, Maryland
.... +William Perdue b: 19 Mar 1797 in MLM, 90 91 92 d: 16 Jul 1836 in West Liberty
.... 3 Thomas Slade b: 11 Aug 1799 in Talbott Hall d: 25 Feb 1876 in Talbott Hall
.... +Charlotte Owings Morris b: 06 Jun 1800 in 7th District Baltimore Co, MD m: 14 Dec 1848 d: 07 Jul 1873 in 7th District Baltimore Co, MD
.... 3 Ariel Slade b: 1802 in Talbott Hall d: 23 Feb 1875
.... +Walter Coleman Walker b: 31 Mar 1792 m: 1826 d: 28 Apr 1874
.... 3 Elizabeth Slade b: 25 Jan 1804 in Maryland d: 19 Sep 1859 in White Hall, Maryland
.... +Benjamin Almony b: 01 Jan 1798 in Maryland m: 17 May 1827 d: 28 Jun 1884 in White Hall, Maryland
...... 2 John Slade b: 1766 in Verdant Valley, Harf Co d: 10 Jul 1855 in Verdant Valley, Harf Co
.... +Elizabeth Ann Hutchins b: 1768 in Maryland m: 1803 d: 1851
.... 3 Sally Ann Slade b: 14 Sep 1805 in Verdant Valley d: 25 Jun 1866 in MLM, LOT20, Houck`s Mill Rd
.... +Richard MaGaw b: 1792 m: 04 Mar 1822 d: 1845
.... 3 Amanda Zana Slade b: 1807 in Verdant Valley, Harf Co d: 01 Apr 1887 in Verdant Valley, Harf Co
.... +Maj Charles William Howard b: 1800 d: 1851

Descendants of John Wilson

```
1 John Wilson  b: Abt. 1740  d: Bef. 1783
.  +Jane Bankhead  b: Abt. 1740  d: Bef. 1819
...... 2 Sarah Wilson  b: Abt. 1770
...... 2 Mary Wilson  b: Abt. 1772
.......... +Unknown Almony  b: Abt. 1770
...... 2 John Wilson  b: Abt. 1774 in Maryland  d: in Maryland
............ 3 David Wilson  b: 1798 in Stablersville
................ +Elizabeth Coe  b: 1808 in Germany
.................... 4 Edwin Wilson  b: 25 Dec 1826  d: 17 Jun 1913 in Graystone Road
........................ +Sarah A. Palmer  b: 1828  m: Abt. 1849  d: 17 Sep 1893 in Graystone Road
............................ 5 Jane Alice Wilson  b: May 1853 in Maryland  d: 1942 in Graystone Road
................................ +Jeramiah Jerry W. Six  b: Dec 1842 in Maryland  d: 1922
............................ 5 Sarah E. Wilson  b: 1854
............................ 5 James A. Wilson  b: 1856
............................ 5 Mary Frances Wilson  b: 1854  d: 1942
............................ 5 Josephine Wilson  b: 1860
............................ 5 Laura Victoria Wilson  b: 25 Jun 1862 in Maryland  d: 16 Jun 1940 in West Liberty
................................ +James Samuel Meredith  b: Jun 1859 in Maryland  d: 1902 in West Liberty
............................ 5 Zora Wilson  b: Abt. 1863
............................ 5 Harvey Nelson Wilson  b: Oct 1866  d: 1946
............................ 5 Jean Wilson  b: Abt. 1874
............................ 5 Fannie Wilson  b: Abt. 1875
............................ 5 Benjamin Franklin Wilson  b: Feb 1865  d: 20 Oct 1953
................................ +Cora Elizabeth Trout  b: 14 Apr 1869  m: 30 Nov 1892  d: 07 Nov 1949
.................... 4 Thomas Wilson  b: 1829
........................ +Amanda  b: 1834
............................ 5 James Wilson  b: 1854
............................ 5 William Wilson  b: 1856
............................ 5 George Wilson  b: 1859
.................... 4 Jane Wilson  b: 1832
.................... 4 Ephriam Wilson  b: 05 Apr 1833 in Maryland  d: 24 May 1911 in Stablersville
........................ +Rosanna Unknown  b: 1845 in Pennsylvania  d: Bef. 1910
............................ 5 Milton Wilson  b: 1872 in Maryland
............................ 5 Minnie Ida Wilson  b: Dec 1874 in Maryland  d: 25 Dec 1955 in Sparks
................................ +Silas Wright Pearce  b: Nov 1862  d: 18 Apr 1948 in White Hall, Maryland
............................ 5 Martha Wilson  b: 1875 in Maryland
............................ 5 Annie F. Wilson  b: 1878 in Maryland  d: in Stablersville
................................ +Ruben T. Wright  b: 27 Jan 1875 in White Hall  d: 22 Sep 1907 in West Liberty
............................ *2nd Husband of Annie F. Wilson:
................................ +Robert M. Miller  b: 04 Nov 1883 in Maryland
............................ 5 Jane Wilson  b: 1880 in Maryland
.................... 4 James Standiford Wilson  b: 15 Jun 1835 in Maryland  d: 25 Sep 1918 in Graystone Rd
........................ +Charlotte Palmer  b: 16 Jul 1838 in Parkton, Maryland  d: 10 Mar 1926
............................ 5 David Bartene Wilson  b: 15 Jul 1858 in Maryland  d: 26 Nov 1940 in Shane, Maryland
................................ +Flora J. Palmer  b: May 1860 in Maryland  m: Abt. 1880  d: 12 Oct 1886 in Shane, Maryland
............................ *2nd Wife of David Bartene Wilson:
................................ +Katie M. Unknown  b: 09 Sep 1869 in Maryland  m: Abt. 1887  d: 24 Feb 1892 in Shane, Maryland
............................ *3rd Wife of David Bartene Wilson:
................................ +Lida E. Hersey  b: 16 Sep 1866  m: 1897  d: 24 May 1934 in West Liberty Cm.
............................ 5 Martha E. Wilson  b: Jun 1859 in Maryland
................................ +John Herbert  b: Abt. 1860
............................ *2nd Husband of Martha E. Wilson:
................................ +Courtland L. Miller  b: 1857 in Pennsylvania  d: 1930
............................ 5 Robert G. Wilson  b: Aug 1871
................................ +Elizabeth E. Unknown  b: Jan 1871
```

.... 4 David Wilson b: 1837 in Stablersville d: 1918
.... +Rachel Slade b: 1837 in Gorsuch Mills d: 1908
.... 5 Abraham Wilson b: Abt. 1860
.... +[1] Laura Procter b: Abt. 1862
.... 5 Frank P Wilson b: 1876 d: 1935
.... 5 David Hutchins Wilson b: Abt. 1862
.... 5 Edith Wilson b: Abt. 1866
.... +Joseph Cathcart b: Abt. 1865
.... 5 Annie Mary Wilson b: 1870 d: 1952
.... +John Joshua Rutledge b: 29 Oct 1873 in Harford Co d: 07 Jul 1954
.... 5 Zora Wilson b: 1874 d: 1938 in Bethel
.... +Samuel A. Turner b: 1869 d: 1909 in Bethel
.... 5 David Hutchins Wilson b: Abt. 1860
.... +Annie Richardson b: Abt. 1860
.... 5 Abraham Wilson b: Abt. 1860
.... +[1] Laura Procter b: Abt. 1862
.... 4 Elizabeth Wilson b: 1840
.... 4 Zane Ann Wilson b: 1842
...... 2 William Wilson b: Abt. 1776
...... 2 Ebenezer Wilson b: Abt. 1778

Joshua Anderson

Joshua Anderson, whose father Benjamin owned a farm near Monkton on My Lady's Manor, patented 829 acres along the present Old York Road, Jordan Saw Mill Road, Gibson Road, Kirkwood Shop Road and Anderson Road. Joshua was a soldier in the Revolutionary War serving as a 2nd Lt. in the Gunpowder Upper Battalion. Joshua was related to the Sparks, Merryman and McComas families. Joshua's daughter Juliet married her cousin William Anderson. Their son Joshua married Mary Jane Bell and daughter Juliet married Benjamin Franklin Jordan. The Anderson children later married into the Bond, Bell, Sutton, Almony, McClung, Kirkwood, Jordan and Wiley families. The Anderson land was divided into five farms after the death of William Anderson in 1853. Sophrona Anderson who married William G. Keller, from Philadelphia, resided on the Old York Farm. John C. R. Standiford later owned the farm and passed it on to his daughter, Annie Elizabeth. George Elmer Cooper who married Rosa Trout, next passed the farm to Cooper's daughter Kathleen and her husband Walter Anderson Bay. Walter Bay was a descendant from Joshua Anderson on his father's side of the family.

Juliet Elizabeth Anderson married Benjamin Franklin Jordan from York County, Pennsylvania and lived on the Old York Road farm later owned by Vernon and Frances Chenoweth. Mary Ann Anderson married John Wesley Anderson and lived on the Kirkwood Shop Road farm. This farm was sold for housing in the 1970's. Benjamin Franklin Anderson stayed on the homestead on Gibson Road where some of the old slave quarters are still standing.. The family graveyard was located on this farm, just west of the lane on Gibson Road. The head stones were probably moved to the West Liberty Cemetery. Carl Anderson, a dairy farmer and his family were the last Andersons to farm near the original Anderson lands.

Descendants of Joshua Anderson

1 Joshua Anderson b: 27 Sep 1755 d: 12 Nov 1823
. +Mary Polly Amos b: Abt. 1776 m: 10 Dec 1791 d: 14 Oct 1825
...... 2 Juliet Elizabeth Anderson b: 02 Dec 1793 in Anderson's Retreat, Balt Co d: 19 Jul 1829
.... +William Anderson b: 03 Jun 1783 d: 27 Oct 1853 in West Liberty
.... 3 Joshua Anderson b: 18 Mar 1814 in 7th District Baltimore Co, MD d: 27 Jan 1851
.... +Mary Jane Bell b: 07 Oct 1814 in Shane, Baltimore Co., Md. d: 11 Apr 1890
.... 4 Joshua James Anderson b: Abt. 1836 in 7th District, Baltimore Co.
.... +Mary Friend
.... 4 Sarah Anderson b: 1836 in 7th District, Baltimore Co.
.... 4 John Westley Anderson b: 17 Jan 1837 in 7th District, Baltimore Co. d: 17 Mar 1899
.... +Sarah Ann Kirkwood b: 28 Jan 1833 in Shane, Maryland m: 30 Nov 1859 d: 30 Apr 1922
.... 4 Juliet Elizabeth Anderson b: 15 May 1839 in 7th District, Baltimore Co. d: 16 Mar 1913 in Baltimore Co.
.... +Col James Almony b: 04 Jul 1829 in Baltimore Co. m: Abt. 1860 d: 04 Aug 1893 in Baltimore Co.
.... 4 Mary Sophronia Anderson b: 14 Sep 1841 in 7th District, Baltimore Co. d: 19 Feb 1907 in Baltimore Co.
.... +William Kirkwood b: 03 Dec 1835 d: 04 Jul 1904 in Baltimore Co.
.... 4 William Anderson b: 1850 in 7th District, Baltimore Co.
.... 3 James Anderson b: 06 Jun 1815 d: 1815
.... 3 Benjamin Franklin Anderson b: 08 Sep 1817 in 7th District Baltimore Co, MD d: 19 Dec 1879 in Baltimore Co.
.... 4 William Franklin Anderson b: in White Hall, MA
.... 3 Son Anderson b: 1819 d: 1819
.... 3 Sophrona Anderson b: 16 Aug 1820 in Gibson Road d: 09 Jun 1878 in 7th District Baltimore Co, MD
.... +William G Keller b: 1820 in Pennsylvania d: Bef. 1860 in 7th District Baltimore Co, MD
.... 4 Mary Keller b: 1842
.... 4 William Keller b: 1845
.... 4 Benjamin F. Keller b: 1851
.... 4 Juliet S. Keller b: 05 Nov 1852 d: 17 Feb 1869
.... 3 Mary Ann Anderson b: 02 Jan 1822 d: 10 Dec 1864
.... +John Westley Anderson b: Abt. 1822
.... 3 Son Anderson b: 14 Mar 1824 d: 04 Apr 1824
.... 3 William Anderson b: 16 Aug 1825 d: 14 May 1870 in Harford Co
.... +Elizabeth Ann Lemmon b: 1823 d: 04 Dec 1899
.... 4 Mararetta Anderson b: Abt. 1846
.... 4 Sophronia Anderson b: Abt. 1848
.... 4 William Franklin Anderson b: 19 Jan 1850 d: 19 Aug 1896 in Harford Co
.... +Rebecca Jackson b: Apr 1854 d: 22 Jun 1917
.... 4 John Thomas Anderson b: 15 Feb 1854 d: 10 Mar 1928
.... +Betty Nelson b: 24 Jun 1854 d: 14 Feb 1945
.... 4 Francis Marion Anderson b: 06 May 1858 d: 01 Feb 1899
.... +Caroline Bradford Wiley b: 1865 d: 1932
.... 4 Andrew Lemmon Anderson b: 07 Aug 1858 d: Sep 1947
.... +Luella Jackson b: 28 Feb 1860 m: 19 May 1881
.... 4 George Lemmon Anderson b: 1862 d: 1936
.... +Martha Charlotte Stansbury
.... 3 Juliet Elizabeth Anderson b: 12 Jul 1827 d: 17 Feb 1886 in 7th District Baltimore Co, MD
.... +Benjamin Franklin Jordan b: 05 Nov 1823 in Pennsylvania d: 25 May 1904 in Baltimore County, Maryland
.... 4 Harriet Jordan b: Abt. 1852
.... 4 Rebecca Jordan b: Abt. 1854
.... +Thomas B. Fulton b: Abt. 1850
.... 4 Mary Sophronia Jordan b: 1856
.... +Unknown Stratton
.... 4 Archibald Steele Jordan b: 1858 d: 1925
.... 4 Benjamin Franklin Jordan b: 29 Dec 1859 d: 25 Jan 1942
.... +Dennille Hall b: 31 Mar 1870 d: 16 Jan 1941
.... 4 John Lawrence Jordan b: Nov 1861 d: Jul 1935 in Wyoming
.... +Janett Liggett b: Mar 1868 in York

.... 4 Rachel Alexander Jordan b: Sep 1864 d: Jan 1937 in York
.... +Samuel Hume Smith b: Abt. 1857 d: Mar 1933
.... 4 James P Jordan b: 21 Sep 1870 in Maryland d: 28 Apr 1949 in West Liberty
.... +Sarah M. Parks b: 24 Apr 1881 in Maryland d: 20 May 1958
.... 4 Otho Jordan b: 1873

Descendants of John Bell

1 John Bell b: 1738 in Co. Stuben, Ireland d: 07 Mar 1824 in Maryland
. +Jane Boyd b: Abt. 1740 in North Hampton, Pa
...... 2 William Bell b: Abt. 1760 d: Abt. 1765
*2nd Wife of John Bell:
. +Mary Kerr b: 22 Aug 1746 d: 06 Jan 1826 in Maryland
...... 2 Rebecca Bell b: 16 Feb 1763 in Baltimore Co., Maryland d: 30 Apr 1846 in Baltimore Co., Maryland
.... +Robert Kirkwood b: 08 Dec 1765 in Harford Co., Maryland d: 16 Dec 1810 in Baltimore Co., Maryland
.... 3 Robert Kirkwood b: 20 Aug 1800 in Baltimore Co., Maryland d: 12 Mar 1881
.... 3 John Bell Kirkwood b: 15 Jul 1803 in Baltimore Co., Maryland d: 04 Jul 1868
.... 3 Mary Bell Kirkwood b: 24 Sep 1805 in Baltimore Co., Maryland d: 03 Oct 1890
.... +William Robinson b: 1795 d: 14 Oct 1849
.... 4 Robert Kirkwood Robinson b: 28 Feb 1833 d: 08 Mar 1920
.... +Abigail Murphy b: 23 Mar 1839 d: 12 Jun 1911
.... 4 Joseph Robinson b: 17 Nov 1834 d: 31 Aug 1873
.... +Margaret Robinson b: 19 Sep 1843 d: 19 Jun 1917
.... 4 Rebecca Jane Robinson b: 24 Dec 1836 d: 17 Mar 1875
.... +Mathew William Nelson Wiley b: 01 Feb 1830 in Monkton, MD d: 17 Aug 1876
.... 4 William Thomas Robinson b: 29 Mar 1839 d: 15 Jan 1919
.... 4 John Calvin Robinson b: 28 Mar 1841 d: 28 May 1904
.... +Emma Robinson b: 16 Jul 1852 d: 14 Aug 1930
.... 4 Mary Elizabeth Robinson b: 25 Jul 1844 d: 25 Jan 1903
.... +Robert Kirkwood b: 1839
.... 4 Rachel Blanche Robinson b: 22 Oct 1846 d: 12 Feb 1920
.... +John Smith Gemmill b: 13 Dec 1844 in York Co d: 26 Sep 1920 in York Co
.... 3 Jane Ann Kirkwood b: 01 Oct 1808 in Baltimore Co., Maryland d: 07 Feb 1885
.... 3 William Henderson Kirkwood b: 09 Oct 1811 in Baltimore Co., Maryland d: Sep 1815
.... 3 Nathaniel Calvin Kirkwood b: 27 Feb 1816 in Baltimore Co., Maryland d: 24 Feb 1902
...... 2 James Bell b: 21 Dec 1776 in Maryland d: 1817 in Shane, Baltimore co., Md.
.... +Sarah Meredith b: 1783 in Shane d: 1860 in Shane, Baltimore co., Md.
.... 3 Joshua M Bell b: 18 Jan 1808 in Openshaw Rd d: 05 Mar 1882
.... +Rachael Green b: 03 May 1817 d: 19 Apr 1900
.... 4 William Bell b: 1843
.... 3 Ann Elizabeth Bell b: 03 Dec 1809 in Shane, Baltimore Co., Md. d: 30 Jun 1876 in Baltimore Co.
.... +Henry Dunnuck Almony b: 1806 in Maryland d: 30 Jun 1860 in Baltimore Co.
.... 4 C. Albert James Bell Almony b: 13 Jun 1834 d: 31 Mar 1909 in White Hall, Maryland
.... +Johanna Hampshire Hoshall b: 12 Jun 1839 d: 27 Oct 1907
.... 4 Mary Cathrine Almony b: Apr 1836 d: 25 Jun 1846
.... 4 William H Almony b: 06 Dec 1837 d: 03 Mar 1913
.... 4 Keziah Jane Almony b: 14 Dec 1840 d: 19 Jan 1851
.... 4 Ephriam Almony b: 1842
.... +Eliza Watkins b: Abt. 1846
.... *2nd Wife of Ephriam Almony:
.... +Mattie Gent b: Abt. 1844
.... 4 Charles Linthicum Almony b: 04 Dec 1846 in Ensor Road d: 31 Jan 1931 in Baltimore Co.
.... +Adaline Frances Quigley b: 28 Aug 1849 in Fawn Grove, York Co. d: 06 Jul 1920 in Baltimore Co.
.... 4 John Westley Almony b: 1850
.... +Alice Bock d: in Ohio
.... 4 Franklin T. Almony b: 06 Aug 1854 in Maryland d: 22 Dec 1903 in Baltimore Co.
.... +Zana Victoria Slade b: 11 Dec 1859 in Maryland d: 01 Sep 1931 in West Liberty
.... 3 John Bell b: 07 Jul 1812 in Shane, Baltimore Co., Md. d: 04 Jul 1872
.... +Elizabeth Bell Meredith b: Abt. 1814 in Shane
.... 4 Jane Bell b: Abt. 1835
.... 3 Mary Jane Bell b: 07 Oct 1814 in Shane, Baltimore Co., Md. d: 11 Apr 1890
.... +Joshua Anderson b: 18 Mar 1814 in 7th District Baltimore Co, MD d: 27 Jan 1851
.... 4 Joshua James Anderson b: Abt. 1836 in 7th District, Baltimore Co.

```
..................        +Mary Friend
..................     4 Sarah Anderson  b: 1836 in 7th District, Baltimore Co.
..................     4 John Westley Anderson  b: 17 Jan 1837 in 7th District, Baltimore Co.  d: 17 Mar 1899
..................        +Sarah Ann Kirkwood  b: 28 Jan 1833 in Shane, Maryland  d: 30 Apr 1922
..................     4 Juliet Elizabeth Anderson  b: 15 May 1839 in 7th District, Baltimore Co.  d: 16 Mar 1913 in Baltimore Co.
..................        +Col James Almony  b: 04 Jul 1829 in Baltimore Co.  d: 04 Aug 1893 in Baltimore Co.
..................     4 Mary Sophronia Anderson  b: 14 Sep 1841 in 7th District, Baltimore Co.  d: 19 Feb 1907 in Baltimore Co.
..................        +William Kirkwood  b: 03 Dec 1835  d: 04 Jul 1904 in Baltimore Co.
..................     4 William Anderson  b: 1850 in 7th District, Baltimore Co.
............    3 Kesiah Bell  b: 26 Oct 1816 in Shane, Baltimore Co., Md.
..............     +Thomas Hale
...... 2 John Bell  b: 11 Apr 1778 in Baltimore Co., Maryland  d: 27 Jun 1826
........  +Lovica Bell  b: Abt. 1778  d: in Fayette Co, Iowa
............ 3 Mary Bell  b: Abt. 1800
..............     +Andrew Boyd
..................     4 Margaret Boyd
..................     4 Elsisa Boyd
..................     4 Andrew W Jr Boyd
..................     4 James Boyd  d: in ILL
..................     4 David Boyd
............ 3 James Bell  b: Abt. 1804  d: in Cottage Grove, WIS
..............     +Emily
............ 3 Agnes Bell  b: Abt. 1806
..............     +David BOYD
............ 3 Lovica Jane Bell  b: Abt. 1808
............ 3 David Bell  b: 1808  d: Nov 1896 in Carroll Co., Ohio
..............     +Nancy  d: 1887
............ 3 Eleanor Bell  b: Abt. 1810
..............     +Nathan Shaw  b: Abt. 1810
............ 3 Rebecca Ann Bell  b: Abt. 1812
............ 3 John Bell  b: 1812  d: 21 Mar 1892
..............     +Elizabeth
............ 3 Elizabeth Mary Bell  b: 1807  d: in NOV, 1859, Harf Co
..............     +[1] Robert McClung  b: 26 Jul 1787 in Monkton, Maryland  d: 17 Oct 1855 in Norrisville, Harford Co., Md.
...... 2 William Bell  b: 08 Sep 1780 in Baltimore Co., Maryland  d: 05 Jun 1860
........  +Jane Coulson  b: 1795
...... 2 Mary Bell  b: 08 Oct 1782 in Baltimore Co., Maryland  d: 05 Dec 1869
...... 2 Elizabeth Bell  b: 08 Apr 1788 in Baltimore Co., Maryland  d: 10 Jul 1844
...... 2 Dr Ephriam Bell  b: 02 Dec 1793 in Baltimore Co., Maryland  d: 02 Aug 1875 in Maryland Line , Md.
........  +Julia Ann Deagon  b: 1803
............ 3 Mary R. S. Bell  b: Abt. 1844
..............     +John E Hurst  b: Abt. 1840
............ 3 Sarah Bell  b: 1845
..............     +Thomas Deford  b: Abt. 1845
..................     4 Robert Bell Deford  b: 1885
..................        +Dorthea H. Unknown
...... 2 Agnes Bell  b: 1768 in Baltimore Co., Maryland  d: 07 May 1819
........  +[1] Robert McClung  b: 26 Jul 1787 in Monkton, Maryland  d: 17 Oct 1855 in Norrisville, Harford Co., Md.
............ 3 Baby McClung  b: 1819
```

Descendants of Josias Grover

1 Josias Grover b: 28 Mar 1733 in England
. +Mary Anderson b: 18 Jan 1735/36 in AA CO m: 25 Dec 1754 in ST JOHNS
...... 2 Benjamin Grover b: 09 Jan 1758
.... +Ann DorseyD'Arcy b: Abt. 1760
...... 2 Elizabeth Grover b: 28 Sep 1760
.... +Jeremiah Talbott b: 1764
...... 2 Drusilla Grover b: 26 Feb 1762
.... +Richard Colgate Talbott b: Abt. 1760
...... 2 Jemima Grover b: 01 Jun 1764
.... +William Mockbee b: Abt. 1762
...... 2 Mary Grover b: 28 Feb 1767
.... +John Allen b: Abt. 1765
...... *2nd Husband of Mary Grover:
.... +John Reed b: Abt. 1765
...... 2 Josiah Grover b: 07 Jul 1770
.... +Martha McClure b: Abt. 1772
...... 2 Abraham Grover b: 20 Jan 1773
...... 2 Sarah Grover b: 10 Mar 1775
.... +John Paul b: Abt. 1773

Josias Grover - John Bell Farm

Looking East toward West Liberty

JOSIAS GROVER

Josias's mother was an Anderson and Josias owned the land next to the Joshua Anderson. His farm included part of the Link Almony farm on Ensor Road and the two farms across from it. The original tract also included part of the James Leffel farm. John Bell, who owned the land after Grover, married Sarah Meredith. Bell was a 1st Lt. in the Deer Creek Battalion in 1776. His daughter Ann, married Henry Dunnick Almony and daughter Mary Jane married Joshua Anderson. The Almony family acquired the land on the North side of Ensor Road from the Joshua Anderson tract. The land on the South side of Ensor Road was sold to Dr. Robert Rankin in 1852. Dr. Rankin was a leader in the West Liberty Church as well as the builder of the house located on the Ensor Road farm. The location of Mrs. Bell's earlier house closer to Ensor road, was shown on an 1850 map. William Bell, brother of John, married Jane Coulson and the farm on the East side of the old York Road was acquired by William Coulson. This farm was owned by Robert McCullough and now owned by James and Jane Leffel.

Dr. Ephriam Bell, a brother of John, was a physician in New Market and a member of the Maryland State Legislature. Agnes Bell, a sister, married Robert McClung the ancestor of the McGinnis family and current owners of the Rankin Farm.

Thomas Gorsuch Rutledge

Rutledge home in "New Market"

Thomas Rutledge surveyed 495 acres called "Rutledge's Labor" in 1787. Thomas was a soldier in the Revolution and involved in evaluation of confiscated proprietary reserve lands in 1782. The Rutledge family owned lands in Harford County near Black Horse. Thomas's children married into the Wantland, Bull, Hunt, Sampson, Hendrix and Gorsuch families. His son, Thomas Gorsuch Rutledge lived in New Market and was active in local affairs. Thomas Gorsuch was a teacher, Justice of the Peace, Judge of the Orphans Court and a member of the School Board. The Rutledge land stretched from the York road along Jordan Saw Mill Road to the Old York Road. The Rosier family later owned several farms belonging to the old tract.

Edward Bond

Edward Bond Surveyed "The Spot" In 1786. This 500-acre tract covered land along the present Lentz, Sampson and Old York roads. Edward was involved in the evaluation of confiscated proprietary reserve lands in 1782. The Pocock, Sampson, Rutledge, Krout and McDonald families are all related to the Bonds. Edward's son George married Jemima Pocock, Ellen Bond married George Stabler, Ross Bond married Mary Jane McDonald and Mary Bond married Abraham Freeland. Ross Bond's daughter Jane Elizabeth married Charles Plowman. Varena married James Thomas Almony and Mary Catharine married James Anderson. The Emerson Ensor family owns the eastern part of the Bond holdings while George Rosier owns the part west of the road. George Bond is buried in a small graveyard across Bond Road behind the old Bond School house. Farming activity around the tree has damaged this cemetery which is located by a lone tree, some two hundred yards from the road.

Samuel Bond

Samuel Bond first surveyed "Bond's Meadows". Bond Meadows was located in the Northeast corner of the Seventh District and extended over into both Harford and York County. George Bond 's children married into the Krout and Sampson families. George lived in Hopewell Twp., York County and died there in 1843. Many of his descendants later moved to Findley, Hancock County Ohio. Dale Bond of Clarkston, Michigan has done extensive research on this family and the Maryland Line history. The Bond family held large acreage in both Harford and Baltimore Counties and were very influential in Colonial affairs..

Isaac Sampson

The Sampson farm lies on the York Road just north of Bee Tree Road. Recent development has surrounded the old cemetery located on the hill in the back of the property. The old house foundation is still visible along a stone wall to the South of the existing main farm house. When David Sampson died in 1862, most of his family had moved to Ohio. Thomas Rutledge carried on a correspondence with David's son Eli, to help settle the estate. The letters are a valuable record of activities occurring during this time period including Lincoln's death. These letters are in Ths possession of the Sampson descendants in Ohio.

John Krout

John Krout's children married into many families around "New Market". These families included the McDonalds, Morris, Waltermire, Orwig, Bond, Free, Anstine, Hendrix, Lowe and Sampson. Many of the Krout family moved to Ohio also. They located near Mt. Blanchard, in Hancock County. They were very successful farmers and large land owners in that county. The land in this area is very flat and fertile, while Northern Baltimore County is more rolling and scenic. Several descendants of John Krout visited the area from Ohio in the summer of 2005. In New Market, the Krout family operated a Post Office and general store as well as a canning factory. One of the Krout farms near Maryland Line is located on Stewartstown Road.

Baltimore County Pioneers- 7th District

Descendants of Thomas Gorsuch Rutledge

```
1 Thomas Gorsuch Rutledge  b: 09 Aug 1759 in Balt Co  d: 06 Jan 1832 in 7th  District Baltimore Co, MD
.  +Mary Matthews  b: Abt. 1760  m: Oct 1782  d: Abt. 1784
*2nd Wife of Thomas Gorsuch Rutledge:
.  +Ruth Hendrix  b: Abt. 1760 in Shrewsbury, PA.  m: 17 Jan 1787  d: Abt. 1790 in New Market, Pa.
...... 2 Elizabeth Ann Rutledge  b: 02 Apr 1787 in New Market, Md.  d: 10 Aug 1839 in Baltimore , Co. Md.
.......... +David Sampson  b: 31 May 1784 in New Market, Md.  m: 09 Feb 1804  d: 24 Aug 1862 in Long Valley, Maryland Line
............ 3 Stephen Sampson  b: Dec 1804  d: 16 Dec 1804
............ 3 Ruth Sampson  b: 06 Nov 1809 in 7TH District  d: 27 Oct 1865 in Hancock Co., Ohio
................ +Elisha Gorsuch  b: 03 Mar 1810 in Gorsuch Mills  m: 12 Feb 1829  d: 07 Mar 1847 in Ohio, Typhoid Fever
............ 3 Eli S. Sampson  b: 12 Feb 1813 in Baltimore County, Maryland  d: 21 Dec 1893 in Ohio
................ +Margaret Ann Krout  b: 15 May 1812 in Baltimore County, Maryland  m: 13 Mar 1835 in Baltimore , Co. Md.  d: 20 Nov
                1892 in Hancock Co. Ohio
............ 3 Elizabeth Jane Sampson  b: 27 Aug 1815 in New Market  d: 11 Feb 1901 in Maryland Line, Md. Line Cm.
................ +James Bond  b: 02 Jan 1808 in New Market, Md.  m: 14 Mar 1834  d: 14 Jan 1891 in Maryland Line
............ 3 Mary Sampson  b: 13 Dec 1817 in Baltimore , Co. Md.  d: 23 Mar 1856 in Baltimore , Co. Md.
................ +Johnsey S. Palmer  b: Abt. 1816 in Baltimore , Co. Md.  d: in Baltimore , Co. Md.
............ 3 Nicholas Sampson  b: 01 Feb 1820 in Baltimore , Co. Md.  d: 18 Aug 1864 in Houcktown, Hancock CO, Ohio
................ +Elizabeth Hunter  b: Abt. 1822  m: 04 Sep 1840
............ 3 David Sampson  b: 14 Aug 1823 in Baltimore , Co. Md.  d: 14 Aug 1824 in Baltimore , Co. Md.
............ 3 Edwin Hindle Sampson  b: 02 Jan 1830 in Maryland  d: 1864 in Houcktown, Ohio
................ +Mary Jane Standiford  b: 23 Aug 1831 in Maryland  m: 25 Feb 1852  d: 1864
...... 2 Ruth Rutledge  b: 19 Oct 1788 in Harford Co  d: 1831 in Balt Co
.......... +Charles Gorsuch  b: 13 Jun 1789 in Gorsuch Mills  m: 05 Jan 1809  d: 06 Feb 1869 in Butler Co , OH
............ 3 Rachel Gorsuch  b: 07 Nov 1809  d: 16 Feb 1883 in ILL
................ +Joseph Lesourd  b: 23 Sep 1811 in Butler Co. Oh.  m: 08 Mar 1832  d: 02 Sep 1883
............ 3 Thomas Gorsuch  b: Abt. 1811 in Gorsuch Mills, MD.  d: in Ohio
................ +Martha Jane Curtis  b: in OH  m: 16 Apr 1840 in butler Co. Oh.  d: in OH
............ 3 Elizabeth Gorsuch  b: Abt. 1813 in Maryland
................ +Robert Allen  b: Abt. 1812
............ 3 Sarah Gorsuch  b: Abt. 1815 in Maryland
................ +Abram Sutton
............ 3 John Westley Gorsuch  b: Abt. 1817 in Maryland
*3rd Wife of Thomas Gorsuch Rutledge:
.  +Sarah Gorsuch  b: 1774 in Balt Co  m: 17 May 1804  d: 1813
...... 2 Mary L Rutledge  b: 1805 in Baltimore Co.  d: 1822 in 7th District Baltimore Co, MD
...... 2 Leah Susan Rutledge  b: 12 Oct 1808 in Baltimore Co.  d: 08 Apr 1895
.......... +Abraham Wilson Downs  b: 1805 in Maryland  m: 02 Apr 1835  d: 16 Sep 1887 in Maryland Line
............ 3 Eli K. Downs  b: 1840
............ 3 John Keller Downs  b: 07 May 1841 in Maryland  d: 04 May 1907 in Maryland Line
................ +Ann Unknown  b: 11 Mar 1845  d: 18 Mar 1903
............ 3 Thomas Rutledge Downs  b: 24 Mar 1844 in Baltimore Co.  d: 17 Oct 1908 in Maryland Line
................ +Susanna Shaver  b: 10 Aug 1843 in Parkton, Md.  m: Abt. 1865  d: 29 Mar 1928
............ 3 G. S. Downs  b: 1851
............ 3 Louisa Downs  b: 09 Sep 1847 in Baltimore Co.  d: 21 Jul 1923 in Maryland Line
...... 2 Joshua Wells Rutledge  b: 31 Jan 1810 in Baltimore Co.  d: 14 Dec 1883 in Pittsburg, Pa.
.......... +Rachel Bell Smiley  b: in Perry Co., Pa.  m: 16 Jun 1836  d: 26 Mar 1837
............ 3 Joshua Smiley Rutledge  b: 19 Mar 1837  d: 12 Oct 1876 in Ohio
................ +Eliza Ann Brady
............ *2nd Wife of Joshua Smiley Rutledge:
................ +Charlotte D Walters  b: 1838  m: 15 Jan 1857  d: 1910 in Montgomery Co., MO.
............ 3 [1] Irene Rutledge  b: 04 Feb 1844  d: 30 Oct 1930 in Pittsburg
............ 3 Alexander Brady Rutledge  b: 22 Nov 1845  d: 18 Feb 1893 in Pittsburg
................ +Mary Jane Harrison  b: Abt. 1848  m: 05 Sep 1871 in PITTS
............ 3 Sarah Ann Rutledge  b: 30 Oct 1847 in Salem, Wayne Co., Pa.  d: 05 Dec 1932 in Pittsburg
................ +John Gillifillan Bryant  m: 03 Aug 1871
```

.... 3 [2] Mary Frances Rutledge b: 06 Nov 1849 d: 09 Sep 1882 in Pittsburg
.... +[3] William H Arthurs
...... *2nd Wife of Joshua Wells Rutledge:
.... +Eliza Ann Brady b: Abt. 1812 m: 26 Mar 1842 in PHILA d: 06 Nov 1891 in Pittsburg
.... 3 [1] Irene Rutledge b: 04 Feb 1844 d: 30 Oct 1930 in Pittsburg
.... 3 Alexander Brady Rutledge b: 22 May 1845
.... 3 Sarah Ann Rutledge b: 30 Oct 1847
.... 3 [2] Mary Frances Rutledge b: 06 Nov 1849 d: 09 Sep 1882 in Pittsburg
.... +[3] William H Arthurs
*4th Wife of Thomas Gorsuch Rutledge:
. +Elizabeth Howard b: 24 Jan 1776 in York Co m: Abt. 1821 d: Abt. 1852 in Baltimore , Co. Md.
...... 2 Thomas Gorsuch Rutledge b: 28 Sep 1822 in 7th Dist, Balt Co , New Market, Md. d: 20 Feb 1899 in New Market, MD
.... +Rebecca Jane Fife b: 14 Jan 1824 in York Co m: 05 Dec 1844 in Baltimore Co. d: 16 Feb 1896 in 7th Dist
.... 3 Rufus Franklin Rutledge b: 27 Mar 1845 in 7th District Baltimore Co, MD
.... +Sarah A. Grove b: 1844 in Pennsylvania
.... 3 Elizabeth Ann Rutledge b: 05 Jan 1847 in 7th District Baltimore Co, MD d: 21 May 1920
.... +Dr Silas Wood Hazeltine b: 23 Sep 1836 in Andover VT m: 24 Dec 1866 in Baltimore , Co. Md. d: 13 Feb 1905 in Baltimore
.... 3 John Fife Rutledge b: 11 Feb 1849 in 7th District Baltimore Co, MD d: 15 Feb 1896 in Maryland Line , Md.
.... +Agnes Jane Sampson b: Dec 1860 m: 16 Oct 1884 d: 18 Dec 1891
.... 3 Mary Louisa Rutledge b: 14 May 1852 in 7th District Baltimore Co, MD d: 30 Mar 1921
.... +Thomas J Meads b: 1851 d: 1935 in Maryland Line
.... 3 Sarah Grace Rutledge b: 09 Mar 1854 in 7th District Baltimore Co, MD d: 1929 in Corbett, Maryland
.... +John Vinton Slade b: 1852 in MLM d: 1909 in Corbett, MD,
.... 3 Leah Susan Rutledge b: 17 Feb 1855 in 7th District Baltimore Co, MD d: 09 Aug 1912
.... +William W Ratcliffe
.... 3 Cornelia Jane Rutledge b: 06 Apr 1861 in 7th District Baltimore Co, MD d: 21 Jun 1861 in Maryland Line

Descendants of Edward Bond

1 Edward Bond b: 12 Jul 1748 in Baltimore Co., Maryland d: Mar 1797 in Baltimore County, Maryland
. +Ruth Sampson b: 24 Nov 1748 in Baltimore Co. m: 23 Mar 1769 d: Bef. 1810 in Baltimore Co.
...... 2 Mary Bond b: Abt. 1775
.... +Abraham Freeland b: Abt. 1785 m: 30 Apr 1802
.... 3 Child Freeland
.... 3 Child Freeland
.... 3 Child Freeland
...... 2 Charles Bond b: 1780 d: 1810 in No children
...... 2 George Sampson Bond b: 04 Jun 1783 in Bond Rd, Baltimore Co. d: 30 Dec 1850 in Maryland Line
.... +Jemima Pocock b: 16 Jan 1789 in Baltimore Co. m: 27 Nov 1804 in Baltimore Co., Md. d: 30 Dec 1850 in Balt Co
.... 3 Elisha Bond b: 30 May 1805 in Bond RD, Maryland Line d: 30 Oct 1884 in Maryland Line, Bond Road
.... +Eliza Pocock b: 07 Jan 1827 d: 18 Dec 1897 in Maryland Line, Bond Road
.... 4 Thomas Bond b: 15 Jul 1849 d: 07 Oct 1853 in Bond Cm., Bond Road
.... 4 Rebecca Jane Bond b: 15 Jul 1851 in Maryland d: 03 Apr 1938 in West Liberty
.... +John S. Hollingshead b: 17 Feb 1854 in Pennsylvania m: Abt. 1875 d: 20 Jul 1918 in West Liberty, Ensor Road
.... 4 Jessie Ross Bond b: 15 May 1857 d: 30 Apr 1899 in New Market Cm.
.... 4 Martha Ellen Bond b: 18 Jul 1864
.... 4 Elizabeth Ann Bond b: 31 Jul 1868
.... 3 Ellen Bond b: 17 Jul 1808 in Bond Road d: Bef. 1830
.... +George Stabler b: 26 Jun 1794 in Stablersville d: 03 Feb 1864 in Stablersville
.... 3 Ann Bond b: 11 Feb 1816 in Bond Road d: 27 Apr 1880
.... +Unknown Morris b: Abt. 1814
.... 3 Harriet S. Bond b: 1820 in Bond Road, Baltimore Co., Md.
.... +Daniel B. Smith b: 29 Nov 1830 in York Co. m: 26 Jan 1854 d: 25 Sep 1901 in Atchinson, Kansas, Wheatland Cm., Horton
.... 4 George A. Smith
.... 4 Adda E. Smith b: 17 Feb 1867 in Horton, Kansas d: 11 Jun 1936
.... +Bailey Wallingford
.... *2nd Husband of Adda E. Smith:
.... +Patrick H. McKeon m: 03 Feb 1894 d: 07 Feb 1902
.... 3 Elizabeth Bond b: 07 Jun 1826 in Bond Road d: 01 Mar 1892
.... 3 Ross Bond b: 14 Oct 1830 in Bond Rd d: 22 Aug 1907 in Maryland Line, Bond Road
.... +Mary Jane McDonald b: 19 Jul 1837 in 7 TH Dist.,Balt Co m: 06 Jan 1859 d: 27 Mar 1898 in Maryland Line, Bond Road
.... 4 Smith Daniel Bond b: 08 Oct 1859 in Bond Road d: 10 Mar 1938 in Maryland Line, Bond Road
.... +Rachel H Kearns b: 11 Sep 1861 m: Abt. 1884 d: 27 Oct 1897
.... *2nd Wife of Smith Daniel Bond:
.... +Margaret A. Baird b: 08 Apr 1855 m: Abt. 1900 d: 03 Apr 1919
.... 4 Jane Elizabeth Bond b: 28 Sep 1861 in Bond Road d: 27 Oct 1926 in Parkton, Maryland
.... +Charles E. Plowman b: Oct 1850 in Balt,Co. m: 06 Jan 1892 d: 27 Feb 1945 in Parkton, Maryland
.... 4 Varena Julia Bond b: 10 Feb 1864 in Bond Road d: 16 May 1922
.... +James Thomas Almony b: 10 Jul 1860 in White Hall, Maryland m: 13 Jan 1886 d: 03 Jan 1929 in Buried Vernon
.... 4 Mary Cathrine Rebecca Bond b: 11 Sep 1865 in Bond Road d: 31 Oct 1934
.... +John James Anderson b: 11 Aug 1869 in Maryland m: 06 Mar 1895 d: 25 Dec 1935
.... 4 Luella Harriet Bond b: 06 May 1867 in Bond Road d: 23 Mar 1868 in Maryland Line, Bond road
.... 4 Sally E. G. Bond b: 09 Apr 1869 in Bond Road d: 22 May 1872 in Maryland Line, Bond Road
.... 4 Lucy M. A. Bond b: 19 Jan 1871 in Bond Road d: 20 Mar 1872 in Maryland Line, Bond Road
.... 4 John Ross Bond b: 26 Jan 1873 in Bond Road d: 16 Aug 1940
.... +Mary Dorcas Kirkwood b: 22 Jan 1869 in Shane d: 28 Jun 1958 in Stewartstown
.... 4 Rosa Eve Bond b: 26 Sep 1875 in Bond Road d: 09 Mar 1881 in Maryland Line
.... 4 Laura Agnes Bond b: 09 Aug 1879 in Bond Road d: 09 Apr 1956
.... +John K. Miller b: Abt. 1876 m: 26 Nov 1902 d: in Red Lion
...... 2 Eleanor Bond b: Abt. 1785 d: 13 Dec 1836
...... 2 Edward Bond b: 1783 d: in Maryland Line

Descendants of Luke Gorsuch Ensor

1 Luke Gorsuch Ensor b: 1776 in Ensor, Manor d: 1851 in Ensor Manor
. +Sarah Hunter Ensor b: 1795 in Maryland m: 04 Apr 1820 d: 1841
...... 2 John Hunter Ensor b: 15 May 1822 in Maryland d: 25 Mar 1903
.... +Elizabeth Chilcoat Ensor b: 1823 in ENSOR MANOR m: 09 Dec 1847 d: 12 Mar 1883 in Maryland
.... 3 Luke Chilcoat Ensor b: 1850
.... 3 Lydia Ensor b: 1852
.... 3 John Edward Ensor b: 23 Jan 1852 in 8TH DIST, Ensor Manor d: 27 Jul 1932 in Sparks, Maryland
.... +Mary Ellen Gorsuch b: 05 Oct 1851 in Frederick CO m: Oct 1864 d: 11 Mar 1921 in Glencoe
.... 4 John H Ensor b: Abt. 1872 d: in Frederick County
.... 4 Elizabeth A Ensor b: Oct 1873
.... 4 William Pinkney Ensor b: Jan 1875
.... 4 Abram Gorsuch Ensor b: Aug 1879
.... 4 [2] James Victor Ensor b: 24 May 1882 in Baltimore County d: 05 Nov 1969
.... +[1] Eureka Philpot Ensor b: 20 Jan 1889 in Mantua Mill Road m: 13 Feb 1909 in ROLAND PARK d: 07 Jul 1956
.... 4 Alexander R Ensor b: Dec 1883 in Baltimore County 8th district
.... +Hester J. Mays b: Feb 1889 in Baltimore County
.... 4 Lawerence E Ensor b: Aug 1888 in Maryland
.... +Addie Wheeler b: 1888 in Maryland
.... 4 Thomas Reverty Ensor b: Apr 1890
.... +Margarette Lamb
.... 3 Sallie Ensor b: 1854
.... 3 William Lewis Ensor b: 18 Nov 1855 in Sparks, Maryland d: 01 Feb 1937 in Sparks, Maryland
.... +Charlotte Ophelia Cole b: 06 Jun 1852 in Butler m: 18 Apr 1885 in COLE HOME d: 24 Nov 1928 in Sparks
.... 4 Leroy J. Ensor
.... 4 Samuel S. Ensor
.... 4 Elizabeth C. Ensor b: 1889
.... +George W. Ensor b: Abt. 1888
.... 4 [1] Eureka Philpot Ensor b: 20 Jan 1889 in Mantua Mill Road d: 07 Jul 1956
.... +[2] James Victor Ensor b: 24 May 1882 in Baltimore County m: 13 Feb 1909 in ROLAND PARK d: 05 Nov 1969
.... 4 Mary Beulah Ensor b: May 1895
.... +Robert Ensor
.... 3 Samuel T. Ensor b: 1857
.... 3 Joseph T. Ensor b: 1861
.... 3 Elijah M. Ensor b: 1865
...... *2nd Wife of John Hunter Ensor:
.... +Anne Nancy Ensor b: Abt. 1800 in Maryland m: Abt. 1867 d: 1867
...... 2 Darby Ensor b: Abt. 1826
...... 2 Ruth Ann Ensor b: 1827 d: 04 Mar 1918
.... +George C. Ensor b: 1820 d: 15 Feb 1881
.... 3 Sarah Ann Ensor b: 09 Jan 1852
.... 3 Samuel Edward Ensor b: 07 May 1853
.... 3 Mary Francis Ensor b: 21 Sep 1854
.... 3 Elijah S. Ensor b: 27 Dec 1855
.... 3 Edward T. Ensor b: 15 Jul 1857
.... 3 Delilah Ensor b: 02 Sep 1859
.... 3 Laura Eugnia Ensor b: 18 Sep 1861
.... 3 George W. Ensor b: 25 Oct 1862
.... 3 John Albert Ensor b: 02 Aug 1864
.... 3 Bettie Florence Ensor b: 04 Mar 1866
.... 3 Maggie Ruply Ensor b: 25 Oct 1867
.... 3 John B. Ensor b: 25 Jul 1869
...... 2 Rachel J. Ensor b: 09 Oct 1829 d: 19 Jun 1905 in Harford Co, Maryland
.... +Shadrach Streett b: 1823 in Harford Co, Maryland m: 10 Jan 1850 d: 25 Jun 1875
...... 2 Sarah J. Ensor b: Abt. 1834
...... 2 Mary K. Ensor b: 05 Feb 1834 d: 19 Nov 1885 in Bethel

```
.......... +Eli Turner  b: 26 Jul 1826  d: 04 Mar 1894 in Bethel
............ 3 Dr Frank Turner  b: 1858
................ +Mary E Hope  b: 12 Mar 1863 in Rocks  m: 17 Jul 1895 in H CO  d: 23 Jan 1930 in MADONNA
............ 3 Sarah Ellen Turner  b: 30 Aug 1860 in Harford Co  d: 02 Jan 1943
...... 2 Thomas E. Ensor  b: Jul 1838  d: in White Hall
...... 2 George Honor Ensor  b: 1841
...... 2 Georgia Honor Ensor  b: 1841
.......... +James Thomas Burns  b: 05 Sep 1833
............ 3 Elsie Burns
............ 3 Edgar Burns  b: Dec 1868
................ +Alverta Virginia Thomas  b: 04 Jun 1871 in Vernon  m: 05 Aug 1891
.................... 4 Carl Burns  b: Oct 1891
.................... 4 May V. Burns  b: Apr 1895
.................... 4 Mabe V. Burns  b: Nov 1898
.................... 4 Henry Polk Burns  b: Mar 1900
.................... 4 Kenneth Burns  b: Abt. 1902
............ 3 J. Howard Burns  b: 1871  d: 1950
............ 3 Clarence Mitchell Burns  b: 25 Apr 1875 in White Hall, Maryland  d: 28 Jul 1949
................ +Ella May Almony  b: 23 Aug 1883 in White Hall, MD  d: 31 Dec 1963 in White Hall, MD
.................... 4 Georgia Frances Burns  b: 17 Feb 1905
.................... 4 Mary Elsie Burns  b: 04 Aug 1907
.................... 4 Ruth Adelaide Burns  b: 03 Sep 1908
.................... 4 Gladys May Burns  b: 11 Nov 1914
........................ +Arnold J Croddy
*2nd Wife of Luke Gorsuch Ensor:
. +Rachel Davis  m: Abt. 1845
```

Edward Bond Land

Looking North toward Maryland Line

The **Edward Bond** land is located on the east side of the Old York Road near Maryland Line. Edward was involved in the evaluation of confiscated proprietary reserve lands in 1782.
The Bond family descends from Peter Bond who was born in Peckham, England abt. 1640.

The farm was owned by the Koller and Snyder families before being bought by Emerson Ensor, a veteran of the Normandy invasion in World War 11. The ancestors of the Emerson Ensor family originally owned land in East Baltimore and later established many farms in the 8th District. The family has ties to the Gorsuch, Cole, Almony and Burns families. The photo shows Maryland Line and Pennsylvania in the distance. Some of this land shown was formerly owned by the Pocock, Ayres and Sparks families. Kevin and Keith Ensor are the current owners of the farm.

Descendants of Samuel James Bond

1 Samuel James Bond b: 1747
. +Cynthia Richardson b: Abt. 1750 m: Abt. 1770
...... 2 Samuel John Bond b: Abt. 1772
.... +Cynthia Richardson b: Abt. 1774 m: 18 Jan 1794 in Harford County
...... 2 George Bond b: 01 Aug 1771 in Harford County d: 1843 in York, Pa.
.... +Elizabeth Davis b: 1775 in Maryland m: Abt. 1797
.... 3 Nancy Ann Bond b: 15 Mar 1799 in New Market d: in Hancock Co., Ohio
.... +John Krout b: 10 Oct 1802 in Baltimore Co. d: 16 Jul 1873 in Ohio
.... 4 Elizabeth Krout b: 01 May 1825 in York, Co., Pennsylvania d: in Missouri
.... +John Ross McDonald b: 1815 in York Co., d: 1867 in Missouri m: 1852 in Maryland
.... 4 Henry Krout b: 17 Jun 1827 in York, Co., Pennsylvania d: 04 Jul 1834
.... 4 Ann Krout b: 14 Dec 1830 in York, Co., Pennsylvania d: 1915 in Ohio
.... +Jacob Hoy
.... 4 John L. Krout b: 06 Dec 1832 in York, Co., Pennsylvania d: 30 Aug 1908 in Ohio
.... +Mary Free b: 17 Dec 1837 d: 31 Oct 1916
.... 4 Mary Krout b: 16 Sep 1834 in York, Co., Pennsylvania d: 16 Nov 1873
.... +John Clark Lowe b: 18 Apr 1809 d: 05 Jul 1898
.... 4 Dr. Adam Nelson Krout b: 30 Dec 1836 in York, Co., Pennsylvania d: 22 Jan 1891
.... +Rachel Ann Orwick
.... 4 Milton Kelly Krout b: 01 Apr 1839 in York, Co., Pennsylvania d: 23 Jan 1862 in Ohio
.... 4 George Wesley Krout b: 14 Oct 1823 in York, Co., Pennsylvania d: 02 Sep 1896 in Mt. Blanchard, Ohio
.... +Jemima Anstine b: 09 Dec 1828 in York Co. d: Abt. 1858 in Ohio m: 1847
.... *2nd Wife of George Wesley Krout:
.... +Elizabeth Sampson b: 08 Mar 1836 in Richland Co., Ohio d: 29 Mar 1910 in Mt. Blanchard, Ohio m: 19 Aug 1858
.... 3 George W. Bond b: Abt. 1800 in New Market d: Abt. 1838
.... +Elizabeth Clarke b: 1803 d: 1873 in Buried Md line
.... 4 William Henry Bond b: 1830 d: 1893 in York
.... 4 Edwin R. Bond b: Abt. 1832
.... 4 Frank Smith Bond b: Abt. 1835
.... 4 Alfred Bond b: 28 Apr 1837 in New Market d: 24 Aug 1929 in York, Prospect Hill Cm.
.... +Elizabeth Hetrick b: 04 Aug 1835 in Shrewsbury Twp d: 23 Apr 1926 in York, Prospect Hill Cm. m: 29 Sep 1859 in Hopewell, York Co
.... 3 James Bond b: 02 Jan 1808 in New Market, Md. d: 14 Jan 1891 in Maryland Line
.... +Elizabeth Jane Sampson b: 27 Aug 1815 in New Market d: 11 Feb 1901 in Maryland Line, Md. Line Cm. m: 14 Mar 1834
.... 4 Eliza Jane Bond b: 31 May 1835 in Maryland Line d: Jul 1891
.... +James Gore b: Abt. 1832 d: in Old Sampson Cm., York Road m: Abt. 1862
.... *2nd Husband of Eliza Jane Bond:
.... +Paul Lloyd b: Abt. 1833 in Baltimore County, Maryland d: 13 Aug 1909 in Baltimore County, Maryland m: Abt. 1867
.... 4 Thomas Gorsuch Bond b: 25 Dec 1836 in Maryland Line d: 11 Feb 1923 in Michigan
.... +Elizabeth Snyder b: Jun 1839 in Ohio d: 1912 in Michigan m: 04 Nov 1859 in Hancock Co., Ohio
.... 4 James Hamilton Bond b: 22 May 1839 in New Market, Maryland d: 24 Nov 1911 in Hancock Co. Ohio
.... +Margaret Elder b: 04 Aug 1837 in Stewartstown, Pa. d: 09 Oct 1909 in Hancock Co., Ohio
.... 4 David Keller Bond b: 11 Jan 1841 in Baltimore County, Maryland d: 07 Oct 1937 in Findley, Ohio
.... +Mary Louise Trone b: Abt. 1842 in New Orleans d: in Columbus, Ohio
.... 4 Jesse Hinkle Bond b: 26 May 1842 in Hopewell, York Co. d: 03 Jun 1915 in Allegan, Michigan
.... +Alvira Siddall b: 12 Oct 1842 d: 09 Nov 1872 in Salem Twp., Michigan
.... *2nd Wife of Jesse Hinkle Bond:
.... +Frances Silizabeth Curtis d: 19 Sep 1887
.... *3rd Wife of Jesse Hinkle Bond:
.... +Lincinda Gulius d: 22 Dec 1897 m: 31 Jul 1889 in Albion, Ind.
.... *4th Wife of Jesse Hinkle Bond:
.... +Alice Miller d: 18 Oct 1906 m: 12 Nov 1902 in Antwerp, Ohio
.... *5th Wife of Jesse Hinkle Bond:
.... +Della Unknown b: 01 Jan 1855 in Definance co., Ohio m: 02 Jul 1907
.... 4 William Moses Bond b: 12 Jun 1844 in Maryland Line d: 17 Nov 1881 in Hancock Co. Ohio

```
................... +Eliza Jane Waltemire  b: in Hancock Co. Ohio  d: 13 Aug 1920 in Hancock Co. Ohio
................ 4 Eli Sampson Bond  b: 21 Nov 1846 in Maryland Line  d: 23 Jan 1911 in Baltimore County
................... +Lorena Jennie Williams  b: 29 Apr 1847 in Oakland, Maryland  d: 16 Jun 1928  m: 06 Dec 1866
................ 4 Francis Westley Bond  b: 03 Feb 1849 in Maryland Line  d: 22 Mar 1933
................... +Laura J. Gilbert  b: 22 Apr 1851 in Baltimore County, Maryland  d: 24 Jun 1898 in Maryland Line
................ 4 Elizabeth Matilda Bond  b: 24 Jul 1850 in New Market, Md.  d: 28 Jan 1922
................... +Dr Thomas M. Wilson  b: 15 Sep 1852 in New Market, Md.  d: 13 Jun 1917 in New Market, Md.  m: 03 Apr 1873
................ 4 Mary Celestia Bond  b: 23 Jun 1853  d: 08 Sep 1853
................ 4 Annie Louise Bond  b: 23 Nov 1854 in New Market, Md.  d: 1942 in Mt. Washington, Maryland
................... +Harry Benton Williams  b: 11 Sep 1848 in Baltimore County  m: 22 Jun 1871 in Bentley Springs, Md.
................ 4 John David Bond  b: 14 May 1857 in New Market, Md.  d: 28 Jan 1928 in Houcktown, Ohio
................... +Sarah Jane Rosier  b: 06 Feb 1859 in Parkton, Md.  d: 08 Sep 1944 in Michigan  m: 29 Apr 1880
........... 3 Mary Jane Bond  b: 20 May 1817 in Baltimore Co., Maryland  d: 25 Nov 1850
.............. +James Standiford  b: 1820 in Baltimore Co., Maryland  d: Aft. 1860 in New Market Cm.  m: 18 Aug 1839 in York Co.
................ 4 William Bond Standiford  b: 24 Jan 1840 in Maryland  d: 06 Mar 1927 in Kalmazoo, Mi.
................... +Drucilla Flagg
................ 4 John W. Standiford  b: 1842
................ 4 Thomas E. Standiford  b: 1845  d: Oct 1870 in Branch, Mi.
................ 4 Henry K. Standiford  b: 22 Nov 1850  d: 24 Jan 1855
........... 3 Joshua Bond  b: 1818 in Harford County  d: Bef. 1888 in Balt,Co.
.............. +Elizabeth Unknown  b: 1821  d: Bef. 1880
................ 4 George Emory Bond  b: 1840 in Maryland  d: 1900 in Mary line Cm.
................... +Susan Hannah Gilbert  b: 1849 in Maryland  d: 03 Sep 1918 in New Market
................ 4 John Westley Bond  b: 1842
................ 4 Ann R. Bond  b: 1844
................ 4 Daniel S. Bond  b: 1846
................... +Rachel A. Unknown  b: 1846
................ 4 James Bond  b: 1847
................ 4 William T. Bond  b: 1848
................ 4 Samuel Bond  b: 1852
........... 3 Elizabeth Bond  b: Abt. 1822
...... 2 John C. Bond  b: Abt. 1800
...... 2 Sallie Bond  b: Abt. 1800
...... 2 William B. Bond  b: Abt. 1802
.......... +Charlotte Howard Richardson  b: 14 Apr 1807
............ 3 Clara Howard Bond  b: 1845 in Harford Co.  d: 1880
............... +P. Bazel Brown
................ 4 Annie Waters Brown  b: 19 Mar 1872  d: 29 Aug 1948
................... +Charles Clinton Holmes  b: 16 Jan 1868 in Monkton  d: 13 May 1940
```

Descendants of George Bond

1 George Bond b: 01 Aug 1771 in Harford County d: 1843 in York, Pa.
. +Elizabeth Davis b: 1775 in Maryland m: Abt. 1797
...... 2 Nancy Ann Bond b: 15 Mar 1799 in New Market d: in Hancock Co., Ohio
.... +John Krout b: 10 Oct 1802 in Baltimore Co. d: 16 Jul 1873 in Ohio
.... 3 Elizabeth Krout b: 01 May 1825 in York, Co., Pennsylvania d: in Missouri
.... +John Ross McDonald b: 1815 in York Co., m: 1852 in Maryland d: 1867 in Missouri
.... 3 Henry Krout b: 17 Jun 1827 in York, Co., Pennsylvania d: 04 Jul 1834
.... 3 Ann Krout b: 14 Dec 1830 in York, Co., Pennsylvania d: 1915 in Ohio
.... +Jacob Hoy
.... 3 John L. Krout b: 06 Dec 1832 in York, Co., Pennsylvania d: 30 Aug 1908 in Ohio
.... +Mary Free b: 17 Dec 1837 d: 31 Oct 1916
.... 3 Mary Krout b: 16 Sep 1834 in York, Co., Pennsylvania d: 16 Nov 1873
.... +John Clark Lowe b: 18 Apr 1809 d: 05 Jul 1898
.... 3 Dr. Adam Nelson Krout b: 30 Dec 1836 in York, Co., Pennsylvania d: 22 Jan 1891
.... +Rachel Ann Orwick
.... 3 Milton Kelly Krout b: 01 Apr 1839 in York, Co., Pennsylvania d: 23 Jan 1862 in Ohio
.... 3 George Wesley Krout b: 14 Oct 1823 in York, Co., Pennsylvania d: 02 Sep 1896 in Mt. Blanchard, Ohio
.... +Jemima Anstine b: 09 Dec 1828 in York Co. m: 1847 d: Abt. 1858 in Ohio
.... *2nd Wife of George Wesley Krout:
.... +Elizabeth Sampson b: 08 Mar 1836 in Richland Co., Ohio m: 19 Aug 1858 d: 29 Mar 1910 in Mt. Blanchard, Ohio
...... 2 George W. Bond b: Abt. 1800 in New Market d: Abt. 1838
.... +Elizabeth Clarke b: 1803 d: 1873 in Buried Md line
.... 3 William Henry Bond b: 1830 d: 1893 in York
.... 3 Edwin R. Bond b: Abt. 1832
.... 3 Frank Smith Bond b: Abt. 1835
.... 3 Alfred Bond b: 28 Apr 1837 in New Market d: 24 Aug 1929 in York, Prospect Hill Cm.
.... +Elizabeth Hetrick b: 04 Aug 1835 in Shrewsbury Twp m: 29 Sep 1859 in Hopewell, York Co d: 23 Apr 1926 in York, Prospect Hill Cm.
...... 2 James Bond b: 02 Jan 1808 in New Market, Md. d: 14 Jan 1891 in Maryland Line
.... +Elizabeth Jane Sampson b: 27 Aug 1815 in New Market m: 14 Mar 1834 d: 11 Feb 1901 in Maryland Line, Md. Line Cm.
.... 3 Eliza Jane Bond b: 31 May 1835 in Maryland Line d: Jul 1891
.... +James Gore b: Abt. 1832 m: Abt. 1862 d: in Old Sampson Cm., York Road
.... *2nd Husband of Eliza Jane Bond:
.... +Paul Lloyd b: Abt. 1833 in Baltimore County, Maryland m: Abt. 1867 d: 13 Aug 1909 in Baltimore County, Maryland
.... 3 Thomas Gorsuch Bond b: 25 Dec 1836 in Maryland Line d: 11 Feb 1923 in Michigan
.... +Elizabeth Snyder b: Jun 1839 in Ohio m: 04 Nov 1859 in Hancock Co., Ohio d: 1912 in Michigan
.... 3 James Hamilton Bond b: 22 May 1839 in New Market, Maryland d: 24 Nov 1911 in Hancock Co. Ohio
.... +Margaret Elder b: 04 Aug 1837 in Stewartstown, Pa. d: 09 Oct 1909 in Hancock Co., Ohio
.... 3 David Keller Bond b: 11 Jan 1841 in Baltimore County, Maryland d: 07 Oct 1937 in Findley, Ohio
.... +Mary Louise Trone b: Abt. 1842 in New Orleans d: in Columbus, Ohio
.... 3 Jesse Hinkle Bond b: 26 May 1842 in Hopewell, York Co. d: 03 Jun 1915 in Allegan, Michigan
.... +Alvira Siddall b: 12 Oct 1842 d: 09 Nov 1872 in Salem Twp., Michigan
.... *2nd Wife of Jesse Hinkle Bond:
.... +Frances Silizabeth Curtis d: 19 Sep 1887
.... *3rd Wife of Jesse Hinkle Bond:
.... +Lincinda Gulius m: 31 Jul 1889 in Albion, Ind. d: 22 Dec 1897
.... *4th Wife of Jesse Hinkle Bond:
.... +Alice Miller m: 12 Nov 1902 in Antwerp, Ohio d: 18 Oct 1906
.... *5th Wife of Jesse Hinkle Bond:
.... +Della Unknown b: 01 Jan 1855 in Definance co., Ohio m: 02 Jul 1907
.... 3 William Moses Bond b: 12 Jun 1844 in Maryland Line d: 17 Nov 1881 in Hancock Co. Ohio
.... +Eliza Jane Waltemire b: in Hancock Co. Ohio d: 13 Aug 1920 in Hancock Co. Ohio
.... 3 Eli Sampson Bond b: 21 Nov 1846 in Maryland Line d: 23 Jan 1911 in Baltimore County
.... +Lorena Jennie Williams b: 29 Apr 1847 in Oakland, Maryland m: 06 Dec 1866 d: 16 Jun 1928
.... 3 Francis Westley Bond b: 03 Feb 1849 in Maryland Line d: 22 Mar 1933

.... +Laura J. Gilbert b: 22 Apr 1851 in Baltimore County, Maryland d: 24 Jun 1898 in Maryland Line
.... 3 Elizabeth Matilda Bond b: 24 Jul 1850 in New Market, Md. d: 28 Jan 1922
.... +Dr Thomas M. Wilson b: 15 Sep 1852 in New Market, Md. m: 03 Apr 1873 d: 13 Jun 1917 in New Market, Md.
.... 3 Mary Celestia Bond b: 23 Jun 1853 d: 08 Sep 1853
.... 3 Annie Louise Bond b: 23 Nov 1854 in New Market, Md. d: 1942 in Mt. Washington, Maryland
.... +Harry Benton Williams b: 11 Sep 1848 in Baltimore County m: 22 Jun 1871 in Bentley Springs, Md.
.... 3 John David Bond b: 14 May 1857 in New Market, Md. d: 28 Jan 1928 in Houcktown, Ohio
.... +Sarah Jane Rosier b: 06 Feb 1859 in Parkton, Md. m: 29 Apr 1880 d: 08 Sep 1944 in Michigan
...... 2 Mary Jane Bond b: 20 May 1817 in Baltimore Co., Maryland d: 25 Nov 1850
.... +James Standiford b: 1820 in Baltimore Co., Maryland m: 18 Aug 1839 in York Co. d: Aft. 1860 in New Market Cm.
.... 3 William Bond Standiford b: 24 Jan 1840 in Maryland d: 06 Mar 1927 in Kalmazoo, Mi.
.... +Drucilla Flagg
.... 3 John W. Standiford b: 1842
.... 3 Thomas E. Standiford b: 1845 d: Oct 1870 in Branch, Mi.
.... 3 Henry K. Standiford b: 22 Nov 1850 d: 24 Jan 1855
...... 2 Joshua Bond b: 1818 in Harford County d: Bef. 1888 in Balt,Co.
.... +Elizabeth Unknown b: 1821 d: Bef. 1880
.... 3 George Emory Bond b: 1840 in Maryland d: 1900 in Mary line Cm.
.... +Susan Hannah Gilbert b: 1849 in Maryland d: 03 Sep 1918 in New Market
.... 3 John Westley Bond b: 1842
.... 3 Ann R. Bond b: 1844
.... 3 Daniel S. Bond b: 1846
.... +Rachel A. Unknown b: 1846
.... 3 James Bond b: 1847
.... 3 William T. Bond b: 1848
.... 3 Samuel Bond b: 1852
...... 2 Elizabeth Bond b: Abt. 1822

Baltimore County Pioneers- 7th District

Descendants of Isaac Sampson

1 Isaac Sampson b: 1753 in Baltimore County, Maryland d: Aug 1836
. +Elizabeth Rutledge b: 09 Aug 1756 in Baltimore County, Maryland d: 19 Oct 1846
...... 2 Sarah Sampson b: Abt. 1778
...... 2 Mary Sampson b: Abt. 1780
.... +John Collett b: Abt. 1780
...... 2 Susannah Sampson b: Abt. 1782
.... +Rutledge b: Abt. 1780
...... 2 David Sampson b: 31 May 1784 in New Market, Md. d: 24 Aug 1862 in Long Valley, Maryland Line
.... +Elizabeth Ann Rutledge b: 02 Apr 1787 in New Market, Md. d: 10 Aug 1839 in Baltimore , Co. Md.
.... 3 Stephen Sampson b: Dec 1804 d: 16 Dec 1804
.... 3 Ruth Sampson b: 06 Nov 1809 in 7TH District d: 27 Oct 1865 in Hancock Co., Ohio
.... +Elisha Gorsuch b: 03 Mar 1810 in Gorsuch Mills d: 07 Mar 1847 in Ohio, Typhoid Fever
.... 3 Eli S. Sampson b: 12 Feb 1813 in Baltimore County, Maryland d: 21 Dec 1893 in Ohio
.... +Margaret Ann Krout b: 15 May 1812 in Baltimore County, Maryland d: 20 Nov 1892 in Hancock Co. Ohio
.... 3 Elizabeth Jane Sampson b: 27 Aug 1815 in New Market d: 11 Feb 1901 in Maryland Line, Md. Line Cm.
.... +James Bond b: 02 Jan 1808 in New Market, Md. d: 14 Jan 1891 in Maryland Line
.... 3 Mary Sampson b: 13 Dec 1817 in Baltimore , Co. Md. d: 23 Mar 1856 in Baltimore , Co. Md.
.... +Johnsey S. Palmer b: Abt. 1816 in Baltimore , Co. Md. d: in Baltimore , Co. Md.
.... 3 Nicholas Sampson b: 01 Feb 1820 in Baltimore , Co. Md. d: 18 Aug 1864 in Houcktown, Hancock CO, Ohio
.... +Elizabeth Hunter b: Abt. 1822
.... 3 David Sampson b: 14 Aug 1823 in Baltimore , Co. Md. d: 14 Aug 1824 in Baltimore , Co. Md.
.... 3 Edwin Hindle Sampson b: 02 Jan 1830 in Maryland d: 1864 in Houcktown, Ohio
.... +Mary Jane Standiford b: 23 Aug 1831 in Maryland d: 1864
...... *2nd Wife of David Sampson:
.... +Matilda Ann Collett b: 15 Nov 1785 in White Hall, Md. d: 29 Nov 1867 in Long Valley, Maryland Line
...... 2 Isaac Sampson b: 24 Jan 1795 in Baltimore Co. d: 24 Nov 1884 in Maryland Line
.... +Keziah Pocock b: 29 May 1801 d: 10 Dec 1879
.... 3 Elizabeth Ellen Sampson b: 08 Jul 1832 in Maryland d: 18 Dec 1886 in Md Line
.... +Agustus Caesar Almony b: 12 Oct 1820 in White Hall, Maryland d: 22 Apr 1881 in Md. Line

Descendants of John Michael Krout

1 John Michael Krout b: 13 Mar 1770 in Pennsylvania d: 08 Aug 1849 in York County
. +Maria Elizabeth Hetrick b: 07 Nov 1776 in York Co. m: Abt. 1792 d: 12 Jun 1855
...... 2 Mary Krout b: 06 Jun 1794 d: 23 Sep 1873
.... +Levi Sampson b: Abt. 1790
...... 2 Jacob Krout b: 1798 in Baltimore Co. d: 1839 in York Co.
.... +Susan Waltermire b: Abt. 1800
.... 3 Joseph Krout b: Abt. 1825
.... 3 Jacob Krout b: Abt. 1827 in Morrow Co., Ohio
.... 3 Elizabeth Krout b: Abt. 1829
.... 3 William Krout b: Abt. 1831
.... +Elizabeth Curry b: 1831
...... 2 Ann Krout b: Abt. 1800 in Baltimore Co. d: Dec 1840
.... +John Orwig b: 20 Apr 1790 d: 1839
...... 2 John Krout b: 10 Oct 1802 in Baltimore Co. d: 16 Jul 1873 in Ohio
.... +Nancy Ann Bond b: 15 Mar 1799 in New Market d: in Hancock Co., Ohio
.... 3 Elizabeth Krout b: 01 May 1825 in York, Co., Pennsylvania d: in Missouri
.... +John Ross McDonald b: 1815 in York Co., m: 1852 in Maryland d: 1867 in Missouri
.... 3 Henry Krout b: 17 Jun 1827 in York, Co., Pennsylvania d: 04 Jul 1834
.... 3 Ann Krout b: 14 Dec 1830 in York, Co., Pennsylvania d: 1915 in Ohio
.... +Jacob Hoy
.... 3 John L. Krout b: 06 Dec 1832 in York, Co., Pennsylvania d: 30 Aug 1908 in Ohio
.... +Mary Free b: 17 Dec 1837 d: 31 Oct 1916
.... 3 Mary Krout b: 16 Sep 1834 in York, Co., Pennsylvania d: 16 Nov 1873
.... +John Clark Lowe b: 18 Apr 1809 d: 05 Jul 1898
.... 3 Dr. Adam Nelson Krout b: 30 Dec 1836 in York, Co., Pennsylvania d: 22 Jan 1891
.... +Rachel Ann Orwick
.... 3 Milton Kelly Krout b: 01 Apr 1839 in York, Co., Pennsylvania d: 23 Jan 1862 in Ohio
.... 3 [2] George Wesley Krout b: 14 Oct 1823 in York, Co., Pennsylvania d: 02 Sep 1896 in Mt. Blanchard, Ohio
.... +Jemima Anstine b: 09 Dec 1828 in York Co. m: 1847 d: Abt. 1858 in Ohio
.... *2nd Wife of [2] George Wesley Krout:
.... +[1] Elizabeth Sampson b: 08 Mar 1836 in Richland Co., Ohio m: 19 Aug 1858 d: 29 Mar 1910 in Mt. Blanchard, Ohio
...... 2 Joseph Krout b: 1803 d: 16 Oct 1883 in Coshocton Co., Ohio
.... +Margaret Morris
.... 3 George W. Krout
.... 3 Elizabeth Krout b: Abt. 1830
.... 3 Charles Krout
.... 3 Joseph Krout
.... 3 Samuel Krout
.... 3 Susan Krout
.... 3 John N. Krout
.... 3 Keziah Krout
.... 3 Benjamin F. Krout b: Abt. 1836
.... 3 Margaret Krout
.... 3 Mary A. Krout
.... 3 Alice Krout
...... 2 Michael Krout b: 1805 in Baltimore Co. d: 02 Oct 1888
.... +Julia A. Lowe b: 1812 in York Co. d: 19 Nov 1896
.... 3 Elizabeth Krout b: Abt. 1835
.... 3 Anna Krout
.... 3 Noah Krout b: Abt. 1825
.... 3 Henry Krout
.... 3 Alice Krout
...... 2 Benjamin Krout b: 14 Aug 1805 in Maryland d: 16 Sep 1875 in Baltimore Co.
.... +Hannah b: 1805 in Maryland
.... 3 Adam Krout b: 1836

```
............ 3 Rebecca Krout  b: 1846
............ 3 Michael Krout  b: Abt. 1830
............ 3 Mary Ann Krout
............ 3 Adam Krout
............ 3 Elizabeth Krout  b: Abt. 1836
............ 3 Noah Krout  b: Abt. 1838
...... 2 Maria Elizabeth Krout  b: 19 Jul 1807 in Pennsylvania  d: 12 May 1880 in Hancock Co., Ohio
.......... +Nicholas Strayer  b: Abt. 1805
...... 2 Henry Krout  b: 1810  d: 15 Nov 1878 in Fairfield, Ohio
.......... +Cristina Strayer  b: 01 Jul 1815  d: 04 Jul 1895
...... 2 Margaret Ann Krout  b: 15 May 1812 in Baltimore County, Maryland  d: 20 Nov 1892 in Hancock Co. Ohio
.......... +Eli S. Sampson  b: 12 Feb 1813 in Baltimore County, Maryland  m: 13 Mar 1835 in Baltimore , Co. Md.  d: 21 Dec 1893 in Ohio
............ 3 Mary Ann Sampson  b: 05 Jan 1830 in Baltimore , Co. Md., New Market  d: in Ohio
................ +William Dety
............ 3 Isaac Sampson  b: 11 Sep 1832 in Baltimore , Co. Md., New Market  d: in Ohio
................ +Sarah Cathrine Dreisbach  d: in Ohio
............ 3 Elizabeth Sampson  b: 22 Jun 1835
................ +Rev A. Sager
............ 3 [1] Elizabeth Sampson  b: 08 Mar 1836 in Richland Co., Ohio  d: 29 Mar 1910 in Mt. Blanchard, Ohio
................ +[2] George Wesley Krout  b: 14 Oct 1823 in York, Co., Pennsylvania  m: 19 Aug 1858  d: 02 Sep 1896 in Mt. Blanchard, Ohio
............ 3 David Hinkle Sampson  b: 11 Sep 1838 in Hancock Co., Ohio  d: 04 Oct 1899
................ +Lenera Seckrider  b: in Ohio
............ *2nd Wife of David Hinkle Sampson:
................ +Malinda Hey  m: 15 Oct 1863
............ 3 Michael W. Sampson  b: 24 Dec 1840 in Hancock Co., Ohio  d: 13 Oct 1844 in Hancock Co., Ohio
............ 3 Clara Ann Sampson  b: 06 Feb 1843 in Hancock Co., Ohio  d: 30 Oct 1844 in Hancock Co., Ohio
............ 3 Sara Jane Sampson  b: 12 Jun 1845 in Baltimore , Co. Md., New Market  d: in Ohio
................ +George Perry Edie  b: in Ohio  d: in Ohio
............ 3 Ruth Gorsuch Sampson  b: 23 Nov 1846 in Hancock Co., Ohio  d: 05 Feb 1927 in Hancock Co., Ohio
................ +John A. Sillik
............ *2nd Husband of Ruth Gorsuch Sampson:
................ +Matthew Gilbert Hammond
............ 3 Isabelle Sampson  b: 05 Mar 1849 in Hancock Co., Ohio  d: 14 Mar 1920 in Hancock Co., Ohio
................ +Daniel Clayton Shields
............ 3 John Sampson  b: 17 Jun 1854  d: 21 May 1866
............ 3 Neomi Sampson  b: 1858
............ 3 Maggie Elizabeth Sampson  b: 1859
...... 2 Noah Krout  b: 1815 in Baltimore Co.  d: 16 Sep 1871 in Lancaster, Fairfield co., Ohio
.......... +Mary Snoke  b: 1821  d: 1892 in Lancaster, Ohio
............ 3 Mary A. Krout  b: Abt. 1844
............ 3 Elizabeth Krout  b: Abt. 1846
............ 3 Angeline Krout  b: Abt. 1848
............ 3 Rachel Krout  b: Abt. 1849
............ 3 John H. Krout  b: Abt. 1850
............ 3 Nancy J. Krout  b: Abt. 1852
............ 3 William D. Krout  b: Abt. 1854
............ 3 Ella Krout  b: Abt. 1856
............ 3 George W. Krout  b: Abt. 1858
...... 2 Adam Henry Krout  b: 1817  d: 27 Sep 1884 in York Co.
.......... +Unknown Standiford
............ 3 William B. Krout  b: Abt. 1840
................ +Sadie Cross  b: 1846 in York Co.  d: 14 Jul 1909 in Baltimore, Maryland
............ 3 Michael Krout  b: Abt. 1830
............ 3 Sarah Ann Krout
............ 3 Mary Jane Krout  d: 20 Jan 1907 in Baltimore , Maryland
................ +Joseph L. League
............ 3 James Krout  b: Abt. 1845
```

.... 3 Colwell Krout
.... 3 Emma Krout d: 09 Aug 1886 in Townsontown, Md.
.... +John E. Flayhart m: 30 Jul 1870
...... 2 Eve Krout b: Abt. 1820 d: Abt. 1820

Baltimore County Pioneers- 7th District

David Gorsuch

David Gorsuch surveyed the property "Goshen", which covered 689 acres along the present Harris Mill Road in 1786. David's father Charles Gorsuch lived near the Western Run in the Eight Election district and was involved in the evaluation of confiscated proprietary reserve lands in 1782. The Gorsuch family owned land along the York Road below Hereford and has many descendants living in the area. David's family constructed a gristmill and sawmill along the Deer Creek and the community became known as Gorsuch Mills. Families connected were: Dunnick, Rutledge, Pearce, LeSourd, Meredith and Tredway. Many of these families later moved to Ohio in the 1800's. Stephen Gorsuch advertised the mill for sale on May 6, 1854. A small Gorsuch graveyard is located on the hill behind where the old mill stood at the crossroads of Gorsuch Mills. The Winemiller family purchased the mill in 1866 and were the last to operate the mill. Gorsuch Mills at one time contained a store, church and blacksmith shop in addition to the gristmill.

Ezekiel Bosley

Ezekiel Bosley surveyed "Fertile Marsh", a 291-acre parcel located along the Harford County Line near Gorsuch Mills. Ezekiel's family has many ties to northern Baltimore County. His wife was Elizabeth Norris and his children all married into local families. Rachel married Abraham Vaughn, Mary married William Norris, Isaac married Elizabeth Hutchins, James married Hannah Hughes, Elizabeth married Walter Perdue, Susanna married James St. Clair and Joseph married Leticia Hutchins.

Abraham McDonald

The **McDonald** family owned several farms in Fawn Township, York County, Pa. Abraham McDonald, settled along the present Harris Mill Road between New Market and Deer Creek. Clark McDonald owned a farm north of Maryland Line. His son, Leib McDonald was a prominent student, educator and athlete. The McDonald's ancestral land was in Glencoe, Southern Scotland and Antrim in Northern Ireland.

Francis Sparks

Francis Sparks was a 2nd Sargent in Captain Cockey's Dragoons serving at Yorktown in 1781. He owned the lands to the east from York Road, along the Harris Mill Road. The Sparks children married into the Kaufman, Pearce and Gosnell families and some descendants later settled on the "Manor". Ruth Sparks married Josiah Pearce and Prudence Sparks married Richard Gosnell. Later generations of the family moved to the Upperco area. Loring Sparks was an Agriculture teacher at Hereford High School and his brother Dave was a prominent farmer in the White House area.

Thomas Pearce

The Pearce Family was an early arrival in Maryland. Thomas Pearce was born at "Molly's Industry", near Towson. His children settled Gorsuch Mills, Shane and White Hall. In Gorsuch Mills, his descendants married into the neighboring families of Gorsuch, Matthews, Perdue, Lee, Sparks, Lytle, Barton, Morris and Slade. Thomas was involved in the evaluation of confiscated proprietary reserve lands in 1782.

Baltimore County Pioneers- 7th District

NEW MARKET 1850- Drawing by Dale Bond

```
              J. CROSS, □              WM. B. KROUT m. SADIE CROSS - 1864
              AT PA LINE
 FREELAND RD.                          TO 83

  □ LUTHER BELL SAMPSON    WM. DAY  □-1    1- □ W.M. STANIFORD - GATE KEEPER
    SON OF ABRAM.          CARPENTER                              G. COOK
                           WHEELWRIGHT □-2  2- ■ JUNK -  HENDRICKS - B. STANIFORD.
           J. KROUT - JOSHUA BOND. □
                      BLACKSMITH SHOP □-3  3- □ NEW
                              SITE
                    SHOEMAKER H. ATWELL ■-4
                           J. KROUT - ■-5   4- ■ ANTHONY TAYLOR ' BLACKSMITH - E. BOND
                              2.1609 - ☒-6   5- ■ M. KROUT BUILT ELIZ. KROUT  J. KROUT 185
 HOTEL                                                    1804              HARMS MILL RD.
 BUILT 1806 BY JOHN BELL  HOTEL   ■-7
 BOUGHT BY HENDRIX - 1906          NEW - □-8  6- ■ DR. E. BELL
                                                DAUGHTERS m. THOM. DEFORD - JOHN HURST
                    P.O. - STORE -  ■-9    7- ■ J. HENDRICKS - STORE ( HURST & DEFORD 1BT
 STORE KEEPER - BEN JORDON                                                          MAY
                                    ☒-10   8- ■ BENJ. STANIFORD
                                              W. HARRIS
              JNO. FIFE - J. WIRTZ. □-11
                                              HANNAH KROUT   W/O BEN J.
                    ABM. MCDONALD ■-12     9- ☒ KROUT        CANNERY
                         TAYOR                 ANN MORRIS   □ CHIMNEY
                                    ☒-13  10-□   H. ROSIER - HORRIE
                                    □-14        RUTLEDGE -
                                                BOCLEY
 ORIG. BUILT - 1838 - M.P. CHURCH - □-15  11 □   LOWE
                              1926
                   PARSONAGE    PARKING LOT
                   BUILT 1831  SCHOOL - HALL- ■-16  12 □ GILES GREEN
 SHOEMAKER - J. CROMER  HEDRICK - □-17    13 □
 HSE OCCUPIED BY - T.G. RUTLEDGE ■-18     14 □ THOMPSON MKT
                      TEACHER - JUDGE                              N
 THOM. MEADS 1900             □-19                                 |
 PURCHASED BY JOHN LEIB.      □-20                             W---+---E
                                                                   |
                       SHED - □ T. WILSON □-21  15-☒ . ROSIER      S
 THOM. M. WILSON. VETERINARY  ☒-22
 m. ELIZ. MATILDA BOND ✱      ☒-23
                     FULTON   □-24        16-□ J. LOWE     MARYLAND LINE
                              ☒-25          □ BLACKSMITH SHOP.    (NEW MKT.)
                              ☒-26          □ BANK - NEW.   MD. HISTORIC TRUST. INVEN
                              □-27        ASBURY METHODIST EPISCOPAL   HOUSE SURVEY
 NEW P.O. - □                STORE        CHURCH SITE 1842-1939
                             GARAGE        (ME CHURCH)              ■ PRE - 1850
                                            M.L. CEMETERY           ☒ - 1850-1880
                       INN - □              EST. 1864               ☒ - 1880-1900
                 ROAD                       □                       □ - 1900-1930
                                            SCHOOL
 ✱ ELIZ. M. WILSON - 1850-1922
  DAUG. JAMES BOND. ELIZ. SAMPSON.                         1852- 17 HOUSE HOLDS
  ELIZ. (SAMPSON) BOND DIED AT THIS HSE                    WITH FURNITURE
      1901
```

Baltimore County Pioneers- 7th District

Descendants of David Gorsuch

1 David Gorsuch b: 23 Nov 1763 in Balt Co d: 06 Oct 1841 in Gorsuch Mills
. +Rebecca Gorsuch b: 06 Mar 1767 in Baltimore , Co. Md. m: 30 Dec 1786 d: 25 Sep 1841 in Gorsuch Mills
...... 2 Eleanor Gorsuch b: 17 Dec 1787 in Gorsuch Mills d: Sep 1825 in Ill.
.... +Thomas Dunnuck b: 25 Aug 1787 in 7th District, Baltimore Co., Md. d: in Ill.
...... 2 Charles Gorsuch b: 13 Jun 1789 in Gorsuch Mills d: 06 Feb 1869 in Butler Co , OH
.... +Ruth Rutledge b: 19 Oct 1788 in Harford Co m: 05 Jan 1809 d: 1831 in Balt Co
.... 3 Rachel Gorsuch b: 07 Nov 1809 d: 16 Feb 1883 in ILL
.... +Joseph Lesourd b: 23 Sep 1811 in Butler Co. Oh. m: 08 Mar 1832 d: 02 Sep 1883
.... 3 Thomas Gorsuch b: Abt. 1811 in Gorsuch Mills, MD. d: in Ohio
.... +Martha Jane Curtis b: in OH m: 16 Apr 1840 in butler Co. Oh. d: in OH
.... 3 Elizabeth Gorsuch b: Abt. 1813 in Maryland
.... +Robert Allen b: Abt. 1812
.... 3 Sarah Gorsuch b: Abt. 1815 in Maryland
.... +Abram Sutton
.... 3 John Westley Gorsuch b: Abt. 1817 in Maryland
...... *2nd Wife of Charles Gorsuch:
.... +[1] Hannah Gorsuch b: 01 Apr 1799 in Charlesborough, Fork MD m: 07 Dec 1831 in MD d: 31 Jul 1885 in Butler Co., OH
.... 3 Elisha Gorsuch b: 26 Sep 1832 in Butler CO. Ohio d: 16 Feb 1874 in Butler Co. Oh.
.... +Sarah Elizabeth Stabler b: 06 Oct 1831 in Butler CO , Ohio m: 29 Mar 1855 in Butler CO d: 14 May 1897 in Butler CO , Ohio
...... 2 Sarah Gorsuch b: 1791 in Maryland d: 1818
...... 2 Elisha Gorsuch b: 24 Dec 1792 in Gorsuch Mills d: 03 Dec 1824 in Gorsuch Mills
.... +[1] Hannah Gorsuch b: 01 Apr 1799 in Charlesborough, Fork MD m: 17 Apr 1823 in MD d: 31 Jul 1885 in Butler Co., OH
.... 3 Rebecca Ann Gorsuch b: Abt. 1824
.... 3 Eleanor Gorsuch b: 24 Jan 1825 in Gorsuch Mills d: 27 Feb 1874 in Butler CO. Ohio
.... +Nicholas Lesourd b: 21 Jun 1816 in Vernon, Md. m: 1841 in Ohio d: 24 Oct 1882 in Butler. OH.
...... 2 Stephen Gorsuch b: 08 Jan 1795 in Gorsuch Mills d: 18 Sep 1878 in Butler Co, OH
.... +Rachel Gorsuch b: 02 Mar 1798 in Fork MD m: 04 Apr 1822 d: 20 Sep 1870 in Butler Co , OH
.... 3 Joseph Gorsuch b: 27 Jan 1823 in Gorsuch Mills d: 1823 in Gorsuch Mills, MD.
.... 3 Nicholas Gorsuch b: 16 Feb 1824 in Gorsuch Mills d: 27 Jun 1872 in Ohio
.... +Sarah Ann Treadway b: 22 Dec 1827 in Gorsuch Mills m: 26 Feb 1850 in Gorsuch mills d: 15 Aug 1890 in Sidney, OH
.... 3 Elisha Gorsuch b: 16 Jul 1825 in Gorsuch Mills d: Dec 1825 in Gorsuch Mills
.... 3 Charles Thomas Gorsuch b: 14 Oct 1826 in Gorsuch Mills Baltimore co. d: 09 Feb 1906 in Bethany, OH
.... +Elizabeth Gorsuch b: 15 Apr 1833 in Gorsuch Mills, Baltimore County m: 01 Jul 1852 in Maryland Line d: 24 Nov 1917 in Butler Co.
.... 3 Rebecca Ann Gorsuch b: 01 Feb 1828 in Gorsuch Mills d: 20 Feb 1912 in Ohio
.... +Alexander Dykes b: 22 Oct 1824 in West Liberty m: 05 Dec 1861 in Gorsuch mills d: 11 Jul 1882 in OH
.... 3 David Gorsuch b: 15 Feb 1830 in Gorsuch Mills d: 1914 in Ohio
.... +Susannah LeSourd b: 27 Jan 1835 in Maryland m: 20 Dec 1857 d: 1924 in Butler Co , OH
.... 3 Mary Gorsuch b: 24 Aug 1831 in Gorsuch Mills d: 25 Nov 1833 in Gorsuch Mills
.... 3 William Gorsuch b: 18 Jan 1834 in Maryland d: in Bethany, Ohio
.... +Mary Jane Cornelius b: 27 Jun 1837 in Baltimore, Maryland d: in Ohio
.... 3 Rachel Gorsuch b: 10 Jan 1836 in Gorsuch Mills d: 08 Nov 1838 in Gorsuch Mills
.... 3 Sarah Jane Gorsuch b: 17 Sep 1837 in Gorsuch Mills d: 1903
.... 3 Hannah Gorsuch b: 23 Feb 1839 in Gorsuch Mills d: in Ohio
.... +William Hershner b: Abt. 1838 d: in Ohio
.... 3 Eleanor Gorsuch b: 12 May 1842 in Gorsuch Mills d: in Ohio
.... +Anthony J. Allen b: 1844 in Pennsylvania d: in Sidney, Ohio
.... 3 Belinda Gorsuch b: 24 Jan 1847 in Gorsuch Mills d: 04 Sep 1900 in Butler Co , OH
.... +Stephen LeSourd b: 04 Apr 1837 in Butler Co , OH m: 05 Sep 1867 d: 03 Apr 1922
...... 2 Nicholas Gorsuch b: 1797 in Maryland d: 1819
...... 2 Mary Gorsuch b: 10 May 1799 in Gorsuch Mills d: 28 Apr 1873 in Butler Co. Ohio
.... +Joseph Curtis b: Abt. 1792 in Gorsuch Mills m: 14 Apr 1819 d: in Butler Co., Ohio
.... 3 Nicholas Curtis
.... 3 Elizabeth Curtis

.... 3 Eleanor Curtis
.... 3 Rebecca Curtis
.... 3 LEVI Curtis
.... 3 Mary Jane Curtis
.... 3 Charles E Curtis b: 1832
...... 2 Rebecca Gorsuch b: 08 Nov 1801 in Gorsuch Mills d: 14 Oct 1875 in Ohio
.... +Levi Curtis b: 08 Sep 1800 in Gorsuch Mills m: 03 Dec 1823 d: 1890 in MD
.... 3 Sarah Elizabeth Curtis
...... *2nd Husband of Rebecca Gorsuch:
.... +Joseph B. Strawbridge b: 29 Jun 1806 in Hopewell m: Sep 1842 in MD d: 19 Dec 1862 in Wayne Co. Richmond, Ind.
.... 3 Mary Strawbridge b: 26 Jun 1833 d: 05 Oct 1861
.... 3 David Strawbridge b: 16 Dec 1834 in Wayne Co. Richmond, Ind. d: 20 Jul 1895 in Chicago, Ill.
.... +Luxima Chloe Nye m: 01 Feb 1859
.... 3 Martha Strawbridge b: 21 Dec 1836 d: 04 Aug 1847
.... 3 Eleanor Strawbridge b: 15 Sep 1838
.... +J. Dunham Hampton
.... 3 William Strawbridge b: 06 Mar 1843 in Wayne Co. Richmond, Ind. d: in Chicago, Ill.
.... +Esther H. Starbuck m: 31 May 1864
.... 3 Joseph Strawbridge b: 02 Apr 1847
...... 2 Ruth Gorsuch b: 01 Nov 1803 d: 10 Nov 1803
...... 2 Ann Gorsuch b: 30 Jan 1806 in Glencoe, Md. d: 01 Oct 1893 in Indiana
.... +Benjamin Lesourd b: 03 Sep 1801 in Vernon, Md. m: 11 Mar 1824 d: 25 Jan 1876 in Ind
.... 3 Sarah Lesourd b: 1826 d: 1895
.... 3 Levi Curtis Lesourd b: 1828 d: 1906
.... 3 Mary Elizabeth Lesourd b: 1829 d: 1869
.... 3 Rachel Eleanor Lesourd b: 1831 d: 1865
.... 3 John Westley Lesourd b: 1833 d: 1861
.... 3 Hannah Lesourd b: 1835 d: 1881
.... 3 Samantha Jane Lesourd b: 1836 d: 1913
.... 3 Martha Lesourd b: 1837
.... 3 Benjamin Jr Lesourd b: 1839 d: 1862
.... 3 David Gorsuch Lesourd b: 1841 d: 1925
.... 3 Francis Asbury Lesourd b: 1845 d: 1885
...... 2 David Gorsuch b: 09 Nov 1808 in Maryland d: 01 May 1816
...... 2 William Gorsuch b: 10 Jul 1813 in Gorsuch Mills d: 18 May 1867 in Indiana
.... +Sarah Ann Gorsuch b: 22 Jul 1819 in Blackhorse, Harford Co., d: 1905 in Indinia
.... 3 Charles Gorsuch b: Abt. 1842
.... 3 Rebecca Ann Gorsuch b: Abt. 1844
.... 3 Martha Jane Gorsuch b: Abt. 1846
.... 3 Frances Amelia Gorsuch b: Abt. 1848
.... 3 John Thomas Gorsuch b: Abt. 1849
.... 3 Laura Gorsuch b: Abt. 1850

Descendants of Thomas Pearce

```
1 Thomas Pearce  b: 1745 in Molly's Industry  d: 1846 in Gorsuch Mills
.  +Unknown Gorsuch  b: Abt. 1747 in Clynmalira, MD  m: 1772  d: Abt. 1780 in Gorsuch Mills ?
...... 2 Thomas Pearce  b: 1775 in Gorsuch Mills  d: 02 Feb 1856
.......... +Elizabeth Cummings  b: Abt. 1775 in Baltimore co., Md.  m: 1795
*2nd Wife of Thomas Pearce:
.  +Mary Perdue  b: Abt. 1761 in 7th District  m: 1779  d: in Gorsuch Mills
...... 2 Benjamin Pearce  b: Abt. 1780
...... 2 Mary Ann Pearce  b: Abt. 1781 in Gorsuch Mills  d: in Harford Co
.......... +William Elliott  b: Abt. 1780 in Harford Co  d: Nov 1842
............... 3 John William Elliott  b: Abt. 1802
............... 3 Grason Elliott  b: Abt. 1804
............... 3 Edward Thomas Elliott  b: Abt. 1805
............... 3 George Elliott  b: Abt. 1806
............... 3 Charles Westly Elliott  b: Abt. 1806
............... 3 Mary Ann Elliott  b: Abt. 1808
............... 3 Bernice Elliott  b: Abt. 1810
...... 2 Dorcas Pearce  b: 1782 in Gorsuch Mills  d: 11 Jan 1871 in 7TH District
.......... +John Webster Lee  b: Abt. 1780  m: 15 Jan 1820
............... 3 Frances Asbury Lee
............... 3 Rachel Lee
............... 3 Thomas Pearce Lee
............... 3 John Westley Lee  b: 01 Sep 1825  d: 06 Oct 1851
............... 3 Josiah Pearce Lee  b: 27 Dec 1829  d: 18 Aug 1887 in Maryland Line
................... +Sophia S. Unknown  b: 01 Oct 1830  d: 20 Oct 1918
...... 2 Sarah Pearce  b: Abt. 1786 in Gorsuch Mills
.......... +James Barton  b: Abt. 1782
...... 2 Nathan Pearce  b: 1784 in Gorsuch Mills  d: 1841 in Baltimore
.......... +Unknown
............... 3 Sarah Ann Pearce  b: Abt. 1806
............... 3 Amon Pearce  b: Abt. 1808
............... 3 Nathan Hinkle Pearce  b: Abt. 1810
............... 3 Isaiah Pearce  b: 1812  d: 27 Jul 1877
............... 3 Thomas Pearce  b: Abt. 1811
............... 3 Josiah Pearce  b: 14 Feb 1812 in Maryland  d: 18 Aug 1879 in 7th District, Balt Co.
................... +Kedelia  b: 01 Sep 1807  d: 09 Feb 1863 in 7th District, Mt.Zion
....................... 4 Samuel D Pearce  b: 07 Feb 1834 in 7th District  d: 09 Apr 1861
....................... 4 James S Pearce  b: 05 Apr 1836  d: 02 Jan 1881 in 7th District
........................... +Nancy  b: 04 Jul 1843  d: 20 Nov 1879 in 7th DIST, Balt Co, Gorsuch Mills
....................... 4 Thomas Pearce  b: 05 Sep 1839 in 7th District  d: in Mt. Zion
............... 3 Eliza Jane Pearce  b: 02 Jan 1821  d: 17 Sep 1884
................... +Lewis Morris  b: 26 Jan 1822 in 7TH District  m: 20 Mar 1845  d: 09 Aug 1874
....................... 4 Alexius Morris  b: 18 May 1846  d: 1922
........................... +Eliza Talbert  b: 1846
....................... 4 Nathan Morris  b: 25 Apr 1850
........................... +Sarah E Billingslea  b: 22 Sep 1859  d: 08 Dec 1947
....................... 4 Thomas A. Morris  b: 1852  d: 1897
........................... +Sarah Harkness  b: 1853  d: 1933
....................... 4 Sophrona Morris  b: 27 May 1857  d: 06 Dec 1924
....................... 4 Emma Jane Morris  b: 13 Jan 1864  d: 30 Aug 1866
...... 2 Isaiah Pearce  b: 1792 in Gorsuch Mills  d: 27 Jul 1857 in Harris Mills, MD
.......... +Nancy Waldow  b: 1797  m: 06 Dec 1820  d: 08 Mar 1868 in Harris Mills, MD
............... 3 Nancy Pearce  b: Abt. 1820
............... 3 John C Pearce  b: 11 Nov 1821 in Harris Mills, MD  d: 18 Sep 1896 in 7th District
................... +Elizabeth A Shean Shane  b: 01 Oct 1819 in 7th District  d: 25 Sep 1893 in 7th District
....................... 4 Eliza Pearce  b: Abt. 1850
```

```
............        4 John Pearce  b: Abt. 1852
............        4 Mary J Pearce  b: 15 Apr 1854  d: 21 Jun 1914
........    3 Thomas Pearce  b: 1824 in Harris Mills, MD
........    3 Micajah Pearce  b: 1826 in Harris Mills, MD  d: 19 Nov 1892 in ML, LOT 12
........      +Sarah Ann Bessler  b: 1818  m: 1847  d: 08 Dec 1897 in MLM LOT 12
............        4 Thomas Wesley Pearce  b: 1848 in MLM LOT 12  d: 1922 in MLM LOT 101
..............          +Carloline Sparks Slade  b: 15 Jan 1846 in MLM LOT 99 100  m: in St James  d: 30 Mar 1918
............        4 Sarah Ann Pearce  b: 21 Jun 1850 in MLM LOT 12  d: 31 Jul 1915
..............          +Charles Henry Standiford  b: 13 Jan 1854 in Gunpowder Manor  m: 27 Apr 1877 in TOWSON  d: 13 Mar 1937
............        4 William H Pearce  b: 15 Oct 1854 in MLM LOT 12  d: 04 Aug 1934 in MLM LOT 12
..............          +Mary Jane
........    3 Levi Pearce  b: 1831 in Harris Mills, Baltimore Co., Md.  d: 14 Nov 1901 in Harris Mills, MD
........      +Lydia Ann Leahy  b: 1835 in Pa.  d: 18 Nov 1901 in Harris Mills, Baltimore Co., Md.
............        4 Laura Louise Pearce  b: 10 Apr 1856 in Harris Mills, Baltimore Co., Md.  d: 07 Nov 1913 in Monkton
..............          +Henry Harvey  b: 12 Mar 1853  d: 02 Dec 1933
............        4 Sallie Ann Fenette Pearce  b: 1862 in Harris Mills, Baltimore Co., Md.  d: 1946
..............          +William Fields
............        4 Wilbur Scott Pearce  b: 09 Sep 1866 in Harris Mills, Baltimore Co., Md.  d: 22 Aug 1897
..............          +Mary Irene Virginia Snyder  b: 14 May 1870  m: 29 Dec 1889 in St James  d: 10 Jun 1956
............        4 Nannie Cathrine Idalvet Pearce  b: 12 Mar 1870 in Harris Mills, Baltimore Co., Md.  d: 10 Oct 1948 in BAALT CO
..............          +Philip Borneman
............        4 Levi Nickolas Pearce  b: Oct 1872 in Harris Mills, Baltimore Co., Md.  d: 1951 in 7TH DIST
..............          +Harriet Minerva Diffenderffer  b: Jan 1873
............        4 Lydia Jennie Pearce  b: 12 Jul 1876 in Harris Mills, Baltimore Co., Md.  d: in Phoenix, MD
..............          +Bernard Dye
............        4 Maude Della Pearce  b: 12 Jul 1876
........    3 Samuel W Pearce  b: 23 Sep 1831 in Harris Mills, Baltimore Co., Md.  d: 05 Aug 1839 in Harris Mills, MD
......  2 Rachel O Pearce  b: 15 Feb 1794 in Gorsuch Mills  d: 20 Jun 1885 in 6th District,
......    +Edward Matthews  b: 31 Jul 1787 in Balt Co  m: 17 Feb 1819 in Home of Thomas Pearce  d: 21 Feb 1865 in 6th District
........    3 William P Matthews  b: 05 May 1820 in Middletown  d: 22 Nov 1887 in Bentley Springs
........      +Amilia Kirschuer  b: 1821
............        4 Mary E. Matthews  b: 1842
............        4 Louisa Matthews  b: 1846
............        4 William K. Matthews  b: 04 Feb 1848
..............          +Anna Pricilla Bosley  b: 21 May 1858  d: 01 Oct 1910
............        4 Charles Matthews  b: 1851
............        4 John Matthews  b: 1853
............        4 Henry Matthews  b: 1858
........    *2nd Wife of William P Matthews:
........      +Jane  b: 1843  m: Abt. 1865
............        4 John T. Matthews  b: 1867
............        4 William H. Matthews  b: 1869
............        4 Minnie Matthews  b: 1874
............        4 Franklin Matthews  b: 1877
........    3 Edward Matthews  b: 15 Jul 1822 in Balt Co  d: 28 Sep 1885 in Balt Co
........    3 Elizabeth Hinkle Matthews  b: 12 Jul 1825 in Middletown  d: 12 Oct 1852 in Balt Co
........    3 Vanard Osinnern Matthews  b: 1826 in Balt Co  d: 30 Oct 1895 in Baltimore
........    3 Ezekiel Matthews  b: 17 Apr 1828 in Bel Air  d: 28 Jan 1903
........      +Martha Ann Beall  b: 07 Jan 1835 in Harford Co  m: 27 Oct 1855  d: 17 Jul 1896 in Hereford
............        4 Charles Lee Matthews  b: 1856  d: 1929
............        4 Cathrine Beall Matthews  b: 1857  d: 1937
............        4 Jarrett Matthews  b: 11 Jul 1859 in Harford Co  d: 13 Aug 1933 in West Liberty
..............          +Ida Ellen Gemmill  b: 20 Nov 1858 in Hopewell, York Co  d: 07 Nov 1936 in Balt Co
............        4 Laura Virginia Matthews  b: 1862  d: 1909
............        4 Scott P Matthews  b: 1864  d: 1897
..............          +Mary E. Unknown  b: Sep 1865 in Balt Co  d: 02 Mar 1899 in Balt Co
............        4 Fannie Elizabeth Matthews  b: 22 Jun 1867 in Hereford  d: 1936
```

.... +William Carrolis b: May 1828 d: Aft. 1900
.... 4 Silas P Matthews b: 20 Jun 1871 in Hereford
.... 3 Rachel Matthews b: 1834 in Middletown
.... 3 George W Matthews b: 1836 in Middletown d: in Parkton
.... +Hannah Wilson b: Abt. 1836
.... 3 Cathrine Hinkle Matthews b: 28 Aug 1840 in Middletown d: 19 Mar 1861 in Balt Co
.... 3 Westley Matthews b: 1847 in Middletown
...... 2 Josiah Pearce b: 1795 in Gorsuch Mills d: in Missouri
.... +Ruth Sparks b: Abt. 1795 in Maryland m: 1816 d: in Missouri
...... 2 Elizabeth Pearce b: 09 Feb 1795 in Gorsuch Mills d: 08 Aug 1868 in Gorsuch Mills
.... +Abraham Slade b: 25 Jan 1791 in Talbott Hall d: 16 Dec 1857 in Graystone Road
.... 3 Van Rensalear Slade b: 08 Dec 1822 in Talbott Hall d: 1856 in Gorsuch Mills
.... +Elizabeth Matthews b: 1827 m: Jan 1843 d: 1864
.... 4 Alice Ann Slade b: 1844 in 7th District
.... +Anstine George Bowman b: 1841 m: 1869 d: 1916
.... 4 Franklin Slade b: 1845 in 7th District d: 29 May 1902 in San Antonio, Tx.
.... 4 Micajah Slade b: 1847 d: 19 Jun 1862 in Hilton Head, SC
.... 4 Abraham Slade b: 27 Jun 1847 in 7th District d: 12 Dec 1932 in Balt
.... +Elizabeth Unkmown b: 1851 in Maryland
.... 4 Josephine Slade b: Abt. 1851
.... 4 Cornelia Victoria Slade b: 28 Apr 1852 in 7th District d: 05 Dec 1922 in White Hall
.... +Henry Ballard Plowman b: 28 Nov 1835 in 7th District m: 14 Feb 1872 d: 14 Aug 1900 in White Hall
.... 4 Laura Elizabeth Slade b: 22 Jul 1854 d: 12 Feb 1909 in Lebenon, Ohio
.... +John B. Beel b: 29 Aug 1950 in Foster, Ohio
.... 3 Franklin Slade b: 16 Apr 1823 d: 27 Sep 1841
.... 3 Silas Slade b: 15 Nov 1830 in Talbott Hall d: 30 Dec 1891 in Gorsuch Mills, MD.
.... +Sarah A Morris b: 20 Sep 1821 in Maryland d: 11 Apr 1887 in Gorsuch Mills
.... 4 Elizabeth A. Slade b: 1857
.... 4 Zana Victoria Slade b: 11 Dec 1859 in Maryland d: 01 Sep 1931 in West Liberty
.... +Franklin T. Almony b: 06 Aug 1854 in Maryland d: 22 Dec 1903 in Baltimore Co.
.... 4 William A. Slade b: 1864
.... +Minnie F. Hersey b: 03 Feb 1870 d: 30 Mar 1890
.... 3 John J Slade b: 1835
.... +Hannah E. Unknown b: 1828
.... 4 E. R. Slade b: 1849
.... 4 Sallie L. Slade b: 1854
.... 4 Zillah T. Slade b: 1859
.... 3 Rachel Slade b: 1837 in Gorsuch Mills d: 1908
.... +David Wilson b: 1837 in Stablersville d: 1918
.... 4 Abraham Wilson b: Abt. 1860
.... +[1] Laura Procter b: Abt. 1862
.... 4 Frank P Wilson b: 1876 d: 1935
.... 4 David Hutchins Wilson b: Abt. 1862
.... 4 Edith Wilson b: Abt. 1866
.... +Joseph Cathcart b: Abt. 1865
.... 4 Annie Mary Wilson b: 1870 d: 1952
.... +John Joshua Rutledge b: 29 Oct 1873 in Harford Co d: 07 Jul 1954
.... 4 Zora Wilson b: 1874 d: 1938 in Bethel
.... +Samuel A. Turner b: 1869 d: 1909 in Bethel
.... 4 David Hutchins Wilson b: Abt. 1860
.... +Annie Richardson b: Abt. 1860
.... 4 Abraham Wilson b: Abt. 1860
.... +[1] Laura Procter b: Abt. 1862
.... 3 Madison Slade b: 31 Mar 1837 d: 08 Jan 1882 in Graystone, Rd
.... +Frances Ellen Lytle b: 22 Sep 1837 in Black Horse m: 08 Nov 1859 d: 21 May 1905
.... 4 Harvey Milton Slade b: 30 Oct 1860 in White Hall, Maryland d: 1927 in Graystone RD, White Hall, Md.
.... +Clara E. Tipton b: 17 Aug 1865 in Maryland m: 27 Jan 1886 d: 22 Jul 1938 in Graystone RD

```
............................ 4 Fannie L. Slade  b: 02 Feb 1863  d: 21 Oct 1899
............................ +Joshua S. Robinson  b: 14 Jan 1853  d: 17 Sep 1889
............................ 4 Zora May Slade  b: 25 Jul 1865 in White Hall RD, Vernon, MD  d: 1916 in Parkton
............................ +James W Ayres  b: 1855  d: 1923
..................... 3 Alice Slade  b: 1846  d: 1849
...... 2 William Pearce  b: 1803 in Gorsuch Mills  d: 21 Sep 1883 in East Lewis TWP, Holt, MO
.......... +Elizabeth Hartman  b: 10 Jan 1805 in Strasburg, Pa.  m: Abt. 1823 in Holt, Mo.  d: 28 Sep 1897 in Monroe,La.
..................... 3 Arthur Pearce  b: 1830
..................... 3 Peter Pearce  b: 06 Mar 1833 in Mo.  d: 25 Jul 1915 in Benard, Mo.
......................... +Rachel Hannah Lytle  b: 24 Jul 1833 in Baltimore Co., Md.  d: 31 Mar 1912 in Benard, Mo.
............................ 4 Eliza Pearce  b: Abt. 1854
............................ 4 William Pearce  b: 03 Nov 1857
............................ 4 Nathaniel Pearce  b: Jan 1859
............................ 4 Laura E. Pearce  b: Aug 1861 in Ia.
............................ 4 Emaline Pearce  b: 1865 in Ia.
............................ 4 Salem Pearce  b: Feb 1868 in Ia.
............................ 4 Jennie Pearce  b: 18 Mar 1870 in Mo.
............................ 4 Frank S. Pearce  b: Jul 1872 in Mo.
............................ 4 Lieurena Pearce  b: Sep 1876
..................... 3 Abraham Pearce  b: 19 May 1838 in Baltimore
......................... +Julia Kunkel
..................... 3 Mary A. Pearce  b: 1839
..................... 3 Franklin S. Pearce  b: 16 Jan 1845
..................... 3 Isaac Pearce  b: 27 Aug 1847
..................... 3 David Pearce  b: 1850
......................... +Ellen  b: 1822
............................ 4 Sarah Elizabeth Pearce  b: 1847
............................ 4 Mary Virginia Pearce  b: 1848
..................... 3 Nicholas Pearce  b: Abt. 1852
..................... 3 Nathan Pearce  b: 1853
..................... 3 Emma Pearce  b: Abt. 1854
```

Descendants of Ezekiel Bosley

1 Ezekiel Bosley b: Abt. 1730 d: 07 Nov 1801 in lots 90, 91, 92
. +Elizabeth Norris b: 30 Dec 1735 in Harford Co. m: 07 Nov 1760 d: in Baltimore County, Maryland
...... 2 Rachel Bosley b: Abt. 1761
.... +Abraham Vaughan b: 27 Oct 1773 m: 15 Dec 1802
...... 2 Mary Bosley b: Abt. 1763
.... +William Norris b: Abt. 1763 m: 22 Nov 1784
...... 2 Issac Bosley b: Abt. 1764
.... +Elizabeth Hutchins b: 1769 m: 17 Feb 1793
.... 3 James Bosley b: Abt. 1794 in Baltimore , Md.
.... +Rachel Hope b: Abt. 1800 in Shelby Ky. m: 23 Sep 1819
.... 3 Mary Bosley b: 1796
.... 3 Elizabeth Bosley b: 10 Dec 1797
.... +William Heaton b: Abt. 1793 m: 13 Jan 1837
.... 3 Letitia Bosley b: 21 Dec 1800
.... 3 Edward Bosley b: 12 Oct 1808 d: 10 Mar 1893 in Owensboro, Ky.
.... +Mary Emeline Stowers b: 25 Nov 1822 m: 25 Nov 1841 d: 16 Feb 1905 in Owensboro, Ky.
...... 2 Hannah Bosley b: Abt. 1765
...... 2 James Bosley b: 1768 in MLM d: 13 May 1850 in St. James
.... +Hannah Hughes b: Abt. 1776 in White Hall, Maryland m: 30 Oct 1799 in St. James d: 14 May 1851 in Vernon UM
.... 3 Elizabeth Bosley b: 12 Nov 1802 d: 23 Jan 1894
.... +Daniel T. Treadway b: 27 Aug 1799 m: 21 Feb 1827 d: 03 Jun 1878
.... 3 Nancy Ann Bosley b: 28 Feb 1804 in St James d: 21 Aug 1893
.... +Unknown Treadway b: Abt. 1802 m: Abt. 1824
.... *2nd Husband of Nancy Ann Bosley:
.... +John Marche McComas b: 29 Feb 1804 m: 14 Jan 1834 d: 24 Apr 1890
.... 3 Norris Bosley b: 16 Nov 1805 in White Hall, Maryland d: 03 Jul 1819
.... 3 Hannah Bosley b: 1807 in Vernon UM d: 05 Oct 1890 in Vernon UM
.... +George Washington Norris b: 06 Mar 1802 in Norrisville m: 22 Feb 1839 d: 28 Sep 1873 in 7th Dist., Baltimore Co.
.... 3 Lucretia V. Bosley b: 03 Oct 1812 d: 14 Jun 1909
.... +Thomas Poteet Smithson b: 20 Sep 1812 in Harford Co. m: 12 Feb 1849 d: 21 Oct 1876
.... 3 Clarinda Bosley b: Abt. 1813
.... +Nicholas Mccomas b: Abt. 1812 m: 12 Dec 1838
.... 3 Mary Ella Bosley b: Abt. 1815
.... +John H Treadway b: Abt. 1812 m: 13 Nov 1834
.... 3 Isaac Bosley b: Apr 1816 d: Apr 1816
.... 3 John Bosley b: 20 Jan 1818 in Vernon, Md. d: 30 Oct 1903 in Vernon, Md., Wesley Chapel
.... +Mary Ann Pearce b: 15 Nov 1828 in MLM lots 87, 88 m: 26 Nov 1851 d: 18 Feb 1906 in Vernon, Md.
...... 2 Elizabeth Bosley b: Abt. 1770 in MLM d: in MLM lot 92
.... +Walter Perdue b: 1766 m: 12 Jun 1790 in St. James d: 1826
.... 3 Labon Perdue b: 12 Jul 1791 in MLM lot 90, 91, 92 d: in MLM lot 58
.... +Rachel Hunter b: 1799 in White Hall, Maryland d: in MLM lot 58
.... 3 Mary Perdue b: 02 Mar 1795 in Balt Co d: in Balt Co
.... +John Slade b: Abt. 1790 in Talbott Hall m: Abt. 1820 d: 1853
.... 3 William Perdue b: 19 Mar 1797 in MLM, 90 91 92 d: 16 Jul 1836 in West Liberty
.... +Ann Slade b: 11 Nov 1797 in Talbott Hall d: 24 Mar 1877 in Parkton, Maryland
.... 3 Rachel Perdue b: Abt. 1798 d: in Baltimore County, Maryland
.... +William Hunter b: 22 May 1797 in White Hall, Maryland d: 1850 in Baltimore County, Maryland
.... 3 Walter Perdue b: 18 Jun 1801 in St James d: 17 Mar 1850
.... 3 John Perdue b: 29 Jun 1804 d: 1874 in St. James
.... +Sarah Hutchins b: 09 Nov 1809 in Harford Co. m: 21 Feb 1832 in St James d: 30 Apr 1878 in Balt,Co.
.... 3 Elizabeth Perdue b: 19 Feb 1807 in MLM lot 90, 91, 92 d: 1884 in Linden MLM
.... +William Given Hutchins b: 18 Mar 1800 m: Abt. 1834 d: 1872
.... 3 Thomas Perdue b: 29 Mar 1809 d: 31 Aug 1877
...... 2 Joseph Bosley b: Abt. 1774 d: Abt. 1835 in Shelby Co. Ky.
.... +Letitia Hutchins b: 1769 m: 26 Feb 1800 d: in Shelby Co. Ky.

.... 3 Nicholas Bosley b: 21 May 1801
.... 3 Mary Bosley b: 12 Jun 1803
.... +George Hammond m: 19 Oct 1833
.... 3 Susanna Bosley b: 1808 d: 09 Apr 1879
.... 3 Elizabeth Bosley b: 05 Apr 1811
.... +Benjamin P. Norris b: 1809 d: in Winemillers Mill area
...... 2 Susanna Bosley b: Abt. 1776
.... +James St. Clair b: Abt. 1775 m: 29 Jun 1799

Descendants of Aquilla McDonald

1 Aquilla McDonald b: 28 Jun 1781 in Hopewell d: 25 Jan 1850 in Stewartstown, Pa.
. +Mary Miller b: 11 Feb 1787 m: 09 Mar 1808 in Crist Luthern, York, Pa. d: 09 Aug 1867 in Stewartstown, Pa.
...... 2 Grizella Ann McDonald b: 1811 d: 1877 in York Co., Pa.
.... +John B. Strawbridge b: 29 Nov 1805 in Fawn Township m: 1840 d: 10 Mar 1878 in New Park
.... 3 John Clarkson Strawbridge b: 01 Sep 1840 d: 28 Aug 1917 in Centre Presbyterian, New Park, Pa.
.... +Sarah Cooper Anderson b: 1845 d: 1919 in Norrisville
.... 3 Mary Ellen Strawbridge b: 27 Nov 1842 d: 21 Aug 1906 in Centre Presbyterian, New Park, Pa.
.... 3 Rachel Ann Strawbridge b: 10 Mar 1845 d: 1919
.... +Richard McDonald b: Abt. 1842 in Harford /Co.
.... 3 Aquilla McDonald Strawbridge b: 10 Jan 1847 d: 05 Jun 1920 in Centre Presbyterian, New Park, Pa.
.... 3 Richard A Strawbridge b: 03 Jan 1849 d: in Marysville Co. Mo.
.... 3 Sarah Jane Strawbridge b: 06 Mar 1851 d: 06 Jun 1905 in Norrisville
.... 3 Franklin Pierce Strawbridge b: 14 Feb 1853 d: in Centre Presbyterian, New Park, Pa.
.... 3 Louisa M. Strawbridge b: 25 May 1855 d: in Centre Presbyterian, New Park, Pa.
.... +John Calvin Wiley b: 16 Mar 1853 m: 1879 d: in Gatcheville
.... 3 Joseph Ross Esq. Strawbridge b: 25 Jul 1858 in Fawn Township d: 14 Oct 1916 in Atlantic City, N. J.
.... +Elizabeth Smyzer
...... 2 Abraham McDonald b: 20 Apr 1811 in Hopewell, York Co. d: 04 Dec 1886 in Maryland Line
.... +Jane Markey b: 15 May 1813 d: 03 Jun 1888
.... 3 Jacob M. McDonald b: 06 Feb 1839 d: 24 Feb 1888 in Maryland Line
.... +Rachel A Miller b: 30 Nov 1831 d: 05 Mar 1873
.... *2nd Wife of Jacob M. McDonald:
.... +Elizabeth b: 1846
.... 3 Mary Jane McDonald b: 19 Jul 1837 in 7 TH Dist.,Balt Co d: 27 Mar 1898 in Maryland Line, Bond Road
.... +Ross Bond b: 14 Oct 1830 in Bond Rd m: 06 Jan 1859 d: 22 Aug 1907 in Maryland Line, Bond Road
.... 3 Eva McDonald b: 15 Sep 1840 in Maryland d: 18 Dec 1910
.... +Daniel Koller b: Oct 1842 in Maryland d: 1915
.... 3 Margaret McDonald b: 1842
.... +Neal
.... 3 Aquilla W. McDonald b: 12 Oct 1844 in Harris Mill Road d: 01 Mar 1914 in Maryland Line
.... +Mary Agnes Bosley b: 14 Dec 1847 in Maryland d: 30 May 1931 in Maryland Line
.... 3 Grizzella A. McDonald b: 06 Feb 1846 d: 19 May 1920
.... +George W. Carr b: 23 Nov 1845 d: 13 Aug 1911 in Maryland Line
.... 3 Rachel E. McDonald b: 20 Jun 1847 d: 07 Jan 1855 in Maryland Line
.... 3 Barbara A. McDonald b: 01 May 1849 d: 12 Aug 1849 in Maryland Line
.... 3 Nancy R. McDonald b: 01 May 1849 d: 05 Aug 1849 in Maryland Line
.... 3 Julia A. McDonald b: 1850
.... +Richard Lee b: 1853
.... 3 Robert McDonald b: 10 Apr 1851 d: 06 Jul 1851 in Maryland Line
...... 2 Eva McDonald b: 1815
.... +Nathaniel B. Bartol b: 1807 m: 25 Nov 1845 in Crist Luthern, York, Pa.
.... 3 Rosanna Bartol b: 1833
.... 3 Sarah Bartol b: 1835
.... 3 Margaret Bartol b: 1846 in Fawn Grove
.... +Jacob Wiest Payne b: 29 Apr 1845 m: Abt. 1868
.... 3 Aquilla Bartol b: 1848
.... +Cathrine T Grove b: 1852 m: Abt. 1880
.... *2nd Wife of Aquilla Bartol:
.... +Elizabeth G. Collins b: 1845 m: 1892
...... 2 John Ross McDonald b: 1815 in York Co., d: 1867 in Missouri
.... +Elizabeth Kurtz b: 1819 m: Abt. 1836 d: 11 Mar 1847 in Saddlers
.... 3 Priscilla E. McDonald b: 18 Jun 1843 in Hopewell d: 19 Sep 1909 in Stewartstown, Pa.
.... +Edward Weist Lanius b: 07 Dec 1839 in Stewartstown, Pa. d: 1925 in Hopewell
.... 3 Elizabeth Jane McDonald
...... *2nd Wife of John Ross McDonald:

".......... +Elizabeth Krout b: 01 May 1825 in York, Co., Pennsylvania m: 1852 in Maryland d: in Missouri
.... 3 Aquilla McDonald b: Abt. 1854
...... 2 Richard McDonald b: 1818 d: 1888 in Harford County, Md.
.... +Tresa Unknown b: 1824
.... 3 Mary McDonald b: 1849
.... 3 Nelson McDonald b: 1852
...... 2 Samuel M. McDonald b: Abt. 1822
...... 2 Aquilla McDonald b: 31 May 1830 in York Co d: 21 Dec 1903 in York Co, Centre Presby
.... +Martha A Gemmill b: 28 Jun 1835 in FAWN m: 27 Jan 1855 in York Co d: 31 Mar 1860 in York Co
.... 3 Benjamin Gemmill McDonald b: 02 Sep 1857 in York Co d: 06 Sep 1919 in York Co
.... +Sarah Adelaide Duncan b: 12 Jan 1855 in FAWN , York Co m: 15 Jan 1880 d: 12 Jun 1935 in York Co
.... 3 William Thomas McDonald b: 04 Jan 1859 in York Co d: 16 Sep 1859 in York Co
.... 3 McDonald b: 24 Mar 1860 in York Co d: 24 Mar 1860
...... *2nd Wife of Aquilla McDonald:
.... +Sarah Elizabeth Gemmill b: 02 Jan 1836 in York Co m: 27 Jan 1862 in York Co d: 16 Sep 1890 in York Co
.... 3 Laura Mary McDonald b: 10 Jan 1864 in York Co d: 12 Jan 1955 in York
.... +James R. Wiley b: 15 Feb 1852 in Pennsylvania m: 13 May 1885
.... 3 Ida Elizabeth McDonald b: 06 Mar 1865 in York Co d: 10 Aug 1932
.... +William Payne Norris b: 29 Jul 1869 in York Co m: 07 Jan 1903 d: 11 Apr 1954 in York Co
.... 3 Amanda Roseela McDonald b: 11 Nov 1868 in York County, Pa. d: 15 Feb 1930
.... +Dr Thomas C. Baldwin b: 1869 in 11 th District, Baltimore Co., Maryland
.... 3 Anna Ettaworth McDonald b: 05 Oct 1869 in York Co d: 26 Dec 1936 in York Co
.... +Samuel Ferquar Reed b: 15 Mar 1864 in York Co m: 17 Oct 1893 d: Sep 1931 in York Co
.... 3 Carrie Victoria McDonald b: 23 Jul 1871 in York Co
.... 3 Margaret Lillie McDonald b: 02 Jun 1873 d: 05 Aug 1890 in York Co
.... 3 James Franklin McDonald b: 05 Apr 1875 in Pennsylvania d: 21 Jun 1941 in York Co
.... +Minerva Grove b: 01 Oct 1874 in Hopewell m: 31 Oct 1901 in York Co d: 27 Jun 1953 in Hopewell
.... 3 Irene McDonald b: 1879
...... 2 William Garretson McDonald b: 16 Jun 1834 d: 20 Apr 1887 in Slate Ridge
.... +Sarah J. Unknown b: 28 Sep 1843 d: 03 Mar 1884 in Slate Ridge
...... 2 Robert McDonald b: 1838
.... +Cathrine b: 1841
.... 3 Mary E. McDonald b: 1861 d: in Egbers, camden, N.J.
.... 3 Richard W. McDonald b: 1862 d: 1924
.... +Rachel A. Unknown b: 1845 d: 1919
.... 3 Lydia A. McDonald b: 1866
.... 3 Emma G. McDonald b: 1870
.... 3 Annie H. McDonald b: 1874
.... +McClellan Gibbs b: 1864
.... 3 Robert Harvey McDonald b: 1875
.... +Fannie Elizabeth Payne b: Abt. 1878
.... 3 Willis R. McDonald b: 1878 d: in Hermanville, Md.

Descendants of Josiah Sparks

```
1 Josiah Sparks  b: Bef. 1720 in Virginia  d: Oct 1764 in New Market, Baltimore Co.
.  +Agnes Wyle  b: Abt. 1715  m: 1749 in St. Anne's
*2nd Wife of Josiah Sparks:
.  +Penelope Brown  m: 15 Jul 1749 in St. Anne, Anne Arundal Co.  d: Abt. 1771 in York Co., Pa.
...... 2 Francis Sparks  b: 1750 in Sparks folly  d: Aft. 1800
..........  +Cassandra Wright  b: in Maryland
............. 3 John T Sparks  b: Abt. 1775 in Maryland  d: 1823 in Pa
............. 3 Josiah Sparks  b: Abt. 1780 in Maryland
............. 3 Wright Sparks  b: 06 May 1785 in Maryland  d: Bef. 1820 in Ind
.................  +Nancy Magnus  d: in Ind.
............. 3 Penelope Sparks  b: 1787 in Maryland
............. 3 Mary Sparks  b: Abt. 1789 in Maryland  d: in Ohio
.................  +John Sharp  b: Abt. 1788
............. *2nd Husband of Mary Sparks:
.................  +Isaac Decker  d: in Ohio
............. 3 Elizabeth Sparks  b: Abt. 1790 in Maryland
.................  +Frederick Kaufman  b: Abt. 1800  m: 31 Mar 1813  d: 1858 in Monkton
............. 3 Ruth Sparks  b: Abt. 1795 in Maryland  d: in Missouri
.................  +Josiah Pearce  b: 1795 in Gorsuch Mills  m: 1816  d: in Missouri
............. 3 Thomas Sparks  b: 1800 in Maryland  d: 1853 in Ohio
.................  +Mary Elizabeth Pierce
............. *2nd Wife of Thomas Sparks:
.................  +Jennie Harwood  b: in Ohio
............. 3 Prudence Sparks  b: 1796 in Maryland  d: 1874
.................  +Richard Gosnell  b: 1797 in Maryland  m: 09 Dec 1820  d: 1877
...... 2 Josias Sparks  b: 1752 in lots50, 51,96  d: 19 Jan 1846 in Sparks Cm lot 50 MLM, Monkton, Md
..........  +Rachel Collett  b: 28 Dec 1748 in Baltimore Co., M  m: Abt. 1778  d: 28 Sep 1818 in Lot 50
............. 3 Rachel Elizabeth Sparks  b: 1774  d: 1860 in 96
.................  +William Carlin  b: 1774 in New Jersey  d: 1847
............. 3 Thomas Sparks  b: 1776 in LOT 50  d: 1825
.................  +Sarah Rampley  b: 29 Jan 1781 in Harford co., Md.  m: 16 Jul 1802  d: 07 Jan 1886 in Green Co. Ind.
............. 3 Sarah E. Sparks  b: 1779  d: 14 May 1851
.................  +John Pitt Mays  b: 12 Jul 1779 in Maryland  m: 04 Sep 1839  d: 20 Sep 1868
............. 3 Ruth Sparks  b: 20 Jul 1781 in Mt. Joy lot 7  d: 25 Mar 1858 in Sparks Cm lot 50 MLM, Monkton, Md
.................  +William Pearce  b: 11 May 1775 in lot 7 Mt Joy  d: 11 Jul 1835 in Mt. Joy, Sparks Graveyard lot 50
............. 3 [2] Aaron Sparks  b: 17 May 1787  d: 31 May 1856
.................  +[1] Elizabeth Sparks  b: 1803  d: 1883
............. 3 Matthew Sparks  b: 02 Mar 1790  d: 02 May 1874 in Westley Chapel
.................  +Mary Ann Johnson  b: 1820  d: 19 Mar 1901
............. 3 Francis Sparks  b: 11 May 1792  d: 26 Nov 1867
.................  +Elizabeth Ellen Shrader  b: 1794  d: 1885
............. 3 Daniel Collett Sparks  b: Dec 1793 in MLM, LOT 96  d: 1863 in White House
.................  +Rachel Curtis  b: 02 Feb 1794 in MLM  m: 19 Jan 1825 in St James  d: 01 Jan 1880 in White House
...... 2 Elijah Sparks  b: 1754  d: 1812
..........  +Annie Anderson  b: 1756  m: 10 Apr 1832  d: 1805
............. 3 Edward A Sparks
.................  +Rachel Mills
............. 3 Josias L Sparks  d: in Ind.
.................  +Rachel McCray
............. 3 Aquilla Sparks
.................  +Dorcas Conway
............. 3 Mary Sparks
.................  +Matthew Drake
............. 3 [1] Elizabeth Sparks  b: 1803  d: 1883
.................  +[2] Aaron Sparks  b: 17 May 1787  d: 31 May 1856
```

```
............ *2nd Husband of [1] Elizabeth Sparks:
............... +Aaron Sparks
............... 3 Elijah Brown Sparks  b: 10 Oct 1807  d: 12 Sep 1888 in 7th district
............... +Elizabeth Anderson  m: 10 Apr 1832  d: in Hereford Baptist
...... 2 Ruth Sparks  b: 1756 in AA CO  d: in MLM
......... +Thomas Anderson  b: 1750 in Monkton, Md.  d: 25 Dec 1801 in MLM
............ 3 Elizabeth Anderson  b: 1777 in MLM  d: Dec 1859 in MLM
............... +William Slade  b: 25 Jul 1775 in MLM  m: 30 Mar 1799 in St James  d: 28 Jun 1849 in MLM
............ 3 Josias Anderson  b: Abt. 1778 in MLM
............... +Comfort Wyle  b: Abt. 1778  m: 1804
............ 3 Thomas Anderson  b: Abt. 1779
............ 3 Nancy Anderson  b: Abt. 1780
............ 3 Aquilla Brown Anderson  b: 18 Nov 1780  d: 14 Jul 1856
............ 3 Penelope Anderson  b: 01 Nov 1786  d: 1794
............ 3 Leonard Anderson  b: 04 Apr 1788
............... +Rebecca
............ 3 Elijah Anderson  b: 19 May 1790
............ 3 John Anderson  b: 28 Oct 1792  d: 10 Sep 1854
............... +Sarah Ann Kirkwood  b: 1804
............ 3 Ruth Anderson  b: 23 Dec 1792  d: 03 Aug 1877
............... +Jacob Hutchins  b: 1785  d: 1824
............ 3 Sarah Ann Anderson  b: 16 Nov 1795 in MLM  d: 17 Jan 1875
............... +John Sheppard Curtis  b: 09 May 1795 in MLM  d: 25 Sep 1871
...... 2 Thomas Sparks  b: 23 May 1758  d: 19 Jan 1815
......... +Rachel Perdue  b: 13 Aug 1758  m: 16 Aug 1779 in St James  d: 1815 in lot58
............ 3 Walter Sparks  b: Abt. 1780  d: in St. Michaels
............ 3 Thomas Sparks  b: Abt. 1782  d: in Ind
............... +Sarah Rampley
............ 3 Penelope Sparks  b: 10 Oct 1787 in Maryland  d: 25 Jan 1858
............... +Charles Robinson  b: 12 Apr 1773 in Maryland  m: 1816  d: 26 Dec 1862
............ 3 Rachel Sparks  b: Abt. 1788
............... +John Sumerwalt  b: Abt. 1785
............ 3 Aquilla Sparks
............ 3 Sarah Sparks
............... +Lawrence Cuddy
............ 3 Laban Sparks  b: 06 Mar 1794 in 8th District  d: 08 Jan 1865
............... +Sarah Green  b: Abt. 1795 in Baltimore Co., Maryland
...... 2 Matthew Sparks  b: 1760  d: 1845 in Schuyler CO, ILL
......... +Prudence Wright  b: 1762  d: 1845 in Schuyler Co., Ill.
............ 3 Leonard Sparks  b: Abt. 1785  d: 1850 in Clay CO, ILL
............... +Hannah Sharp
............ 3 Levi Sparks  b: Abt. 1786  d: 1850 in Schuyler CO, ILL
............ 3 Cassandra Sparks  b: Abt. 1788
............... +Silas Roberts
............ 3 Ruth Sparks  b: Abt. 1790
............ 3 Elizabeth Sparks  b: Abt. 1792
............ 3 Lemuel Sparks  b: 1794 in Balt Co  d: 1855 in Schuyler CO, ILL
............... +Nancy Jane Bartlow
............ 3 Penelope Sparks  b: 1804 in Balt Co  d: 1876 in Schuyler CO , ILL
............... +James Blackburn
............ 3 James Sparks  b: 1811
```

Descendants of Adam Miller Hendrix

1 Adam Miller Hendrix b: 1729 d: 1788 in Shrewsbury, PA.
. +Unknown m: 25 Oct 1744
...... 2 Abraham Hendrix b: Abt. 1745 in Shrewsbury, PA. d: 11 Nov 1825 in Bath Co., Ky.
...... 2 Isaac Hendrix b: Abt. 1742 in Shrewsbury, PA. d: 03 Jul 1817 in York Co.
.... +Jane Unknown b: 1740 m: Abt. 1770 d: 1815
.... 3 John Hendrix b: 23 Mar 1804 in Parkton d: 08 May 1879 in Maryland, 7th District
.... +Maria Unknown b: 05 May 1818 in Pennsylvania d: 02 May 1895 in Maryland Line
.... 4 John W. Hendrix b: 1841 in Maryland
.... +Elnora McCubbin b: 1845
.... 4 Emma F. Hendrix b: 29 Mar 1842 d: 27 Sep 1912 in Maryland Line
.... 4 Hester A. Hendrix b: 05 Nov 1844 in Baltimore Co. d: 27 Sep 1912 in Maryland Line
.... 4 Mary R. Hendrix b: 1847
.... 4 Laura v. Hendrix b: 13 Oct 1849 in Baltimore Co. d: 13 Dec 1854 in Maryland Line
.... 4 [1] William H. Hendrix b: 1852 in Maryland d: 1937
.... +[2] Blanche O. Kroh b: 1872 in Maryland d: 1960
.... 4 Jacob Frank Hendrix b: 08 Jul 1854 d: 27 Sep 1912 in Maryland Line
.... 4 Isabella H. Hendrix b: 21 Aug 1858 d: 14 Aug 1860 in Maryland Line
.... 4 Walter Hendrix b: 1867
.... 3 Adam Hendrix b: 1814 d: 1876
.... +Isabelle Murray
.... 3 Isaac Hendrix b: Abt. 1801
.... 3 Thomas Hendrix b: Abt. 1803
.... 3 Joseph Hendrix b: Abt. 1804
.... 3 Hannah Hendrix b: Abt. 1805
.... 3 Ruth Hendrix b: Abt. 1806
.... 3 Joshua Hendrix b: 1810 in Maryland d: Aft. 1892 in Wiseburg
.... +Mary Eva Anstine b: 1816 in Pennsylvania
.... 4 Margaritta Hendrix b: 1839
.... 4 Elizabeth Hendrix b: 1841
.... 4 Agustus Hendrix b: 1843
.... 4 Margaret Maggie Hendrix b: 1844
.... 4 Mary Ann Hendrix b: 1847 d: 1917
.... 4 Lucretia Hendrix b: 1853
.... 4 Ida L. Hendrix b: 1858
.... 4 [1] William H. Hendrix b: 1852 in Maryland d: 1937
.... +[2] Blanche O. Kroh b: 1872 in Maryland d: 1960
.... *2nd Wife of Joshua Hendrix:
.... +Mary Wantland b: Abt. 1818
...... 2 Dorcus Hendrix b: Abt. 1754 in Shrewsbury, PA. d: 1827 in Bean Cove, Va.
.... +Amos Dicken b: Abt. 1752
...... 2 Adam Hendrix b: 26 Jan 1757 in Shrewsbury, PA. d: 07 Nov 1836 in Pennsylvania
.... +Rachel Klingman Yost b: 1755 m: Abt. 1780 d: 04 Aug 1842
.... 3 Darcus Hendrix b: 12 Jun 1786
.... +Jacob Sumwalt
.... 3 Joseph Hendrix b: 04 Apr 1788 d: in New Market
.... +Agnes McDonald b: 1785 m: 1810
.... 4 Adam Hendrix b: Abt. 1814 d: in Howard Co., Mo.
.... 4 John M. Hendrix b: 06 Jan 1816 d: in Preble Co. Ohio
.... +Rebecca Murray b: 21 Jan 1817
.... 4 Sarah A. Hendrix b: Abt. 1817 d: in Freeland, Md.
.... 4 Daniel Hendrix b: Abt. 1819 d: in New Freedom, Pa.
.... 4 Joseph W. Hendrix b: Abt. 1820 d: in New Oxford, Pa.
.... 4 Washington Hendrix b: Abt. 1822 d: in New Freedom, Pa.
.... 4 Isaac Hendrix b: Abt. 1824 d: in New Freedom, Pa.
.... 4 Assenth Hendrix b: Abt. 1826 d: in New Freedom, Pa.

```
............         3 Rachel Hendrix  b: 04 Apr 1891  d: in York Co.
............           +Joshua Green  b: 12 Feb 1781 in Baltimore Co., Maryland  d: 13 Sep 1848
............         3 Julia Hendrix  b: Abt. 1789  d: in Ohio
............           +Unknown Tracey  b: Abt. 1788
............         3 Dr Isaac Hendrix  b: 01 Oct 1799  d: 20 Jul 1880 in Shrewsbury, Pa.
............         3 Ruth Hendrix  b: 22 Jul 1794 in Shrewsbury, Pa.  d: 1815
............           +Peter Koller  b: 31 Jan 1788 in Shrewsbury, Pa.  d: 1870
..............          4 Elizabeth Koller  b: 04 Sep 1811 in Pennsylvania  d: 12 Dec 1880 in Shane
..............            +Patrick Kean Curry  b: 16 Dec 1806 in Killarney, ireland  m: 1828  d: 30 Nov 1881 in Shane
..............          4 Isaac Koller  b: 28 Feb 1813
..............            +Eliza Jane Unknown  b: 09 Aug 1841
..............          *2nd Wife of Isaac Koller:
..............            +Eva Klinefelter
......   2 Ruth Hendrix  b: Abt. 1760 in Shrewsbury, PA.  d: Abt. 1790 in New Market, Pa.
..........     +Thomas Gorsuch Rutledge  b: 09 Aug 1759 in Balt Co  m: 17 Jan 1787  d: 06 Jan 1832 in 7th District Baltimore Co, MD
............         3 Elizabeth Ann Rutledge  b: 02 Apr 1787 in New Market, Md.  d: 10 Aug 1839 in Baltimore , Co. Md.
............           +David Sampson  b: 31 May 1784 in New Market, Md.  m: 09 Feb 1804  d: 24 Aug 1862 in Long Valley, Maryland Line
..............          4 Stephen Sampson  b: Dec 1804  d: 16 Dec 1804
..............          4 Ruth Sampson  b: 06 Nov 1809 in 7TH District  d: 27 Oct 1865 in Hancock Co., Ohio
..............            +Elisha Gorsuch  b: 03 Mar 1810 in Gorsuch Mills  m: 12 Feb 1829  d: 07 Mar 1847 in Ohio, Typhoid Fever
..............          4 Eli S. Sampson  b: 12 Feb 1813 in Baltimore County, Maryland  d: 21 Dec 1893 in Ohio
..............            +Margaret Ann Krout  b: 15 May 1812 in Baltimore County, Maryland  m: 13 Mar 1835 in Baltimore , Co. Md.  d: 20
                          Nov 1892 in Hancock Co. Ohio
..............          4 Elizabeth Jane Sampson  b: 27 Aug 1815 in New Market  d: 11 Feb 1901 in Maryland Line, Md. Line Cm.
..............            +James Bond  b: 02 Jan 1808 in New Market, Md.  m: 14 Mar 1834  d: 14 Jan 1891 in Maryland Line
..............          4 Mary Sampson  b: 13 Dec 1817 in Baltimore , Co. Md.  d: 23 Mar 1856 in Baltimore , Co. Md.
..............            +Johnsey S. Palmer  b: Abt. 1816 in Baltimore , Co. Md.  d: in Baltimore , Co. Md.
..............          4 Nicholas Sampson  b: 01 Feb 1820 in Baltimore , Co. Md.  d: 18 Aug 1864 in Houcktown, Hancock CO, Ohio
..............            +Elizabeth Hunter  b: Abt. 1822  m: 04 Sep 1840
..............          4 David Sampson  b: 14 Aug 1823 in Baltimore , Co. Md.  d: 14 Aug 1824 in Baltimore , Co. Md.
..............          4 Edwin Hindle Sampson  b: 02 Jan 1830 in Maryland  d: 1864 in Houcktown, Ohio
..............            +Mary Jane Standiford  b: 23 Aug 1831 in Maryland  m: 25 Feb 1852  d: 1864
............         3 Ruth Rutledge  b: 19 Oct 1788 in Harford Co  d: 1831 in Balt Co
............           +Charles Gorsuch  b: 13 Jun 1789 in Gorsuch Mills  m: 05 Jan 1809  d: 06 Feb 1869 in Butler Co , OH
..............          4 Rachel Gorsuch  b: 07 Nov 1809  d: 16 Feb 1883 in ILL
..............            +Joseph Lesourd  b: 23 Sep 1811 in Butler Co. Oh.  m: 08 Mar 1832  d: 02 Sep 1883
..............          4 Thomas Gorsuch  b: Abt. 1811 in Gorsuch Mills, MD.  d: in Ohio
..............            +Martha Jane Curtis  b: in OH  m: 16 Apr 1840 in butler Co. Oh.  d: in OH
..............          4 Elizabeth Gorsuch  b: Abt. 1813 in Maryland
..............            +Robert Allen  b: Abt. 1812
..............          4 Sarah Gorsuch  b: Abt. 1815 in Maryland
..............            +Abram Sutton
..............          4 John Westley Gorsuch  b: Abt. 1817 in Maryland
......   2 Thomas Hendrix  b: 1759 in Shrewsbury, PA.  d: in South Carolina
......   2 Tamer Hendrix  b: Abt. 1764 in Shrewsbury, PA.  d: in Adams Co., Pa.
..........     +Francis Coulson  b: Abt. 1760
......   2 Elizabeth Hendrix  b: Abt. 1765  d: in Beford Co., Pa.
..........     +David Long  b: Abt. 1764
*2nd Wife of Adam Miller Hendrix:
 . +Mary Freeland  b: Abt. 1735  m: Abt. 1770
```

Descendants of Shadrach Green

1 Shadrach Green b: 16 Jul 1747 in Baltimore Co., Maryland d: 29 Oct 1822 in Baltimore Co., Maryland
. +Rachel Smith b: 1758 in Baltimore Co., Maryland d: 1847 in Baltimore Co., Maryland m: 1776
...... 2 Elizabeth Green b: 03 Jan 1777 in Baltimore Co., Maryland
.... +James Given b: Abt. 1775
...... 2 Nancy Ann Green b: 17 Oct 1778 in Baltimore Co., Maryland d: 31 Mar 1849 in Carroll Co. Md.
.... +Joshua Bosley b: Abt. 1777 d: 29 Jun 1846 m: 11 Aug 1801
.... 3 James Bosley b: Abt. 1804
.... +Mary Sellers
.... 3 Rachel Bosley b: Abt. 1806
.... +Abendago Jackson
.... 3 Kesiah Bosley b: Abt. 1808
.... +Joshua Coltrider
.... 3 Joshua Bosley b: 1810
.... 3 Belinda Bosley b: Abt. 1813
.... +George Sellers
.... 3 Shadrach Bosley b: 28 Jan 1816 d: 29 Jul 1847
.... +Sarepta Sater m: 05 Jun 1837
.... 3 Thomas Bosley b: 1820
...... 2 Joshua Green b: 12 Feb 1781 in Baltimore Co., Maryland d: 13 Sep 1848
.... +Rachel Hendrix b: 04 Apr 1891 d: in York Co.
...... *2nd Wife of Joshua Green:
...... +Lydia Carl b: Abt. 1784
.... 3 Westley Green b: 07 Mar 1818 d: 30 Mar 1892
.... +Sarah Meredith b: 27 Jul 1818 d: 17 Aug 1904
.... 3 Rachael Green b: 03 May 1817 d: 19 Apr 1900
.... +Joshua M Bell b: 18 Jan 1808 in Openshaw Rd d: 05 Mar 1882 m: 12 Apr 1853
.... 4 William Bell b: 1843
...... 2 Temperance Green b: 10 Sep 1783 in Baltimore Co., Maryland d: 1835
.... +John Pitt Mays b: 12 Jul 1779 in Maryland d: 20 Sep 1868 m: 10 Mar 1807 in Baltimore , Md.
.... 3 Elizabeth Ann Mays b: 1808 d: Mar 1892 in Mt. Carmel Cm.
.... +Robert Miller b: 1797 d: 1869 in Mt. Carmel Cm. m: 1830
.... 4 John Grafton Miller b: 29 Aug 1835 d: 18 Apr 1911 in Mt. Carmel
.... +Hester Gorsuch b: 23 May 1844 in Mt. Carmel d: 01 Dec 1872
.... 4 Thomas Miller b: Abt. 1835
.... +Margaret A. Benson b: Jul 1836
.... 4 Hannah Ann Miller b: 1837
.... +Joshua Fowble Benson b: 14 Dec 1821 in Near Mt. Carmel 5th District m: 1856
.... 4 Rachel Jane Miller b: 1832
.... +Rev. Joshua Lemmon Benson b: 26 Jan 1831
.... 4 Laura Miller b: 1841
.... 4 Emma Miller b: 1843
.... 4 Milton Miller b: 1849
.... 4 Silas Miller b: Jun 1853 d: in 5th District, Baltimore County
.... +Ida F. Markland b: Mar 1856
.... 3 John C. Mays b: 1808 d: 30 Oct 1887 in Hereford Med Cm.
.... +Harriet Foster b: 1800 in Baltimore Co., Md. d: 03 Dec 1884 in Hereford Med Cm. m: 11 Mar 1834
.... 4 Maranda Mays b: 1837
.... 4 Nicholas Foster Mays b: 13 Nov 1838 in Baltimore Co. , Md. d: 07 Jul 1914 in Hereford Med Cm.
.... +Margaret Ann Wilhelm b: 18 Mar 1850 in Baltimore Co. , Md. d: 20 Mar 1920 in Hereford Med Cm.
.... 4 George H. Mays b: 31 Mar 1840 in Baltimore , Md. d: 03 Mar 1915 in Hereford Methodist
.... +Emily b: Apr 1845 d: 1920 in Hereford Methodist
.... 4 John T. Mays b: 04 Jan 1842 d: 20 Feb 1910 in Hereford Med Cm.
.... +Fannie A. Unknown b: 21 Jul 1851 d: 17 Dec 1898
.... 4 Sopharine Mays b: 1846
.... 3 Thomas Mays b: 1813 in Baltimore Co.

.... +Barbara Unknown b: 1820
.... 4 James Mays b: 1846 in Baltimore Co.
.... 4 John Mays b: 1848 in Baltimore Co.
.... 3 John Pitt Mays b: 02 Mar 1817 in Baltimore Co. d: 02 Jun 1896 in Baltimore Co.
.... +Martha E. Mellor b: 1825 in Baltimore Co. m: Abt. 1846
.... 4 Sarah Temperance Mays b: 1848 in Baltimore Co. d: 18 Aug 1900 in Glencoe
.... +Thomas Talbott Gorsuch b: 17 Sep 1845 in Gorsuch's Retirement, Balt Co d: 12 Apr 1923 in Balt Co m: 20 Feb 1866
.... 4 Rachel Emma Mays b: Sep 1849 in Baltimore Co. d: 18 Apr 1918
.... +William Hutchins Little b: 16 May 1842 d: 1922 in Hill House, Parkton
.... 4 George Albert Mays b: 21 Sep 1852 in Baltimore Co. d: Sep 1915
.... +Elizabeth Ann Sterling b: 1856 in Balt Co d: 1919
.... 4 John F. Mays b: 13 Mar 1854 in Baltimore Co. d: 27 Apr 1878
.... +Harriet Unknown b: 1856
.... 4 William M. Mays b: Feb 1855 in Baltimore Co. d: 17 Feb 1873
.... +Mary F. Unknown b: Jun 1857 in Baltimore Co.
.... 4 Charles H Mays b: 06 Mar 1861 in Baltimore Co. d: 31 Jul 1933 in Balt,Co.
.... +Sarah Florence Elliott b: Jan 1863 in Balt,Co. d: 1934 in Balt,Co.
.... *2nd Wife of John Pitt Mays:
.... +Dorcas Hicks b: 16 Aug 1825 in Baltimore Co. d: 05 Mar 1862 m: Abt. 1860
...... 2 Benjamin Green b: 08 Jul 1787 in Baltimore Co., Maryland
...... 2 Thomas Green b: 1789 in Baltimore Co., Maryland
...... 2 Matilda Green b: 23 Jun 1792 in Baltimore Co., Maryland
.... +Abraham Miles b: 1795 in Maryland
.... 3 Elizabeth Miles b: 1824 in Maryland
.... 3 April Miles b: 1816 in Maryland
.... 3 Tabitta Miles b: 1818 in Maryland
.... 3 Rev Nelson Reed Miles b: 1826 in Maryland
.... +Cecelia Lavinia Mayes b: 1833 m: Abt. 1860
.... 4 Otis T. Miles b: 1854
.... 4 John W. Miles b: 1856
.... 4 William T. Miles b: 1858
.... +Mary Elizabeth Cole b: 1862 m: 15 Feb 1888
.... 4 Ella M. Miles b: 1860
.... 4 Winefred F. Miles b: 19 Jun 1863 d: 11 Jan 1942
.... +Daniel Webster Bosley b: 03 Aug 1857 in Baltimore County d: 24 Aug 1925 m: 24 Dec 1885
.... 4 Nelson Miles b: 1865
.... 4 Sarah Elizabeth Miles b: 05 Jun 1867 d: 08 May 1933 in Hereford
.... +Samuel Parkin Cole b: 04 Oct 1864 d: 22 Feb 1926
.... 4 Cecilia Lavinia Miles b: 19 Jun 1870 in Balt Co d: 27 Mar 1944 in HEREFORD
.... +Clarence Gorsuch Cole b: 20 Mar 1873 in GORSUCH'S TAVERN d: 20 Mar 1915 in VERONA
.... *2nd Husband of Cecilia Lavinia Miles:
.... +Walter Elmer Johnson
.... 4 Clinton Miles b: Abt. 1872
.... 4 Herbert Miles b: Abt. 1874
.... 3 Sarah Miles b: 1829 in Maryland
.... 3 Joshua Miles b: 1834 in Maryland
.... +Virginia Unknown b: 1844 in Maryland
.... 4 Harry Miles b: 1858
.... 4 Florence Miles b: 1859
.... 4 Howard Miles b: 1861
.... 4 Nelson Miles b: 1865
.... 4 Eugene Miles b: 1868
.... 3 Cathrine Miles b: 1841 in Maryland
.... 3 John Miles b: 1841 in Maryland
.... +Martha E. Unknown b: 1845
.... 4 Harry Miles b: Mar 1864 in Maryland
.... +Rose E. Unknown b: Oct 1865 in Maryland

```
................  4 Clarence D. Miles  b: 1867 in Maryland
................    +Lillian Benson  b: 1868 in Maryland
................  4 Dora I. Miles  b: 1870
................    +Calvin D. Price  b: 17 Jan 1869 in Baltimore, Co., Maryland
................  *2nd Husband of Dora I. Miles:
................    +Calvin D. Price  b: 17 Jan 1869 in Balt,Co.
...... 2 Sarah Green  b: Abt. 1795 in Baltimore Co., Maryland
..........  +Laban Sparks  b: 06 Mar 1794 in 8th District  d: 08 Jan 1865
............. 3 Shadrach Green Sparks  b: Abt. 1840 in Sparks, Maryland
................  +Susannah Stewart  m: 06 Sep 1865
................  4 Shadrack Green Sparks  b: Abt. 1867
................  4 Richard B Sparks  b: Abt. 1869
................  4 Reverdy B Sparks  b: Abt. 1871
................  4 Annie E Sparks  b: Abt. 1873
................  4 Laban Sparks  b: Abt. 1870
................    +Grace Waggner
............. 3 Rachel Sparks
................  +Joseph Stewart
............. 3 Matilda Sparks
................  +Abraham Cole  b: Abt. 1820
............. 3 Cecilia Sparks
................  +Joseph PARSONS
...... 2 Susan Green  b: 1796 in Baltimore Co., Maryland
...... 2 Ariann Green  b: 1797 in Baltimore Co., Maryland
...... 2 Rachel Green  b: 1800 in Baltimore Co., Maryland
...... 2 William Green  b: 14 Nov 1800 in Baltimore Co., Maryland
```

Descendants of Blois Wright

```
1 Blois Wright  b: 17 Nov 1735
.  +Mary Talbott  b: 29 Nov 1737
...... 2 Cassandra Wright  b: in Maryland
..........  +Francis Sparks  b: 1750 in Sparks folly  d: Aft. 1800
...............  3 John T Sparks  b: Abt. 1775 in Maryland  d: 1823 in Pa
...............  3 Josiah Sparks  b: Abt. 1780 in Maryland
...............  3 Wright Sparks  b: 06 May 1785 in Maryland  d: Bef. 1820 in Ind
..................  +Nancy Magnus  d: in Ind.
...............  3 Penelope Sparks  b: 1787 in Maryland
...............  3 Mary Sparks  b: Abt. 1789 in Maryland  d: in Ohio
..................  +John Sharp  b: Abt. 1788
...............  *2nd Husband of Mary Sparks:
..................  +Isaac Decker  d: in Ohio
...............  3 Elizabeth Sparks  b: Abt. 1790 in Maryland
..................  +Frederick Kaufman  b: Abt. 1800  d: 1858 in Monkton
...............  3 Ruth Sparks  b: Abt. 1795 in Maryland  d: in Missouri
..................  +Josiah Pearce  b: 1795 in Gorsuch Mills  d: in Missouri
...............  3 Thomas Sparks  b: 1800 in Maryland  d: 1853 in Ohio
..................  +Mary Elizabeth Pierce
...............  *2nd Wife of Thomas Sparks:
..................  +Jennie Harwood  b: in Ohio
...............  3 Prudence Sparks  b: 1796 in Maryland  d: 1874
..................  +Richard Gosnell  b: 1797 in Maryland  d: 1877
...... 2 Thomas Wright  b: 1759  d: 1818
...... 2 Prudence Wright  b: 1762  d: 1845 in Schuyler Co., Ill.
..........  +Matthew Sparks  b: 1760  d: 1845 in Schuyler CO, ILL
...............  3 [2] Leonard Sparks  b: Abt. 1785  d: 1850 in Clay CO, ILL
..................  +[1] Hannah Sharp
...............  3 Levi Sparks  b: Abt. 1786  d: 1850 in Schuyler CO, ILL
...............  3 Cassandra Sparks  b: Abt. 1788
..................  +Silas Roberts
...............  3 Ruth Sparks  b: Abt. 1790
...............  3 Elizabeth Sparks  b: Abt. 1792
...............  3 Lemuel Sparks  b: 1794 in Balt Co  d: 1855 in Schuyler CO, ILL
..................  +Nancy Jane Bartlow
...............  3 Penelope Sparks  b: 1804 in Balt Co  d: 1876 in Schuyler CO , ILL
..................  +James Blackburn
...............  3 James Sparks  b: 1811
...... *2nd Husband of Prudence Wright:
..........  +John Sharp  b: Abt. 1760
...............  3 John Sharp  b: Abt. 1784
...... 2 Elizabeth Wright  b: 1768  d: 1840
..........  +Benjamin Sharp
...............  3 [1] Hannah Sharp
..................  +[2] Leonard Sparks  b: Abt. 1785  d: 1850 in Clay CO, ILL
...... 2 Bloys Wright  b: 1772  d: 1843
..........  +Jane Gillispie  d: in Gratiot, Licking Co., Ohio
...............  3 Mary Talbott Wright
...............  3 Jane Wright
...............  3 Nathan Wright
...............  3 Isaac Wright
...............  3 John G Wright
...............  3 Sarah Wright  b: in Harford Co
...............  3 Matthew Wright  b: in Ohio
...............  3 James Wright  b: in Ohio
```

.... 3 William Wright b: Abt. 1796
.... 3 Thomas Wright b: Abt. 1800
...... 2 John Talbott Wright b: 15 Jul 1774 d: 10 Jul 1845
.... +Maacha Low b: Abt. 1775 in Maryland Line
.... 3 William Wright b: 1792
.... +Elinor Henderson
.... 3 John Wright b: 1793
.... +Agnes Gordon
.... 3 Caleb Wright b: 22 Sep 1799 d: 29 May 1880 in Ayres Chapel
.... +Elizabeth RUTLEDGE Gilbert b: Abt. 1804 d: 1826
.... *2nd Wife of Caleb Wright:
.... +Ann Elizabeth Gilbert b: Abt. 1807
.... *3rd Wife of Caleb Wright:
.... +Ann Garrett b: 14 May 1809 d: 02 Mar 1885 in Ayres Chapel
.... 3 [4] Joshua Low Wright b: 04 Sep 1801 d: 27 Mar 1877
.... +Julian Webb
.... *2nd Wife of [4] Joshua Low Wright:
.... +[3] Mary Farnandis Wright b: 21 Oct 1814 d: 19 Mar 1894
...... *2nd Wife of John Talbott Wright:
.... +Margaret Elizabeth Wilgis b: 14 Feb 1801 d: 25 Jan 1875
.... 3 Mary E Wright b: 06 Aug 1828 d: 1905
.... +Thomas Bayne
.... 3 Elizabeth Ann Wright b: 06 Aug 1829 in Wrights Prospect, Shawsville, Harford Co. Md. d: 13 Feb 1872 in Mt. Joy, West Liberty Um
.... +Josiah Sparks Pearce b: 14 Apr 1818 in Baltimore Co. d: 17 Oct 1886 in Mt. Joy, West Liberty Um
.... 3 Cassandra Wright b: 1832
.... +Unknown Kaufman b: Abt. 1830
.... 3 Henry Slicer Wright b: 05 Oct 1837 in Wrights Prospect d: 22 May 1907
.... +Sarah Elizabeth Rogers b: Jan 1840 d: 17 Aug 1883
.... *2nd Wife of Henry Slicer Wright:
.... +Susan Cuddy b: 05 Jul 1856 in Stablersville d: 23 Nov 1905
.... 3 John W Wright b: 1838
.... +Eizabeth A. B. Unknown b: 1840
.... *2nd Wife of John W Wright:
.... +Elizabeth Garrett b: Abt. 1850
.... 3 Emory P. Wright b: 08 Oct 1840 d: 22 May 1864
...... 2 William Wright b: 1778 in Harford co. d: 1855 in Telegraft, Rd, Harford Co
.... +Amelia Smithson b: 1787 in Harford Co. d: 1858 in Harford Co.
.... 3 Johanna Wright b: 1805
.... +Henry Slater
.... 3 [3] Mary Farnandis Wright b: 21 Oct 1814 d: 19 Mar 1894
.... +[4] Joshua Low Wright b: 04 Sep 1801 d: 27 Mar 1877
.... 3 Sarah Ann Wright b: Abt. 1815 d: 1882
.... 3 Elizabeth D Wright b: Abt. 1816
.... +Rudolph Johns b: Abt. 1813
.... 3 Daniel S Wright b: Abt. 1818
.... +Jane Forrester b: Abt. 1818
.... 3 Susanna Wright b: Abt. 1819
.... 3 William Wright b: 1820 in Baltimore Co. d: in Bethel
.... +Elizabeth Ayres b: Abt. 1820
.... *2nd Wife of William Wright:
.... +Charlotte A. McClung b: 1827 in Norrisville d: 1853 in Norrisville
.... 3 Emily Wright b: 1821 d: 05 Jul 1899 in St. Pauls
.... +William Glenn McComas b: 1808 d: 02 Aug 1861 in St. Pauls
.... 3 James Lawrence Wright b: Abt. 1824
.... 3 Thomas Wright b: Abt. 1825
.... 3 Joshua Wells Wright b: 15 Feb 1826 in Harford Co. d: 24 Mar 1899 in St. Pauls

.... +Hannah Amos b: 07 Apr 1819 in Harford Co.
.... *2nd Wife of Joshua Wells Wright:
.... +Margaret Anderson b: Abt. 1828 d: in McKendree
.... *3rd Wife of Joshua Wells Wright:
.... +Hannah Amos b: 07 Apr 1819 in Harford Co. d: 27 Aug 1902 in St. Pauls
.... 3 William Wright b: 22 Apr 1826 d: 18 Dec 1898
.... +Elizabeth C Ayres b: Abt. 1824
.... 3 John Wesley Wright b: 23 Feb 1823 d: 18 Dec 1898
.... +Mary J Peters
.... *2nd Wife of John Wesley Wright:
.... +Mary Elizabeth Herbert b: 1838 d: 1916

Descendants of Edward Matthews

```
1 Edward Matthews  b: 1761 in Edinburg, Scotland  d: 08 Sep 1829 in Balt Co, Bk 14 Pg 362
.  +Sarah Tracey  b: 1762 in Baltimore Co., Md.  d: 16 Apr 1837 in Balt Co, Gunpowder Bap
...... 2 Agnes Frances Matthews  b: 1781  d: 11 Oct 1861 in Balt Co
...... 2 Rachel Matthews  b: 1784  d: 27 Apr 1863
...... 2 Edward Matthews  b: 31 Jul 1787 in Balt Co  d: 21 Feb 1865 in 6th District
.......... +Rachel O Pearce  b: 15 Feb 1794 in Gorsuch Mills  d: 20 Jun 1885 in 6th District,
.............. 3 William P Matthews  b: 05 May 1820 in Middletown  d: 22 Nov 1887 in Bentley Springs
.................. +Amilia Kirschuer  b: 1821
.............. *2nd Wife of William P Matthews:
.................. +Jane  b: 1843
.............. 3 Edward Matthews  b: 15 Jul 1822 in Balt Co  d: 28 Sep 1885 in Balt Co
.............. 3 Elizabeth Hinkle Matthews  b: 12 Jul 1825 in Middletown  d: 12 Oct 1852 in Balt Co
.............. 3 Vanard Osinnern Matthews  b: 1826 in Balt Co  d: 30 Oct 1895 in Baltimore
.............. 3 Ezekiel Matthews  b: 17 Apr 1828 in Bel Air  d: 28 Jan 1903
.................. +Martha Ann Beall  b: 07 Jan 1835 in Harford Co  d: 17 Jul 1896 in Hereford
.............. 3 Rachel Matthews  b: 1834 in Middletown
.............. 3 George W Matthews  b: 1836 in Middletown  d: in Parkton
.................. +Hannah Wilson  b: Abt. 1836
.............. 3 Cathrine Hinkle Matthews  b: 28 Aug 1840 in Middletown  d: 19 Mar 1861 in Balt Co
.............. 3 Westley Matthews  b: 1847 in Middletown
...... 2 Deborah Ann Matthews  b: 1789  d: 19 Dec 1854 in Maryland
.......... +Jacob Stabler  b: 05 Mar 1795  d: 20 Feb 1868
.............. 3 William Stabler  b: Abt. 1814
.................. +Elizabeth Unkmown
.............. 3 Jarred Stabler  b: Abt. 1816
.................. +Margaret
.............. 3 Sarah Stabler  b: Abt. 1818
.................. +Jarris Hyster
.............. 3 Daniel Stabler  b: 1827
.................. +Cathrine  b: 1837  d: 1918
...... 2 Comfort Elizabeth Matthews  b: 1798 in Bentley Springs  d: 19 Jan 1863 in Balt Co
.......... +Thomas Wantland  b: 02 Jan 1787  d: in Gunpowder Baptist, Freeland, Md.
.............. 3 Rachel Wantland  b: Abt. 1817
.................. +John Hamptman  b: Abt. 1815
.............. 3 Mary Wantland  b: Abt. 1818
.................. +Joshua Hendrix  b: 1810 in Maryland  d: Aft. 1892 in Wiseburg
.............. 3 Westley Joseph Wantland  b: 1822  d: 1872
.................. +Mary J. Unknown  b: 1832  d: 1872
.............. 3 Jane Wantland  b: Abt. 1825
.............. 3 Thomas E. Wantland  b: Abt. 1829
.................. +Lydia Michael  b: Abt. 1837
...... 2 Sarah W Matthews  b: 1798  d: 15 Aug 1852 in Balt Co, Gunpowder Bap
.......... +George BRIGGS  d: in Gunpowder Bap
...... 2 William T Matthews  b: 1802 in Balt Co  d: 1862 in Balt Co, Gunpowder Bap
.......... +Mary Curfman  b: Abt. 1804
.............. 3 Rosana Matthews  b: Abt. 1832
.............. 3 Sarah Jane Matthews  b: 05 May 1833
.................. +Randolf Young  b: 19 May 1831  d: 16 Mar 1907
.............. 3 Davie Matthews  b: 1835
.............. 3 Rachel Ann Matthews  b: 21 Sep 1836
.............. 3 Elizabeth Matthews  b: 1838
.............. 3 William Westley Matthews  b: 09 Nov 1838
.............. 3 Edward Clarke Matthews  b: 1840
.............. 3 Eli Free Matthews  b: 1843
.............. 3 Mary Elizabeth Matthews  b: 1844
```

```
.............. 3 Naomi Francis Matthews  b: 1846
.............. 3 John Curfman Matthews  b: 1850
...... 2 Charlotte Matthews  b: 15 Nov 1803 in Balt Co
.......... +Micajah Tracey  b: 1801 in Maryland
.............. 3 John M. Tracey  b: 06 Mar 1823
.................. +Margaret
.............. 3 Sarah Tracey  b: 01 Feb 1825
.................. +William Wilson  b: Abt. 1824  d: in Gunpowder Bap
.............. 3 Edward M. Tracey  b: 1830
.............. 3 William W. Tracey  b: Aug 1834
```

Baltimore County Pioneers- 7th District

LOCATION OF RESIDENTS 1850-Drawing by Dale Bond

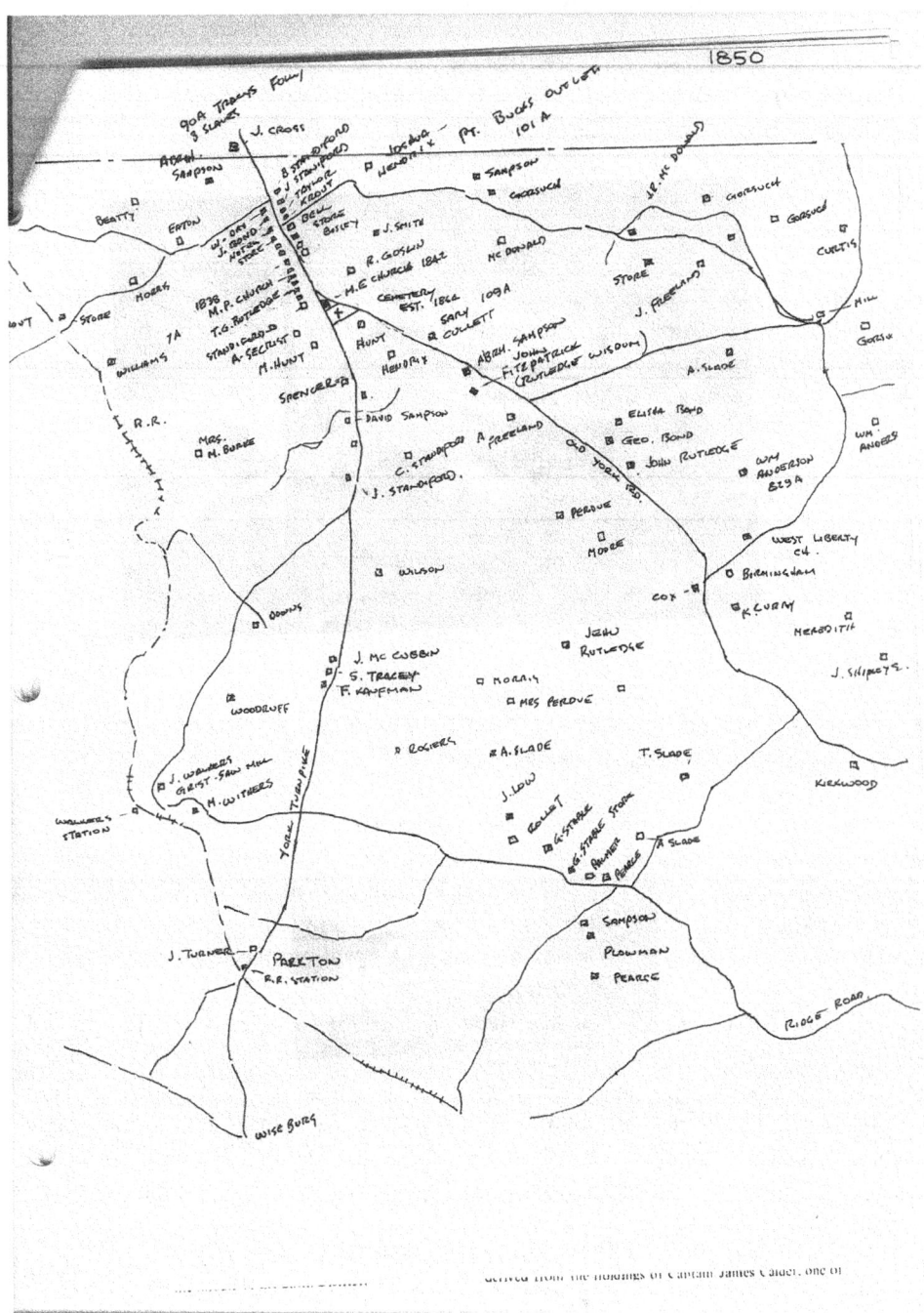

VINCENT STANDIFORD

The Standiford s owned **"Standifers Range"** located on both sides of the York Road. John Standiford married his neighbor, Jane Rutledge and their children married into the Gosnell, Hunt, Sampson, Rosier and Almony families. Vincent Standiford married Charity Gosnell. Charity Ann Standiford married Willie Hunt and Mary Jane married Edward Sampson. Vincent's son John R. Standiford married Keziah Almony and Joshua R. Standiford married Mary Jane Rosier. Elizabeth married James Franklin Almony and William F. Standiford married Francis M. Rosier. The Standiford family originally came from England and first settled on the Manor. The old log home on York road was a Standiford home. Adolphis Standiford was a teacher and lived in Maryland Line.

JOHN LAWSON

John Lawson patented "Lawson's Pleasant Hills" in 1787. This 602-acre property stretched from the York Road West along the Freeland Road to meet "Wantlands Folly" owned by Thomas Wantland. Lawson's land was located partially in York county. John Lawson's daughter married Joshua Low. The Lowe family has extensive members in both York and Harford County.

SAMUEL MORRIS

Further west of Maryland Line, the ancestors of Morris Meadow's owner, Clyde Morris, were the most influential. **Samuel Morris** surveyed "Dreary Wilderness" containing 148 acres in 1786. Samuel was involved in the evaluation of confiscated proprietary lands in 1782. Samuel Morris Junior, also patented a large tract. Joseph Morris surveyed the 242 acre "North Hampton" in 1786. Clyde Morris has built a thriving campground on his farm and added a museum of the area just recently.

THOMAS WANTLAND

Nearby, **Thomas Wantland** surveyed the 332-acre "Wantlands Folly" in 1786 also. Thomas was involved in the evaluation of confiscated proprietary lands in 1782.

JOHN FREELAND

John Freeland had an adjoining 106-acre tract laid out in 1787 as well as other holdings. John was involved in evaluation of confiscated proprietary lands in 1782. George Freeland, born about 1785, married Mary Bond. The town of Freeland had a post office, store, hotel and railroad station.

THOMAS HUNT

Going south from Maryland Line, **Thomas Hunt** surveyed the 256-acre Hunt's Hollow in 1787. Thomas was involved in evaluation of confiscated proprietary lands in 1782. The Hunt family owned land in the Monkton area before coming to this area. Matthew Hunt appears on the 1850 map as the owner of Maryland Line farm. Willie Hunt married Charity Ann Standiford daughter of neighbor Joshua P. Standiford. Hugh Hunt married Leah L. Wilson, George W. Hunt married Elizabeth Slade, Clarence W. Hunt married Alice Thomas and Leah Grace Hunt married Oscar Simpson.

ADAM HENDRIX

The Hendrix family owned the former Inn just north of New Market along the York Road. The Hendrix graveyard lies near the south end of the house.

Descendants of Thomas Hunt

1 Thomas Hunt b: Abt. 1740 in Mine Run Hundred d: Abt. 28 Dec 1833 in Baltimore, Co. Md., New Market
. +Ann Wiley b: Abt. 1740
...... 2 William Hunt b: Abt. 1765
.... +Elizabeth Unknown
.... 3 George Hunt b: 12 Oct 1788
.... 3 Ruth Hunt b: 09 Feb 1792
...... 2 Thomas Hunt b: Abt. 1775
...... 2 Noah Hunt b: 1780
.... +Margaret Bull b: 17 Feb 1787 in Maryland d: 03 Jul 1857 in Maryland Line
.... 3 Willie Hunt b: 1816 in Baltimore Co. d: 28 Apr 1882 in Maryland Line
.... +Charity Ann Standiford b: 1824 in Baltimore Co.
.... 4 Thomas Hunt b: 1841
.... +Martha Keys b: Abt. 1844
.... 4 Levinia Hunt b: 1843
.... 4 Susan Hunt b: 1844
.... 4 Mary Hunt b: 1847
.... 4 Margaret Hunt b: 1849
.... 3 Thomas Hunt b: 1826 in Baltimore, Co. Md., New Market d: Aft. 1880 in Baltimore, Co. Md., New Market
.... +Hanna Unknown b: 1829 in Maryland d: Bet. 1860 - 1870
.... 4 Susan Hunt b: 1853
.... 4 Tillie A. Hunt b: 1856
.... 4 Henry Hunt b: 1857 d: in Freeland
.... 4 John Noah Hunt b: 03 Apr 1858 in Maryland d: 31 May 1932 in Maryland Line
.... +Emma Irene Wilson b: 09 Dec 1864 in Baltimore Co. d: 12 May 1926
.... 4 Lizzy Hunt b: 1862
.... 4 Hugh Wilson Hunt b: 11 Jul 1864 in Bentley Springs d: 02 Jan 1939 in Parkton, Maryland
.... +Leah L. Wilson b: 16 Aug 1869 m: 14 Jan 1886 in Stablersville d: 18 Sep 1923
.... *2nd Wife of Hugh Wilson Hunt:
.... +Ellen V. Unknown b: 1878 in England m: Abt. 1905
.... 4 Rosie Hunt b: 1867
...... 2 Matthew Hunt b: 1785 in Baltimore Co. d: 1851 in Maryland Line
.... +Elleanor Wadlow b: 1795 d: 17 Feb 1876
.... 3 John W. Hunt b: 31 Oct 1825 in Baltimore Co. d: 26 Jun 1882 in Maryland Line
.... +Julia A. Kidd b: 11 May 1829 d: 30 Dec 1903
.... 4 Annie B. Hunt b: 24 Aug 1869 d: 09 Nov 1883
.... 4 William Wiley Hunt b: 1859
.... 3 Nancy Hunt b: 1830 in Baltimore Co.
.... +John W. Macabee b: Abt. 1827
.... 3 Joshua Hunt b: 1835 in Baltimore Co. d: 29 Oct 1873 in Maryland Line
.... +Margaret R. Unknown b: 08 Apr 1836 d: 01 Feb 1914
.... 4 John T. Hunt b: 03 Jul 1871 in Baltimore Co. d: 20 Aug 1889 in Maryland Line
.... 4 Grace Hunt b: Abt. 1872
.... 4 William Hunt b: Abt. 1865
.... 4 Charles Hunt b: Abt. 1867
.... 3 Julia A. Hunt b: Abt. 1832
.... +Lawrence Morris b: Abt. 1830 d: in Pine Grove Cm.
.... 3 Temperance Hunt b: Abt. 1834
.... +Emanuel Wilson b: Abt. 1830 d: in Schuylkill Co., Pa.
.... 3 Sarah Hunt b: Abt. 1836
.... +William Ruhl b: Abt. 1835
.... 3 Hannah Hunt b: 11 Feb 1822 d: 12 Dec 1906 in Parkton, MD.
.... +Hosea Rosier b: 18 Mar 1827 in Maryland d: 12 Mar 1899 in Parkton, MD.
.... 4 William S. Rosier b: 16 Mar 1853 in Parkton, MD. d: 22 Jun 1917 in Maryland Line
.... +Annie Maria Almony b: 05 Aug 1857 d: 04 Oct 1948
.... 4 James MacCord Rosier b: 15 Jan 1855 d: 26 Jun 1860 in Maryland Line

```
................... +Laura V. Jones  b: Dec 1865  d: 10 Jan 1927 in Baltimore City, Maryland
................. 4 Benson D. Rosier  b: 1860  d: 1934 in Parkton, MD.
................... +Margaret  b: 02 Sep 1860  d: 05 Dec 1883
................... *2nd Wife of Benson D. Rosier:
................... +Anna Elizabeth Echtol  b: 07 Oct 1865  d: 18 Jan 1949 in Maryland Line
............ 3 Elizabeth Hunt  b: Abt. 1838
............... +Unknown Krammer
...... 2 Mary Hunt  b: 22 Mar 1787
...... 2 Enock Hunt  b: 25 Feb 1789 in Maryland  d: 01 Jan 1850 in Maryland Line
...... 2 Hannah Hunt  b: Abt. 1786
...... 2 Sarah Hunt  b: Abt. 1787
.......... +Unknown Gendy
...... 2 Cassander Hunt  b: Abt. 1788
.......... +Unknown Evins
...... 2 Charlotte Hunt  b: Abt. 1789
.......... +Unknown Chuffey
...... 2 Penelope Hunt  b: Abt. 1790
.......... +Unknown Downs  b: Abt. 1785
...... 2 John Hunt  b: Abt. 1785
...... 2 Wiley Hunt  b: Abt. 1784
```

Descendants of John Samuel Morris

1 John Samuel Morris b: Abt. 1760 in Wales
..... 2 John Samuel Morris b: 1795 in Freeland, Md. d: 1855 in 6th District, Mt. Zion Cm.
.... +Jemima Palmer b: 30 Nov 1804 in Maryland m: 01 Jul 1841 d: 1881 in 6th District
.... 3 George Palmer Morris b: 20 Nov 1842 in 6th District, Baltimore Co., Md. d: 14 Jan 1920 in Cm., Mt. Zion
.... +Louisa Jane Wilhelm b: Dec 1847 d: in Cm., Mt. Zion
.... 4 Emma Morris b: 13 Jan 1870 in Freeland, Md. d: 30 Nov 1960 in Cm., Mt. Zion
.... +Robert Benson b: 1865 d: 1942
.... 4 Serina Morris b: 12 Jun 1872 in Freeland, Md. d: 28 Mar 1937 in Cm., Steltz
.... +William Harrison Masemore b: 18 Nov 1873
.... 4 Ada Morris b: Sep 1880 in Freeland, Md. d: 1956 in Cm., Mt. Zion
.... 4 Clarence Upton Morris b: Nov 1882 in Freeland, Md.
.... +Florence Robinson b: Abt. 1885
.... 4 Howard K. Morris b: 1884 in Freeland, Md. d: 11 Dec 1886 in Cm., Mt. Zion
.... 4 Florence V. Morris b: Sep 1887 in Freeland, Md.
.... +William Franklin Hare m: 09 Dec 1903
.... 4 Hattie Morris b: May 1889 in Freeland, Md.
.... 4 Ernest A. Morris b: 1892 in Freeland, Md. d: Aug 1987 in Cm., Mt.Zion
.... +Edith Simpson b: 1894 d: 1980 in Cm., Mt. Zion
.... 3 Ellenora Morris b: 23 Dec 1844 d: 11 Nov 1928 in Cm., Mt. Zion
.... 3 John Samuel Morris b: 24 Mar 1846 in Baltimore Co. d: 18 Jan 1926 in Baltimore City
.... +Elizabeth Cooper b: 1843 in Maryland
.... 4 Sarah C. Morris b: 1864
.... 4 George Morris b: 1869
.... 4 Herbert Clinton Morris b: 11 Nov 1872 d: 1921
.... 4 Harvey Morris b: 11 Nov 1872 d: 07 Jul 1932
.... 4 Edwin Morris b: 01 Nov 1874
.... 4 Wilbur Oscar Morris b: 16 Dec 1877 d: 1953 in Philadelphia, Mt. Zion Cm.
.... +Reba Vivian Lentz b: 26 Jan 1880 d: 1975
.... 4 Oscar Morris b: 1880
.... 4 Myrtle Gertrude Morris b: 1882
.... 4 Stella Morris b: 1887
.... 4 Sarah Morris b: 1864
.... 4 Charles Henry Morris b: 1870 d: 1948
.... 4 Lettie Morris b: 1885
.... +Thomas McConnell b: 29 Aug 1879 d: Apr 1965

Descendants of Vincent Standiford

1 Vincent Standiford b: Abt. 1750
...... 2 Benjamin Standiford b: Abt. 1775
...... 2 Joshua P. Standiford b: 24 Aug 1780 in Maryland Line d: 20 Aug 1873 in Md. Line
.... +Jane Rutledge b: 20 Aug 1795 in Maryland Line m: 20 Mar 1822 in Baltimore, Co., Md. d: 15 Sep 1879 in Md. Line
.... 3 John C. R. Standiford b: 17 Apr 1824 d: 24 Nov 1908 in Zion
.... +Lavina Hannigan b: 28 Sep 1819 d: 29 Apr 1900 in Mt. Zion
.... 4 Joshua P. Standiford b: Abt. 1849
.... 4 Annie Elizabeth Standiford b: Jun 1851 in Balt Co d: 1933 in West Liberty
.... +Samuel Shaver Cooper b: Mar 1845 in 5th Dist m: 09 Oct 1869 d: 1921 in West Liberty
.... 4 Mary Standiford b: 1854
.... 4 Priscilla Elizabeth Standiford b: 1857
.... +Joshua H. L. Boyer
.... 4 John C. B. Standiford b: 18 Jun 1861 d: 03 Jun 1887 in Graham, Mo Mt. Zion
.... 3 Vincent Standiford b: 27 Mar 1827 in Baltimore Co. d: 28 Apr 1898 in Maryland
.... +Charity C. Gosnell b: 27 Jul 1829 in Baltimore Co. m: Abt. 1849 d: 26 Aug 1892
.... 4 Mary Frances Standiford b: 01 Apr 1850 in Baltimore Co. d: 22 Sep 1936
.... +Thomas Leonard Harris b: 04 Jan 1858 d: 22 Mar 1899
.... 4 Sarah Jane Standiford b: 1852 in Baltimore Co.
.... +Unknown
.... 4 Kyantha Nancy Standiford b: 1854 in Baltimore Co.
.... +William Seitz b: Abt. 1840
.... 4 John R. Standiford b: 06 Jul 1856 in Baltimore Co. d: 14 Aug 1907 in Maryland Line
.... +Keziah Almony b: 01 Oct 1854 d: 12 Nov 1908
.... 4 Joshua R. Standiford b: Jan 1860 in Baltimore Co. d: 1938 in Maryland Line
.... +Mary Jane Rosier b: May 1858 d: 1945
.... 4 Elizabeth Celesta Standiford b: 18 Mar 1861 in Parkton d: 28 Oct 1894 in Md Line
.... +James Franklin Almony b: 26 Dec 1859 in Maryland m: Abt. 1890 d: 23 May 1931 in Md Line
.... 4 William F. Standiford b: 10 Feb 1864 in Baltimore Co. d: 11 Feb 1918
.... +Francis M. Rosier b: 14 May 1867 d: 24 Dec 1915
.... 3 Charity Ann Standiford b: 1824 in Baltimore Co.
.... +Willie Hunt b: 1816 in Baltimore Co. d: 28 Apr 1882 in Maryland Line
.... 4 Thomas Hunt b: 1841
.... +Martha Keys b: Abt. 1844
.... 4 Levinia Hunt b: 1843
.... 4 Susan Hunt b: 1844
.... 4 Mary Hunt b: 1847
.... 4 Margaret Hunt b: 1849
.... 3 Mary Jane Standiford b: 23 Aug 1831 in Maryland d: 1864
.... +Edwin Hindle Sampson b: 02 Jan 1830 in Maryland m: 25 Feb 1852 d: 1864 in Houcktown, Ohio
.... 4 Eli A. Sampson b: Abt. 1855
.... 4 Anne A. Sampson b: Abt. 1858
.... 4 Mary L. Sampson b: Abt. 1858
.... 4 Lora F. Sampson b: Abt. 1859
.... 4 Hinkle E. Sampson b: Abt. 1864
...... 2 Clement Standiford b: 10 Feb 1783 in Maryland Line d: Jun 1868 in Maryland Line
.... +Mary Fitzpatrick b: 18 May 1791 in Maryland d: 1879
.... 3 James A. Standiford b: 23 Jan 1818 d: 1913
.... +Sarah Caldwallader Carter b: 23 Oct 1828
.... 4 Charles Arthur Standiford b: 08 Nov 1866 d: 11 Jan 1954
.... +Jennifer Ferris b: 1867 d: 20 Feb 1958
.... 4 Marie Standiford
.... 4 J. Milton Standiford b: 1864 d: 1928
.... +Sarah Marissa Casey b: 1865 d: 1939
.... 3 Joshua Standiford b: 1826
.... 3 John Standiford b: 1831 d: 1899 in Maryland Line

```
................ +Sarah Miller  b: 1833  d: 1915
..................... 4 John William G. Standiford  b: 1856  d: 1892
..................... 4 Howard T Standiford  b: 1858 in Maryland  d: 1943
........................ +Cathrine Hampshire  b: 1864 in Maryland  d: 1922
..................... 4 Giles D. M. Standiford  b: 1862  d: 1918 in Maryland Line
..................... 4 William T. Standiford  b: 1856  d: 1892 in Maryland Line
...... 2 Vincent Standiford  b: Abt. 1785
```

Descendants of Jesse Pocock

```
1 Jesse Pocock  b: 20 Jun 1760 in Balt Co  d: 14 Sep 1845 in Delaware, Definance Co., Ohio
.  +Cathrine Price  b: Abt. 1760
...... 2 Jemima Pocock  b: 16 Jan 1789 in Baltimore Co.  d: 30 Dec 1850 in Balt Co
.......... +George Sampson Bond  b: 04 Jun 1783 in Bond Rd, Baltimore Co.  m: 27 Nov 1804 in Baltimore Co., Md.  d: 30 Dec 1850 in
            Maryland Line
............. 3 [2] Elisha Bond  b: 30 May 1805 in Bond RD, Maryland Line  d: 30 Oct 1884 in Maryland Line, Bond Road
................. +[1] Eliza Pocock  b: 07 Jan 1827  d: 18 Dec 1897 in Maryland Line, Bond Road
..................... 4 [3] Thomas Bond  b: 15 Jul 1849  d: 07 Oct 1853 in Bond Cm., Bond Road
..................... 4 [4] Rebecca Jane Bond  b: 15 Jul 1851 in Maryland  d: 03 Apr 1938 in West Liberty
......................... +[5] John S. Hollingshead  b: 17 Feb 1854 in Pennsylvania  m: Abt. 1875  d: 20 Jul 1918 in West Liberty, Ensor Road
..................... 4 [6] Jessie Ross Bond  b: 15 May 1857  d: 30 Apr 1899 in New Market Cm.
..................... 4 [7] Martha Ellen Bond  b: 18 Jul 1864
..................... 4 [8] Elizabeth Ann Bond  b: 31 Jul 1868
............. 3 Ellen Bond  b: 17 Jul 1808 in Bond Road  d: Bef. 1830
................. +George Stabler  b: 26 Jun 1794 in Stablersville  d: 03 Feb 1864 in Stablersville
............. 3 Ann Bond  b: 11 Feb 1816 in Bond Road  d: 27 Apr 1880
................. +Unknown Morris  b: Abt. 1814
............. 3 Harriet S. Bond  b: 1820 in Bond Road, Baltimore Co., Md.
................. +Daniel B. Smith  b: 29 Nov 1830 in York Co.  m: 26 Jan 1854  d: 25 Sep 1901 in Atchinson, Kansas, Wheatland Cm., Horton
..................... 4 George A. Smith
..................... 4 Adda E. Smith  b: 17 Feb 1867 in Horton, Kansas  d: 11 Jun 1936
......................... +Bailey Wallingford
..................... *2nd Husband of Adda E. Smith:
......................... +Patrick H. McKeon  m: 03 Feb 1894  d: 07 Feb 1902
............. 3 Elizabeth Bond  b: 07 Jun 1826 in Bond Road  d: 01 Mar 1892
............. 3 Ross Bond  b: 14 Oct 1830 in Bond Rd  d: 22 Aug 1907 in Maryland Line, Bond Road
................. +Mary Jane McDonald  b: 19 Jul 1837 in 7 TH Dist.,Balt Co  m: 06 Jan 1859  d: 27 Mar 1898 in Maryland Line, Bond Road
..................... 4 Smith Daniel Bond  b: 08 Oct 1859 in Bond Road  d: 10 Mar 1938 in Maryland Line, Bond Road
......................... +Rachel H Kearns  b: 11 Sep 1861  m: Abt. 1884  d: 27 Oct 1897
..................... *2nd Wife of Smith Daniel Bond:
......................... +Margaret A. Baird  b: 08 Apr 1855  m: Abt. 1900  d: 03 Apr 1919
..................... 4 Jane Elizabeth Bond  b: 28 Sep 1861 in Bond Road  d: 27 Oct 1926 in Parkton, Maryland
......................... +Charles E. Plowman  b: Oct 1850 in Balt,Co.  m: 06 Jan 1892  d: 27 Feb 1945 in Parkton, Maryland
..................... 4 Varena Julia Bond  b: 10 Feb 1864 in Bond Road  d: 16 May 1922
......................... +James Thomas Almony  b: 10 Jul 1860 in White Hall, Maryland  m: 13 Jan 1886  d: 03 Jan 1929 in Buried Vernon
..................... 4 Mary Cathrine Rebecca Bond  b: 11 Sep 1865 in Bond Road  d: 31 Oct 1934
......................... +John James Anderson  b: 11 Aug 1869 in Maryland  m: 06 Mar 1895  d: 25 Dec 1935
..................... 4 Luella Harriet Bond  b: 06 May 1867 in Bond Road  d: 23 Mar 1868 in Maryland Line, Bond road
..................... 4 Sally E. G. Bond  b: 09 Apr 1869 in Bond Road  d: 22 May 1872 in Maryland Line, Bond Road
..................... 4 Lucy M. A. Bond  b: 19 Jan 1871 in Bond Road  d: 20 Mar 1872 in Maryland Line, Bond Road
..................... 4 John Ross Bond  b: 26 Jan 1873 in Bond Road  d: 16 Aug 1940
......................... +Mary Dorcas Kirkwood  b: 22 Jan 1869 in Shane  d: 28 Jun 1958 in Stewartstown
..................... 4 Rosa Eve Bond  b: 26 Sep 1875 in Bond Road  d: 09 Mar 1881 in Maryland Line
..................... 4 Laura Agnes Bond  b: 09 Aug 1879 in Bond Road  d: 09 Apr 1956
......................... +John K. Miller  b: Abt. 1876  m: 26 Nov 1902  d: in Red Lion
...... 2 Ann Pocock  b: 15 Mar 1794
.......... +Unknown Eton  b: Abt. 1792
...... 2 Eli Pocock  b: 29 Mar 1796
.......... +Cathrine Kinstrick
...... 2 Charity Pocock  b: 22 Apr 1798
.......... +James Farrell
...... 2 Eleanor Pocock  b: 22 Apr 1800
...... 2 Israel Pocock  b: 01 Oct 1802 in Baltimore Co., Md.  d: 20 Mar 1889 in Maryland Line
.......... +Ruth Gorsuch  b: 26 Feb 1804 in Balt Co  m: 23 Feb 1821 in Baltimore , Co. Md.  d: 04 Mar 1847
............. 3 Elizabeth Ann Pocock  b: 1822  d: 1824
```

```
............ 3 Daniel Beckley Pocock  b: 15 Sep 1824 in 7 th District  d: 27 Jan 1907 in Navarre, Ohio
............... +Susanna Rockhold  b: 04 Apr 1830 in 7th District, Balt Co, Gorsuch Mills  m: 26 Jul 1849  d: 11 Dec 1906 in Navarre, Ohio
.................. 4 Ruth Ann Pocock  b: 1850  d: 1851
.................. 4 Rebecca Jane Pocock  b: 1852  d: 1928
.................. 4 Elizabeth Matilda Pocock  b: 1853  d: 1856
.................. 4 James Franklin Pocock  b: 1856  d: 1914
.................. 4 Charles Francis Pocock  b: 1858  d: 1859
.................. 4 Isreal Beckley Pocock  b: 1859
.................. 4 Elisha Gorsuch Pocock  b: 1861  d: 1927
.................. 4 Mary Margaret Pocock  b: 1866  d: 1896
............ 3 [1] Eliza Pocock  b: 07 Jan 1827  d: 18 Dec 1897 in Maryland Line, Bond Road
............... +[2] Elisha Bond  b: 30 May 1805 in Bond RD, Maryland Line  d: 30 Oct 1884 in Maryland Line, Bond Road
.................. 4 [3] Thomas Bond  b: 15 Jul 1849  d: 07 Oct 1853 in Bond Cm., Bond Road
.................. 4 [4] Rebecca Jane Bond  b: 15 Jul 1851 in Maryland  d: 03 Apr 1938 in West Liberty
..................... +[5] John S. Hollingshead  b: 17 Feb 1854 in Pennsylvania  m: Abt. 1875  d: 20 Jul 1918 in West Liberty, Ensor Road
.................. 4 [6] Jessie Ross Bond  b: 15 May 1857  d: 30 Apr 1899 in New Market Cm.
.................. 4 [7] Martha Ellen Bond  b: 18 Jul 1864
.................. 4 [8] Elizabeth Ann Bond  b: 31 Jul 1868
............ 3 Rebecca Jane Pocock  b: 1829  d: 1922
............ 3 Mary Ellen Pocock  b: 1831  d: 1834
............ 3 Cathrine Pocock  b: 1834  d: 1838
............ 3 Jessie Price Pocock  b: 1836  d: 1838
............ 3 James Franklin Pocock  b: 25 Jan 1839  d: 12 Aug 1923
............ 3 George W Pocock  b: 1842  d: 1871
............ 3 Israel Putnam Pocock  b: 1845  d: 1854
...... 2 Mary Pocock  b: 09 Feb 1806
......... +Jarrard Rutledge  b: 06 May 1809  d: 20 Jul 1857 in Wiseburg Cm.
............ 3 Elizabeth Rutledge  b: 1830 in Baltimore Co., Maryland
............ 3 Catherine Rutledge  b: 1833 in Baltimore Co., Maryland
............ 3 Julian Rutledge  b: 1835 in Baltimore Co., Maryland
............ 3 Jesse Rutledge  b: 1840 in Baltimore Co., Maryland
............ 3 Mary J. Rutledge  b: 1841 in Baltimore Co., Maryland
............ 3 William H. Rutledge  b: 1845 in Baltimore Co., Maryland
............ 3 Chariety Rutledge  b: 1849 in Baltimore Co., Maryland
...... 2 Asenath Pocock  b: 02 Dec 1807
...... 2 Juliet Elizabeth Pocock  b: 29 Jan 1810
...... 2 Keziah Pocock  b: 29 May 1801  d: 10 Dec 1879
......... +Isaac Sampson  b: 24 Jan 1795 in Baltimore Co.  d: 24 Nov 1884 in Maryland Line
............ 3 Elizabeth Ellen Sampson  b: 08 Jul 1832 in Maryland  d: 18 Dec 1886 in Md Line
............... +Agustus Caesar Almony  b: 12 Oct 1820 in White Hall, Maryland  d: 22 Apr 1881 in Md. Line
.................. 4 Keziah Almony  b: 01 Oct 1854  d: 12 Nov 1908
..................... +John R. Standiford  b: 06 Jul 1856 in Baltimore Co.  d: 14 Aug 1907 in Maryland Line
.................. 4 Annie Maria Almony  b: 05 Aug 1857  d: 04 Oct 1948
..................... +William S. Rosier  b: 16 Mar 1853 in Parkton, MD.  d: 22 Jun 1917 in Maryland Line
.................. 4 James Franklin Almony  b: 26 Dec 1859 in Maryland  d: 23 May 1931 in Md Line
..................... +Elizabeth Celesta Standiford  b: 18 Mar 1861 in Parkton  m: Abt. 1890  d: 28 Oct 1894 in Md Line
..................... *2nd Wife of James Franklin Almony:
..................... +Priscilla Elizabeth Rutledge  b: 1865 in Maryland  m: Abt. 1895  d: 10 Aug 1939 in White Hall, Maryland
.................. 4 Thomas E W Almony  b: 03 Apr 1866  d: 13 Jan 1881 in Md Line
```

Descendants of Thomas Wilson

1 Thomas Wilson b: Abt. 1800 in Baltimore Co., Maryland d: Abt. 1848
. +Jemima Collett b: Abt. 1800 in Baltimore Co., Maryland
...... 2 Delilah Wilson b: Abt. 1826
.... +Adam Curry b: Abt. 1825
...... 2 John T. Wilson b: 21 Apr 1828
.... +Hannah Walker b: 15 Nov 1831
...... 2 Daniel Wilson b: Abt. 1832
...... 2 Eli Wilson b: 1836
.... +Ariel Young b: Abt. 1838
...... *2nd Wife of Eli Wilson:
.... +Elizabeth Jane Walker b: 1837
...... *3rd Wife of Eli Wilson:
.... +Annabella Sly b: Abt. 1840 d: 1887
...... 2 Mary Ann Wilson b: 1838
.... +John Burroughs b: Abt. 1836
...... 2 Elizabeth Wilson b: 1840
.... +David Harris b: Abt. 1836
...... 2 Cornelius Wilson b: 03 Jun 1842 in Maryland d: 01 Dec 1929
.... +Eliza Emma Young b: 19 Apr 1852 in Maryland d: 03 Aug 1929
.... 3 Samuel Young Wilson b: 10 May 1872 in Maryland d: Jul 1950
.... +Rebecca Jane Anstine b: 25 Jul 1874 in Stewartstown, Pa. d: 04 Jan 1944
.... 3 Eli Daniel Wilson b: 29 Nov 1874 in Maryland d: 16 Jun 1947
.... +Clara Bell Krout b: Abt. 1877 d: 24 Nov 1977
.... 3 Thomas W. Wilson b: 16 Jul 1877 in Maryland d: 14 May 1966
.... +Ida Cotter d: 23 Sep 1974
.... 3 Mary Wilson b: 20 Jan 1880 in Maryland d: 03 Oct 1965
.... +Elmer Ellsworth Shaver b: Abt. 1880 d: 03 Jun 1920
.... 3 Katherine Wilson b: Jan 1883 in Maryland d: 1927
.... +Henry C. McCullough b: Abt. 1880
.... 3 Grace Annie Wilson b: 22 Feb 1884 in Maryland d: 19 Nov 1960
.... 3 Margaret E. Wilson b: 06 May 1886 in Maryland d: 27 Mar 1991
.... +Claude Hare b: Abt. 1885 d: 10 Feb 1956
.... 3 Frank Lindsay Wilson b: 05 May 1888 in Maryland d: 15 Mar 1950 in Maryland
.... +Mary Agnes Schuppert b: Abt. 1890 in Maryland d: 01 Jun 1965
.... 3 George W. Wilson b: 10 Oct 1890 in Maryland d: 02 Dec 1938
.... 3 John W. Wilson b: 18 Aug 1893 in Maryland d: 03 Jul 1982
.... +Bessie Trabert b: Abt. 1895
.... 3 Nellie Pauline Wilson b: 09 Jun 1898 in Maryland d: 29 Nov 1993
...... 2 Margaret Jane Wilson b: 1847
.... +Unknown Curry b: Abt. 1845
...... 2 Silas Wilson b: 1849

James Calder

James Calder owned 3836 acres around Parkton in 1798 and was undoubtedly the largest landowner in the district. Captain James Calder was from a prominent family in Inverness, Scotland. After fighting on the losing side in the battle of Culloden, he escaped to this county and purchased land in the Parkton area. Being a surveyor, he was able to acquire a number of tracts north of present day Parkton, which he named for the family estate in Scotland ,"Castle Calder". During the Revolutionary War, Captain Calder went to Canada. Some Scots had to pledge not to take up arms against the King of England as a condition for their being allowed to leave Scotland. Calder was the County Surveyor before and after the war. His daughter Mary married Thomas Little and daughter Sarah married Captain James Turner. The Little and Turner families were from the "Manor". Granddaughter Miranda Turner married James Harris and Eleanor Turner married James Rampley. The Harris family later operated the Harris Mill east of New Market. Margaret Calder married Davis B. Parke of whom the town was later named . Miranda Harris' daughters, Luella and Calder, were instrumental in starting Parke Memorial Church. James Calder, his wife Margaret, daughter Margaret and Davis Parke were re buried under the new church. The Calder property passed from each generation through the daughters until Marian Turner Clark's death. Cousins in South Carolina inherited the land and recently sold part of the farm for development.

Hugh Cameron

Hugh Cameron came to this country from Scotland and settled next to fellow countryman James Calder. Hugh Cameron settled on land surveyed by Daniel Curfman called "Curfman Stradt", an 857-acre tract patented in 1800. Most of the Curfman family later moved to Frederick County. Hugh married Sarah Walker and married second to Rachel Walker, daughters of Daniel Walker and Prudence Perdue. Hugh's daughter Mary married Thomas Vaughn Hunter. The Walkers were also related to the Fosters and all operated mills. Later generation, Richard Cameron operated the White Hall Mill for many years. The old Cameron home has presently been renovated after years of neglect.

Daniel Walker

Daniel's descendants married Camerons, Hunters, Slades and Lowes. During the Civil War, a group of Union soldiers were camped near the Walker farm guarding the railroad bridges. During the night, one of the soldiers shot at a mysterious figure walking nearby. The next day, Mr. Walker came to the camp looking for a lost cow. The cow was found shot dead nearby. The Walker farm was located on Walker Road above Parkton. Walker Road was changed to Stablersville in the late nineteen hundreds for no apparent reason.

CALDER DESCENDANT HOME REPLACED ORIGINAL HOUSE

Photo by Betty Hammond

Parkton Hotel

Descendants of Capt James Calder

1 Capt James Calder b: 1729 in Elgin, Scotland d: 11 Aug 1808 in Mine Run Hundred - Parkton
. +Margaret Bagnel b: 1754 in Ireland d: 12 Apr 1829 in Parkton MD
...... 2 George E Calder b: 1779 in Parkton d: 1809 in Parkton
...... 2 Margaret Calder b: 1781 in Parkton d: 1860 in Parkton
.... +Davis B. Parke b: 1781 d: 1831 in Parkton, buried Parke Mem. Church
.... 3 Mararetta Parke b: 1817 in Parkton d: 1835 in Parkton
...... 2 Mary Calder b: Abt. 1784 in Parkton
.... +Thomas Little b: 1774 d: 15 Nov 1849
.... 3 Charles Little b: 1814 d: 1846
.... +Miranda Hutchins b: 1809 d: 1897
.... 3 George Little b: 06 Jun 1822 in Parkton, Md. d: 28 Jan 1878 in Parkton, Md.
.... +Mary C. Kerr b: 28 Jan 1821
...... 2 Rebecca Calder b: 1789 in Parkton d: 1801 in Parkton
...... 2 Charlotte Calder b: 1795 in Mine Run Hundred, Parkton
.... +Michael Withers b: 1778 in Pennsylvania
.... 3 Susan Withers b: 1812 in Baltimore Co.
.... 3 Edwin Withers b: 1824 in Baltimore Co.
.... 3 Charlotte Withers b: 1836 in Baltimore Co.
...... 2 Sarah Calder b: 24 May 1796 in Parkton d: 11 May 1874
.... +James Turner b: 07 Nov 1783 m: 22 Apr 1811 in Hopewell, York Co d: 28 Mar 1861 in Castle Caulder, Parkton MD
.... 3 Margaret Turner d: 19 Sep 1895
.... +Elbert Grandison Emack b: 20 Feb 1804 in Versailles, France d: 12 Sep 1886
.... 3 George Washington Turner d: in Ind
.... +Caroline Verry
.... 3 James Calder Turner b: 03 Mar 1813 in Wiseburg, MD d: 24 Apr 1882 in Habersham Co., Georgia
.... +Jane Mary McLeod b: 12 Apr 1812 in Washington DC m: 20 Apr 1838
.... 3 Mary Ann Turner b: 30 Jan 1814 d: 30 Nov 1851
.... +John Moore Price b: 30 Nov 1800 in Wiseburg, MD m: 27 Mar 132 d: 04 Sep 1858 in Parkton
.... 3 Martha Turner b: 15 Aug 1815 d: 02 Mar 1822
.... +Thomas Kurtz Turner b: 1811 d: 19 Nov 1900
.... 3 Rachel Turner b: 15 Aug 1818 d: 02 Mar 1822 in Bethel
.... 3 Miranda Turner b: 28 Sep 1825
.... +James C Harris b: 22 Dec 1817 m: 28 Sep 1848 d: 30 Aug 1866
.... 3 Eleanor Turner b: 15 Nov 1829 d: 25 Jan 1901
.... +James Rampley b: 25 Oct 1819 in Harford Co m: 1850 d: 27 Aug 1901

Descendants of Hugh Cameron

```
1 Hugh Cameron  b: Abt. 1775 in Scotland  d: 15 Nov 1831
.  +Sarah Walker  b: 31 Aug 1784  d: 24 Mar 1815 in Cameron Cm,Parkton
...... 2 William Cameron  b: Abt. 1801
...... 2 Eveline Cameron  b: Abt. 1802  d: 26 Sep 1823
...... 2 Elizabeth Cameron  b: 27 Jul 1806  d: 28 Dec 1866
...... 2 Daniel W Cameron  b: 10 Sep 1811  d: 28 Jul 1904
...... 2 James W. Cameron  b: 01 Mar 1814  d: 03 Feb 1870 in Cameron Cm,Parkton
.......... +Mary W. Uhler  b: 15 Aug 1820  d: 28 Dec 1891 in Mt. Zion
.............. 3 Frank Cameron
.................. +Serena Mackey  b: 12 Apr 1857  d: 15 Jul 1922
...................... 4 F. Horace Cameron  b: 09 Jan 1883  d: 07 Jan 1912 in Mt Zion
.............. 3 John M. Cameron  b: 1842  d: 1892 in Mt. Zion
.................. +Eleanor Peeling  b: 1848  d: 1931 in Mt Zion
...................... 4 Mary Cameron  b: Abt. 1870
.......................... +Billet
...................... 4 James P. Cameron  b: 1872
.............. 3 George Hugh Cameron  b: 03 Sep 1844  d: 17 Mar 1928
.................. +Mary Jane Shunk  b: 14 Mar 1855 in Spring Grove, Pa.  m: 01 May 1878 in Bentley Springs  d: 02 Oct 1937
...................... 4 Harry Gladfelter Cameron  b: 17 Mar 1879
...................... 4 Benjamin Franklin Cameron  b: 31 Mar 1880 in Maryland  d: 11 Oct 1963
.......................... +Mary Mollie Royston  b: 23 Jan 1883 in Maryland  d: 02 Jun 1959 in Mt Zion
...................... 4 Daniel Webster Cameron  b: 22 Sep 1881  d: 08 Aug 1958
...................... 4 Mamie Margaret Cameron  b: 02 Dec 1883  d: 1943
.......................... +Charles V. Masemore  b: 11 Mar 1873  d: 26 Dec 1947
...................... 4 Grover Cleveland Cameron  b: 27 May 1885
...................... 4 Francis Folsom Cameron  b: 02 Nov 1887
.......................... +Unknown Chenoweth  b: Abt. 1886
...................... 4 Robert Lee Cameron  b: 19 Dec 1888
...................... 4 Euhla Cameron  b: 1889  d: 17 Apr 1924
...................... 4 Joseph S. Cameron  b: 25 Jul 1893  d: 08 Oct 1918 in France
...................... 4 Annie Cameron  b: 27 May 1891
.......................... +Chester Royston  b: 14 Jun 1891  m: 04 Apr 1910
.............. 3 Elizabeth A. Cameron  b: 30 Sep 1851
.................. +Jasper Jones  b: 23 Mar 1849  d: 28 Feb 1919
.............. 3 William J. Cameron  b: 1852  d: 1926 in Mt Zion
.................. +Isabelle Stiffler  b: 1862  d: 1926 in Mt Zion
...................... 4 Daniel Walker Cameron  b: 1882  d: 1947
.......................... +Sarah Elizabeth Royston  b: 01 Oct 1881  d: 01 Feb 1974
...................... 4 Robert Norris Cameron  b: 1883  d: 14 Jan 1964 in Parkton
.......................... +Emma R. Ensor  b: Jan 1888  m: Abt. 1910  d: 1975 in Parkton
...................... 4 Mary Cameron  b: 1888  d: 1961 in Mt Zion
.......................... +Charles O. Thorne  b: 1876  d: 1949
*2nd Wife of Hugh Cameron:
.  +Rachel Walker  b: 12 Aug 1790  d: Abt. 1866
...... 2 Jane Cameron  b: Abt. 1821
.......... +Joseph Skinner  m: 02 Jul 1846
.............. 3 Mary E. Skinner
...... 2 Mary Cameron  b: 1822 in Maryland  d: 17 Dec 1904 in White Hall, Maryland
.......... +Thomas Vaughan Hunter  b: 18 Jul 1807 in White Hall, Maryland  d: 05 Mar 1889 in White Hall, Maryland, Vernon Cm.
.............. 3 Frances Lytle Hunter  b: 28 Jan 1855 in White Hall, Maryland  d: 04 Jul 1941 in Monkton, Maryland
.................. +William Pearce  b: 26 Jul 1842  d: 22 Feb 1924 in Monkton, Md.
.............. 3 Ida Elizabeth Hunter  b: 1858  d: 1933
.............. 3 Thomas Cameron Hunter  b: 11 May 1866  d: 23 May 1949
.................. +Clara M. Luckey  b: 1867  d: 1953
.............. 3 Anna L Marion Hunter  b: Abt. 1868
```

```
...... 2 Joseph Cameron  b: Abt. 1824
............ 3 Frank Cameron  b: Abt. 1850
............ 3 Harry Cameron  b: Abt. 1852
............ 3 Gertrude Cameron  b: Abt. 1854
............ 3 Ann Cameron  b: Abt. 1856
............ 3 Alice Cameron  b: Abt. 1858
................ +William G. Little
...... 2 Margaret Cameron  b: 04 Mar 1827  d: 26 Mar 1898
.......... +Edward M. Walker  b: Abt. 1825  m: 26 Mar 1898
...... 2 Cathrine Cameron  b: 21 Jan 1820  d: 24 Apr 1896
...... 2 Adeline Cameron  b: Abt. 1829
...... 2 Lucinda Amelia Cameron  b: Abt. 1830  d: Abt. 1902
```

Descendants of Daniel Walker

```
1 Daniel Walker  b: 1752  d: 18 Dec 1820
.  +Prudence Perdue  b: Abt. 1762 in 7th District  m: 05 Nov 1783  d: May 1841
...... 2 Sarah Walker  b: 31 Aug 1784  d: 24 Mar 1815 in Cameron Cm,Parkton
.......... +[1] Hugh Cameron  b: Abt. 1775 in Scotland  d: 15 Nov 1831
.............. 3 William Cameron  b: Abt. 1801
.............. 3 Eveline Cameron  b: Abt. 1802  d: 26 Sep 1823
.............. 3 Elizabeth Cameron  b: 27 Jul 1806  d: 28 Dec 1866
.............. 3 Daniel W Cameron  b: 10 Sep 1811  d: 28 Jul 1904
.............. 3 James W. Cameron  b: 01 Mar 1814  d: 03 Feb 1870 in Cameron Cm,Parkton
.................. +Mary W. Uhler  b: 15 Aug 1820  d: 28 Dec 1891 in Mt. Zion
...... 2 Catherine Walker  b: 1786
.......... +John Sellman Cox
.............. 3 Daniel Cox
.............. 3 Selman Cox
...... 2 Christopher Walker  b: 06 Mar 1788
.............. 3 Daniel Walker  b: Abt. 1815
...... 2 Rachel Walker  b: 12 Aug 1790  d: Abt. 1866
.......... +[1] Hugh Cameron  b: Abt. 1775 in Scotland  d: 15 Nov 1831
.............. 3 Jane Cameron  b: Abt. 1821
.................. +Joseph Skinner  m: 02 Jul 1846
.............. 3 Mary Cameron  b: 1822 in Maryland  d: 17 Dec 1904 in White Hall, Maryland
.................. +Thomas Vaughan Hunter  b: 18 Jul 1807 in White Hall, Maryland  d: 05 Mar 1889 in White Hall, Maryland, Vernon Cm.
.............. 3 Joseph Cameron  b: Abt. 1824
.............. 3 Margaret Cameron  b: 04 Mar 1827  d: 26 Mar 1898
.................. +Edward M. Walker  b: Abt. 1825  m: 26 Mar 1898
.............. 3 Cathrine Cameron  b: 21 Jan 1820  d: 24 Apr 1896
.............. 3 Adeline Cameron  b: Abt. 1829
.............. 3 Lucinda Amelia Cameron  b: Abt. 1830  d: Abt. 1902
...... 2 Walter Coleman Walker  b: 31 Mar 1792  d: 28 Apr 1874
.......... +Ariel Slade  b: 1802 in Talbott Hall  m: 1826  d: 23 Feb 1875
...... 2 Joseph Walker  b: 16 Jul 1794  d: 07 Jan 1877
...... 2 John Walker  b: 07 Apr 1796
.......... +Catherine Lowe  b: 1799
...... 2 Mary Walker  b: 05 Sep 1799  d: 25 Sep 1880
.......... +William Shauck  b: 03 Jun 1799  d: 12 Jun 1858
.............. 3 Jarrett Shauck
```

CHRISTIAN STABLER

The **Stabler** Family first settled in the Shrewsbury area before buying "Hopewell" near Parkton. The family operated a gristmill, general store and post office along Stablersville Road. The family also started Stabler's Church and cemetery. Christian Stabler married Elizabeth Hershner and moved to Baltimore County where son George married Ellen Bond and married second, Susanna Collett. Jacob Stabler married Deborah Ann Matthews, John Stabler married Elizabeth Miller, Adam Stabler married Hannah LeSourd and Elizabeth Stabler married David Pearce. Margretta Stabler, of Daniel, married Thomas Cole Pearce and the Pearce family of Belfast, descend from this marriage. Henry Stabler operated a store and post office out of his home in Stablersville. Many of the Stabler family moved to Ohio during the 1800's along with many other families from the Seventh District. The Stabler land was first leased and cleared by George Chalk Norris before the Revolutionary War.

EDWARD GRANT TURNBAUGH

Edward Grant Turnbaugh's descendants have owned the George Stabler farm in recent years. Edward Grant Turnbaugh was born to Isaac Turnbaugh and Frances Rebecca Divan Foster. Their farm was located on Benson and Yoeho Road in the fifth District. Edward's children and grandchildren married into many local families. Sarah Louise Turnbaugh married John Walter Streett, Clarence Walter Turnbaugh married Carrie Dailey, Charles Franklin married Leona Herbert, Vincent Earl Turnbaugh married Elsie Rosier, Benjamin Leroy married Anna May Dell, Allen Leroy married Ruth Standiford, Frances May married Ernest Tracey and Ralph Daily Turnbaugh married Jean Carolyn Benson. Steve Turnbaugh, the highly successful Hereford Football coach, is the son of Ralph and Jean. Lois Hale, former teacher and vice-principal at Seventh District School was also a granddaughter of Edward Grant Turnbaugh.

JOHN ROSIER

John Rosier, from York County, patented "Hunter's Delight" on Downs Road in 1786. John's Son Abijah Rosier married first Mary Morris and second Dorcas Williams. John Rosier Jr. married Elizabeth Ann Slade, daughter of John Slade and Mary Perdue. Mary's father, Walter Perdue, purchased a large section of land originally a part of "Mount Joy". This tract was located between 'Talbott Hall", owned by the Slade family, and 'Hunters Delight". John Rosier Junior sold the farm about 1860 and moved to Rollo, Missouri where descendants still live. Thomas R. Downs, whose daughter Eleanor J. Downs married William Joseph Dailey, owned both the old Rosier farm and the Perdue farm. Carrie M. Daily married Clarence Walter Turnbaugh. Doctor Robert Kondner presently owns the original John Rosier farm.

JAMES TRACEY

James Tracey's descendant, **Doctor Richard Wilson Tracey**, a farmer, veterinarian and Board of Education member was a much beloved member of the Bentley Springs community. Dr. Tracy married Mellie Keech and was one of the first recipients of the Outstanding Alumni Awards of the Sparks-Hereford Alumni Association. Salem Tracey was his great-grandfather, and the Traceys were closely related to the Wilson and Rosier Families.

WALTER PERDUE

The **Perdue** family was established on My Lady's Manor before some members moved to the present Seventh District. Walter Perdue owned a large parcel called "Yellow Breeches', located between " Bakers Meadows" and "Rutledge's Labor". This farm was originally part of "Mount Joy" and is located on the present day Downs Road.

Descendants of Christian Stabler

```
1 Christian Stabler  b: 23 Jul 1764 in York Co, Pa  d: 06 Dec 1846 in Stablersville, Balt Co
.  +Elizabeth Herschner  b: 18 Jul 1764 in York Co, Pa  m: 1790  d: 16 Oct 1811 in Stablersville
...... 2 George Stabler  b: 26 Jun 1794 in Stablersville  d: 03 Feb 1864 in Stablersville
..........  +Ellen Bond  b: 17 Jul 1808 in Bond Road  d: Bef. 1830
...... *2nd Wife of George Stabler:
..........  +Susanna Collett  b: 16 May 1794 in 7th District, Baltimore Co.  m: 1831 in Stablersville  d: 10 Jun 1856 in Stablersville
............ 3 Henry Stabler  b: 05 Jun 1823 in Stablersville  d: 13 Oct 1904 in Stablersville
................  +Caroline Matilda Buck  b: 1825 in Maryland  m: 10 May 1849  d: 05 Dec 1894
............ 3 Sarah Elizabeth Stabler  b: 25 Aug 1824 in Stablersville  d: 16 Dec 1897 in Gorsuch Mills
................  +Samuel McClung Billingslea  b: 26 Dec 1814 in Maryland  m: 1841  d: 08 Jun 1892 in Gorsuch Mills
............ 3 Moses C Stabler  b: 27 Dec 1828 in Stablersville  d: 09 Apr 1835
............ 3 Rachel Ann Stabler  b: 21 Jun 1831 in Stablersville, Maryland  d: 14 Feb 1882
................  +Westley Billingslea  b: Abt. 1809
............ *2nd Husband of Rachel Ann Stabler:
................  +Westley Royston Cuddy  b: 21 Jan 1828 in Baltimore Co.  m: 24 Jun 1849  d: 10 Oct 1905
............ 3 Rebecca Ruth Stabler  b: 1836  d: 31 Dec 1836
............ 3 George Washington Stabler  b: 04 Jul 1841  d: 12 May 1911 in Huron, Atchison, Kansas
...... 2 Jacob Stabler  b: 05 Mar 1795  d: 20 Feb 1868
..........  +Deborah Ann Matthews  b: 1789  m: 1812  d: 19 Dec 1854 in Maryland
............ 3 William Stabler  b: Abt. 1814
................  +Elizabeth Unkmown
............ 3 Jarred Stabler  b: Abt. 1816
................  +Margaret
............ 3 Sarah Stabler  b: Abt. 1818
................  +Jarris Hyster
............ 3 Daniel Stabler  b: 1827
................  +Cathrine  b: 1837  d: 1918
...... 2 Henry Stabler  b: 16 Nov 1796 in York County, Pennsylvania  d: 22 Apr 1814
...... 2 John Stabler  b: 1799  d: 1851 in Stark Co., Ohio
..........  +Elizabeth Miller
............ 3 Christian Stabler
............ 3 Mary Ann Stabler
............ 3 Daniel Stabler
............ 3 John Stabler
............ 3 Rebecca Stabler
...... 2 Adam Stabler  b: 31 Mar 1799 in Stablersville  d: 12 Jul 1855 in Butler CO, Ohio
..........  +Hannah Lesourd  b: 07 Jul 1804 in Vernon, MD  m: 27 Apr 1825  d: 31 Dec 1886 in Butler CO, Ohio
............ 3 Mary Ann Stabler  b: 04 Mar 1826 in Butler CO, Ohio  d: 26 Feb 1900
................  +Joshua Lowe  b: 1822  m: 23 Dec 1845 in Ohio  d: 1851
............ 3 Thomas Stabler  b: 10 Mar 1828  d: 24 Jul 1828
............ 3 Christian Stabler  b: 14 Nov 1829 in 7TH District, Baltimore co.  d: 22 May 1907 in Butler CO, Ohio
................  +Hannah Lesourd  b: 01 Oct 1830 in Butler CO., Ohio  m: 05 Jan 1853 in Butler CO.  d: 25 Dec 1895 in Butler CO., Ohio
............ 3 Sarah Elizabeth Stabler  b: 06 Oct 1831 in Butler CO , Ohio  d: 14 May 1897 in Butler CO , Ohio
................  +Elisha Gorsuch  b: 26 Sep 1832 in Butler CO. Ohio  m: 29 Mar 1855 in Butler CO  d: 16 Feb 1874 in Butler Co. Oh.
............ 3 Benjamin L Stabler  b: 11 Aug 1834  d: 11 Apr 1889
................  +Mary Jane Hinds  b: 21 May 1846  d: 08 Nov 1883
............ 3 John W Stabler  b: 05 Jan 1837  d: 24 Jan 1874
................  +Elizabeth J Williamson  b: 20 Feb 1836  d: 18 Jun 1912
............ 3 Daniel F Stabler  b: 13 Nov 1840 in Stablersville  d: 16 Apr 1889 in Ohio
................  +Rachel Ann Lesourd  b: 30 Jan 1842 in Butler Co.  m: 30 Oct 1862
............ 3 Stephen G Stabler  b: 21 Sep 1843  d: 15 Jun 1918
................  +Sarah E Hinds  b: 03 Dec 1843  d: 12 Aug 1872
............ 3 Alfred Griffith Stabler  b: 04 Aug 1848  d: 06 Dec 1914
................  +Susie Williamson  b: 13 Dec 1853  d: 1927
...... 2 Christian Stabler  b: 30 Sep 1800 in York Co  d: 12 Aug 1850 in Stablersville
```

```
.......... +Sarah Gorsuch  b: 1807 in Gorsuch Mills  m: 01 Jun 1825 in Stablerville  d: 21 Nov 1881 in Stablersville
..............  3 Charles Stabler  b: Abt. 1834
..............  3 Elizabeth Stabler  b: Abt. 1841
..............  3 Elisha Stabler  b: 19 Jun 1837  d: 03 Mar 1868
..................  +Henrietta Gillespie
..............  3 Hester Ann Stabler  b: 16 Mar 1840  d: 21 Dec 1922 in Gatchaville, Pa.
..................  +Westley Gillispie  b: Abt. 1840
..............  3 John Stabler  b: 07 Oct 1843  d: 13 Apr 1924
..................  +Narcissa Ann Muller  b: 29 Dec 1846
..............  3 Edmund Stabler  b: 02 Feb 1846 in Stablersville  d: 03 Jun 1905
..................  +Rebecca Ann Cuddy  b: 17 Nov 1852 in Maryland  d: 30 Dec 1934
..............  3 Thomas William Stabler  b: 30 Jun 1848  d: 23 Jun 1862
......  2 Daniel E Stabler  b: 18 Mar 1804 in York Co  d: 18 Nov 1865 in Stablersville
..........  +Ann Elizabeth Stabler  b: 11 Mar 1810 in York Co  m: 14 Sep 1828  d: 15 Jul 1895 in Stablersville
..............  3 Sarah Jane Stabler  b: 02 Mar 1830 in Stablersville  d: 17 Aug 1876 in Ohio
..................  +John Plowman  b: 24 May 1822 in Baltimore , Co., Maryland  m: 1846  d: 22 Sep 1907 in Glide Rock, Nebraska
..............  3 Adam Joseph Stabler  b: 14 Aug 1832 in Stablersville  d: 17 Oct 1888 in Wiseburg
..................  +Rebecca Pearce  b: 20 Feb 1839 in MLM, LOT 87 88  d: 04 May 1901 in Wiseburg
..............  3 Susanna Stabler  b: 1834  d: 10 Apr 1854
..............  3 Elizabeth Ann Stabler  b: 05 Jul 1837 in Stablersville  d: 25 Sep 1915
..............  3 Anna Mary Stabler  b: 07 May 1840 in Stablersville  d: 14 Mar 1856
..............  3 Margretta Stabler  b: 1843 in Stablersville  d: 27 Jan 1888 in Belfast
..................  +Thomas Cole Pearce  b: 23 Dec 1831 in MLM, 87 88  d: 27 Mar 1911 in Belfast, Md.
......  2 Elizabeth Stabler  b: 16 Sep 1808 in York Co  d: 24 Aug 1890 in Gilmer, TWP, Adama CO, IL
..........  +David Pearce  b: 18 Mar 1807 in Lot 7, 7TH Dist., Baltimore Co.  m: 27 Feb 1829 in MD  d: 16 Dec 1878 in Gilmer TWP, Adams
           CO, ILL
..............  3 Mary Ann Pearce  b: 26 Jan 1829 in Balt Co  d: 06 Jul 1907 in Mt Plesant, ILL
..................  +William Conrad Lawless  b: 07 Jan 1829 in Kentucky  m: 01 Feb 1855  d: 15 Feb 1898 in Mt Pleasant, ILL
..............  3 Sarah Ruth Pearce  b: 15 Aug 1832 in Balt Co  d: 23 Dec 1869 in Quincy, ILL
..................  +Edward A. Yeargain  m: 29 May 1851 in Adams CO, ILL
..............  3 Elizabeth Stabler Pearce  b: 02 Sep 1834 in Balt Co  d: 07 Mar 1916 in Adams CO, ILL
..................  +John Quincy Lawless  b: 01 Dec 1826 in Kentucky  m: Feb 1862 in ILL  d: 01 Jan 1916 in ILL
..............  3 Thomas David Pearce  b: 03 Dec 1836 in Butler CO, Ohio  d: in ILL
..................  +Rachel Pearce  b: Abt. 1838
..............  3 John Christian Pearce  b: 25 Aug 1839 in ButlerCO, Ohio  d: 30 Jun 1915 in West Point, ILL
..................  +Sarah E Powell  m: Apr 1868
*2nd Wife of Christian Stabler:
.  +Anna Maria Seitz  b: Abt. 1767 in York County, Pennsylvania  m: 11 Apr 1812 in York Co  d: 19 Mar 1845 in STABLERSVILLE
```

Descendants of Isaac Turnbaugh

```
1 Isaac Turnbaugh  b: 1828  d: 01 Mar 1903
.  +Francis Rebecca Diven Foster  b: 04 Apr 1846  d: Jul 1936
...... 2 Emory P. Turnbaugh
...... 2 Edward Grant Turnbaugh  b: 22 Dec 1865 in Maryland  d: 05 Apr 1937
.......... +Laura Emma Mays  b: 13 Jul 1869 in Maryland  d: 13 Mar 1909
.............. 3 Alice Virginia Turnbaugh  b: 05 Aug 1889 in Maryland  d: 25 Jul 1959
.................. +George M. Hale  b: 05 Aug 1889 in Maryland  d: 06 Feb 1959
.............. 3 Edward Allen Turnbaugh  b: 02 Sep 1890
.................. +Blanche Elinor Wagner  b: 17 Jun 1891
.............. 3 Charles Franklin Turnbaugh  b: 23 Apr 1892  d: 1966
.................. +Anna Louise Talbott  b: 19 Jun 1895
.............. 3 C. Edna Turnbaugh  b: 1893  d: 1894
.............. 3 Clarence Walter Turnbaugh  b: 21 Jan 1895  d: 12 Jul 1977
.................. +Carrie M. Dailey  b: 1898
.............. 3 Harry Ned Turnbaugh  b: May 1896  d: 1970 in Parkton
.............. 3 Leroy Turnbaugh  b: 15 May 1898  d: 25 Mar 1971 in Parkton
.............. 3 Calvin Turnbaugh  b: Jan 1900 in Maryland  d: 1945
.................. +Zeca A. Miller  b: Abt. 1902 in Maryland  d: 1964
.............. 3 George Westley Turnbaugh  b: 1901  d: 1902
.............. 3 Helen Turnbaugh  b: 1902
.............. 3 James Stanley Turnbaugh  b: 1904  d: 1913
.............. 3 Mary Louise Turnbaugh  b: 1906  d: 1979
.............. 3 Cora M. Turnbaugh  b: 1908  d: 1908
...... 2 Jacob C. Turnbaugh  b: 17 Jan 1867
.......... +Elizabeth A. Johnson  b: 1869  d: 1923
.............. 3 Gilbert Turnbaugh  b: 1898  d: 1898
.............. 3 Annie Mable Turnbaugh  b: 12 Feb 1900 in Baltimore Co.  d: 03 Nov 1977
.................. +William Henry Mays  b: 02 Nov 1889 in Baltimore Co.  d: 22 Oct 1948 in Baltimore Co.
.............. 3 Ernest Johnson Turnbaugh  b: 18 Aug 1903
.................. +Irene Morford Mays  b: 05 Nov 1904 in Baltimore Co.
.............. 3 Vesta Elizabeth Turnbaugh  b: 31 Dec 1906
.............. 3 Sara Mildred Turnbaugh  b: 06 Aug 1909
.................. +Christian G. Hoover
...... 2 Annie M. Turnbaugh  b: 1872  d: 18 Jan 1951
.......... +Silas M. Peregoy  b: 10 Dec 1873  d: 1960
...... 2 James Walter Turnbaugh  b: 23 Feb 1874  d: 22 Apr 1940
.......... +Katherine F. Bruehl  b: 02 Apr 1890  d: 1976
...... 2 Isaac Newton Turnbaugh  b: 1876
.......... +Fannie G. Mays  b: 1880  d: 02 Sep 1913
.............. 3 Marie Turnbaugh  b: 17 Sep 1906
.................. +Hobart Mays  b: 06 May 1898
.............. 3 Elmer Turnbaugh  b: 27 Feb 1908
.................. +Bertha Davis
.............. 3 Anna May Turnbaugh  b: 24 May 1910
.................. +Carl Peregoy  b: 13 Feb 1916
...... 2 Margaret Turnbaugh  b: Abt. 1880
.......... +Howard C. Burton  b: 1878  d: 1926
.............. 3 Eugene Burton
```

Descendants of John Rosier

1 John Rosier b: Abt. 1760 d: Abt. 1799
. +Elizabeth b: Abt. 1760
...... 2 Moses Rosier
...... 2 William Rosier b: 1795
.... +Rachel Unknown b: Abt. 1798
...... 2 George Rosier b: Abt. 1782
...... 2 Elizabeth Rosier b: Abt. 1783
...... 2 Mary Rosier b: Abt. 1784
...... 2 Susanna Rosier b: Abt. 1785
...... 2 John Rosier b: 1785 in Pa 1850 census d: 16 Sep 1867 in Parkton, Md.
.... +Mary Ann Unknown b: 1780 m: Abt. 1810 d: 05 Aug 1848 in Parkton, MD.
.... 3 Abijah Rosier b: 1805 in Baltimore County, Maryland d: 1863 in Parkton, MD.
.... +Dorothy Dorcas Williams b: 1813 m: Abt. 1828 d: 30 Jul 1858 in Parkton, Maryland
.... 4 Margaret Rosier b: Abt. 1829 d: Bef. 1870 in Baltimore , Co. Md., New Market
.... 4 Eliza Jane Rosier b: Abt. 1830
.... +Unknown Stump
.... 4 Dennis Rosier b: 10 Jul 1835 in Parkton, MD. d: 23 Jan 1883 in Parkton, MD.
.... +Cathrine Jane Through b: 18 Aug 1836 in York, Pennsylvania m: Abt. 1858 d: 30 Jul 1907
.... 4 Hannah Jane Rosier b: 1838
.... 4 Lewis Rosier b: Oct 1840 in Parkton, MD. d: 1906 in Parkton, MD.
.... +Amanda Unknown b: 1841 d: 1895
.... *2nd Wife of Lewis Rosier:
.... +Eliza Unknown b: Jan 1850
.... 4 John Rosier b: 1841
.... 4 George Washington Rosier b: 03 Apr 1841 in Parkton, MD. d: 26 May 1929 in Seneca Co., Ohio
.... +Amelia Foght b: 1844 m: 14 Aug 1864 in Seneca Co., Ohio d: 13 Jul 1866
.... *2nd Wife of George Washington Rosier:
.... +Caroline Yambert b: 26 Apr 1840 m: 27 Nov 1867 d: 12 Jul 1920
.... 4 Mary Ann Rosier b: 1843
.... +Unknown Hedrick b: Abt. 1840
.... 4 William Thomas Rosier b: 1845
.... +Sarah E. Unknown b: 1852
.... 4 Elizabeth Rosier b: 1850
.... 4 Abijah Rosier b: 25 Sep 1852 in Parkton, Md. d: 28 Mar 1928 in Parkton, MD.
.... +Susanna Shaver b: 10 Aug 1843 in Parkton, Md. d: 29 Mar 1928
.... *2nd Wife of Abijah Rosier:
.... +Eliza Tracey b: 03 May 1846 d: 12 Dec 1904 in Parkton, MD.
.... 4 Sarah Cathrine Rosier b: Oct 1854 d: 23 Jun 1913 in Baltimore County, Maryland
.... +Benjamin Franklin Almony b: 10 May 1851 m: 22 Jun 1876 in Baltimore , Md. d: 20 Sep 1894
.... 4 Julia Ann Rosier b: 20 Oct 1855 in Parkton, MD. d: 16 Aug 1918 in Parkton, MD.
.... +Henry Wickersham Simpson b: 1856 in Maryland m: 24 Mar 1878 d: 1927 in Maryland Line
.... 4 Dorcas Ann Rosier b: 19 Nov 1857 in Parkton, MD. d: 06 Apr 1921
.... +Unknown Almony b: Abt. 1855
.... *2nd Wife of Abijah Rosier:
.... +Mary Morris m: Bef. 1828
.... *3rd Wife of Abijah Rosier:
.... +Margaret Paules m: Abt. 1860
.... 4 Nicholas Westley Rosier b: 22 Mar 1861 in Parkton, Md. d: 25 Oct 1928 in York, Pa.
.... +Louise Hoover b: Abt. 1862 m: Abt. 1890
.... 4 James MacCord Rosier b: 09 Sep 1862 d: 07 Jan 1927 in Freeland, Bur Maryland Line
.... +[1] Laura V. Jones b: Dec 1865 m: Abt. 1885 d: 10 Jan 1927 in Baltimore City, Maryland
.... 4 Jacob Elmer Rosier b: 27 May 1869 in Parkton, Md. d: 12 Mar 1928 in Maryland Line
.... +Luly M. Jones b: 23 Dec 1880 m: 1896 d: 27 Jan 1941
.... 3 John W. Rosier b: 24 May 1816 in Maryland d: 11 Nov 1899 in Meadville, Mo. Linn Co.

```
................ +Elizabeth Ann Slade  b: 15 Mar 1825 in Talbott's Hall, Baltimore Co., Md. lot3  m: 27 Aug 1848  d: 09 Sep 1899 in
                 Meadville, Mo. Linn Co.
................... 4 Joshua Rosier  b: 1849
................... 4 Pleasant Hunter Rosier  b: 1849
................... 4 Hannah Rosier  b: Abt. 1851
................... 4 Aquilla W. Rosier  b: 1851
................... 4 Edward Rosier  b: 1853
................... 4 Elizabeth Ann Rosier  b: 1855
................... 4 Dennis Rosier  b: 1857
................... 4 Mary Jane Rosier  b: May 1858  d: 1945
....................... +Joshua R. Standiford  b: Jan 1860 in Baltimore Co.  d: 1938 in Maryland Line
................... 4 Cathrine Rosier  b: Abt. 1860
................... 4 Laura L. Rosier  b: Abt. 1864
............ 3 Westley Rosier  b: 1826 in Parkton, Md.  d: in Parkton, Md.
................ +Harriet  b: 1826  m: Abt. 1852  d: in Parkton, Md.
................... 4 Cathrine Kate Rosier  b: 1850
................... 4 Daniel Rosier  b: 1852
................... 4 Agnes Rosier  b: 1854
................... 4 John Rosier  b: Nov 1856  d: 21 Feb 1897
....................... +Annie Unknown  b: Apr 1857
................... 4 Wiliam Rosier  b: 1859
............ *2nd Wife of Westley Rosier:
................ +Mary A. Rosier  b: 1836  m: Abt. 1866
................... 4 George Albert Rosier  b: 06 Nov 1868 in White Hall, Maryland  d: 07 May 1953 in White Hall, Md.
....................... +Harriet Lavinia Dailey  b: 23 Dec 1872 in White Hall, Maryland  d: 30 Jul 1947 in White Hall, M
................... 4 Nancy J. Rosier  b: 03 Jun 1870  d: 14 Apr 1924
....................... +Thomas Mitchell Bull  b: 15 Sep 1866  d: 14 Jan 1943
................... 4 May C. Rosier  b: 1873
................... 4 Alice E. Rosier  b: 1876
....................... +George Frank Ensor  b: Abt. 1873
............ 3 Hosea Rosier  b: 18 Mar 1827 in Maryland  d: 12 Mar 1899 in Parkton, MD.
................ +Hannah Hunt  b: 11 Feb 1822  d: 12 Dec 1906 in Parkton, MD.
................... 4 William S. Rosier  b: 16 Mar 1853 in Parkton, MD.  d: 22 Jun 1917 in Maryland Line
....................... +Annie Maria Almony  b: 05 Aug 1857  d: 04 Oct 1948
................... 4 James MacCord Rosier  b: 15 Jan 1855  d: 26 Jun 1860 in Maryland Line
....................... +[1] Laura V. Jones  b: Dec 1865  d: 10 Jan 1927 in Baltimore City, Maryland
................... 4 Benson D. Rosier  b: 1860  d: 1934 in Parkton, MD.
....................... +Margaret  b: 02 Sep 1860  d: 05 Dec 1883
................... *2nd Wife of Benson D. Rosier:
....................... +Anna Elizabeth Echtol  b: 07 Oct 1865  d: 18 Jan 1949 in Maryland Line
............ 3 Hannah Jane Rosier  b: 1838  d: 20 Oct 1827
................ +John Slade  b: Abt. 1820
```

Descendants of James H. Tracey

1 James H. Tracey b: Abt. 1765 in Baltimore County, Maryland d: Bef. 1840
. +Sarah Cross b: 1785 in Baltimore County, Maryland d: 1857
...... 2 Elizabeth Betsy Tracey b: 1801 in Maryland
.... +Thomas Jr. Williams b: 1800 in Maryland m: 21 Aug 1824
.... 3 Susan Williams b: 1832 in Baltimore Co.
.... 3 James Williams b: 1835 in Baltimore Co.
.... 3 Rachel Williams b: 1837 in Baltimore Co.
.... 3 Thomas Williams b: 1838 in Baltimore Co.
.... 3 Nelson Williams b: 1840 in Baltimore Co.
.... 3 Jacob Williams b: 1842 in Baltimore Co.
.... 3 Richard Williams b: 1847 in Baltimore Co.
.... 3 Victor Williams b: 1849 in Baltimore Co.
.... 3 Gibson Williams b: 1838 in Baltimore Co.
.... +Elizabeth Williams b: Abt. 1844
.... 4 Cathrine Williams b: Abt. 1864
.... 4 Laura Williams b: Abt. 1867
.... 4 Frank Williams b: Abt. 1870
...... 2 Salem Tracey b: 1805 in Maryland d: Aft. 1880 in Parkton, Md.
.... +Sarah Williams b: 06 Jun 1804 in Baltimore County, Maryland m: 01 Nov 1832 in York, Pa. d: 14 Jun 1865 in Parkton
.... 3 Susanna Tracey b: 1834
.... 3 Jesse Tracey b: 1834 in Parkton, Md. d: in Parkton, Md.
.... +Sarah L. Unknown b: 1839 d: in Parkton, Md.
.... 4 Emmanuel E. Tracey b: 1870 in Parkton, Md.
.... 4 Pleasant S. Tracey b: 1871 in Parkton, Md.
.... 4 Belinda Tracey b: 1873 in Parkton, Md.
.... 4 Walter C. Tracey b: Apr 1874 in Parkton, Md.
.... +Lucinda R. Rosier b: Sep 1879 in Parkton, Md.
.... 4 John F. Tracey b: 1876 in Parkton, Md.
.... 3 Elias Tracey b: 1837 in Parkton, Md.
.... +Amanda Rosier b: 1842 m: Abt. 1865
.... 4 Sarah Tracey b: 1869
.... 4 Agnes Tracey b: 1872
.... 4 Harry E Tracey b: 1873
.... 4 Alfred Tracey b: 1875
.... 4 Eli Tracey b: 1877 in Parkton, Md. d: Sep 1942
.... +Viola Mary b: 1882 in Pennsylvania
.... 4 Geneva Tracey b: Abt. 1880
.... 4 Herbert Clarence Tracey b: 29 Dec 1883 in Maryland d: 16 Sep 1943 in Parkton, Md.
.... +Alyce Irene Wilson b: 05 Aug 1885 in Maryland m: Jan 1905 d: 11 Dec 1970
.... 4 Samuel Eaton Tracey b: Abt. 1884
.... 4 Crayton Salem Tracey b: 16 Oct 1885 d: 29 Sep 1942
.... +Elsie Norris Wilson b: 04 Jun 1889 in Parkton, Maryland d: 28 Oct 1959
.... 4 John Tracey b: Abt. 1886
.... 3 Amanda Tracey b: 1849
...... 2 Annie Tracey b: 13 Apr 1810
.... +John Leaf b: 02 Feb 1804
...... 2 Amos Tracey b: 12 Jan 1811 in Parkton, Md. d: 16 Oct 1866 in Muskingum, Ohio
.... +Cassander Hampshire b: Abt. 1817 m: 01 Nov 1836 in Baltimore County d: Aft. 1880
.... 3 Mary Elizabeth Tracey b: 10 Oct 1837
.... 3 William Tracey b: 18 Oct 1839
.... 3 John David Tracey b: 08 Feb 1842
.... 3 James Franklin Tracey b: 19 Oct 1844
.... 3 George Washington Tracey b: 26 Jun 1847
.... +Mary E. Curfman m: 06 Apr 1880
.... 3 Matha Ellen Tracey b: 30 Sep 1849

```
............ 3 Jasper Newton Tracey  b: 19 Aug 1854
............ 3 Justis Wilson Tracey  b: 19 Aug 1854
............ 3 Benjamin Preston Tracey  b: 13 Dec 1856
............ 3 William Arthur Tracey  b: 19 Oct 1859
............ 3 Sarah Jane Tracey  b: 14 Nov 1863
............ 3 Edward Amos Tracey  b: 28 Dec 1863
......   2 John Tracey  b: 1811 in Parkton, Md.  d: Bef. 1880
..........   +Cathrine Nace  b: 06 Feb 1818 in Baltimore County, Maryland  m: Jan 1838  d: 24 Dec 1912
............ 3 George Tracey  b: 1841
............ 3 Susan Tracey  b: Abt. 1844
............ 3 Thomas Edward Tracey  b: Aug 1847 in Parkton, Md.
................   +Laura Tracey  b: Dec 1857
.................... 4 Arthur Tracey  b: Jul 1877
.................... 4 Walter H. Tracey  b: Jan 1879
.................... 4 Salem N. Tracey  b: Nov 1885
.................... 4 Nora D. Tracey  b: Jun 1887
.................... 4 Goldie C. Tracey  b: Apr 1889
.................... 4 Margaret E. Tracey  b: Mar 1893
.................... 4 Mable V. Tracey  b: Jun 1895
.................... 4 John Taylor Tracey  b: 16 Aug 1901
............ 3 Mary Elizabeth Tracey  b: 1855
............ 3 Oliver H. Tracey  b: 1858
......   2 James Tracey  b: Abt. 1815 in Parkton, Md.
..........   +Mary Polly Nace  b: 30 Dec 1813  d: 11 Sep 1870 in Baltimore County, Maryland
............ 3 John Tracey  b: Abt. 1840
............ 3 Peter Tracey  b: Abt. 1841
............ 3 Jacob Tracey  b: 28 Jan 1843
............ 3 Michael Tracey  b: Abt. 1845
............ 3 James Westley Tracey  b: 1847
............ 3 Elizabeth Tracey  b: Abt. 1850
............ 3 Nelson Tracey  b: Abt. 1854
............ 3 Serena Tracey  b: 1857
......   *2nd Wife of James Tracey:
..........   +Mary J. Unknown  b: Abt. 1835
......   2 Gilson Tracey  b: 31 Aug 1816 in Parkton, Md.  d: 16 Feb 1904
..........   +Jane Wilson  b: Abt. 1826  m: 15 Feb 1844  d: Aft. 16 Feb 1804
......   2 Curtis Tracey  b: Abt. 1819 in Parkton, Md.
..........   +Anna Mary Stump  b: 23 Dec 1819 in Baltimore County, Maryland
............ 3 Sarah Tracey  b: Abt. 1840
............ 3 Daniel Tracey  b: Abt. 1841
............ 3 John Tracey  b: Abt. 1844
............ 3 Ellen Tracey  b: Abt. 1845
............ 3 James Tracey  b: Abt. 1848
............ 3 Henry Tracey  b: Abt. 1850
............ 3 Cathrine Tracey  b: Abt. 1850
............ 3 Anna Mary Tracey  b: Abt. 1855
............ 3 Samuel S. Tracey  b: 21 Sep 1858
......   2 Ellen Tracey  b: Abt. 1830 in Baltimore County, Maryland
..........   +Henry Bogue
```

Descendants of Luke Ensor

```
1 Luke Ensor  b: 1800  d: 1838 in Texas War
.  +Rachel Ensor  b: Abt. 1802  m: 1824
...... 2 William Ensor  b: 31 Aug 1826 in Baltimore  d: 25 Sep 1912 in 7TH District
..........  +Julia Ann Shaul  b: 1824 in 5th Dist, Baltimore Co., Maryland  m: Oct 1850
.............. 3 Noah F Ensor  b: Jun 1851  d: 09 Apr 1932 in 7th dist
..................  +Annie M. Unknown  b: Dec 1849
...................... 4 Clarence D. Ensor  b: Jul 1873 in Maryland
..........................  +Queen Mary Sutton  b: 30 Jan 1875 in Monkton, MD.  d: 1971 in West Liberty
...................... 4 William G. Ensor  b: Oct 1874
..........................  +Minnie E. Hollingshead  b: Nov 1880
...................... 4 Harry F. Ensor  b: Sep 1879 in Maryland  d: 1953 in West Liberty
..........................  +Sallie E. Nelson  b: 02 Mar 1884  d: 03 Apr 1903 in West Liberty
...................... 4 Luke E. Ensor  b: Nov 1882 in Maryland  d: 1956 in Parkton
..........................  +Mary Maudice Thomas  b: Nov 1889 in Maryland
...................... 4 Roy C. Ensor  b: Feb 1884
..........................  +Sara E. Unknown  b: 1889
...................... 4 Emma R. Ensor  b: Jan 1888  d: 1975 in Parkton
..........................  +Robert Norris Cameron  b: 1883  m: Abt. 1910  d: 14 Jan 1964 in Parkton
...................... 4 Isabell Ensor  b: Abt. 1889
..........................  +Unknown Pearce  b: Abt. 1888
...................... 4 Hazel Ensor  b: Abt. 1890
.............. 3 Luke E Ensor  b: Mar 1853 in Parkton, Maryland
..................  +Maggie P. Unknown  b: Oct 1892
.............. 3 Peter William Ensor  b: 25 Sep 1854 in Maryland  d: 24 Jul 1943 in Parkton, Maryland
..................  +Elizabeth E. Miller  b: 09 Mar 1855 in Pennsylvania  d: 07 Dec 1948
...................... 4 Julia Ann Ensor  b: 20 Jul 1892 in Parkton  d: 21 May 1970
..........................  +J. Walter Shaul
...................... 4 Ariel Menta Ensor  b: Apr 1894  d: in York
..........................  +Unknown Bailey
.............. 3 Anna R Ensor  b: 1858
.............. 3 Harry Ensor  b: 1860
```

Descendants of Walter Perdue

1 Walter Perdue b: 1766 d: 1826
 . +Elizabeth Bosley b: Abt. 1770 in MLM m: 12 Jun 1790 in St. James d: in MLM lot 92
 ...... 2 Labon Perdue b: 12 Jul 1791 in MLM lot 90, 91, 92 d: in MLM lot 58
 .... +Rachel Hunter b: 1799 in White Hall, Maryland d: in MLM lot 58
 .... 3 Laban Perdue b: 1828
 .... 3 John Perdue b: Abt. 1830
 ...... 2 Mary Perdue b: 02 Mar 1795 in Balt Co d: in Balt Co
 .... +John Slade b: Abt. 1790 in Talbott Hall m: Abt. 1820 d: 1853
 .... 3 [2] Abraham Slade b: 1821 in White Hall, Maryland d: in White Hall, Maryland
 .... +[1] Mary Slade Perdue b: 21 Oct 1819 in Parkton, Maryland m: 1838 d: 06 May 1839
 .... 3 Elizabeth Ann Slade b: 15 Mar 1825 in Talbott's Hall, Baltimore Co., Md. lot3 d: 09 Sep 1899 in Meadville, Mo. Linn Co.
 .... +John W. Rosier b: 24 May 1816 in Maryland m: 27 Aug 1848 d: 11 Nov 1899 in Meadville, Mo. Linn Co.
 .... 3 John Slade b: 15 Oct 1826
 .... +Elizabeth b: 1827
 .... 3 Benjamin A Slade b: 1828 in 7th District Baltimore Co, MD d: 1870 in Ohio
 .... +Cathrine Boyle
 .... 3 Mary Slade b: 1829 in Monkton d: 1870 in Ohio
 .... +Josuha Francis Pearce b: 1826 in Mt. Joy, West Liberty Um m: 1848 d: 1870 in Ohio
 ...... 2 William Perdue b: 19 Mar 1797 in MLM, 90 91 92 d: 16 Jul 1836 in West Liberty
 .... +Ann Slade b: 11 Nov 1797 in Talbott Hall d: 24 Mar 1877 in Parkton, Maryland
 .... 3 [1] Mary Slade Perdue b: 21 Oct 1819 in Parkton, Maryland d: 06 May 1839
 .... +[2] Abraham Slade b: 1821 in White Hall, Maryland m: 1838 in White Hall, Maryland
 .... 3 Elizabeth Perdue b: 1824 d: 1899
 .... +John Ayres b: 31 Dec 1824 in Maryland d: 1865
 .... 3 Hannah Perdue b: 21 Dec 1827 d: 07 Jun 1918
 .... +John Robert Jackson b: 25 Dec 1812 m: 13 Jun 1844 d: 27 Jul 1900
 ...... 2 Rachel Perdue b: Abt. 1798 d: in Baltimore County, Maryland
 .... +William Hunter b: 22 May 1797 in White Hall, Maryland d: 1850 in Baltimore County, Maryland
 .... 3 Curtis Hunter d: 1823
 .... 3 [4] Josephine Hunter b: in White Hall, Maryland d: in MLM lot 90
 .... +[3] William Thomas Perdue b: 21 Apr 1834 d: 1897 in MLM lot 90
 ...... 2 Walter Perdue b: 18 Jun 1801 in St James d: 17 Mar 1850
 ...... 2 John Perdue b: 29 Jun 1804 d: 1874 in St. James
 .... +Sarah Hutchins b: 09 Nov 1809 in Harford Co. m: 21 Feb 1832 in St James d: 30 Apr 1878 in Balt,Co.
 .... 3 Mary Elizabeth Perdue b: 29 Dec 1832 d: 1886
 .... +Charles Quinlan
 .... 3 [3] William Thomas Perdue b: 21 Apr 1834 d: 1897 in MLM lot 90
 .... +[4] Josephine Hunter b: in White Hall, Maryland d: in MLM lot 90
 .... 3 Walter Perdue b: 26 Jun 1836 in MLM lot 92 d: 27 Nov 1899 in MLM lot 92
 .... +Lovisah Hope Nelson b: 1852 m: 1878 d: 1920
 .... 3 John Perdue b: 1838 in MLM d: 1896
 .... +Anna Holmes b: 1844 in Baltimore Co. m: 18 May 1876 d: 1911
 .... 3 Carvel Richard Perdue b: 02 Feb 1844 in Baltimore County, Maryland d: 1894
 .... +Mary Emma Taylor Richardson b: 1856 d: 1879
 .... 3 Eleanor Ellen Sparks Perdue b: 1846 in MLM lot 92 d: 08 Nov 1909 in Loafer's Lodge, MLM
 .... +Richard McGaw Howard b: 1840 m: 30 Oct 1866 in St. James d: 1903 in Loafer's Lodge, MLM
 ...... 2 Elizabeth Perdue b: 19 Feb 1807 in MLM lot 90, 91, 92 d: 1884 in Linden MLM
 .... +William Given Hutchins b: 18 Mar 1800 m: Abt. 1834 d: 1872
 .... 3 Emily Elizabeth Hutchins b: 1835 d: 1917
 .... +Dr J. S. Reed m: 1857
 .... *2nd Husband of Emily Elizabeth Hutchins:
 .... +Young Owen Wilson m: Abt. 1860
 .... 3 William Hutchins b: 23 Jul 1837 in MLM d: 17 Jan 1908 in LINDON
 .... +Martha Jane Hutchins b: 1848 m: 1885 d: 1923
 .... 3 Margaret Ellen Hutchins b: 1840 in MLM d: 1917

.... +Benjamin Denmead b: Abt. 1840
.... 3 William Hutchins b: 1837
.... 2 Thomas Perdue b: 29 Mar 1809 d: 31 Aug 1877

Robert Gillis patented "Gillis' Garden in 1789. His daughter, Levinia Sharp Gillis, married **Doctor James Moore** who was the ancestor of many persons on White Hall Road. His son, John Moore, married Elizabeth Ann Burns and daughter Elizabeth married William H. Nelson. William's daughter Hannah Ann married David Newton Thomas. David Thomas's son William Newton married Kate King, Nora May married Charles Preston and Raymond Findley Thomas married Annie May Wright. John Thomas Moore married Mary Jane Burns and his grandson David Greene, a retired University of Maryland Cooperative Extension Agent, operates Greene's Sheep farm on White Hall Road with his wife Nancy. David is also a descendant of the John Burns family. Another descendant, Lillian Evelyn Moore married White Hall Postmaster Edward Loring Best and did extensive research on the White Hall area and family genealogy.

Adam Burns first purchased land in the White Hall area in 1787. Adam married Mary Bull and granddaughter Amanda Jane married Squire Henry Wiers. Henry Polk Burns married Sarah Elizabeth Nelson. Sarah Nelson's Grandfather John Nelson lived on the Manor, but son Richard Nelson married Delilah Wiers and William H. Nelson married Elizabeth Moore. Sons Jarrett and John Nelson both married daughters of Jonathon Plowman. Jonathon Plowman's mother and Mount Joy Owner Edward Johnson's wife were sisters. Jonathon Plowman became the owner of much of Mount Joy in the White Hall area. Most of the farms between Graystone Road and White Hall Road below Vernon road belonged to the Burns, Nelson, Moore, and Weirs families.

Isaac Bull who married Elizabeth Ann Slade is closely tied to most White Hall families. Mary Bull married Adam Burns, Josiah Slade Bull married Rebecca Norris, William Bull married Delilah Sampson and Josiah Slade Bull's daughter Belinda Jane married Isaac Garrett. The Bull family owned farms between White Hall and Wiseburg.

The Nelson family descends from **William Nelson**, born about 1720, and Hannah Johnson. They are heavily tied to the Hope, Wiley and Hutchins families. Grandson John Nelson and wife Hannah Hutchins were the parents with many ties to White Hall.
Richard Hutchins Nelson married Delilah Wiers; William H. Nelson married Elizabeth Moore, Elizabeth Nelson married Shadrack Rutledge Gilbert, Jarrett Nelson married Susanna Plowman, Amanda Nelson married John Hutchins, Mary Ann Nelson married Abraham Gilbert and John Hutchins Nelson married Mary Ann Plowman. The Plowman sisters were descendant from the owner of the original "Mount Joy" tract. William Thomas "Billy" Nelson was a famous Maryland softball pitcher and dairy farmer on White Hall Road

William Pearce was a brother of Thomas Pearce. His descendants married into most of the families around the White Hall- Vernon area. His son David, married Elizabeth Stabler and son Josiah married Elizabeth Wright of the Shawsville area. From this marriage, Margaret Ruth married James Thomas Curry, Joseph Wright Pearce married Mary Frances Lytle, Thomas Emory married Kathrine Maria Stabler and Silas Wright Pearce married Minnie Ida Wilson. Cassandra Pearce married Edward Wiley Norris and Joshua Francis Pearce married Mary Slade. Mary Ann Pearce's daughter Margaret married Arthur Shane.

White Hall Milk Shippers

First row
John Nick Norris, William Norris, Nelson Richardson, Egbert Norris, Richard Wiley, Ben Garrett, Charlie Wagner, --, Robert Bacon, Howard Burns, John Thomas Ayres, --, Tom Curry Station Agent, Second row- Tom Lytle, John T. Moore, John T. Amos, Harry Rosier Third Row(--), Henry Fowble, --, Harry Almony, Nick Lytle, Thomas Parrish, Leonard Slade, Oscar Almony, Lum Slade, --,-- Fourth row-Kroh, Ray Slade, March McComas, Henry Burns, Tom Hunter, John Burns,--, Tommy Elliott, Lilburn Nelson

WHITE HALL BASEBALL TEAM

Descendants of Isaac Bull

1 Isaac Bull b: 03 Feb 1726/27 d: 1783
. +Hannah Robertson b: 1728 in Maryland m: 23 Jan 1748/49 in St. George
...... 2 Rachael Bull b: 05 Mar 1755
*2nd Wife of Isaac Bull:
. +Elizabeth Ann Slade b: 1738 in LOT 38 m: 26 May 1761 in St. George, p269 d: Bef. 1802 in Harford Co
...... 2 Isaac Bull b: 25 May 1766
...... 2 Mary Bull b: 01 Jan 1769
.... +Adam Burns b: 10 Dec 1763 m: 15 Apr 1795 d: 14 Jun 1854 in White Hall, Maryland
.... 3 Betsy Ann Burns b: 06 Mar 1796 d: 21 Jun 1859
.... 3 John Burns b: 22 Oct 1797 in Baltimore County, Maryland d: 22 Dec 1878 in White Hall, Maryland
.... +Marab Roberts b: 27 Mar 1807 in Harford Co. d: 30 Nov 1890 in White Hall, Maryland
.... 3 William Bull Burns b: 27 Dec 1800 in White Hall, Maryland d: 20 Dec 1879 in Weisburg
.... +Hannah Bull b: Mar 1808 in Monkton, Maryland d: in White Hall, Maryland
.... 3 Balinda Bull Burns b: 22 Aug 1807
.... +Benjamin Burns b: 21 Dec 1806
.... *2nd Husband of Balinda Bull Burns:
.... +James Thomas Collett b: Abt. 1805 m: 12 Dec 1865
...... 2 Josias Slade Bull b: 1771
.... +Rebecca Norris b: Abt. 1770 m: 27 Oct 1791 in St James
.... 3 Ann Bull b: 25 Jul 1793
.... 3 Lucy Smith Bull b: 07 Dec 1795
.... 3 Betsey A Bull b: 04 Dec 1796
.... 3 Rebecca Bull b: 20 Mar 1798
.... 3 Belinda Jane Bull b: 05 Aug 1800
.... +John Cottrell Rutledge b: 1738 in Maryland m: 04 Aug 1821 d: 05 May 1828 in Baltimore County
.... *2nd Husband of Belinda Jane Bull:
.... +Isaac Garrett b: 1802 m: 05 Aug 1839
.... 3 Josias Slade Bull b: 19 Jan 1801
.... 3 John Bull b: 30 Dec 1802
.... 3 Elisha Bull b: 30 Oct 1804
.... 3 Edward Parish Bull b: 11 Jun 1807
.... 3 Susanna Bull b: 13 Feb 1809
...... 2 William Bull b: Abt. 1775 d: 12 Nov 1822
.... +Deliliah Sampson b: Abt. 1780 m: 08 Jun 1799 d: Abt. 1830
...... *2nd Wife of William Bull:
.... +Delilah Cole b: 1775 m: Abt. 1800
...... 2 Belender Bull b: Abt. 1865
.... +Unknown Sampson b: Abt. 1864

Descendants of Adam Burns

1 Adam Burns b: 10 Dec 1763 d: 14 Jun 1854 in White Hall, Maryland
. +Mary Bull b: 01 Jan 1769 m: 15 Apr 1795
...... 2 Betsy Ann Burns b: 06 Mar 1796 d: 21 Jun 1859
...... 2 John Burns b: 22 Oct 1797 in Baltimore County, Maryland d: 22 Dec 1878 in White Hall, Maryland
.... +Marab Roberts b: 27 Mar 1807 in Harford Co. d: 30 Nov 1890 in White Hall, Maryland
.... 3 William Burns b: 18 Jun 1829 d: 1864 in Civil War
.... 3 Mary Jane Burns b: 01 Jun 1831 d: 30 Aug 1888 in White Hall, Maryland
.... +James Thomas Moore b: 03 Oct 1829 m: 17 Jan 1860 d: 21 Dec 1901 in White Hall, Maryland
.... 3 James Thomas Burns b: 05 Sep 1833
.... +Georgia Honor Ensor b: 1841
.... 3 John Wesley Burns b: 20 Nov 1834 in White Hall, Maryland d: 21 Nov 1913
.... +Elizabeth A. Cooper b: 1841 m: Abt. 1862 d: 02 Feb 1893 in Weisburg
.... 3 Amanda Jane Burns b: 10 Dec 1836 d: 06 Jul 1931 in White Hall, Maryland
.... +Squire Henry Wiers b: 29 Feb 1824 m: Abt. 1850 d: 16 Feb 1896 in White Hall, Maryland
.... 3 Adam Burns b: 29 Jan 1839 d: 23 Feb 1864 in Civil War Libby Prison
.... 3 Belinda Ann Burns b: 17 Feb 1841
.... 3 Benjamin France Burns b: 15 Jul 1843
.... +Emma
.... 3 Henry Polk Burns b: 26 Jan 1846 in White Hall, Maryland d: 21 Feb 1914 in White Hall
.... +Sarah Elizabeth Nelson b: 09 Mar 1849 in White Hall, Maryland m: Abt. 1874 d: 16 Oct 1947 in White Hall
...... 2 William Bull Burns b: 27 Dec 1800 in White Hall, Maryland d: 20 Dec 1879 in Weisburg
.... +Hannah Bull b: Mar 1808 in Monkton, Maryland d: in White Hall, Maryland
.... 3 William Bull Burns b: 17 Aug 1826
.... 3 John Moore Burns b: 16 Jan 1827
.... 3 Mary Elizabeth Ann Burns b: 10 Oct 1829
.... 3 Rachel Belinda Burns b: 26 Dec 1831
.... 3 James Jarrett Burns b: 19 Apr 1835
.... 3 Richard Nicholas Burns b: 17 Feb 1838 in White Hall, Maryland d: 10 Oct 1891 in White Hall, Maryland
.... +Rachel Ann Burns b: 13 Jun 1832 in Towson, Maryland m: 25 Oct 1864 in Towson d: 06 Feb 1908 in White Hall, Maryland
...... 2 Balinda Bull Burns b: 22 Aug 1807
.... +Benjamin Burns b: 21 Dec 1806
.... 3 Rachel Ann Burns b: 1842
.... 3 Betsy Morre Burns b: 1844
.... 3 John Thomas Burns b: 1847 d: 1920
.... +M. Frances b: 03 Dec 1852 d: 01 Jun 1886
.... 3 Mary Belinda Burns b: 1849
...... *2nd Husband of Balinda Bull Burns:
.... +James Thomas Collett b: Abt. 1805 m: 12 Dec 1865

Descendants of Robert Gillis

1 Robert Gillis b: Abt. 1745
. +Elizabeth Sharp b: Abt. 1745 m: Abt. 1765
...... 2 Thomas Gillis b: 12 Jan 1766
...... 2 John Gillis b: 08 Oct 1767
...... 2 Sarah Gillis b: 07 Feb 1772
.... +William Mossman b: Abt. 1800
...... 2 William Gillis b: 25 Mar 1774
...... 2 Elizabeth Gillis b: 03 May 1776 d: 04 Nov 1854
.... +Capt Samuel Davidson b: 23 Jan 1765 in South Carolina m: 27 Nov 1800 d: 25 Dec 1854 in South Carolina
.... 3 Polly Davidson b: 29 Aug 1802
.... +Joseph Jameson b: 06 Feb 1801 in Blairsville, S. C. m: 07 Aug 1823 d: 01 Jun 1899 in South Carolina
.... 3 [2] Col Robert G. Davidson b: 28 Jul 1805 d: 31 Dec 1881
.... +Mary Neely b: Abt. 1806 m: Abt. 1827
.... *2nd Wife of [2] Col Robert G. Davidson:
.... +[1] Elizabeth Caroline Moore b: 10 Mar 1826 m: 16 Dec 1859 d: 02 Jan 1884
.... 4 [3] Levinah Rebecca Davidson b: 06 Nov 1860
.... 4 [4] Son Davidson b: 1861
.... 4 [5] Daughter Davidson b: 04 Sep 1864
.... 4 [6] Sarah Elizabeth Davidson b: 18 Nov 1865 d: 23 May 1928 in White Hall, Maryland
.... +[7] James Franklin Grant b: 24 Sep 1860 m: 01 Sep 1881 in Union Co. South Carolina
.... 4 [8] James John Davidson b: 24 Oct 1867 d: 01 Sep 1873
.... 3 John G. Davidson b: 28 Jul 1805 d: 14 Nov 1861 in Charlottsville, Va.
.... +Jane S. Hamilton b: 18 May 1810 d: 20 Jan 1891
.... 3 Rebecca Davidson b: 16 Jan 1808
.... 3 Sarah Davidson b: 16 Jul 1810
.... +Joshua P. Dawkins
.... 3 Martha Davidson b: 04 May 1813 d: 11 May 1816
.... 3 William Thomas Davidson b: 19 May 1817 d: 05 Jun 1854
...... 2 Rebecca Gillis b: 22 Aug 1778
...... 2 William Robert Gillis b: 11 Dec 1780
...... 2 James Gillis b: 05 Apr 1783
...... 2 David Gillis b: 10 Aug 1785
.... +Anna Provost LeSourd b: 05 Dec 1793 m: 08 Oct 1823 in Baltimore , Md. d: 28 Dec 1877 in Topeka, ILL.
.... 3 Elizabeth Gillis b: Abt. 1820
...... 2 Hannah Gillis b: 10 Aug 1785
...... 2 Levinah Sharp Gillis b: 10 Aug 1787 d: Bef. 1850
.... +Dr James Reed Moore b: 12 Jul 1792 m: 13 May 1823 d: 05 Sep 1870
.... 3 John James Moore b: Abt. 1824
.... 3 [1] Elizabeth Caroline Moore b: 10 Mar 1826 d: 02 Jan 1884
.... +[2] Col Robert G. Davidson b: 28 Jul 1805 m: 16 Dec 1859 d: 31 Dec 1881
.... 4 [3] Levinah Rebecca Davidson b: 06 Nov 1860
.... 4 [4] Son Davidson b: 1861
.... 4 [5] Daughter Davidson b: 04 Sep 1864
.... 4 [6] Sarah Elizabeth Davidson b: 18 Nov 1865 d: 23 May 1928 in White Hall, Maryland
.... +[7] James Franklin Grant b: 24 Sep 1860 m: 01 Sep 1881 in Union Co. South Carolina
.... 4 [8] James John Davidson b: 24 Oct 1867 d: 01 Sep 1873
.... 3 James Thomas Moore b: 03 Oct 1829 d: 21 Dec 1901 in White Hall, Maryland
.... +Mary Jane Burns b: 01 Jun 1831 m: 17 Jan 1860 d: 30 Aug 1888 in White Hall, Maryland
.... 4 James Oscar Moore b: 09 Feb 1863 in White Hall, Maryland d: 25 Apr 1927 in Jarrettsville, Maryland
.... +Georgianna Magness b: 29 Aug 1874 d: 02 Mar 1941 in Jarrettsville, Maryland
.... 4 John Thomas Moore b: 15 Nov 1866 in Gillis Garden d: 28 May 1951 in White Hall, Maryland
.... +Levinah Ellen Grant b: 26 Dec 1882 in Wilkensville, South Carolina m: 19 Nov 1901 d: 06 Jul 1959 in White Hall, Maryland
.... 4 Mary Emma Moore b: 10 Jan 1868

Baltimore County Pioneers- 7th District

Descendants of Robert Nelson

```
1 Robert Nelson  b: Abt. 1760  d: 1806
.  +Sarah Johnson  b: 1750  m: 23 Apr 1782  d: 1782
...... 2 James Nelson  b: Abt. 1780  d: 1853
.......... +Elizabeth Rutledge  b: 19 Jan 1793  m: 15 Dec 1809 in St. James, Baltimore Co.
............... 3 [2] Robert Nelson  b: 1811  d: 1884
................... +[1] Elizabeth Bowen Nelson  b: 1810  d: 1894
............... 3 Betaye Nelson  b: Abt. 1812
............... 3 Joshua Nelson Nelson  b: 1814  d: 1881
................... +Margaret Ruth MILLS  b: 1821  d: 1920
...... 2 William Nelson  b: 1782  d: 1851
.......... +Hannah Hutchins  b: 1783 in Maryland  m: 1804  d: 1833
............... 3 Sarah Nelson  b: 1805  d: 1865
................... +William Glenn
............... 3 [1] Elizabeth Bowen Nelson  b: 1810  d: 1894
................... +[2] Robert Nelson  b: 1811  d: 1884
............... 3 Nicholas Hutchins Nelson  b: 15 Dec 1812  d: 1874
................... +Hannah Ann Hope  b: 06 Sep 1815  m: 14 Jan 1836  d: 09 May 1857 in Bethel
...... 2 John Nelson  b: 1786  d: 1857
.......... +Hannah Hutchins  b: 1787  d: 1860
............... 3 Richard Hutchins Nelson  b: 29 Sep 1811  d: 04 Apr 1866
................... +Delilah Wiers  b: 12 Jul 1811 in adams Garden  d: 06 Mar 1896
............... 3 Sarah Nelson  b: 10 Jan 1813  d: 15 Mar 1855
................... +James D Hope  b: 20 Jan 1811  m: 25 Feb 1836  d: 05 Jan 1891
............... 3 Hannah Nelson  b: Abt. 1814
............... 3 William H Nelson  b: 1815
................... +Elizabeth Moore  b: 1815
............... 3 Elizabeth Nelson  b: 1817  d: 1887
................... +Shadrack Rutledge Gilbert  b: 10 Dec 1821 in Harford Co.  m: 01 Aug 1891  d: 1891
............... 3 Jarrett Nelson  b: 1819  d: 1900
................... +Susanna Plowman  b: 1825  d: 1895
............... 3 Amanda Zana Nelson  b: 1822  d: 1901
................... +John Stansbury Hutchins  b: 1818  d: 1881
............... 3 Mary Jane Nelson  b: 1825  d: 1878
................... +Abraham A Gilbert  b: 1824 in Delightful rocks  m: 1848  d: 1864
............... 3 James Nelson  b: 1826  d: in Vernon
............... 3 John Hutchins Nelson  b: 1829  d: 1891
................... +Mary Ann Plowman  b: 1827  d: 1905
...... 2 Elizabeth Nelson  b: Abt. 1790  d: 1872
.......... +James Rampley  b: 25 Oct 1786 in Harford Co. Md.  m: 03 Jan 1812  d: 09 Jan 1858 in Md.
............... 3 William Nelson Rampley  b: 1825  d: 1894
................... +Martha Elizabeth Streett  b: 1825 in Harford Co, Maryland  d: 06 Jun 1907
............... 3 Robert Nelson Rampley  b: 1817  d: 1899
................... +Frances R. Maul  b: 11 Nov 1829  m: 14 Feb 1850
............... 3 Nelson Rampley  b: 1818
............... 3 James Rampley  b: 25 Oct 1819 in Harford Co  d: 27 Aug 1901
................... +Eleanor Turner  b: 15 Nov 1829  m: 1850  d: 25 Jan 1901
...... 2 Nathan Nelson  b: 1792 in MLM  d: 17 Oct 1866 in Bishops Lot, MLM
.......... +Penelope Rutledge Talbott  b: 1798  m: Abt. 1817  d: 1825
............... 3 Thomas Nelson
................... +Louisa McPhail
............... 3 Nathan Nelson  b: Abt. 1818
................... +Mary Hope Hutchins  b: 1822  d: 1883
............... 3 Joshua Nelson  b: 1820  d: 1875 in Houcks Mill Rd
................... +Ellen Hope  b: 31 Aug 1822  d: 23 Jun 1899
...... *2nd Wife of Nathan Nelson:
```

```
.......... +Penelope Slade  b: 20 Sep 1809 in Bush, River, Upper Hundred  m: Abt. 1830  d: 28 Jan 1872 in MLM
.............. 3 Charles Nelson  b: Abt. 1829
.................. +Lida Preston
.............. 3 Robert Nelson  b: Abt. 1830
.................. +Margaret Hunter  b: Abt. 1830
.............. 3 Mary Nelson  b: Abt. 1832
.................. +Charles Stromenger
.............. 3 Sarah Nelson  b: Abt. 1834
.................. +William H. Carroll
.............. 3 James H Nelson  b: 1839  d: 22 Feb 1913 in Washington DC
.................. +Caroline Missouri Wiley  b: 10 Jun 1840 in Monkton, MD  d: 21 Dec 1917
```

Descendants of William Pearce

1 William Pearce b: 11 May 1775 in lot 7 Mt Joy d: 11 Jul 1835 in Mt. Joy, Sparks Graveyard lot 50
. +Ruth Sparks b: 20 Jul 1781 in Mt. Joy lot 7 d: 25 Mar 1858 in Sparks Cm lot 50 MLM, Monkton, Md
...... 2 Rachel Pearce b: Abt. 1801
...... 2 Elizabeth Pearce b: Abt. 1803
...... 2 William Pearce b: Abt. 1800
.... +Sarah A. Shepperd b: 1808 in Monkton, lot 57 d: 1899 in St Johns, Baldwin, Md.
...... 2 Mary Ann Pearce b: 24 Feb 1802 in Mt. Joy, Baltimore County d: 16 Jan 1899 in Clynmalira
.... +Joseph Pearce b: Apr 1795 in Mt.Joy 7th Dist, Balt. Co., Md. d: 22 Aug 1870 in Clynmalira
.... 3 Elizabeth Pearce b: 1819
.... +Nicholas Shock b: Abt. 1815
.... 4 Josephine Shock b: Abt. 1839
.... 4 John Shock b: Abt. 1841
.... 4 Mary A. Shock b: Abt. 1843
.... 4 Martha Shock b: Abt. 1845
.... 4 Nicholas Shock b: Abt. 1847
.... 4 Crawford Shock b: Abt. 1849
.... 3 John Cole Pearce b: 30 Dec 1820 d: 24 Mar 1890 in Towson,Md. Prospect Hill
.... +Sarah Achia Wood b: 01 May 1836 d: 23 Jun 1930 in Towson,Md. Prospect Hill
.... 4 Richard Wood Pearce b: 1857
.... 4 Annie Pearce b: 1860
.... +Rev Thomas Eigelberger
.... 4 John Cole Pearce b: 1862 d: 28 Sep 1920
.... +Priscillia A. Francies b: 1871 d: 25 Oct 1925
.... 4 William Taggart Pearce b: 03 Jan 1864 d: 21 Sep 1938
.... +Ella Garman b: Abt. 1867 d: 02 Feb 1943
.... 4 Thomas Gott Pearce b: 07 Nov 1870 d: 11 Jul 1955
.... +Charlotte Stevens Wright b: Abt. 1870 d: 05 Jan 1956
.... 3 Margaret E Pearce b: 14 Mar 1822 in Clynmalira, Monkton, Md. d: 28 Feb 1884 in Shane, Md.
.... +Arthur Shane b: 07 Jan 1816 m: 15 Feb 1849 d: 19 Oct 1876 in Shane, Md.
.... 4 Mary Susan Shane b: 21 Mar 1850 d: 07 Mar 1872
.... +[1] John Thomas Almony b: 28 Jun 1849 in West Liberty m: Abt. 1872 d: 29 Mar 1899
.... 4 Annie Elizabeth Shane b: 17 Feb 1852 d: 08 Feb 1917 in West Liberty
.... +[1] John Thomas Almony b: 28 Jun 1849 in West Liberty m: Abt. 1873 d: 29 Mar 1899
.... 4 William F. Shane b: 21 Nov 1853 d: 1909 in West Liberty
.... +Elizabeth Jane McCann b: 1855 d: 1940
.... 4 Emma Jane Shane b: 25 Nov 1858 d: 08 Oct 1852
.... 4 Ella Dorcas Shane b: 29 Apr 1867 d: 10 Jul 1943
.... +Clinton R. Kirkwood b: 21 Dec 1869 d: 18 Jun 1945 in Shane
.... 3 Mary J. Pearce b: 1830 in Maryland d: 20 Jun 1908 in Maryland
.... +Elijah Chilcoat b: 22 Jul 1831 in Maryland
.... 4 John Pearce Chilcoat b: 17 Aug 1856
.... +Laura Alloway
.... 4 George Rufus Chilcoat b: 05 Dec 1854
.... +Ruth L. Brooks b: 23 Feb 1857 in Baltimore, Co., Maryland d: 06 Oct 1949
.... 4 Elijah F. Chilcoat b: Jan 1858
.... 4 Lewis Edward Chilcoat b: 13 Nov 1861
.... 4 Ozella C. Chilcoat b: 12 Nov 1861
.... 4 Howard Greenberry Chilcoat b: Jun 1865
.... 4 Florence Chilcoat b: 1868
.... 3 Rachel Pearce b: 1831
.... +Unknown Canoles b: 1830
.... 4 Emeline Canoles b: Abt. 1855
.... 4 William Canoles b: Abt. 1857
.... 4 Elizabeth Canoles b: Abt. 1857
.... 4 John A. Canoles b: Abt. 1859

```
................... 4 Mary J. Canoles  b: Abt. 1861
............... 3 Rufus T. Pearce  b: 1831
................... +Miranda M. Cox
................... 4 John Crawford Pearce  b: Abt. 1857
................... 4 Ida Pearce  b: Abt. 1859
................... 4 Joseph Pearce  b: Abt. 1860
................... 4 Blanche Pearce  b: Abt. 1870
............... 3 Eliza Moore Pearce  b: 02 Sep 1833 in Baltimore County  d: 16 Nov 1902 in Maryland
................... +William Parlett Corbin  b: 03 Oct 1829 in Baltimore County  d: 20 Jan 1869 in Maryland
................... 4 Mary Lenora Corbin  b: 18 Apr 1867  d: 01 Sep 1893
................... 4 Georgette Corbin  b: 23 Jul 1853  d: 06 Feb 1874
................... 4 Elizabeth Ann Corbin  b: 18 Nov 1855  d: 05 Oct 1924
................... 4 John Putnam Corbin  b: 01 May 1861
................... 4 William Parlett Corbin  b: 25 Jan 1865  d: 10 Jun 1868
............... 3 Lavinia Pearce  b: 1835
................... +Riley Seth Williamson  b: 1833  m: 1854
................... 4 Ann Elizabeth Williamson  b: 1857
............... 3 Zany Amanda Pearce  b: 1838  d: in Columbus Ohio
................... +John J. Fogal  b: 1830  d: in Columbus, Ohio
................... 4 Oscar L. Fogal  b: 1863
................... 4 Frank Fogal  b: Abt. 1869
............... 3 Greenbury Arpheus Pearce  b: 23 Jul 1840 in Baltimore  d: 09 Mar 1915 in Waugh UM, Glen Arm, Md.
................... +Martha Jane Simms  b: 13 May 1847 in Maryland  m: 02 Oct 1869  d: 05 Apr 1927 in Long Green
................... 4 E. Frank Pearce  b: 05 Aug 1870
................... 4 William Silas Pearce  b: 19 Nov 1872
................... 4 Eleanor E. Pearce  b: 24 May 1874
....................... +Unknown Hardwick
................... 4 John Cole Pearce  b: 16 Nov 1876 in Glen Arm  d: 1944 in Maryland
....................... +Annie Florence Obitz  b: 1879  d: 1960 in Baltimore
................... 4 Mary Jane Pearce  b: 05 Nov 1878
....................... +W. W. Smith
....................... *2nd Husband of Mary Jane Pearce:
....................... +Dave Bond
................... 4 Joseph L. Pearce  b: 10 Dec 1880  d: in Baltimore County
....................... +Annette Sophie Wetzel  b: Mar 1889  d: 05 Jan 1952 in Kingsville
................... 4 Arthur Pearce  b: 13 Feb 1883  d: 22 Jul 1892
................... 4 Martha Estella Pearce  b: 10 Mar 1887
....................... +Frank Brown  b: Abt. 1886
....................... *2nd Husband of Martha Estella Pearce:
....................... +Unknown Zubrowski
............... 3 Ruth T. Pearce  b: 1841
............... 3 Eleanor Ella Pearce  b: 1845  d: 22 May 1877 in Towson
................... +John E. Sheridan  b: Abt. 1844
............... 3 William Silas Pearce  b: 14 Dec 1848  d: 16 Dec 1912 in St. Marys P.E. Baltimore, Md.
................... +Sarah Elizabeth Francis  b: 1850  d: 15 Oct 1922 in St. Marys P.E. Baltimore, Md.
................... 4 Emma Gertrude Pearce  b: 07 Mar 1883
....................... +William Lattin
................... 4 Charles Wesley Pearce  b: 10 Sep 1885  d: 09 Jan 1989
................... 4 Zany Amanda Pearce  b: 27 Apr 1872  d: 1945
................... 4 Sarah Ann Pearce  b: 07 Feb 1874  d: 1947
................... 4 Florence Pearce  b: 18 Jan 1881
....................... +Charles Edward Shipley  b: Abt. 1880
................... 4 Ella Edith Pearce  b: 06 Feb 1876
................... 4 Clara Frances Pearce  b: 02 Jul 1878
................... 4 Ethel Lavina Pearce  b: 15 Oct 1891
....................... +Charles Kerr  b: 1890
................... 4 William Crawford Pearce  b: 1889  d: 1891
```

```
...... 2 David Pearce  b: 18 Mar 1807 in Lot 7, 7TH Dist., Baltimore Co.  d: 16 Dec 1878 in Gilmer TWP, Adams CO, ILL
.......... +Elizabeth Stabler  b: 16 Sep 1808 in York Co  m: 27 Feb 1829 in MD  d: 24 Aug 1890 in Gilmer, TWP, Adama CO, IL
............... 3 Mary Ann Pearce  b: 26 Jan 1829 in Balt Co  d: 06 Jul 1907 in Mt Plesant, ILL
................... +William Conrad Lawless  b: 07 Jan 1829 in Kentucky  m: 01 Feb 1855  d: 15 Feb 1898 in Mt Plesant, ILL
....................... 4 Orville Henry Lawless  b: 1855  d: 1927
....................... 4 John Thomas Lawless  b: 1858  d: 1908
....................... 4 Elizabeth Margaret Lawless  b: 1859  d: 1939
....................... 4 David Oliver Lawless  b: 1861  d: 1928
....................... 4 Mary Ann Lawless  b: 1863  d: 1947
....................... 4 William Wilbur Lawless  b: 1864  d: 1938
....................... 4 James Albert Lawless  b: 1871  d: 1871
....................... 4 Charles Clarence Lawless  b: 1873  d: 1949
............... 3 Sarah Ruth Pearce  b: 15 Aug 1832 in Balt Co  d: 23 Dec 1869 in Quincy, ILL
................... +Edward A. Yeargain  m: 29 May 1851 in Adams CO, ILL
............... 3 Elizabeth Stabler Pearce  b: 02 Sep 1834 in Balt Co  d: 07 Mar 1916 in Adams CO, ILL
................... +John Quincy Lawless  b: 01 Dec 1826 in Kentucky  m: Feb 1862 in ILL  d: 01 Jan 1916 in ILL
............... 3 Thomas David Pearce  b: 03 Dec 1836 in Butler CO, Ohio  d: in ILL
................... +Rachel Pearce  b: Abt. 1838
............... 3 John Christian Pearce  b: 25 Aug 1839 in ButlerCO, Ohio  d: 30 Jun 1915 in West Point, ILL
................... +Sarah E Powell  m: Apr 1868
....................... 4 Mary Elizabeth Pearce  b: 12 Dec 1867 in Adams Co. , ILL  d: in West Point , ILL
....................... 4 George T Pearce  b: 27 Jan 1872  d: 25 Dec 1935 in Adams Co., ILL
........................... +Amy Boyd  b: 16 Aug 1871 in Pa  m: 14 Feb 1895  d: 18 Jun 1961 in Houston Twp., Adams Co., ILL
....................... 4 David Otho Pearce  b: 1876  d: 1878
...... 2 Josiah Sparks Pearce  b: 14 Apr 1818 in Baltimore Co.  d: 17 Oct 1886 in Mt. Joy, West Liberty Um
.......... +Elizabeth Ann Wright  b: 06 Aug 1829 in Wrights Prospect, Shawsville, Harford Co. Md.  d: 13 Feb 1872 in Mt. Joy, West Liberty
Um
............... 3 John Talbott Pearce  b: 1852  d: 21 Jul 1936 in Mount Carmel
................... +Hannah Price  b: Abt. 1855  d: Bef. 1936
....................... 4 Olevia Pearce
........................... +Thomas Rosier
....................... 4 Addie Pearce
........................... +George Zouck
....................... 4 Grace Pearce  b: Abt. 1880
........................... +Samuel J. Dichter
............... 3 Margaret Ruth Pearce  b: 15 Apr 1854  d: 14 Jan 1950 in Towson,
................... +James Thomas Curry  b: Aug 1848 in Baltimore Co., Maryland  m: 16 May 1878  d: 10 Jan 1930 in New Freedom, Pa.
....................... 4 James Irving Curry  b: 1879 in Baltimore Co., Maryland  d: 11 Apr 1963 in Utah
....................... 4 Carl Leroy Curry  b: 1883 in Baltimore Co., Maryland  d: 1952 in New Freedom , Pa
........................... +Lida Hoshall  b: 1887 in Balt Co, MD  m: 1909  d: 1949 in New Freedom, Pa
....................... *2nd Wife of Carl Leroy Curry:
........................... +Ethel Decker  m: Abt. 1950
....................... 4 Bettie R. Curry  b: 1892 in Baltimore Co., Maryland
........................... +Unknown Farnum  d: in Aberdeen
....................... 4 Lillian Curry  b: Abt. 1894 in Baltimore Co., Maryland
........................... +Harry Williams  b: Abt. 1892
............... 3 Joseph Wright Pearce  b: Aug 1854  d: 1930
................... +Mary Frances Lytle  b: Nov 1858  d: 1930
....................... 4 Lydia Beulah Pearce  b: 05 May 1880 in White Hall, Maryland  d: 10 Jul 1968
........................... +Oscar Vernon Streett  b: 16 Feb 1876 in Harford Co.  m: 28 Mar 1914  d: 26 Jul 1969 in Baltimore County, Maryland
....................... 4 Charles Leroy Pearce  b: 30 Nov 1881 in Maryland  d: 18 Apr 1956
........................... +Nellie Beatrice Scarborough  b: 30 Jul 1881 in Maryland  d: 03 Mar 1947
....................... 4 Minerva Pearce  b: 02 Feb 1883 in Vernon  d: 01 May 1921
........................... +Jacob Edmund Forwood  b: Abt. 1880 in Maryland  m: 26 Oct 1904 in Vernon
....................... 4 Jessie Viola Pearce  b: 14 Sep 1884  d: 17 Mar 1960 in White Hall, MD
........................... +William R Rampley  b: 08 Dec 1877  m: 28 Feb 1906 in Vernon  d: 12 Jan 1946
....................... 4 Harry Gladden Pearce  b: 05 Jul 1890 in Maryland  d: 07 Dec 1960 in White Hall, Maryland, Vernon Cm.
```

```
................ +Annie Estella Burns  b: 13 Nov 1896 in Maryland  m: Abt. 1920  d: 1962
............ 3 William H Pearce  b: 30 Aug 1855  d: 24 Feb 1856
............ 3 Thomas Emory Pearce  b: 1857 in Mt. Joy, Lot 7, 7th District  d: 20 Jan 1899 in Stablersville
................ +Kathrine Maria Stabler  b: 18 Mar 1858 in Stablersville  m: 27 May 1885 in Stablersville  d: 14 Feb 1922 in Towson
.................... 4 Elmer Pearce  b: Abt. 1886
.................... 4 Alice Virgie Pearce  b: Oct 1885  d: 1979
........................ +Harry M. Buris
.................... 4 Fannie Pearce  b: May 1887  d: 1943
........................ +Raymond Yarison
.................... 4 Goldie Lillian Pearce  b: Oct 1889  d: 1952
........................ +Dr Oliver S. Lloyd
.................... 4 Carrie Estelle Pearce  b: 1890  d: 1890
.................... 4 Thomas Carroll Pearce  b: 14 Dec 1890 in Stablersville  d: 1952
........................ +Viola Johnson
.................... 4 Bertha Eleanor Pearce  b: Oct 1895
........................ +Welty F. Burgee
.................... 4 Beulah Grace Pearce  b: Nov 1896  d: 1980
........................ +Leon Debois
.................... 4 Gladys Minerva Pearce  b: Apr 1899  d: 1954
........................ +Henry Boyd Fisher
............ 3 Silas Wright Pearce  b: Nov 1862  d: 18 Apr 1948 in White Hall, Maryland
................ +Minnie Ida Wilson  b: Dec 1874 in Maryland  d: 25 Dec 1955 in Sparks
.................... 4 Betty E Pearce  b: 27 Feb 1890 in White Hall, MD  d: 04 Feb 1943
........................ +J. Ralph Grove  b: 05 Mar 1893 in York  d: 10 Nov 1946
.................... 4 Elva M. Pearce  b: May 1895  d: in York
........................ +Unknown Mundis
.................... 4 Clarence N. Pearce  b: 1899 in Maryland  d: 1979
........................ +Cora Mildred Meredith  b: 1900 in Maryland  d: 1983
.................... 4 Millard Wallace Pearce  b: 1901  d: 1979 in York Road, Parkton, Md.
........................ +May Charlotta Lytle  b: 28 May 1898  m: Abt. 1922  d: 1925
.................... *2nd Wife of Millard Wallace Pearce:
........................ +Isabelle Thelma Ensor  m: Abt. 1925
.................... *3rd Wife of Millard Wallace Pearce:
........................ +Jennie Hare  b: 04 Nov 1905 in Baltimore County  m: Abt. 1938  d: 29 Jan 1971
............ 3 Cassandra Pearce  b: 1865 in Mount Joy lot 7  d: 1957 in New Park, PA.
................ +Edward Wiley Norris  b: 04 Sep 1859 in Harford Co.  m: 1883 in York Co  d: 16 Apr 1932 in New Park, Pa.
.................... 4 Clarence Emory Norris  b: 23 Apr 1883 in Harford Co  d: 12 Feb 1958 in York Co
........................ +Clara M Stansbury  b: Sep 1883 in Fawn Twp.  d: 1945 in York Co
.................... 4 Milford C. Norris  b: 1885
.................... 4 Wilbur Paul Norris  b: 1889 in Norrisville
........................ +Mertyle E. Marsteller  b: 1891 in New Park  d: 14 Aug 1968 in New Park
............ 3 Ella Pearce  b: 1868
................ +Harmon Davis  b: 1859
.................... 4 Son Davis  b: 1887  d: 26 Oct 1887
............ 3 Bettie Pearce  b: 1871  d: 02 May 1890
................ +John C. Anstine  b: Abt. 1870
.................... 4 Bettie Anstine  b: May 1890  d: 20 Nov 1890
...... 2 Josuha Francis Pearce  b: 1826 in Mt. Joy, West Liberty Um  d: 1870 in Ohio
.......... +Mary Slade  b: 1829 in Monkton  m: 1848  d: 1870 in Ohio
............ 3 William Slade Pearce
...... 2 Thomas C. Pearce  b: 1810 in Mt Joy  d: 1891
.......... +Jemima Hutchins  b: 1818 in Atlanta Hall, Monkton, Md.  m: 1836  d: 1891 in Columbus, Ill.
............ 3 Joshua Pearce  b: 1816 in Stablersville  d: in Columbus, Ill.
................ +Mary Hill  b: 1829
.................... 4 William Pearce  b: 1849
.................... 4 George Pearce  b: Abt. 1851
.................... 4 Laura Pearce  b: Abt. 1852
```

```
.................... 4 Loula Pearce  b: Abt. 1854
............. 3 William Hutchins Pearce  b: Abt. 1837 in Columbus, ILL  d: 18 Jan 1858
............. 3 Mary Pearce  b: 07 Sep 1839 in Columbus, ILL  d: 10 Nov 1902 in Liberty, Quicey, ILL
................ +Creighton Slade  b: 14 May 1830 in 7th District Baltimore Co, MD  m: 25 Jan 1866  d: 06 Jan 1924 in Quincy, ILL.,
                Columbus Cm.
.................... 4 Mary Alverta Slade  b: 12 Jul 1866  d: 14 Oct 1867
.................... 4 Emma Slade  b: 17 Aug 1872  d: 10 May 1888
.................... 4 Ada Slade  b: 23 Aug 1875
.................... 4 William Slade  b: 12 May 1880  d: 17 Jan 1934
............. 3 John Hutchins Pearce  b: 1841  d: 1919
............. 3 Thomas J Pearce  b: 1843  d: 1912
```

Baltimore County Pioneers- 7th District

Descendants of Early Families in White Hall Area

Baltimore County Pioneers- 7th District

JOSEPH NORRIS

The **Norris** Family was among the earliest settlers in the White Hall area, with leases dated as early as 1743. Joseph Norris, 1704-1784, was the ancestor of many White Hall residents. His daughter Elizabeth married Ezekiel Bosley and their granddaughter Nancy Ann Bosley, married John March McComas of McComas Road. John Norris married Mary Bond; Rachel married Gist Vaughn; Mary married William St. Clair; Joseph married Elizabeth Cole and Edward married Mary Wyle. Edward's son, John Chalk Norris, established " Hopewell", a 265 acre parcel on Stablers Road before the creation of "Mount Joy". Christian Stabler from York County later bought the land. George Washington Norris' sons John and George became Doctors. Clarinda Norris married Peter Hunter and William Henry Norris married Emma Jamima Richardson. William Henry's grandsons, Pearce Bosley Norris and William Norris still live on the original Norris Lands. Edward Norris's daughter, Sophia Charlotte Norris, married Benjamin Payne and their daughter Mary married Robert McClung.

ROBERT MCCLUNG

The first **Robert McClung** came from Ireland and settled on the Manor in 1763. Robert's farm was on the present Shepperd Road and currently owned by Sportscaster, Jim McKay. **Joseph McClung** married Cloe Riston. Grandson, Robert McClung married first Agnes Bell, sister of Doctor Ephraim Bell and second, married Mary Payne. His descendants from the second marriage include the Anderson Family and McGinnis families of Shane. After the War of 1812, several family members moved to Butler County, Ohio. The McClung cemetery is located on Shepperd Road across from old Holmes residence and the head stones were removed by a previous owner.

EDWARD PARRISH

Edward Parrish served in the Revolutionary War under Captain Carvel Hall. He married Delia Norris in 1789 and married second Clemency Hughes in 1821. His son, Norris Bosley Parrish, married Elizabeth O. Lytle. Edward's, daughter, Elizabeth Parrish, married John Royston. The Parrish farm was located on the South side of White Hall Road next to the Norris farm. The first Edward Parrish came to America from Yorkshire, England in 1635. The family held extensive holdings in Baltimore City and Baltimore County.

ABRAHAM RISTON

The Riston name was sometimes spelled Royston. They lived next to the Johnsons, Norris', Hughes and McClung. A small grave site on the Parrish Farm, contains Abraham, John and Jesse Riston who all died in 1818.

Descendants of Joseph Norris

```
1 Joseph Norris  b: 20 Feb 1704/05 in Herring Creek, Anne Arundal Co.  d: Apr 1784 in Harford Co.
. +Mary Talbot  b: Abt. 1705  m: Abt. 1730
...... 2 Elizabeth Norris  b: 30 Dec 1735 in Harford Co.  d: in Baltimore County, Maryland
.......... +Ezekiel Bosley  b: Abt. 1730  m: 07 Nov 1760  d: 07 Nov 1801 in lots 90, 91, 92
............ 3 [2] Rachel Bosley  b: Abt. 1761
................ +[1] Abraham Vaughan  b: 27 Oct 1773  m: 15 Dec 1802
............ 3 Mary Bosley  b: Abt. 1763
................ +William Norris  b: Abt. 1763  m: 22 Nov 1784
............ 3 Issac Bosley  b: Abt. 1764
................ +Elizabeth Hutchins  b: 1769  m: 17 Feb 1793
............ 3 Hannah Bosley  b: Abt. 1765
............ 3 James Bosley  b: 1768 in MLM  d: 13 May 1850 in St. James
................ +Hannah Hughes  b: Abt. 1776 in White Hall, Maryland  m: 30 Oct 1799 in St. James  d: 14 May 1851 in Vernon UM
............ 3 Elizabeth Bosley  b: Abt. 1770 in MLM  d: in MLM lot 92
................ +Walter Perdue  b: 1766  m: 12 Jun 1790 in St. James  d: 1826
............ 3 Joseph Bosley  b: Abt. 1774  d: Abt. 1835 in Shelby Co. Ky.
................ +Letitia Hutchins  b: 1769  m: 26 Feb 1800  d: in Shelby Co. Ky.
............ 3 Susanna Bosley  b: Abt. 1776
................ +James St. Clair  b: Abt. 1775  m: 29 Jun 1799
...... 2 John Norris  b: 10 Sep 1737  d: 17 Mar 1787
.......... +Mary Bond  b: Abt. 1740  m: 19 Jan 1758
............ 3 Joseph Smith Norris
............ 3 Delia Norris  b: Abt. 1760 in White Hall  d: 1819 in White Hall Road
................ +Edward Parrish  b: 27 Apr 1757 in Baltimore , Co., Maryland  m: 11 Mar 1789 in Dar Magazine  d: 06 Aug 1835 in White Hall Road
............ 3 Charlotte Norris  b: Abt. 1766
............ 3 Mary Norris  b: Abt. 1767
............ 3 Susanna Norris  b: Abt. 1768
............ 3 Rebecca Norris  b: Abt. 1770
................ +Josias Slade Bull  b: 1771  m: 27 Oct 1791 in St James
...... 2 Rachel Norris  b: 21 Jul 1739  d: in White Hall, Maryland
.......... +Gist Vaughn  b: Abt. 1732  m: 02 Mar 1769  d: 1800
............ 3 Rachel Vaughan  b: 25 Jun 1770
............ 3 John Vaughan  b: 27 Nov 1771
............ 3 [1] Abraham Vaughan  b: 27 Oct 1773
................ +[2] Rachel Bosley  b: Abt. 1761  m: 15 Dec 1802
............ 3 Benjamin Vaughan  b: 22 Jul 1775  d: 20 Apr 1806
............ 3 Elizabeth Vaughan  b: 07 Mar 1777 in Harford Co.  d: 05 Jul 1850 in White Hall, Maryland
................ +Peter Grubb Hunter  b: 1775  m: 24 Feb 1796  d: 04 Nov 1838 in Wiseburg Cm.
............ 3 Gist Vaughan  b: 07 Sep 1780
................ +Rebecca Unknown  b: 1810
...... 2 Susanna Norris  b: 1741
.......... +Walter Wyle  b: 08 May 1742  m: 29 Dec 1763
...... 2 Mary Norris  b: 01 Jun 1742
.......... +William Sinclair  b: 1750  m: 02 Mar 1769  d: 1804
............ 3 Willimena Sinclair  b: Abt. 1775
...... 2 Hannah Norris  b: 28 May 1743
...... 2 Joseph Norris  b: 18 Apr 1745
.......... +Elizabeth Cole  b: Abt. 1746
...... 2 Willimina Norris  b: 28 Mar 1747
.......... +Vincent Bosley  b: Abt. 1746  m: 28 Mar 1771
............ 3 James Bosley  b: Abt. 1773
............ 3 Bosley  b: Abt. 1774
............ 3 Mary Bosley  b: Abt. 1776
............ 3 Benniah Bosley  b: Abt. 1778
```

.... 3 Joseph Vincent Bosley b: 1778 d: 19 Dec 1848 in Norrisville
.... +Mary Cathcart b: 1790 in Norrisville d: 1856 in Norrisville
...... 2 Benjamin Norris b: 17 Jan 1748/49
...... 2 Edward Norris b: 08 Apr 1741 in Harford Co, Maryland d: Oct 1781
.... +Mary Wyle b: 20 Dec 1735 in Clynmalira, MLM m: 19 Sep 1754 in ST Johns, Kingsville d: Aft. 1790 in Norrisville
.... 3 George Chalk Norris b: 1763 in Norrisville
.... +Elizabeth Hughes b: Abt. 1770 m: Abt. 1790
.... 3 John Vincent Norris b: 30 Apr 1767 in Norrisville, Maryland d: 19 May 1849 in Norrisville, Maryland
.... +Mary Wiley b: 1779 d: 19 May 1851
.... 3 Jonathan Norris b: Abt. 1769
.... 3 Althelia Norris b: Abt. 1770
.... +James Tyrrell
.... 3 Elizabeth Norris b: Abt. 1772
.... +William Hudson b: Abt. 1772
.... 3 Mary Norris b: Abt. 1776
.... 3 Sophia Charlotte Norris b: 20 Mar 1779 d: 18 Apr 1835 in Norrisville
.... +Benjamin Payne b: 1765 in Norrisville d: 28 Jul 1821 in Norrisville
...... 2 Temperance Norris b: 02 Feb 1753
...... 2 James Norris b: 29 Mar 1756

Descendants of George Chalk Norris

1 George Chalk Norris b: 1763 in Norrisville
. +Elizabeth Hughes b: Abt. 1770 m: Abt. 1790
...... 2 Edward Norris b: 15 Sep 1791 in Harford Co. d: 17 Jun 1875
.... +Elizabeth Seitz b: 02 Apr 1805 d: 06 Nov 1884
.... 3 Edward Norris b: 1825
.... 3 James W Norris b: 1826
.... 3 Mary A Norris b: Abt. 1829
.... 3 Daniel Norris b: 1830
.... 3 Andrew Norris b: 1832
.... 3 George Washington Norris b: 04 Sep 1835 in Harford Co. d: 16 Sep 1913 in New Park, PA.
.... +Mary Elizabeth Wiley b: 20 May 1835 in Maryland d: 21 Jul 1897
.... 3 Elizabeth J Norris b: 1838
.... 3 Jonathan Norris b: 1839
.... 3 Nicholas Norris b: 1841
.... 3 William Norris b: 1843 in Harford County, Md. d: 1904
.... +Elizabeth Payne b: 1841 in Harford County, Md. m: 02 Dec 1864 d: 1924
.... 3 Eliza Norris b: 1846
.... 3 Benjamin Norris b: Abt. 1850
...... 2 Daniel Treadway Norris b: 27 Oct 1793 d: 1873
...... 2 Mary Norris b: 07 Nov 1794
...... 2 Esron Hughes Norris b: 21 Sep 1795
...... 2 Greenberry Wiley Norris b: 30 Jan 1800 in White Hall Road
.... +Elizabeth b: 1795
...... 2 George Washington Norris b: 06 Mar 1802 in Norrisville d: 28 Sep 1873 in 7th Dist., Baltimore Co.
.... +Hannah Bosley b: 1807 in Vernon UM m: 22 Feb 1839 d: 05 Oct 1890 in Vernon UM
.... 3 Dr John Norris b: 07 Mar 1840
.... 3 William Henry Norris b: 23 Oct 1841 in Vernon UM d: 08 Dec 1915 in Vernon UM
.... +Emma Jamima Richardson b: 02 Apr 1848 m: Abt. 1869 d: 15 Nov 1926
.... 3 Dr George Norris b: 01 Jul 1846
.... 3 Clarinda Norris b: 28 Mar 1845 in White Hall, Maryland d: 13 Jan 1904 in White Hall, Maryland
.... +Peter S. Hunter b: 1841 in White Hall, Maryland d: 07 Jul 1891 in White Hall, Maryland

Baltimore County Pioneers- 7th District

Descendants of Edward Parrish

1 Edward Parrish b: 27 Apr 1757 in Baltimore , Co., Maryland d: 06 Aug 1835 in White Hall Road
. +Delia Norris b: Abt. 1760 in White Hall m: 11 Mar 1789 in Dar Magazine d: 1819 in White Hall Road
...... 2 Elizabeth Parrish b: Abt. 1790 in Baltimore Co. d: in Baltimore Co.
.... +John Royston b: 1790 in Baltimore Co. m: 17 Apr 1815 d: in 6 TH District
.... 3 Jesse Riston Royston b: 1816 in Baltimore Co. d: 1890
.... +Sophia Charlotte Payne b: 20 Sep 1804 m: 20 May 1844 d: 1891
.... 3 John E. Riston Royston b: 1818 in Baltimore Co. d: Aft. 1872 in lived in Montgomery Co., Indiana 1872
.... +Tilitha Unknown b: Abt. 1820 in Maryland
.... 4 John F. Riston b: 1856 in Ohio
.... 4 Cassius Riston b: 1857
.... 4 Jacob K. P. Riston b: 1859
.... 4 Syphonia Riston b: 1861
...... *2nd Husband of Elizabeth Parrish:
.... +Unknown Norris m: Abt. 1825
*2nd Wife of Edward Parrish:
. +Clemency Hughes b: 20 May 1782 in White Hall m: 09 Mar 1821 d: 04 Apr 1862
...... 2 Norris Bosley Parrish b: 22 Jan 1822 in Baltimore , Co., Maryland d: 1900 in Baltimore Co.
.... +Elizabeth O. Lytle b: 1821 d: 1906 in Baltimore Co.
.... 3 Edward Moore Parrish b: Dec 1846 d: 30 May 1905
.... +Sabra Ellen Henderson b: 12 Sep 1846 m: 25 Feb 1873 d: 05 Oct 1916
.... 4 Mary Elizabeth Parrish
.... 4 Clarence Miller Parrish b: 09 Jun 1874
.... 4 Walter Henderson Parrish b: 16 Aug 1875 d: 1959
.... +Anna Mary Norris
.... 5 Mary Parrish d: 16 Aug 1973 in Vernon
.... 4 Lillian Edna Parrish b: 04 Apr 1877 d: 22 Dec 1941
.... +James Austin Wheeler b: 1874 d: 09 Feb 1965 in Bel Air
.... 5 H. Edward Wheeler b: Abt. 1900
.... 5 Austin Wheeler b: Abt. 1902
.... 5 Unknown Wheeler
.... +Sterling Edwards
.... 5 Unknown Wheeler
.... +Roland Hamilton
.... 4 William Caldwell Parrish b: 31 Jan 1879 d: 14 Oct 1933
.... +Annetta Etz m: 23 Jun 1904
.... 4 Leland Parrish b: 30 Jan 1881 d: 19 Mar 1881
.... 4 Eliza Susan Parrish b: 04 Apr 1884 d: 22 Dec 1949
.... +William T. Anderson b: Abt. 1880
.... 4 Sabra Ellen Parrish b: Jan 1886
.... +George Brown
.... 4 David Edward Parrish b: 17 Nov 1887
.... 4 Edward N Parrish b: 15 Jun 1892 d: 14 May 1930
.... +Amelia Etz m: 1887
.... 3 Thomas L Parrish b: 1848 d: 26 Nov 1937 in White Hall, Maryland
.... +Margaret B Wallace b: 1849 m: 10 Jan 1871 d: 1925 in White Hall, Maryland
.... 4 Samuel R Wallace Parrish b: 05 Mar 1872 d: 1961
.... +Lena K. Unknown b: 1875 d: 1946
.... 4 Charles Norris Parrish b: Jun 1874
.... 4 Margaret Elizabeth Onion Parrish b: 11 Jun 1884 d: 01 Apr 1968
.... +Millard Black
.... 3 Nicholas Morgan Parrish b: 1855 d: 11 Feb 1919
.... +Laura Frances Henderson b: 15 Dec 1849 m: 03 Sep 1884 d: 12 Sep 1931 in Vernon
.... 4 Elizabeth Ireland Parrish b: 27 Oct 1885 d: 1956
.... 4 Caldwell Henderson Parrish b: 21 Aug 1889 d: 13 Aug 1891
.... 3 Elizabeth Parrish b: 1856

...... 2 Edward Parrish b: Abt. 1824 in Baltimore Co. d: Abt. 1827

Descendants of Abraham Riston Royston

1 Abraham Riston Royston b: 10 Jul 1737 in Baltimore County d: 1790 in Baltimore Co.
  +Elianor Farlow b: Abt. 1740 m: 11 Nov 1762 in St. Johns and St. Georges d: in Baltimore Co.
...... 2 Cloe Riston Royston b: 1760 in Vernon, Maryland d: in Monkton, MD
.... +Joseph McClung b: 20 May 1763 in Mine Run 100, Balt Co, Maryland m: 08 Oct 1783 in MLM d: 10 Apr 1834 in Sheppard Rd, Monkton, MD
.... 3 Rebecca McClung b: 12 Aug 1784 in Monkton, MD d: 1856
.... +James Billingslea b: 1775 in Harford Co. m: Abt. 1805 d: 02 Oct 1814 in Baltimore County, Maryland
.... *2nd Husband of Rebecca McClung:
.... +Capt Lawson Cuddy b: 26 May 1780 m: Abt. 1820
.... 3 Rachel McClung b: 15 May 1786 in Monkton, MD
.... +Aquillia Thompson b: Abt. 1785 m: 03 Jan 1808
.... 3 Robert McClung b: 26 Jul 1787 in Monkton, Maryland d: 17 Oct 1855 in Norrisville, Harford Co., Md.
.... +Agnes Bell b: 1768 in Baltimore Co., Maryland m: 20 Feb 1817 in Harford Co, MD d: 07 May 1819
.... *2nd Wife of Robert McClung:
.... +Mary Payne b: 1799 in Norrisville, Maryland m: 03 Feb 1823 in Harford Co, MD, Norrisville Methodist d: 01 May 1834 in Norrisville
.... *3rd Wife of Robert McClung:
.... +Elizabeth Mary Bell b: 1807 m: 20 Nov 1847 d: in NOV, 1859, Harf Co
.... 3 Joseph McClung b: 07 Apr 1789 in Monkton, Md , Balt Co d: 05 Feb 1883 in Warren Co., Mason, Ohio
.... +Charity Hair b: 26 Jan 1798 m: 1815 d: 05 Dec 1892 in Ohio
.... 3 Mary McClung b: 01 Jul 1791 in Monkton, MD d: 1835 in Sweet Air , MD
.... +James Wilson b: 1780 d: 18 Mar 1844 in Sweet Air, Baltimore Co.
.... 3 Samuel Francis McClung b: 13 Apr 1793 in Monkton, MD d: 09 Sep 1861 in Mason, Ohio
.... +Susanna Hair b: 08 May 1799 in Baltimore County, Maryland m: 18 Feb 1818 in Baltimore Co., Md. d: 26 May 1839 in Mason, Ohio
.... *2nd Wife of Samuel Francis McClung:
.... +Mary Decker b: 27 Mar 1798 in Pa. m: 15 Dec 1842 d: 07 Nov 1881 in Mason, Ohio
.... 3 Margaret McClung b: 08 Jun 1795 in Monkton, MD
.... +Joseph McClung b: Abt. 1795
.... 3 Thomas R McClung b: 19 Oct 1799 in Monkton, MD d: 29 Mar 1836 in Monkton, Md
.... +Margaret Pocock b: 21 Feb 1802 d: 1834
.... 3 Elizabeth McClung b: 06 Mar 1801 in Monkton, MD
.... +William Hill b: Abt. 1800
...... 2 Abraham Riston Royston b: 1764 in Baltimore Co. d: 06 Mar 1818 in Parrish Farm, White Hall
.... +Elizabeth Parrish b: Abt. 1766
...... *2nd Wife of Abraham Riston Royston:
.... +Susanna Hughes b: Abt. 1762 m: 29 Oct 1790
.... 3 John Riston Royston b: 1791 d: 1818 in White Hall, Maryland, on Parrish Farm
.... 3 Jesse Riston Royston b: 1797 d: 1818 in White Hall, Maryland, on Parrish Farm
...... 2 Joshua Royston b: Abt. 1767 d: in Mine Run, Baltimore Co.
.... +Mary Holland b: Abt. 1768 m: 22 Sep 1786
.... 3 Joshua Royston b: Abt. 1790
.... +Martha Streett b: Abt. 1792
...... 2 Jesse Royston b: Abt. 1773 in Maryland
.... +Ann Unknown b: in Maryland
.... 3 Sarah Royston b: 05 Aug 1800
.... +John Lesourd b: 04 Sep 1796 m: 09 Oct 1817 d: 15 Apr 1872 in ILL
.... 3 John Royston b: Abt. 1813 d: in Liberty Twp., Butler Co., Ohio
.... +Tabitha Unknown
.... 3 Jonas Royston b: Abt. 1817
.... 3 Mariah Royston b: 07 Mar 1820

Descendants of Robert McClung

```
1 Robert McClung  b: 1740 in Ireland  d: 1784 in Balt Co, MD
.  +Mary Unknown  m: 27 Nov 1759 in Swede's Church, Phila  d: Aft. 1790 in Mine Run, Baltimore Co.
...... 2 William McClung  b: Abt. 1760
...... 2 Ruth McClung  b: 1761 in Probably Ireland  d: 08 Feb 1838 in Phoenix, MD.
.......... +John Royston  b: 1762 in Ireland  m: 18 Dec 1784 in Baltimore  d: 11 Sep 1822 in Phoenix, Md.
.............. 3 Thomas Royston  b: 25 May 1787 in Baltimore Co., Maryland  d: 06 Oct 1823 in Baltimore Co.
.............. 3 Robert Royston  b: 16 Nov 1788 in Baltimore Co.  d: 03 Dec 1872 in Hess Road, Baltimore County
.................. +Sarah M Bowen  b: 1797 in Baltimore County  d: 12 Sep 1885
.............. 3 John Royston  b: 1790 in Baltimore Co.  d: in 6 TH District
.................. +Elizabeth Parrish  b: Abt. 1790 in Baltimore Co.  m: 17 Apr 1815  d: in Baltimore Co.
.............. *2nd Wife of John Royston:
.................. +Sarah  m: Abt. 1814
.............. *3rd Wife of John Royston:
.................. +Rachel Collett  b: 03 Sep 1789  m: 01 Oct 1816
.............. 3 William Royston  b: 1801 in Baltimore County  d: 26 Aug 1857 in 11 TH District, Baltimore Co.
.................. +Elizabeth Fuller  b: 1801 in Baltimore County  m: 02 Aug 1821 in Jessup Ledger  d: 26 Feb 1870
.............. 3 Mary Royston  b: 1794 in Baltimore Co.
.................. +John Kidd  b: 1801 in Edinburgh, Scotland
.............. 3 Ruth Royston  b: Abt. 1796 in Baltimore Co.
.................. +Elisha Green  b: Abt. 1795  m: 29 May 1823 in Chas. Jessup Ledger
.............. 3 Caleb C. Royston  b: Jun 1797 in Baltimore Co.  d: 24 Jan 1860 in 6th District
.................. +Mary Bosley  b: 1807  m: 28 Oct 1826  d: 05 Jun 1845 in Royston Cm.
.............. *2nd Wife of Caleb C. Royston:
.................. +Sophia Cole  b: 23 Sep 1818  m: 1832  d: 13 Dec 1905
.............. 3 Elizabeth Royston  b: Abt. 1798 in Baltimore Co.
.................. +Samuel Benson  b: Abt. 1795  m: 01 May 1814
.............. 3 Margaret Royston  b: Abt. 1800 in Baltimore Co.
.................. +William P. Mills
.............. 3 Joshua Royston  b: Abt. 1801 in Baltimore Co.  d: 22 Dec 1883 in Baltimore
.................. +Mary Ann Shelley  b: 1810
.............. 3 Westley A. Royston  b: 15 Jan 1804 in 10 TH District  d: 17 Dec 1892 in Baltimore Co.
.................. +Mary Ellen Fuller  b: 1808  m: 11 Sep 1827 in Baltimore , Md.  d: 05 Jan 1873
...... 2 Thomas McClung  b: Bef. 1763 in Ireland
.......... +Nancy Graham
.............. 3 Robert McClung  b: Abt. 1785  d: in Ohio
.................. +Tutwiller  d: in Perry Co., Ohio
.............. 3 Isaac McClung  b: Abt. 1790  d: in Marysville, Ohio
.............. 3 Thomas McClung  b: 1792  d: 1879
.................. +Unknown Sanderson
...... 2 Joseph McClung  b: 20 May 1763 in Mine Run 100, Balt Co, Maryland  d: 10 Apr 1834 in Sheppard Rd, Monkton, MD
........ +Cloe Riston Royston  b: 1760 in Vernon, Maryland  m: 08 Oct 1783 in MLM  d: in Monkton, MD
.............. 3 Rebecca McClung  b: 12 Aug 1784 in Monkton, MD  d: 1856
.................. +James Billingslea  b: 1775 in Harford Co.  m: Abt. 1805  d: 02 Oct 1814 in Baltimore County, Maryland
.............. *2nd Husband of Rebecca McClung:
.................. +Capt Lawson Cuddy  b: 26 May 1780  m: Abt. 1820
.............. 3 Rachel McClung  b: 15 May 1786 in Monkton , MD
.................. +Aquillia Thompson  b: Abt. 1785  m: 03 Jan 1808
.............. 3 Robert McClung  b: 26 Jul 1787 in Monkton, Maryland  d: 17 Oct 1855 in Norrisville, Harford Co., Md.
.................. +Agnes Bell  b: 1768 in Baltimore Co., Maryland  m: 20 Feb 1817 in Harford Co, MD  d: 07 May 1819
.............. *2nd Wife of Robert McClung:
.................. +Mary Payne  b: 1799 in Norrisville, Maryland  m: 03 Feb 1823 in Harford Co, MD, Norrisville Methodist  d: 01 May 1834 in Norrisville
.............. *3rd Wife of Robert McClung:
.................. +Elizabeth Mary Bell  b: 1807  m: 20 Nov 1847  d: in NOV, 1859, Harf Co
.............. 3 Joseph McClung  b: 07 Apr 1789 in Monkton, Md , Balt Co  d: 05 Feb 1883 in Warren Co., Mason, Ohio
```

Balitimore County Pioneers- 7th District

```
................    +Charity Hair  b: 26 Jan 1798  m: 1815  d: 05 Dec 1892 in Ohio
............    3 Mary McClung  b: 01 Jul 1791 in Monkton, MD  d: 1835 in Sweet Air , MD
............    +James Wilson  b: 1780  d: 18 Mar 1844 in Sweet Air, Baltimore Co.
............    3 Samuel Francis McClung  b: 13 Apr 1793 in Monkton, MD  d: 09 Sep 1861 in Mason, Ohio
................    +Susanna Hair  b: 08 May 1799 in Baltimore County, Maryland  m: 18 Feb 1818 in Baltimore Co., Md.  d: 26 May 1839 in
                Mason, Ohio
............    *2nd Wife of Samuel Francis McClung:
................    +Mary Decker  b: 27 Mar 1798 in Pa.  m: 15 Dec 1842  d: 07 Nov 1881 in Mason, Ohio
............    3 Margaret McClung  b: 08 Jun 1795 in Monkton, MD
................    +Joseph McClung  b: Abt. 1795
............    3 Thomas R McClung  b: 19 Oct 1799 in Monkton, MD  d: 29 Mar 1836 in Monkton, Md
................    +Margaret Pocock  b: 21 Feb 1802  d: 1834
............    3 Elizabeth McClung  b: 06 Mar 1801 in Monkton, MD
................    +William Hill  b: Abt. 1800
......    2 Rebecca McClung  b: Abt. 1765 in Monkton, Baltimore County Maryland
..........    +James Birmingham  b: Abt. 1762 in Harford Co.  m: 02 May 1784  d: 27 Jan 1795
............    3 Margret Birmingham  b: Abt. 1785
............    3 Mary Birmingham  b: 24 Jul 1786  d: 29 Jul 1875
................    +John Garrison  b: 26 Mar 1786  m: 08 Jan 1812
............    3 Matthew Birmingham  b: 10 Oct 1787  d: 26 Sep 1866
................    +Elizabeth Unknown  b: 12 Sep 1795  d: 15 Oct 1863
............    3 James Birmingham  b: Abt. 1791
............    3 Robert Birmingham  b: Abt. 1792
............    3 Samuel Birmingham  b: 20 Feb 1794  d: 12 Mar 1860
................    +Phebe Beazell  b: 30 Nov 1794
............    3 Rebecca Birmingham  b: Abt. 1795
......    2 Samuel McClung  b: 05 Mar 1765 in Baltimore Co. , Md.  d: 1850 in Hanover Twp, Beaver Co, Florence, Pa
..........    +Charlotte Fugate  b: Abt. 1764 in Monkton, Baltimore Co., Md.  m: 12 Jan 1803 in Baltimore Co.  d: 1853 in Washington Co., Pa.
............    3 Adam McClung  b: 1805 in Maryland  d: Aft. 1884 in Jackson Co., Ohio
................    +Alice Coole  b: Abt. 1805 in Brook Co. WVA.  m: 15 Dec 1829  d: 24 Jan 1870 in Jackson County, Ohio
............    3 Caleb McClung  b: Abt. 1806 in Frankfort Spring, Hanover TP, Beaver Co, PA  d: 1879 in Frankfort Spring, Hanover Tp.,
                Beaver Co., PA.
................    +Sarah Duncan  b: 12 Jul 1810  d: in Florence, PA.
............    *2nd Wife of Caleb McClung:
................    +Rachel Hartford  b: Abt. 1808
............    *3rd Wife of Caleb McClung:
................    +Maria Shannon
............    3 Mary Polly McClung  b: Abt. 1808
................    +Unknown Saxton
............    3 Mordecai McClung  b: 29 May 1809 in Maryland  d: 27 Feb 1879 in Lick, Jackson Co., Ohio
................    +Nancy Wilson  b: 1816 in Washington Co., Pa.  m: 1837 in WASHINGTON CO PA  d: Abt. 1896 in Jackson County, Ohio
......    2 Rachel McClung  b: Abt. 1767 in Monkton, Baltimore County Maryland
..........    +Thomas Gorsuch  b: Abt. 1765  m: 15 Dec 1787 in Baltimore , Md.
............    3 Charles Gorsuch  b: 1789
......    2 Elizabeth McClung  b: 24 Nov 1770 in Monkton, Baltimore County Maryland
..........    +William Jones  b: Abt. 1770  m: 24 Mar 1789
......    2 Nancy Ann McClung  b: Abt. 1771 in Monkton, Baltimore County Maryland
..........    +Benjamin Davis  m: 15 May 1792
......    2 Mary McClung  b: Abt. 1773 in Monkton, Baltimore County Maryland  d: 28 Jan 1861 in Jackson County, Ohio
..........    +John Gorsuch  b: Abt. 1755 in Balt Co  m: 18 Oct 1791 in Baltimore Co.  d: Abt. 1840 in moved 1792 to Washington County, Pa.
............    3 John Gorsuch  b: Abt. 1795  d: in Meigs Co., Ohio
................    +Rachel Singer
............    3 Mary Gorsuch  b: 08 Apr 1797 in Washington Co., Pa.  d: 26 Oct 1878 in Jackson County, Ohio
................    +Peter Stiffler  b: 09 May 1797  d: 30 Apr 1837 in Jackson County, Ohio
............    *2nd Husband of Mary Gorsuch:
................    +Ezekiel Masters  m: 27 May 1856  d: 1874
............    3 Thomas Gorsuch  b: Abt. 1808  d: 13 Oct 1859 in moved 1830 to Jackson Co., Ohio
```

.... +Anna Gilmore b: Abt. 1812 d: 27 Oct 1882 in Jackson County, Ohio
.... 3 Rebecca Gorsuch b: Abt. 1809
.... +Caleb Clark b: Abt. 1806
.... 3 David Gorsuch b: Abt. 1810
.... +Sarah Hanlin

1917 TRIP TO GETTYSBURG

Webster Anderson family in Overland Car
Harry Yost family in Jeffry Car
Tydings McGinnis family in Dodge Car

Thomas Ayres

Thomas Ayres, born 1755, was a native of Scotland, was very influential in the Shawsville area as well as owning land near Maryland Line. Thomas served as a private in the Maryland Line from 1776-1780. His descendants owned many farms along the Shawsville - Norrisville Road. Thomas married John Almony's daughter Elizabeth. His daughter Dorcas Ayres, married Jacob Bradenbaugh, John Ayres married Amelia Hitchcock and Susannah Ayres married Nicholas Hutchins from the Manor.

George Elliott

George Elliott who married Keziah Anderson, bought land from Edward Johnson as early as 1743. The family owned several holdings between Vernon and White Hall, which has now become the Graystone Golf course. Benjamin Elliott married Alice McClung, and Rachel Elliott married John Burns. Abraham Elliott married Margaret Cunningham and their children married into many White Hall families including the Bacon, Bradenbaugh, Wilson and Meredith families. John Elliott Mays Junior of Hereford is also a descendant of George Elliott.

John Garrett

John Garrett married Elizabeth Turnbaugh and son Benjamin Howard Garrett married Amanda Nelson. Benjamin's daughter Mary Emma Garrett married James Buchannan Davis, grandfather of Grafton Miller. Charles Howard Garrett's son Francis Dawes Garrett was the former Principal of Seventh District Elementary School. Charles Samuel Garrett's daughter Frances Ellen married Vernon Chenoweth, son of Howard Chenoweth who owned the farm on Old York Road. James Benjamin Garrett, who was a standout basketball player at Hereford High School, still lives on Garrett Road.

Thomas Lytle

The marriage of Thomas Lytle to Chariety McComas eventually tied the Lytle family to most of the surrounding families. Thomas' father, George was involved in the evaluation of confiscated proprietary reserve land in 1782 and also married a McComas. The Lytle house, sitting beside the railroad tracks in White Hall, is thought to be the first house built in the town.

Daniel Shaw

Daniel was a Captain of Baltimore County Militia Company No. 5 in August 1776, under Col. Edward Cockey's Battalion.

Descendants of Thomas Ayres

1 Thomas Ayres b: 1751 in Scotland d: 13 Mar 1836 in Maryland
. +Elizabeth Almony b: 1756 in Baltimore, Co., Maryland m: 11 Jan 1779 d: 04 Aug 1856 in Harford Co.,Maryland
...... 2 Nancy Ann Ayres b: 24 May 1780 in Maryland d: Bef. 1870
.... +William Rampley b: Abt. 1778 m: 23 Jan 1802 in Balt,Co. d: Mar 1841
.... 3 Dorcas Rampley
.... 3 Elizabeth Rampley b: 28 May 1803 in Harford Co d: 10 May 1843 in Harrison CO, Ohio
.... +John Streett Amos b: 23 Feb 1804 in Harford Co m: 04 Feb 1824 in Harford Co. d: 27 Apr 1847 in Harrison CO, Ohio
.... 3 Thomas A Rampley b: Abt. 1807 d: 1860
.... +Mary Susan Demoss b: Abt. 1809 m: 07 Dec 1837
.... 3 William Rampley b: 1818 d: 1880
.... +Eleanor
...... 2 Dorcas Ayres b: 28 Dec 1782
.... +Jacob Bradenbaugh b: in Harford Co., Maryland
.... 3 Jacob Bradenbaugh b: 20 Sep 1812 in Harford Co., Maryland d: 23 Sep 1849 in Harford Co., Maryland
.... +Elizabeth Ann Almony b: 1819 in Baltimore Co. d: 05 Feb 1893 in Harford Co., Maryland
.... 3 Thomas Bradenbaugh
.... +Margaret A Elliott b: 1818 m: 17 Mar 1837
.... 3 Mary Susan Bradenbaugh b: 14 May 1818 d: 18 Mar 1901
.... +Richard Hutchins b: 1813 d: 1887
.... 3 Nancy Ann Bradenbaugh b: 30 Nov 1820 in Balt,Co. d: 16 Jun 1890 in Balt,Co.
.... +Thomas Andrew Elliott b: 1814 in Balt,Co. m: 26 Jul 1841 d: 17 Jul 1896 in White Hall, Maryland
...... 2 John Ayres b: 04 Dec 1784 d: 10 Mar 1852 in Maryland
.... +Amelia Hitchcock b: 04 Dec 1788 d: 03 May 1862 in Maryland
.... 3 Eliza Ayres
.... +Unknown Porter
.... 3 Mary Susan Ayres
.... 3 William Hitchcock Ayres b: 1814
.... 3 Nancy Ann Ayres b: 1826 d: 02 Jan 1894
.... +Ezekiel J. Richardson b: 1824 m: 09 Mar 1846 d: 23 Mar 1900
.... 3 Margaret Ayres b: Abt. 1830
.... +Elijah Rockhold b: Abt. 1830 m: 30 Dec 1851
...... *2nd Wife of John Ayres:
.... +Rachel Dunnuck b: 24 Jun 1793 in Baltimore Co.
.... 3 Elizabeth C Ayres b: Abt. 1824
.... +William Wright b: 22 Apr 1826 d: 18 Dec 1898
.... 3 Rachel Ann Ayres b: 09 Mar 1827
.... 3 Ruth Ellen Ayres b: 06 Jun 1831
...... 2 Elizabeth Ayres b: 19 Aug 1787 d: 08 Mar 1876 in Maryland
...... 2 Joshua Ayres b: 13 May 1790
...... 2 James Ayres b: 07 Jun 1793 d: 21 Dec 1816 in Stubenville Ohio
...... 2 Susanna Ayres b: 07 Feb 1796 d: 03 Mar 1860 in Stubanville Ohio
.... +Nicholas Hutchins b: 1791 m: 31 Jul 1816 d: 1876
.... 3 Elizabeth E. Hutchins b: 1817 d: 1855 in Ohio
.... 3 William James Hutchins b: 1819 in Jefferson Co. Ohio
.... +Mary Glass
.... 3 Thomas Ayres Hutchins b: 1822
.... 3 Dewitt Clinton Hutchins b: 1824 in Steubenville,Ohio
...... 2 Mary Ayres b: 30 Jan 1799 d: 29 Jan 1800
...... 2 Thomas Jefferson Ayres b: 15 Apr 1801 in Baltimore, Co., Maryland d: 16 Nov 1886 in Harford Co.,Maryland
.... +Elizabeth Almony b: 18 Apr 1803 in Baltimore, Co., Maryland d: 25 Oct 1886 in Maryland
.... 3 John Ayres b: 31 Dec 1824 in Maryland d: 1865
.... +Elizabeth Perdue b: 1824 d: 1899
.... 3 Elizabeth Ayres b: 24 Feb 1827 in Maryland d: 04 Feb 1880 in Maryland
.... +William Harrison Almony b: Apr 1814 in Baltimore Co. m: 31 Dec 1859 d: 09 Aug 1892 in Maryland
.... 3 Dorcas Ayres b: 10 Apr 1830 in Maryland

```
............ 3 Thomas Jefferson Ayres  b: 09 Mar 1833 in Maryland  d: 17 Jun 1910 in Maryland
................ +Alice Ann Norris  b: 21 Jul 1834  m: 1865  d: 27 Nov 1917 in Maryland
............ 3 Ann Ayres  b: 16 Nov 1835 in Maryland
................ +John Wiley  b: Abt. 1834
............ 3 Mary S Ayres  b: 25 Feb 1839 in Maryland
............ 3 Benjamin A Ayres  b: 07 Apr 1841 in Maryland
................ +Julia Schrodes  b: Abt. 1842
```

Descendants of George Elliott

1 George Elliott b: Abt. 1744 in Balt Co d: Nov 1824 in Balt.,Co.
. +Keziah Theresa Anderson b: Abt. 1730 in Balt Co m: 20 Jun 1769 in St John's, AA CO d: Aft. 1825
...... 2 Benjamin Elliott b: Abt. 1770 in Balt,Co. d: 08 May 1840 in Butler Co. Ohio
.... +Alice McClung b: Abt. 1770 in Balt,Co. m: Abt. 1795 in Balt,Co. d: 04 Jun 1826 in Butler Co. Ohio
.... 3 Abraham Elliott b: 19 Feb 1797 in Balt,Co. d: 23 Aug 1869 in Shelby Co. Ohio
.... +Cathrine R. Mullally b: 04 Apr 1796 in Va. m: 23 Aug 1821 in Butler Co. Ohio d: 06 Oct 1877 in Shelby Co. Ohio
.... 4 Mary Jane Elliott b: 26 Jan 1822
.... 4 Joseph M. Elliott b: Abt. 1829
.... +Elizabeth m: Abt. 1848 in Butler Co. Ohio d: in Shelby Co. Ohio
.... 4 Benjamin A. Elliott b: 10 Dec 1830
.... +Amanda D. Staley b: 1840 m: 12 Jan 1860 in Logan Co. Ohio d: 1918 in Shelby Co. Ohio
.... 3 Benjamin Ezra Elliott b: 03 Nov 1802 in Balt,Co. d: 28 Jan 1881 in Cincinnati, Ohio
.... +Asenath C. Varney b: 18 Jan 1812 m: 05 Feb 1832 in Cincinnati, Ohio d: 29 Oct 1863 in Cincinnati, Ohio
.... 4 Ann Elizabeth Elliott b: 25 Mar 1833
.... +John D. Jennings m: 04 Oct 1855 in Cincinnati, Ohio d: 03 Apr 1862
.... 4 Martha Elliott b: 08 Nov 1834
.... 4 Mary Elizabeth Elliott b: 01 Oct 1836
.... +John K. Sterrett b: Abt. 1835 m: 04 Oct 1855 in Cincinnati, Ohio
.... 4 Caroline Augusta Elliott b: 26 Aug 1838
.... 4 Alice M. Elliott b: 07 Apr 1841
.... +George M. Middleton m: 20 Jun 1865 in Cincinnati, Ohio
.... 4 William Woodnut Elliott b: 13 Feb 1843
.... +Emily Gertrude Fries b: 25 Mar 1845 in Columbiana Co. Ohio m: 10 Dec 1868 in Cincinnati, Ohio d: 09 Jul 1927 in Cincinnati, Ohio
.... 4 Ezra Taylor Elliott b: 15 Nov 1845
.... +Victoria W. Ellison m: 15 Sep 1885 in Cincinnati, Ohio
.... 4 Amelia Sterrett Elliott b: 12 Dec 1849
.... 4 Charles Acton Elliott b: 05 Mar 1855
.... +Kathrine Talley
.... *2nd Wife of Charles Acton Elliott:
.... +Daisy Cumming
.... 3 Mary Elliott b: 27 Jul 1805
.... +John McGuire m: 14 Jan 1836 in Butler Co. Ohio d: Abt. 1842 in Butler Co. Ohio
.... 3 Elizabeth Elliott b: 24 Jul 1809
.... +Bazil Moore m: 31 Oct 1830 in Butler Co. Ohio
.... 3 Delilah Crayton Elliott b: 30 Jun 1812 in Md.
...... *2nd Wife of Benjamin Elliott:
.... +Cathrine m: Aft. 1826 in Butler Co. Ohio
...... 2 Leonard Elliott b: 06 Apr 1784 in Baltimore Co. d: 17 Jan 1862 in Shelby Co, Ohio
.... +Jemima Ramley b: Abt. 1785 in Harford Co m: 18 Aug 1804 in MD d: Bef. 1822 in Ohio
.... 3 Keziah Elliott b: 08 Sep 1805 in Baltimore
.... +John Holden b: Abt. 1790 in Va. d: Jun 1880 in Adams Co. Ill.
.... 4 Joseph Holden b: Abt. 1832
.... 4 Sarah L. Holden b: Abt. 1842
.... 3 George Elliott b: 22 Feb 1807 in Baltimore Co.
.... 3 Sarah Gibson Elliott b: 1809
.... +George Shepperd b: Abt. 1808 m: 26 Jan 1843 in Butler Co. Ohio
.... 3 Ariel Elliott b: 11 Feb 1812 in Balt,Co. d: 24 Jun 1846 in Darke Co. Ohio
.... +Jarrett Mutchner b: 17 Sep 1809 in Md. m: 30 Jan 1834 in Butler Co.,Ohio d: 06 Jun 1888 in Bethel, Wayne Co. Ind.
.... 4 Elizabeth Mutchner b: 28 Apr 1835
.... +Joseph Burgess
.... 4 Rachel Ann Mutchner b: 07 Feb 1840
.... +McClure
.... 4 Philip Mckandree Mutchner b: 07 Feb 1840 d: 16 Feb 1847
.... 3 James Ramley Elliott b: 24 Feb 1813 in Balt,Co. d: 28 Jan 1893 in Mulbery, Clinton Co. Ind.

.... +Maria Augusta Davis b: 20 Dec 1818 in Butler Co. Ohio m: 13 Oct 1835 in Butler Co. Ohio d: 12 Mar 1900 in Mulbery, Clinton Co. Ind.
.... 4 Almon D. Elliott b: 10 Jan 1840 d: 21 Mar 1915 in Battle Ground, Tippecanoe Co. In.
.... +Charity Murphy b: 1839 in Ohio m: 15 Nov 1859 in Clinton Co. In. d: 1878 in In.
.... *2nd Wife of Almon D. Elliott:
.... +Harriet Murphy b: Dec 1849 in Ohio m: 1880 in In. d: May 1916 in In.
.... 4 William Riley Elliott b: 14 Jan 1843 in Butler Co. Ohio d: 24 Jul 1844 in Butler Co. Ohio
.... 4 Nancy S. Elliott b: 26 Nov 1844 in West Chester, Butler Co. Ohio d: 26 Jul 1916 in Frankfort, Clinton Co. In.
.... +George Duckworth Blinn b: 09 Jul 1837 m: 28 Jan 1867 in Clinton Co. In. d: 23 Apr 1918 in Frankfort, Clinton Co. In.
.... 4 John C. Elliott b: 06 Apr 1847 in Butler Co. Ohio d: 11 Dec 1873 in Mulbery, Clinton Co. Ind.
.... +Caroline V. Wolf b: 10 Feb 1847 in Boonsboro, Washington Co. Pa. m: 20 Feb 1866 in Shelby Co., Ohio d: 04 Apr 1892 in In.
.... 4 Ann Augusta Elliott b: 18 Feb 1850 in Butler Co. Ohio d: 26 Dec 1899 in Mulbery, Clinton Co. Ind.
.... +Robert W. Peters b: 1842 in Madison Twp. Clinton Co. In. d: 1908 in Madison Twp. Clinton Co. In.
.... 4 James Rampley Elliott b: 26 Nov 1852 in Butler Co. Ohio d: 16 Apr 1917
.... +Sarah F. Combs b: Abt. 1856 in In. m: 15 May 1874 in Clinton Co. In.
.... 4 Frank Boyd Elliott b: 23 Nov 1854 in Butler Co. Ohio d: 07 May 1939 in Cincinnati, Ohio
.... +Ellen Jane Steckel b: 26 Mar 1856 in Clinton Co. In. m: 10 Nov 1878 in Clinton Co. In. d: 04 Mar 1904 in Mulbery, Clinton Co. Ind.
.... *2nd Wife of Frank Boyd Elliott:
.... +Ida J. Clark b: 21 Aug 1862 in Clinton Co. In. m: 26 Feb 1907 in Jacksonville, Fl. d: 11 Dec 1936 in San Diego, Cal.
.... 4 Orlando Bush Elliott b: Sep 1858 in Clinton Co. In. d: 18 Mar 1943 in Clinton Co. In.
.... +Carrie Bell Boyles b: 15 May 1862 in Clinton Co. In. m: 02 Nov 1881 in Clinton Co. In. d: 30 Jul 1936 in Clinton Co. In.
.... 3 Elizabeth Elliott b: 1815
.... +Noswanger
.... 3 William Elliott b: 1817
.... 3 Serena Elliott b: 1819
.... 3 Jemima Elliott b: 1821 in Butler Co. Ohio
.... +Daniel Souder b: Abt. 1819 in Md. m: 25 Nov 1841 in Shelby Co., Ohio d: in Ohio
.... 4 Lucretia Souder b: Abt. 1843
.... 4 Sarah E. Souder b: Abt. 1846
.... 4 Margaret Souder b: Abt. 1849
.... *2nd Wife of Leonard Elliott:
.... +Melinda Holden b: 05 Dec 1803 in Ohio m: 19 Jan 1822 in Butler CoO, Ohio d: 30 Dec 1850 in Shelby, Ohio
.... 3 John H. Elliott b: 25 Dec 1822 in Butler Co. Ohio d: 27 Mar 1895 in Pemberton, Shelby Co. Ohio
.... +Jane Burditt b: 30 Jan 1821 m: 11 Mar 1843 in Shelby Co. Ohio d: 04 Jan 1856 in Shelby Co. Ohio
.... 4 Elizabeth M. Elliot b: Abt. 1843
.... 4 George Elliott b: 27 Apr 1847
.... 4 Female Elliot b: Sep 1848
.... 4 Sarah Maria Elliot b: 03 Oct 1851 d: 28 Apr 1926 in Shelby Co. Ohio
.... +Thomas J. Davidson b: 09 Feb 1854 in Vandalia, Montgomery Co. Ohio m: 08 Dec 1881 in Shelby Co. Ohio d: 01 Nov 1928 in Shelby Co. Ohio
.... *2nd Wife of John H. Elliott:
.... +Sarah Burditt b: 03 May 1825 in Shelby Co. Ohio m: 06 Dec 1856 d: 29 Oct 1897 in Shelby Co. Ohio
.... 4 William Taylor Elliot b: 21 Oct 1858
.... +Henrietta F. Barringer b: 27 Aug 1859 m: 19 Oct 1882 d: 19 May 1921 in Shelby Co. Ohio
.... 4 John Burditt Elliot b: 22 Aug 1867
.... +Minnie Ross b: Abt. 1875 m: 28 Sep 1898 d: 20 Mar 1961 in Cincinnati, Ohio
.... 3 Emmaline Elliott b: 03 Aug 1826
.... +Jacob Kerns b: Abt. 1824 in Ohio m: 20 Mar 1844
.... 4 Joseph L. Kerns b: 08 Jun 1845
.... 4 Stephen Woodruff Kerns b: 1849
.... 4 Cyrus Kerns b: Jun 1852
.... 4 Serena Kerns b: Abt. 1862
.... 3 Leonard Taylor Elliott b: 26 Dec 1827 d: 24 Jan 1888 in Shelby Co. Ohio
.... +Elizabeth Kemp b: Abt. 1830

```
............        4 Irwin O. Elliott  b: 1855 in Shelby Co. Ohio  d: 1913
................      +Mary E. Tatham  b: 1858 in ohio  m: 09 Mar 1876  d: 22 Oct 1916 in Shelby Co. Ohio
............        4 Lilly Elliott  b: Abt. 1858
................      +T. F. Shaw  b: Abt. 1856  m: 28 Jan 1879
........    *2nd Wife of Leonard Taylor Elliott:
..............   +Jane Moore  m: 10 Feb 1853 in Champaign Co. Ohio
..........     3 Rachel Jane Elliott  b: 26 Nov 1829 in Shelby Co. Ohio  d: 26 Mar 1873 in Shelby Co. Ohio
................     +Joseph L. Kemp  b: Abt. 1822 in Shelby Co. Ohio  d: 30 May 1886 in Shelby Co. Ohio
............        4 Mary M. Kemp  b: 08 Jan 1849
............        4 Margaret V. Kemp  b: Abt. 1851
............        4 Martha E. Kemp  b: Abt. 1853
............        4 Joseph O. Kemp  b: Abt. 1861
..........     3 Mariah H. Elliott  b: 1831
..........     3 Serena W Elliott  b: Abt. 1833
................     +Henry Idel  b: Abt. 1824 in Va.  m: 28 Oct 1852
............        4 Martha B. Idel  b: Abt. 1853
............        4 Oro May Idel  b: 23 Nov 1867
......  2 Abraham Elliott  b: 22 Jan 1792 in Balt,Co.  d: 19 Oct 1857 in Anderson's Retreat, Baltimore Co.
........   +Margaret Cunningham  b: 1790 in Ireland  m: 13 Oct 1809 in Balt. Co.  d: 15 Feb 1867 in Balt. Co.
..........     3 Maria Elliott  b: 10 Sep 1810 in Baltimore Co.  d: 04 Apr 1887 in Balt,Co.
................     +Benjamin Bosley  b: 07 Dec 1805 in Balt Co  m: 01 Dec 1830 in Balt,Co.  d: 23 Jan 1864 in Balt,Co.
............        4 Elizabeth Green Bosley  b: 13 Oct 1831
............        4 Mary Virginia Bosley  b: 19 Oct 1833
............        4 Samuel Bosley  b: 31 Jul 1835 in MLM, LOT79  d: 16 Jan 1916 in MLM
..................        +Cecelia Scott  b: 17 Feb 1839  d: 25 Jan 1906
............        4 Margaret Elizabeth Bosley  b: 20 Apr 1837 in Monkton  d: 30 Jun 1915 in Wesley Chapel
..................        +Samuel Slicer Tipton  b: 1830 in LOT 78  d: 28 May 1904 in westley Chapel
............        4 Abraham Elliott Bosley  b: 08 Jan 1839
............        4 Henry Smith Bosley  b: 10 Dec 1841  d: 26 Sep 1872
............        4 Edward Denmead Bosley  b: 20 May 1843
............        4 William Talbott Bosley  b: 08 Apr 1845
............        4 James Chamers Bosley  b: 11 Sep 1847  d: 26 Jul 1910
..................        +Mary Elizabeth Sparks  b: 02 Aug 1854  d: 13 Jun 1929
............    *2nd Wife of James Chamers Bosley:
..................        +Mary Ellen Sparks  b: 1852  d: 1952
............        4 Sarah Ellen Bosley  b: 17 Jan 1851
..........     3 Sarah White Elliott  b: 24 May 1812  d: 19 Dec 1892 in Md.
................     +John B. Henderson  b: 28 Aug 1811  m: 14 Sep 1837  d: 07 Aug 1886 in Md.
............        4 John Wesley Henderson  b: 30 Nov 1841  d: 10 Jul 1912 in Md.
..................        +Frances A. Unknown  b: 04 Apr 1843  d: 16 Sep 1920 in Md.
............        4 Upton B. Henderson  b: 02 Jun 1847  d: 25 Mar 1917 in Md.
..................        +Sarah V. Unknown  b: 30 Apr 1851  d: 09 Mar 1934 in Md.
..........     3 Mary Jane Elliott  b: 25 Aug 1813 in Balt,Co.  d: 03 Mar 1884 in Balt,Co.
................     +Peter Grubb Hunter  b: 1812 in Balt,Co.  d: 11 Oct 1861 in Balt,Co.
............        4 Ellen Hunter  b: 1837 in Balt,Co.  d: 1921
..................        +Edward Jr Heffner  b: 1845  d: 1887
............        4 Bette Hunter  b: 24 Nov 1839  d: 07 Nov 1921
............        4 Abraham Curtis Hunter  b: 19 Jul 1841 in Balt,Co.  d: 29 Aug 1861 in BAlt,Co.
............        4 Pleasant C Hunter  b: 24 May 1844  d: 06 Jan 1933
..................        +Gertrude Gross  d: 17 Oct 1936
............        4 Margaret Hunter  b: 08 Jul 1847  d: 12 Oct 1879
..................        +Robert Nelson  b: Abt. 1846
............        4 Peter Grubb Hunter  b: 22 Apr 1849  d: 27 Jul 1885
..................        +Elizabeth Bacon  b: 30 Aug 1846  d: 22 Jun 1929
............        4 Rebecca Jane Hunter  b: May 1852  d: 12 Jan 1937 in Baltimore
..................        +James N. Frederick  b: Oct 1849  m: 04 Jan 1888  d: Abt. 1929 in Parkton, Maryland
............        4 John Brown Hunter  b: 12 Aug 1855  d: 26 Jul 1928
```

```
................... +Olevia R Bacon  b: 04 Apr 1849  d: 04 Feb 1937
............ 3 Thomas Andrew Elliott  b: 1814 in Balt,Co.  d: 17 Jul 1896 in White Hall, Maryland
................ +Nancy Ann Bradenbaugh  b: 30 Nov 1820 in Balt,Co.  m: 26 Jul 1841  d: 16 Jun 1890 in Balt,Co.
.................... 4 Mary Elizabeth Elliott  b: 05 Jan 1843
.................... 4 Thomas Elliott  b: Nov 1843 in Vernon, Maryland  d: 28 Jun 1936 in White Hall, Maryland
........................ +Salie A. Wilson  b: Jul 1850  d: 03 May 1930 in White Hall, Maryland
.................... 4 William Elliott  b: 04 Jan 1844
........................ +Emma Elizabeth Piersol  b: Mar 1854
.................... 4 Jacob Elliott  b: 11 Jun 1850
........................ +Mary Virginia Bacon  b: 20 Mar 1848  m: 1867 in Balt,Co.  d: 23 Jun 1937 in Balt,Co.
.................... 4 Frank P. Elliott  b: 20 Nov 1852 in Balt,Co.  d: 03 Feb 1880 in Balt,Co.
.................... 4 Dorcas Cecelia Elliott  b: 14 Nov 1855  d: 15 Aug 1946 in White Hall, Maryland
.................... 4 Abraham James Elliott  b: Nov 1858 in Balt,Co.  d: 16 Apr 1943
........................ +Mollie Wheeler  b: Nov 1861 in MD.  d: 1932
............ 3 Margaret A Elliott  b: 1818
................ +Thomas Bradenbaugh  m: 17 Mar 1837
.................... 4 Margaret Bradenbaugh  b: Abt. 1842
.................... 4 Oliver Bradenbaugh  b: Abt. 1843
.................... 4 Brown Bradenbaugh  b: Abt. 1843
.................... 4 Caroline Bradenbaugh  b: Abt. 1845
.................... 4 Thomas Bradenbaugh  b: Abt. 1845
.................... 4 Jacob Bradenbaugh  b: Abt. 1846
.................... 4 Eliza Bradenbaugh  b: Abt. 1848
............ 3 Keziah Anderson Elliott  b: 11 Sep 1819  d: 05 Mar 1898
............ 3 Robert Elliott  b: 14 Apr 1821
................ +Sarah Jane Meredith  b: 04 Jun 1828  d: 25 Apr 1893
.................... 4 Abraham Oliver Elliott  b: 05 Feb 1850 in Balt,Co.
........................ +Louise Bennett
.................... 4 Charles Meredith Elliott  b: 20 Dec 1850 in Balt,Co.
........................ +Mary Amanda Jenners  b: 02 Jan 1848  m: 08 Jul 1874 in Balt,Co.
........................ *2nd Wife of Charles Meredith Elliott:
........................ +Annie Rebecca Brundige  b: Oct 1855  m: 05 Jul 1892
.................... 4 Samuel Meredith Elliott  b: 29 Sep 1852 in Balt,Co.  d: 1885 in Adams, Co., ILL
........................ +Mary Francis Lytle  b: 1856 in Adams Co. Ill.  d: 1936 in Adams Co., ILL
.................... 4 Robert Vinton Elliott  b: 16 Feb 1854 in Balt,Co.
........................ +Safronia Tandry
.................... 4 Edwin Dorsey Elliott  b: 17 Sep 1855 in White Hall, Md.  d: 29 Mar 1950 in Manhattan Beach, Los Angeles, Cal.
........................ +Desie Buford  b: 24 Sep 1860 in Pulaski, Giles Co. Tenn.  m: 17 Nov 1883 in San Berardino, Cal.  d: 04 Jul 1915 in Los
                         Angeles, Cal.
.................... 4 Luella Jane Elliott  b: 17 Jul 1857 in Balt,Co.  d: Jan 1881 in Adams Co. Ill.
........................ +Josiah Bennett
.................... 4 Ida Elliott  b: 24 Mar 1859 in Balt,Co.
........................ +Frank Olmstead
.................... 4 Margaret Belinda Elliott  b: 19 Dec 1860 in Balt,Co.  d: 18 Aug 1881 in Adams Co. Ill.
........................ +Lewis Strickler
.................... 4 Sarah Henderson Elliott  b: 08 Nov 1862 in Balt,Co.
........................ +Edgar Strickler
.................... 4 Mary Francis Elliott  b: 08 Jan 1865 in Balt,Co.
........................ +E C Lochard
.................... 4 Clarence Elmer Elliott  b: 15 Mar 1867 in Balt,Co.
........................ +Alice Barrow  b: Abt. 1868
.................... 4 Carrie Viola Elliott  b: 08 Oct 1870 in Ill.
........................ +Elmer Wink
.................... 4 Wilbur Micajah Elliott  b: 19 Apr 1873 in Ill.
............ 3 Elizabeth Ann Elliott  b: 24 Dec 1823 in Balt,Co.  d: 01 Mar 1801 in Balt,Co.
............ 3 George Washington Elliott  b: 01 May 1828 in Balt,Co.  d: 27 Mar 1905 in Balt,Co., Vernon
................ +Elizabeth E. Hicks  b: 14 Jan 1832 in Baltimore County, Maryland  m: 23 Oct 1858  d: 21 Feb 1906
```

```
................     4 Sarah Florence Elliott  b: Jan 1863 in Balt,Co.  d: 1934 in Balt,Co.
.........................  +Charles H Mays  b: 06 Mar 1861 in Baltimore Co.  d: 31 Jul 1933 in Balt,Co.
................     4 John E. Elliott
................     4 Walter H. Elliott
............  3 Abraham James Elliott  b: 19 Aug 1834 in Baltimore Co.  d: 09 Sep 1914 in Vernon
......  2 Rachel Elliott  b: 1800 in Balt,Co.
..........  +John Burns  b: 1795 in Balt,Co.
............   3 Sarah Jane Burns  b: 1826
............   3 Mary E. Burns  b: 1831
............   3 John B. Burns  b: 1843
............   3 Mortimer Burns  b: 1846
............   3 Charles J. Burns  b: 1849
```

Descendants of John Garrett

1 John Garrett b: 1770 d: 1814 in Baltimore Co.
. +Elizabeth
...... 2 John Garrett b: 1796 in Children in bible owned by Margaret Ann Garrett of Monkton d: 16 May 1866
.... +Nancy Ann Turnbaugh b: 02 Jul 1800 m: 30 Mar 1825 d: 11 Feb 1879
.... 3 Benjamin Howard Garrett b: 10 Mar 1826
.... 3 Margaret Ann Garrett b: 06 Jun 1827
.... +Tracey m: Abt. 1848
.... *2nd Husband of Margaret Ann Garrett:
.... +Solomon Wolfgang b: 13 Jun 1825 m: Abt. 1852 d: 28 Feb 1907
.... 4 Dora A. Wolfgang
.... +Hare
.... 3 Mary Garrett b: 29 Jun 1831
.... 3 Martha Ellen Garrett b: 08 Apr 1834
.... 3 Susanna Lavinia Garrett b: 16 May 1837 d: Abt. 1838
.... 3 John Amos Garrett b: 09 Mar 1839
...... 2 Benjamin Garrett b: 1798 in Maryland d: 1870
.... +Elizabeth Turnbaugh b: 1805 in Maryland m: 20 Mar 1823 d: 1886
.... 3 Mary Patterson Garrett b: Abt. 1825
.... 3 Martha E. Garrett b: Abt. 1826
.... +Corbett
.... 3 Jehu Garrett b: 1830
.... 3 Benjamin Howard Garrett b: Nov 1831 in White Hall, Maryland, d: 1903 in Buried Vernon
.... +Amanda C. Nelson b: Mar 1850 in White Hall, Maryland, d: 1927 in Buried Vernon
.... 4 Mary Emma Garrett b: 1871 in Maryland d: 15 Apr 1950
.... +James Buchannan Davis b: 1856 in Pennsylvania d: 17 Mar 1945 in Shane
.... *2nd Husband of Mary Emma Garrett:
.... +James Benjamin Davis b: 1856 d: 1945 in Buried West liberty
.... 4 Charles Howard Garrett b: Dec 1875 in White Hall, Maryland d: 16 May 1937 in White Hall, Maryland
.... +Betti Dawes Molesworth b: Aug 1883 in Maryland m: Abt. 1905 d: 1959 in White Hall, Maryland
.... 4 Clara May Garrett b: 1878 d: 1967
.... +J Marche Lytle b: 1870 m: 10 Jul 1901 d: 09 Apr 1951 in Buried Vernon
.... 4 Benjamin A. Garrett b: May 1882
.... 3 Elizabeth A. Garrett b: 1836
.... +Hobblen
.... 3 Joanna L. Garrett b: 1837
.... +Whieley
.... 3 Margaret E. Garrett b: 1839
.... 3 Hester A. Garrett b: 1841
.... 3 Ann Garrett b: 1846
.... 3 Caroline Garrett b: 1849
.... 3 John R. Garrett b: Abt. 1850
...... 2 Nancy Garrett b: Abt. 1799

Descendants of Daniel Shaw

1 Daniel Shaw b: Abt. 1743 d: 1807
. +Prudence Bosley b: 1737 m: 14 Apr 1763
...... 2 Joshua Shaw b: Abt. 1765 d: Nov 1838
.... +Alice Hutchins b: Abt. 1768
.... 3 Nicholas Hutchins Shaw b: 1787
.... 3 Anne Shaw b: Abt. 1790
.... +Unknown Mcnabb
.... 3 Daniel Shaw b: Abt. 1792
.... 3 Edward P. Shaw b: Abt. 1794
.... 3 James Shaw b: Abt. 1796
.... 3 Mary Shaw b: Abt. 1800
.... +Unknown Wadsworth
.... 3 Elizabeth Shaw b: 25 Dec 1800 in Vernon d: 19 Jan 1877
.... +Thomas Norris b: 24 Feb 1800 in Vernon d: 21 Mar 1880 in Hunter Mill Road
.... 4 Norris
.... 4 Nicholas J Norris b: 14 Mar 1825 d: 28 Oct 1882
.... 4 Elizabeth Norris b: 29 Dec 1829 d: 14 Jul 1907
.... 4 Rachel Ann Norris b: 28 Apr 1832
.... +Stephen Miller b: Abt. 1830
.... 4 Alice Ann Norris b: 21 Jul 1834 d: 27 Nov 1917 in Maryland
.... +Thomas Jefferson Ayres b: 09 Mar 1833 in Maryland m: 1865 d: 17 Jun 1910 in Maryland
.... 4 Mary Miranda Norris b: 16 Mar 1836 d: 30 Jul 1913
.... 4 Molly Norris b: 06 Mar 1838
.... 4 Thomas J Jr Norris b: 06 Nov 1840 in Vernon, Baltimore Co. d: 28 Mar 1907
.... +Mary Cathrine Ayres b: 22 Mar 1847 d: 14 Oct 1878
.... 3 Jesse Shaw b: Abt. 1802
.... 3 William Shaw b: Abt. 1804
...... 2 William Shaw b: Abt. 1766
...... 2 Elizabeth Shaw b: Abt. 1768

Descendants of Thomas Lytle

1 Thomas Lytle b: 27 Feb 1788 d: 05 Jan 1853
. +Delia Anderson m: 14 May 1807
*2nd Wife of Thomas Lytle:
. +Charity McComas b: 1797 m: 24 Apr 1817 d: 02 Aug 1864
...... 2 William Lytle b: Abt. 1819
...... 2 Nicholas Day Lytle b: 1820 d: 15 Jan 1895
.... +Sarah Amanda Hughes b: 1833 m: 04 Dec 1863 d: 12 Oct 1879
.... 3 Harry Elmer Lytle b: 15 Mar 1864 d: 29 Apr 1929 in Graystone rd. White Hall, Md., Vernon UM
.... +Sarah Luella McGinnis b: 16 Apr 1876 in Openshaw Rd, White Hall , MD d: 29 Apr 1928 in White Hall, Md.
.... 3 Thomas Grant Lytle b: 22 Sep 1864 d: 1925
.... 3 Wilbur B Lytle b: 22 Feb 1866 d: 16 Jul 1866
.... 3 Charles R Lytle b: 31 Jan 1869 in White Hall d: 25 Aug 1936 in White Hall, Maryland
.... +Mary Gertrude Herbert b: 1870 d: 1952 in White Hall, Maryland
.... 3 Ann Hughes Lytle b: 27 Jun 1871 d: 02 Aug 1964
.... 3 Nicholas McComas Lytle b: 01 Nov 1873 d: 1926
.... 3 Edgar Hughes Lytle b: 09 Aug 1876 d: 20 May 1915
.... 3 Amanda Victoria Lytle b: 17 Oct 1878
...... 2 Elizabeth O. Lytle b: 1821 d: 1906 in Baltimore Co.
.... +Norris Bosley Parrish b: 22 Jan 1822 in Baltimore , Co., Maryland d: 1900 in Baltimore Co.
.... 3 Edward Moore Parrish b: Dec 1846 d: 30 May 1905
.... +Sabra Ellen Henderson b: 12 Sep 1846 m: 25 Feb 1873 d: 05 Oct 1916
.... 3 Thomas L Parrish b: 1848 d: 26 Nov 1937 in White Hall, Maryland
.... +Margaret B Wallace b: 1849 m: 10 Jan 1871 d: 1925 in White Hall, Maryland
.... 3 Nicholas Morgan Parrish b: 1855 d: 11 Feb 1919
.... +Laura Frances Henderson b: 15 Dec 1849 m: 03 Sep 1884 d: 12 Sep 1931 in Vernon
.... 3 Elizabeth Parrish b: 1856
...... 2 Julia P Lytle b: 1826 in Hunter Mill RD , White Hall, MD d: 1911 in Vernon
.... +William Slade b: 30 Sep 1822 in 7th District Baltimore Co, MD m: Abt. 1845 d: 1905 in Vernon, MD , West Liberty
.... 3 Delilah Ann Slade b: 23 Mar 1847 in Vernon d: 13 Oct 1892
.... +John Bosley Pearce b: 20 Jun 1837 in MLM, LOT87 m: 18 Sep 1866 d: 26 Aug 1920 in MLM, LOT89
.... 3 Mary F Slade b: 10 Jun 1849 d: 26 Sep 1853
.... 3 Ella Slade b: 1852 d: 1868
...... 2 James Onion Lytle b: 01 Feb 1828 in Blackhorse, d: 1898 in Columbus, ILL.
.... +Ann Slade b: 03 Dec 1832 in 7th District Baltimore Co, MD m: 16 Jan 1854 in Balt Co, MD d: 1911 in Quincy, ILL., Columbus Cm.
.... 3 Charles Lytle b: Abt. 1855
.... +Winnie Thompkins
.... 3 Nathan Lytle b: Abt. 1856
.... 3 William Clayton Lytle b: Abt. 1857 in Columbus, ILL d: in QUINCY, ILL
.... +Margaret Elizabeth Lawless b: 1866 d: 1948
.... 3 Emma Lytle b: Abt. 1858
.... +Frank Lummis
.... 3 Jennie Lytle b: 1861 d: 1935
.... 3 Mary Francis Lytle b: 1856 in Adams Co. Ill. d: 1936 in Adams Co., ILL
.... +Samuel Meredith Elliott b: 29 Sep 1852 in Balt,Co. d: 1885 in Adams, Co., ILL
...... 2 Thomas Lytle b: May 1830 d: 10 Nov 1909 in White Hall, Maryland
.... +Eleanor H. Treadway b: Mar 1833 d: 18 Aug 1903
.... 3 William Lytle b: Oct 1855 d: 17 Aug 1939 in White Hall, Maryland
.... 3 Mary Frances Lytle b: Nov 1858 d: 1930
.... +Joseph Wright Pearce b: Aug 1854 d: 1930
.... 3 Elizabeth M Lytle b: 12 Jun 1863 d: 09 Aug 1927
.... +Charles M. Cathcart b: 1862 m: 24 Dec 1884
.... 3 Thomas Winfield Lytle b: 1866 in White Hall, Maryland d: 29 Feb 1940 in White Hall, Maryland
.... +Annie M. Burns b: Oct 1871 in White Hall, Maryland d: in White Hall, Maryland
.... *2nd Wife of Thomas Winfield Lytle:

.... +Annie M. Burns b: 1863 d: 1953 in Weisburg
.... 3 D Owen Lytle b: 1867 d: 17 Feb 1945 in White Hall, Maryland
.... +Ida Robinson b: 1878 d: 1931 in White Hall, Maryland
.... 3 J Marche Lytle b: 1870 d: 09 Apr 1951 in Buried Vernon
.... +Clara May Garrett b: 1878 m: 10 Jul 1901 d: 1967
...... 2 Amanda Mary Lytle b: 31 Mar 1833 in Blackhorse, d: 15 Apr 1897 in Liberty, Adams Co., Quincey, ILL
.... +Abraham Slade b: 01 Feb 1828 in 7th District Baltimore Co, MD m: 23 Jan 1855 in MD d: 17 Dec 1902 in Quincy, ILL., Columbus Cm.
.... 3 Julia Slade b: Abt. 1857 in Baltimore Co.
.... +Ed Simmonds
.... 3 Della Slade b: Abt. 1858 in Baltimore Co.
.... +James Limb
.... 3 Seldon Slade b: Abt. 1860 in Baltimore Co.
.... +Alta Six b: 1878 d: 1966
.... 3 Laura Slade b: Abt. 1862 in Baltimore Co.
.... +George Stewart
.... 3 Lida Slade V b: 07 Dec 1863 in Baltimore Co. d: 05 Sep 1887 in ILL
.... +Edson Benjamin Oles Dean
.... 3 Charles Slade b: Abt. 1864 in Baltimore Co.
.... 3 Emma Slade b: 1865 in Baltimore Co. d: 1891
.... +George Cassius Dean b: 1866
.... 3 Nathan Slade b: Abt. 1866 in Baltimore Co.
.... 3 William Clayton Slade b: Abt. 1868 in Baltimore Co.
.... 3 Ella May Slade b: 1869 d: 1928
...... 2 Mary Susan Lytle b: 1836 d: in Bethel
.... +Joshua Guyton Luckey b: 04 Nov 1826 in Black Horse m: 29 Dec 1853 d: 24 Mar 1899 in Bethel Cm.
.... 3 Charity Luella Luckey
.... +Nicholas Nelson b: 24 Feb 1861 d: 1933
.... 3 Ella Luckey
.... +Lawrence Roberts
.... 3 Laura Luckey
.... +Edgar Henderson
.... 3 Bessie Luckey
.... +Robert Delgar
.... 3 Virginia Luckey
.... +Samuel Miskimmons Kirkwood b: 11 Sep 1859 d: 22 Jun 1917
.... 3 Octavia A Luckey b: 22 Oct 1854 d: 1938
.... +John Thomas Nelson b: 1848 d: 1924
.... 3 James B Luckey b: 05 Nov 1855 d: 1946
.... +Ida Amos
.... 3 Edward T Luckey b: 1858 d: 1935
.... +Hannah Elizabeth Nelson b: 13 Jul 1856 m: 19 Dec 1883 d: 15 Feb 1914
.... 3 Clara M. Luckey b: 1867 d: 1953
.... +Thomas Cameron Hunter b: 11 May 1866 d: 23 May 1949
...... 2 Frances Ellen Lytle b: 22 Sep 1837 in Black Horse d: 21 May 1905
.... +Madison Slade b: 31 Mar 1837 m: 08 Nov 1859 d: 08 Jan 1882 in Graystone, Rd
.... 3 Harvey Milton Slade b: 30 Oct 1860 in White Hall, Maryland d: 1927 in Graystone RD, White Hall, Md.
.... +Clara E. Tipton b: 17 Aug 1865 in Maryland m: 27 Jan 1886 d: 22 Jul 1938 in Graystone RD
.... 3 Fannie L. Slade b: 02 Feb 1863 d: 21 Oct 1899
.... +Joshua S. Robinson b: 14 Jan 1853 d: 17 Sep 1889
.... 3 Zora May Slade b: 25 Jul 1865 in White Hall RD, Vernon, MD d: 1916 in Parkton
.... +James W Ayres b: 1855 d: 1923
...... 2 Asenath Charity Lytle b: 28 May 1840 d: 10 Oct 1906
.... +Josiah Carlin b: 12 May 1836 d: 10 Jan 1910
.... 3 Laura Frances Carlin b: 23 Nov 1863 d: 16 Mar 1920
.... +William Ward
.... 3 Sarah Mae Carlin b: 09 Nov 1867 d: 02 Feb 1945

.... +Thomas Jefferson Ayres b: 28 May 1858 m: 28 Jan 1891 d: 12 Aug 1931
.... 3 Elizabeth Ellen Carlin b: 13 Nov 1873 d: 14 Aug 1951

Baltimore County Pioneers- 7th District

Lt. RICHARD HUTCHINS

The Hutchins family is connected to many families in the 7th and 10th Districts. Richard was a 2nd Lt. in the Maryland Line during the Revolutionary War. Many of the old stone homes along Troyer Road were built by Hutchins relatives.

His descendants include the following families: Slade, Howard, Mc Gaw, McClung, Hope, Wiley, Shaw, Payne, Norris, Bradford, Nelson, Huges, Holmes, Perdue, Hawkins, Pearce, Garrison and Glenn.

LUKE WYLE

Luke Wyle Sr. came to Baltimore County from Herring Creek, Anne Arundal County. His family were members of the Church of England and no doubt were attracted to come to Baltimore County by advertisements in 1734 from Thomas Berewood. Luke Wyle Jr. fought in the Revolutionary War.

JOSIAH SHEPPERD

Josiah Shepperd's farm was located near Monkton. Some of his later descendants lived on Graystone Road. Harold Shepperd saw heavy action on Iwo Jemima in World War 11.

ALEXANDER MCCOMAS

Alexander McComas was the ancestor of many residents of the area between Vernon and the Harford County Line along Hunter Mill Road and McComas Road. Some of the families actually lived near the line in the Tenth District but are closely tied to the area. Alexander's daughter Elizabeth married George Lytle, Alexander married Susan Amos and Nicholas Day McComas married Elizabeth Onion. Hannah McComas married James Whitaker Slade. Marian Elizabeth McComas, a descendant of Alexander also, married Charles Samuel Garrett of Garrett Road. The McComas family has long been established in both Harford County and early Baltimore County.

Descendants of William Carlin

1 William Carlin b: 1774 in New Jersey d: 1847
. +Rachel Elizabeth Sparks b: 1774 d: 1860 in 96
...... 2 Thomas Carlin b: Abt. 1802 d: 1847
...... 2 James A Carlin b: 1803 in Harford Co d: 1855
.... +Rachel Annie Sparks b: 24 Apr 1803 in Harford Co m: 04 Mar 1825 in Baltimore Co., M d: 14 May 1851 in Sparks Burial, Balt Co, Md.
.... 3 James Carlin b: Abt. 1835
.... +Mary Ellen Ring b: Abt. 1836 m: 1853
.... 3 Ellen Virginia Carlin b: 04 Nov 1840 in Harford Co d: 04 Feb 1919 in Baltimore County
.... +David Sutton b: 22 Oct 1838 in Baltimore Co., M m: 25 Apr 1863 in Baltimore Co., M d: 07 Nov 1918 in Maryland
...... 2 Ruth Carlin b: 1804
...... 2 Josiah Carlin b: 18 Mar 1806 d: 20 Jul 1878 in Adams Co. Ill.
.... +Elizabeth Ann Hughes b: 06 Oct 1812 in Baltimore Co. d: 23 Nov 1884 in Adams Co., ILL
.... 3 Mary Susan Carlin b: 05 Mar 1835 d: 22 Oct 1887
.... +Robert C Sterrett b: 01 Sep 1826 m: 15 Dec 1853 d: 22 Dec 1887 in Hancock Co., Ill.
.... 3 Daniel Hughes Carlin b: 30 Jul 1836 d: 18 Nov 1909
.... +Lucy A Pearce
.... 3 William Carlin b: 18 Oct 1837 in MD d: 24 Feb 1912 in Columbus, ILL.
.... +Delilah Slade b: 12 May 1841 d: 28 Feb 1870 in Columbus, ILL
.... *2nd Wife of William Carlin:
.... +Matilda Lyon
.... 3 James Thomas Carlin b: 21 Oct 1839 d: 10 Apr 1922
.... +Clarissa Mortin
.... 3 Elijah Carlin b: 07 Aug 1842 d: 30 Jan 1907
.... 3 Franklin Carlin b: 27 Oct 1844 d: 21 Jul 1897
.... +Hannah Brian b: 11 Mar 1848 m: 05 Jan 1868
.... 3 Josiah Carlin b: 05 Sep 1848 d: 26 Sep 1899
.... +Eva Hester
.... 3 Sarah Elizabeth Carlin b: 01 Apr 1850 d: 10 Oct 1885
.... 3 John Oliver Carlin b: 22 May 1852
.... +Martha Hester
.... 3 Rachel E Carlin b: 03 Apr 1857
...... 2 Aaron Carlin b: 1808 d: 1840
.... +Rachel Ann Collett b: 1836
.... 3 Aaron Carlin b: Abt. 1835
.... +Albritt Sutton
...... 2 William Carlin b: 1812 in Maryland d: 1890 in McKendree Cm. Blackhorse, Harford Co. Md.
.... +Sarah Poteet b: 1807 d: 13 Oct 1873 in McKendree Cm. Blackhorse, Harford Co. Md.
.... 3 Maria Elizabeth Carlin b: 1835 d: 22 Jan 1898
.... +Christoper Slade b: 12 Jun 1825 in 7th District Baltimore Co, MD m: 08 Feb 1853 in MD d: 03 Jul 1906 in 7th District Baltimore Co, MD
.... 3 Josiah Carlin b: 12 May 1836 d: 10 Jan 1910
.... +Asenath Charity Lytle b: 28 May 1840 d: 10 Oct 1906
...... 2 Rachel Carlin b: 1817 d: 1908

Descendants of William Curtis

1 William Curtis b: 1760 d: 1859
. +Ann Shepperd b: 1767
...... 2 Elizabeth Curtis
...... 2 Rachel Curtis b: 02 Feb 1794 in MLM d: 01 Jan 1880 in White House
.... +Daniel Collett Sparks b: Dec 1793 in MLM, LOT 96 d: 1863 in White House
.... 3 William Curtis Sparks b: 03 Mar 1827 in 10 DIST d: 12 Oct 1911 in 5th Dist Mt Carmel
.... +Susanna Hoover b: 12 May 1828 in Maryland d: 01 Jul 1916 in St. Abraham's Luthern
.... 3 Josiah Alfred Sparks b: 10 Nov 1829 in Maryland d: 20 Feb 1907 in White House
.... +Sarah Ann Ensor b: 1829 in Maryland d: 1896
.... 3 John Sheppard Sparks b: in Maryland
.... 3 Levi Sparks
...... 2 John Sheppard Curtis b: 09 May 1795 in MLM d: 25 Sep 1871
.... +Sarah Ann Anderson b: 16 Nov 1795 in MLM d: 17 Jan 1875
.... 3 Amanda Young Curtis b: 30 Apr 1823 in Clynmalira d: 20 Jan 1903
.... +Jackson Wilson b: 10 Jun 1821 in Baltimore, MD d: 27 Dec 1903 in Baltimore County
.... 3 Mary E Curtis b: 15 Jul 1826 d: 10 Mar 1917
.... 3 Ann Eliza Curtis b: 27 Apr 1828 in Clynmaria d: 27 May 1911
.... 3 Charles Henry Clay Curtis b: 07 Jun 1830 d: 25 Jan 1911
.... 3 Matilda S Curtis b: 19 Sep 1832 d: 08 Feb 1882
.... 3 William Harrison Curtis b: 04 Nov 1836 in Clynmaria d: 14 Jan 1929 in Blathnia, Cambria, Warren, MD
.... +Anna Barbara Gunter
...... 2 Thomas Curtis b: 20 Jan 1799
...... 2 Levi Curtis b: 1801 d: 1890
.... +Cathrine Jane Merryman b: 22 Feb 1812 in Balt Co d: 03 Jun 1888 in BC
.... 3 John Curtis
.... 3 Annie Elizabeth Curtis b: 16 Apr 1832 d: 28 May 1918
.... 3 Martha Garrison Curtis b: 27 Jun 1835 d: 09 May 1881
.... +John Parker b: 1818 d: 1892
.... 3 Marion Manilla Curtis b: 04 Jun 1837 d: 21 Oct 1876
.... 3 William Thomas Curtis b: 22 Aug 1842 d: 29 Jan 1929
.... +Helen A. Hutchins b: 1843
.... 3 Susan Worthington Curtis b: 18 Jan 1845
.... 3 Nicholas James Merryman Curtis b: 25 Dec 1846
.... 3 Arabella Stansbury Curtis b: 07 Jun 1848
.... 3 Cathrine Jane Curtis b: 09 Aug 1850
.... 3 LEVI Curtis b: 13 Sep 1853 d: 19 Jan 1854
...... 2 Sarah Curtis b: 16 Sep 1803 in MLM d: 19 Jan 1878 in New Madison, Ohio
.... +William Pearce b: 1802 d: 1861
...... *2nd Husband of Sarah Curtis:
.... +Greenberry Wyle Pearce b: 28 Jan 1800 in Clynmalira d: 25 Nov 1855 in New Madison, ohio
.... 3 William Crawford Pearce b: 04 Nov 1827 in Balt Co d: 1850
.... 3 Mary C Pearce b: 17 Nov 1829 d: 1850
.... 3 John Westley Pearce b: 15 Feb 1832 d: 11 Mar 1832
.... 3 Charles Henry Pearce b: 06 May 1833 d: 01 Nov 1879
.... 3 Ann Elizabeth Pearce b: 01 Feb 1835 in Balt Co d: 20 Sep 1911 in New Madison
.... 3 Thomas Riley Pearce b: 02 Oct 1838 in New Madison d: 21 Apr 1925 in Darke Co, Ohio
.... 3 Rachel Elizabeth Pearce b: 08 Apr 1841 d: 28 Jun 1888
.... 3 Levi Wilson Pearce b: 12 May 1843 in New Madison d: 30 Jun 1913
.... 3 Amanda Jane Pearce b: 06 Jul 1846
.... 3 Francis Marion Pearce b: 28 Jan 1849 d: 08 May 1913 in Greenville, Ohio
...... 2 William Curtis b: 25 Aug 1805 in MLM
.... +Sarah Wisner
.... 3 Rachel Curtis b: 1847
.... 3 Mary Curtis b: 1849
...... 2 Eli Curtis b: 17 Aug 1807 in Monkton d: 07 Oct 1876 in MLM

.... +Frances Merryman b: 1809 d: 26 Feb 1887 in Balt Co
.... 3 Mary Ann Shepard Curtis b: 03 Jun 1845 d: Feb 1847
.... 3 William Curtis b: 17 Dec 1846 d: Apr 1847
.... 3 George Worthington Curtis b: 01 Mar 1848 d: 23 May 1899
.... 3 Charles Merryman Curtis b: 27 Jan 1851 d: 24 Apr 1897
...... 2 Ann Curtis b: 1808
.... +David Hoover b: 02 May 1831
...... 2 Eliza Curtis b: 17 Jun 1815

Descendants of Lt Richard Hutchins

1 Lt Richard Hutchins b: 21 Jun 1741 in MLM, Sweet Air d: 29 Jul 1826 in Harford Co.,Maryland
. +Philiszana Standeford Standiford b: 1741 in Baltimore Co. , Md. d: 23 Dec 1819 in Harford Co., Maryland
...... 2 Elizabeth Ann Hutchins b: 1768 in Maryland d: 1851
.... +John Slade b: 1766 in Verdant Valley, Harf Co d: 10 Jul 1855 in Verdant Valley, Harf Co
.... 3 Sally Ann Slade b: 14 Sep 1805 in Verdant Valley d: 25 Jun 1866 in MLM, LOT20, Houck`s Mill Rd
.... +Richard MaGaw b: 1792 d: 1845
.... 3 Amanda Zana Slade b: 1807 in Verdant Valley, Harf Co d: 01 Apr 1887 in Verdant Valley, Harf Co
.... +Maj Charles William Howard b: 1800 d: 1851
...... 2 Sarah Hutchins b: 1771 in Maryland d: 12 Feb 1848
.... +John MCGAW b: 1769 d: 1818
...... 2 Thomas Hutchins b: 25 Jul 1773 in Atlanta Hall , Monkton Md d: Sep 1847 in Houck Mill Rd, Monkton Md
.... +Lovisah Hope b: 1783 in Hope Farm, Bethel, Harford Co d: 17 Feb 1844 in Houck Mill Rd, Monkton Md
.... 3 Elizabeth Ann Hutchins b: 1804 in Monkton, MD, Baltimore Co d: 26 Oct 1872 in Monkton , Balt Co, MD
.... +John Wiley b: 30 Mar 1790 in Norrisville, Harford Co d: 17 Jan 1868 in Houcks Mill Rd, Monkton , MD
.... 3 Hannah Hutchins b: 1806 d: 14 Oct 1880
.... 3 Anna Hutchins b: 1809 d: 25 Sep 1884
.... +Harrison Shaw b: 05 Mar 1815 d: 28 Dec 1885
.... 3 Amanda Zana Hutchins b: 19 Aug 1811 in Atlanta Hall, MLM d: 22 Sep 1894 in Norrisville, Maryland
.... +Dr. Josiah Payne b: 1816 d: 04 Feb 1839 in Black Horse
.... *2nd Husband of Amanda Zana Hutchins:
.... +John Stevenson Norris b: 30 Aug 1801 in Norrisville d: 03 Jun 1879 in Norrisville
.... 3 Richard Hutchins b: 1813 d: 1887
.... +Mary Susan Bradenbaugh b: 14 May 1818 d: 18 Mar 1901
.... 3 Lovisia Hutchins b: 1818 d: 14 Jan 1906
.... +John Bradford b: 1813 d: 1887
.... 3 Nicholas Hutchins b: 1821 d: 19 Mar 1895
.... +Martha E Nelson b: 22 Jul 1829 in Bishops Lott, MLM d: 23 Oct 1860 in MLM
.... 3 Mary Hope Hutchins b: 1822 d: 1883
.... +NATHAN Nelson b: 1819 d: 1893
.... *2nd Husband of Mary Hope Hutchins:
.... +Nathan Nelson b: Abt. 1818
.... 3 Sarah McGaw Hutchins b: 29 Jul 1815 d: 21 Dec 1879
.... +William Nelson Hughes b: 1814 d: 10 Apr 1897
...... 2 Nicholas Hutchins b: 1775 in Maryland d: 24 May 1845
...... 2 William Hutchins b: 16 Aug 1779 in Baltimore, Co., Maryland d: 15 Apr 1860
.... +Mary Rampley b: 02 May 1782 in Harford Co., Md. d: 12 Sep 1862
.... 3 Zana Ann Hutchins b: 28 Jan 1808 in Baltimore Co. d: 17 Dec 1876 in Balt,Co.
.... +John Bacon Holmes b: 21 Sep 1801 in Baltimore Co. d: 08 Nov 1882 in Monkton
.... 3 Sarah Hutchins b: 09 Nov 1809 in Harford Co. d: 30 Apr 1878 in Balt,Co.
.... +John Perdue b: 29 Jun 1804 d: 1874 in St. James
.... 3 Elizabeth Hutchins b: 1811 d: 1828
.... 3 John Standiford Hutchins b: 1814 d: 1881
.... +Mary Jane Hawkins b: 1830 d: 1903
.... 3 Richard McGaw Hutchins b: 1817 d: 1884
.... 3 Jemima Hutchins b: 1818 in Atlanta Hall, Monkton, Md. d: 1891 in Columbus, Ill.
.... +Thomas C. Pearce b: 1810 in Mt Joy d: 1891
.... 3 Mary Ann Hutchins b: 1822 d: 1889
.... +Alfred Selman Garrison b: 09 Oct 1820 d: 02 Sep 1884
...... 2 Hannah Hutchins b: 1783 in Maryland d: 1833
.... +William Nelson b: 1782 d: 1851
.... 3 Sarah Nelson b: 1805 d: 1865
.... +William Glenn
.... 3 Elizabeth Bowen Nelson b: 1810 d: 1894
.... +Robert Nelson b: 1811 d: 1884
.... 3 Nicholas Hutchins Nelson b: 15 Dec 1812 d: 1874

.... +Hannah Ann Hope b: 06 Sep 1815 d: 09 May 1857 in Bethel

Descendants of Josiah Shepperd

1 Josiah Shepperd b: 1762 d: 1858
...... 2 Elias Shepperd b: Abt. 1797
.... +Mary Bell b: Abt. 1800
...... 2 John Shepperd b: Abt. 1798
.... +Elizabeth Pearce b: 24 Apr 1798 d: 25 May 1843
.... 3 Ann Elizabeth Shepperd
.... 3 Rachel Rebecca Shepperd
.... 3 John William Shepperd
...... 2 James Shepperd b: 1798 in Baltimore County d: 1851
.... +Rachel Talbott Pearce b: 24 Apr 1798 in Baltimore County d: 19 Sep 1861
.... 3 James Albert Shepperd b: 1840 in Baltimore County d: 1909
.... +Margaret Jane Noland b: Jun 1844 in Pa. d: 1925
.... 4 James Matthew Shepperd b: 1866 in Shepperd's Corner, Monkton, MD. d: 1951
.... +Susan Elizabeth Henderson b: 1872 d: 1939
.... 5 Eva Leona Shepperd b: 27 Nov 1893 d: 20 Jul 1975 in Westley Chapel
.... +Streett Baldwin Fogal b: 01 Feb 1888 d: 04 Apr 1969
.... 5 James Albert Shepperd b: 24 Oct 1896 d: 30 Jul 1972
.... +Gladys Lucia Gaines b: 24 Jun 1896
.... 5 Amelia Elizabeth Shepperd b: 19 Nov 1899
.... +Walter Norris Billingsley b: 28 Jul 1900
.... 5 Charles Pearce Shepperd b: 07 Jul 1901 in Maryland
.... +Anne Olivia Meredith b: 31 Mar 1905 in Maryland d: 16 Mar 1960 in Graystone Rd., White Hall
.... 5 Leonard Edward Shepperd b: 23 Sep 1902
.... +Josephine Miller b: 17 Feb 1904
.... 5 Margaret Olivia Shepperd b: 08 Dec 1903
.... 5 Josephine Millen Shepperd b: 17 Feb 1904
.... 5 Arthur Henderson Shepperd b: 06 Feb 1907 d: 21 Jun 1978 in Loudan Cem
.... +Florence Disney
.... 4 Margaret Shepperd b: 1869 in Balt,Co.
.... 4 Sarah Shepperd b: 1871 in Balt,Co.
.... 4 Francis Shepperd b: 1874 in Balt,Co.
.... 4 John W. Shepperd b: 1876 in Balt,Co.
.... 4 Wilmer Daniel Shepperd b: 30 Oct 1877 in Balt,Co. d: 23 Jul 1947
.... +Mary Alice Watson b: 05 Jul 1880 in Baltimore City d: 04 Jun 1944 in Catonsville, Md.
.... 5 John Carroll Shepperd b: 23 Jul 1900 in Balt,Co. d: 06 Aug 1959
.... +Eleanor Richardson Price b: 21 Aug 1902 in Balt,Co.
.... 5 Eleanor Margaret Shepperd b: 21 Aug 1902 in Baltimore County, Maryland
.... +Charles Coale b: Abt. 1900
.... 5 Greenbury Pearce Shepperd b: 13 May 1904 in Baltimore County, Maryland
.... 5 George Leon Shepperd b: 21 Jun 1905 in Balt,Co.
.... 5 Alice Shepperd b: Abt. 1907 in Balt,Co.
.... 5 Wilmer Thomas Shepperd b: 06 Aug 1910 in Balt,Co. d: 1991
.... 5 Dorothy Shepperd b: Abt. 1912 in Balt,Co.
.... 5 Catharine Virginia Mota Shepperd b: 16 Feb 1914 in Balt,Co.
.... 5 Neal Shepperd b: 09 Oct 1917
.... 4 Greenberry Shepperd b: 1880 in Balt,Co.
...... 2 Mary Shepperd b: 1803
...... 2 Josias Shepperd b: Abt. 1800
...... 2 Elizabeth Shepperd b: Abt. 1802
.... +Asbel Price
...... 2 Sarah A. Shepperd b: 1808 in Monkton, lot 57 d: 1899 in St Johns, Baldwin, Md.
.... +William Pearce b: Abt. 1800

Descendants of Luke Wyle

1 Luke Wyle b: 29 Mar 1740 in St. John's, Baltimore Co. d: Bef. 1781
. +Cassandra Carr b: Abt. 1742
...... 2 William Benjamin Wyle b: Abt. 1760 d: in Garrard Co. Ky. about 1800
.... +Sarah Royston b: 1758
...... 2 Comfort Rebecca Wyle b: 1760 in Harford Co. d: 1829
.... +Joseph Pearce b: 1752 in Towson d: 09 Feb 1829 in Maryland
.... 3 William Crawford Pearce b: Abt. 1798 d: 17 Dec 1823
.... +Eleanor Johnson b: 29 Sep 1799 d: 09 Apr 1887
.... 4 David Johnson Pearce b: 21 Jul 1818 in Gorsuch Mills, Baltimore Co. d: 01 Feb 1904 in Phoenix, Clynmaria Cm.
.... +Ellen S. Ensor b: 26 Dec 1821 d: 19 Jan 1896 in Phoenix, Clynmalira Cm.
.... 4 Mary Elizabeth Pearce b: 25 Feb 1820
.... 4 Sarah Johnson Pearce b: 05 Mar 1822 in MLM d: 22 Mar 1909
.... +John Brandon Slade b: 24 Apr 1819 in MLM d: 24 Feb 1852
.... 3 Luke Wiley Pearce b: Abt. 1784 d: 1848
.... 3 John A Pearce b: 1790
.... 3 Joseph Pearce b: Apr 1795 in Mt.Joy 7th Dist, Balt. Co., Md. d: 22 Aug 1870 in Clynmalira
.... +Mary Ann Pearce b: 24 Feb 1802 in Mt. Joy, Baltimore County d: 16 Jan 1899 in Clynmalira
.... 4 Elizabeth Pearce b: 1819
.... +Nicholas Shock b: Abt. 1815
.... 4 John Cole Pearce b: 30 Dec 1820 d: 24 Mar 1890 in Towson,Md. Prospect Hill
.... +Sarah Achia Wood b: 01 May 1836 d: 23 Jun 1930 in Towson,Md. Prospect Hill
.... 4 Margaret E Pearce b: 14 Mar 1822 in Clynmalira, Monkton, Md. d: 28 Feb 1884 in Shane, Md.
.... +Arthur Shane b: 07 Jan 1816 d: 19 Oct 1876 in Shane, Md.
.... 4 Mary J. Pearce b: 1830 in Maryland d: 20 Jun 1908 in Maryland
.... +Elijah Chilcoat b: 22 Jul 1831 in Maryland
.... 4 Rachel Pearce b: 1831
.... +Unknown Canoles b: 1830
.... 4 Rufus T. Pearce b: 1831
.... +Miranda M. Cox
.... 4 Eliza Moore Pearce b: 02 Sep 1833 in Baltimore County d: 16 Nov 1902 in Maryland
.... +William Parlett Corbin b: 03 Oct 1829 in Baltimore County d: 20 Jan 1869 in Maryland
.... 4 Lavinia Pearce b: 1835
.... +Riley Seth Williamson b: 1833
.... 4 Zany Amanda Pearce b: 1838 d: in Columbus Ohio
.... +John J. Fogal b: 1830 d: in Columbus, Ohio
.... 4 Greenbury Arpheus Pearce b: 23 Jul 1840 in Baltimore d: 09 Mar 1915 in Waugh UM, Glen Arm, Md.
.... +Martha Jane Simms b: 13 May 1847 in Maryland d: 05 Apr 1927 in Long Green
.... 4 Ruth T. Pearce b: 1841
.... 4 Eleanor Ella Pearce b: 1845 d: 22 May 1877 in Towson
.... +John E. Sheridan b: Abt. 1844
.... 4 William Silas Pearce b: 14 Dec 1848 d: 16 Dec 1912 in St. Marys P.E. Baltimore, Md.
.... +Sarah Elizabeth Francis b: 1850 d: 15 Oct 1922 in St. Marys P.E. Baltimore, Md.
.... 3 Rachel Talbott Pearce b: 24 Apr 1798 in Baltimore County d: 19 Sep 1861
.... +James Shepperd b: 1798 in Baltimore County d: 1851
.... 4 James Albert Shepperd b: 1840 in Baltimore County d: 1909
.... +Margaret Jane Noland b: Jun 1844 in Pa. d: 1925
.... 3 Elizabeth Pearce b: 24 Apr 1798 d: 25 May 1843
.... +John Shepperd b: Abt. 1798
.... 4 Ann Elizabeth Shepperd
.... 4 Rachel Rebecca Shepperd
.... 4 John William Shepperd
.... 3 Greenberry Wyle Pearce b: 28 Jan 1800 in Clynmalira d: 25 Nov 1855 in New Madison, ohio
.... +Sarah Curtis b: 16 Sep 1803 in MLM d: 19 Jan 1878 in New Madison, Ohio
.... 4 William Crawford Pearce b: 04 Nov 1827 in Balt Co d: 1850
.... 4 Mary C Pearce b: 17 Nov 1829 d: 1850

.... 4 John Westley Pearce b: 15 Feb 1832 d: 11 Mar 1832
.... 4 Charles Henry Pearce b: 06 May 1833 d: 01 Nov 1879
.... 4 Ann Elizabeth Pearce b: 01 Feb 1835 in Balt Co d: 20 Sep 1911 in New Madison
.... 4 Thomas Riley Pearce b: 02 Oct 1838 in New Madison d: 21 Apr 1925 in Darke Co, Ohio
.... 4 Rachel Elizabeth Pearce b: 08 Apr 1841 d: 28 Jun 1888
.... 4 Levi Wilson Pearce b: 12 May 1843 in New Madison d: 30 Jun 1913
.... 4 Amanda Jane Pearce b: 06 Jul 1846
.... 4 Francis Marion Pearce b: 28 Jan 1849 d: 08 May 1913 in Greenville, Ohio
...... 2 Greensbury Wyle b: Abt. 1762
.... +Rachel Pearce
.... 3 Comford Wiley
...... 2 Walter Wyle b: Abt. 1762
...... 2 Vincent Wiley b: Abt. 1763
.... +Sarah Sutton b: 28 Jul 1749 in Baltimore Co. d: 24 Jan 1789
.... 3 Thomas Sutton Wiley b: 31 Aug 1783 in Maryland
.... 3 William Wiley b: 20 Oct 1785 in Maryland
.... 3 John Stephenson Wiley b: 05 Jun 1789 in Maryland
.... 3 Sarah Wyle b: Abt. 1776 in Maryland
.... +John W Dunnuck b: Abt. 1780 in Baltimore Co.
.... 4 Joseph Sutton Dunnuck b: 22 Dec 1797 d: 11 Apr 1856
.... 4 Luke Wyle Dunnuck b: 22 Nov 1799 in St James
...... 2 John Wyle b: Abt. 1763
...... 2 Joshua Wyle b: Abt. 1766
.... +Rachel Gallion b: Abt. 1770
.... 3 Andrew Wyle b: 1771 d: 21 Sep 1822 in Maryland
.... +Sarah Dunnuck b: Abt. 1781 in Baltimore Co.
.... 4 Joseph Dunnuck Wyle b: 11 Oct 1796
.... 4 Joshua C Wiley b: Abt. 1802
...... 2 Hannah Wyle b: Abt. 1770
...... 2 Mary Wyle b: Abt. 1772
...... 2 Esther Wyle b: Abt. 1773
.... +John Stevenson

Dr. Edward Johnson

Dr. Edward Johnson, was Mayor of Baltimore City and a large land owner. He patented "Mt Joy" consisting of 2,261 acres in 1792. This land stretched from Parkton to Monkton. Jonathan Plowman, a wealthy business man in Baltimore held extensive leases on land in this area before the Revolutionary War. Jonathan's daughter Anne, married Dr. Johnson's son Edward Jr. Dr. Johnson was appointed guardian for Plowman's children after his death. A court case evolved with the Norris's over the ownership of some of the leased land that was purchased after 1782. John Norris had acted as an agent for Johnson in managing the leased land for Johnson. Edward Norris worked with James Calder in some of his survey work and had claim to some of the land along the present Stablersville Road. George Chalk Norris, son of Edward, held title to the farm later bought by the Stabler family. Jonathan Plowman, the third, sold off parcels of land to later settlers in the area. Many families in the White Hall and Parkton areas descend from the Plowmans.

Moses Collett

Moses Collett was the ancestor of many White Hall residents. Moses born in 1725 married Elizabeth Wiley. Son Stephen Collett married Ann Gorsuch, Rachel Collett married Josiah Sparks, and Moses Junior married Rachel Cross. Rachel Collett Sparks had eight children. Rachel Elizabeth Sparks married William Carlin who lived near Black Horse, Ruth Sparks married William Pearce and Daniel Sparks married Rachel Curtis. David Sparks and Loring Sparks of Upperco are descendant from this marriage. Mary Ann Pearce, daughter of William, married Joseph Pearce and their daughter, Margaret E. Pearce, married Arthur Shane. Josiah Sparks Pearce married Elizabeth Ann Wright and their great-grandson Wendell Russell Pearce lives on the old Pearce property on the White Hall Road. Wendell Pearce, an outstanding baseball and softball player and teammate of pitcher, William 'Billy" Nelson. Wendall and Billy were members of a state championship softball team. Moses Collett Junior and Rachel Cross were the ancestors of Harford County Genealogist, William Smithson.

William Johnson

William Johnson owned " Johnson's Choice", a 220-acre section, located on the north and south side of White Hall Road. William's daughter Elizabeth married John V. Hunter and two of their children married Slades. Annie Hunter married Christopher Columbus Slade and Charles Hunter married Mary Slade. Part of the farm on the North side of White Hall Road was later owned by Ross Almony and is currently owed by Owen and Ann Bricker.

Gist Vaughn

Gist Vaughn surveyed a large tract of land in White Hall east of Hunter Mill Road. Gist was a Captain in Baltimore County Militia in August 1776 and a Major in Col. Thomas Gist's Upper Battalion in 1777. His son Abraham Vaughn married Rachel Bosley and Elizabeth Vaughn married Peter Grub Hunter. Elizabeth Vaughn Hunter's children married into many families in the White Hall area. William Hunter married Rachel Perdue, Ann Hunter married John Wise Jr., John Hunter married Elizabeth Johnson, Thomas Hunter married Elizabeth Cameron, Peter Grubb Hunter married Mary Jane Elliott and Elizabeth Hunter married William Henry Slade. Thomas V. Hunter ran a farm machinery business and John Wise operated the paper mill in White Hall. John V. Hunter's daughter Annie Hunter married Christopher Columbus Slade. The children of this marriage included Elizabeth Slade who married Andrew Leroy Anderson, James Elmer Slade who married Nellie Ray Almony and Ella May Slade who married Russel Calvin Shaw.

Descendants of Jonathon Plowman

1 Jonathon Plowman b: 1734 in England d: 22 May 1776
. +Rebecca Arnold b: Abt. 1735 m: 07 Oct 1762 in Calvert Co. d: 1780
...... 2 Rebecca Plowman b: Abt. 1760
.... +Robert Ballard b: in VA m: 13 Jul 1780
.... 3 John Ballard
.... 3 Henry Ballard
.... 3 William Ballard
.... 3 Edward Ballard
...... 2 Ann Plowman b: Abt. 1761 in Baltimore d: 15 Nov 1795
.... +Edward Jr Johnson b: Abt. 1760 in Baltimore m: 31 Mar 1791 d: Bef. 1838 in Baltimore
.... 3 Edward Johnson b: 29 Dec 1791
.... 3 William Johnson b: 04 Feb 1793 in Baltimore d: 27 Nov 1813 in Baltimore
.... 3 Marie Caroline Johnson b: Abt. 1794 in Baltimore
.... +George E. Franklin b: Abt. 1792 m: 14 Jun 1848 in Baltimore , Md.
...... 2 Jonathon Plowman b: 23 Dec 1754 in Owings Mills d: 1790 in Baltimore
.... +Hannah Loveall b: 12 Jan 1772 in Baltimore County m: 21 Feb 1785
.... 3 Jonathon Plowman b: 13 Dec 1792 in St James d: 1850 in 214 Acres Mt Joy, Aj Weirs
.... +Hannah Unknown b: 1800
.... 4 Susanna Plowman b: 1825 d: 1895
.... +Jarrett Nelson b: 1819 d: 1900
.... 4 Mary Ann Plowman b: 1827 d: 1905
.... +John Hutchins Nelson b: 1829 d: 1891
.... 4 Martha Plowman b: 1834
.... +Joshua E. Rutledge b: 15 Oct 1819 in Maryland d: 12 Dec 1896
.... 4 Henry Ballard Plowman b: 28 Nov 1835 in 7th District d: 14 Aug 1900 in White Hall
.... +Cornelia Victoria Slade b: 28 Apr 1852 in 7th District m: 14 Feb 1872 d: 05 Dec 1922 in White Hall
.... 4 Charles E. Plowman b: Oct 1850 in Balt,Co. d: 27 Feb 1945 in Parkton, Maryland
.... +Jane Elizabeth Bond b: 28 Sep 1861 in Bond Road m: 06 Jan 1892 d: 27 Oct 1926 in Parkton, Maryland
...... 2 Mary Plowman b: 1765 d: 1799
.... +William McLaughlin m: 20 Feb 1787 in 11 BA 10 d: 10 Feb 1795 in Sheriff of Baltimore Co.

Descendants of Gist Vaughn

1 Gist Vaughn b: Abt. 1732 d: 1800
. +Rachel Norris b: 21 Jul 1739 m: 02 Mar 1769 d: in White Hall, Maryland
...... 2 Rachel Vaughan b: 25 Jun 1770
...... 2 John Vaughan b: 27 Nov 1771
...... 2 Abraham Vaughan b: 27 Oct 1773
.... +Rachel Bosley b: Abt. 1761 m: 15 Dec 1802
...... 2 Benjamin Vaughan b: 22 Jul 1775 d: 20 Apr 1806
...... 2 Elizabeth Vaughan b: 07 Mar 1777 in Harford Co. d: 05 Jul 1850 in White Hall, Maryland
.... +Peter Grubb Hunter b: 1775 m: 24 Feb 1796 d: 04 Nov 1838 in Wiseburg Cm.
.... 3 William Hunter b: 22 May 1797 in White Hall, Maryland d: 1850 in Baltimore County, Maryland
.... +Rachel Perdue b: Abt. 1798 d: in Baltimore County, Maryland
.... 3 Rachel Hunter b: 1799 in White Hall, Maryland d: in MLM lot 58
.... +Labon Perdue b: 12 Jul 1791 in MLM lot 90, 91, 92 d: in MLM lot 58
.... 3 Ann Hunter b: 1801 in Baltimore Co. d: 10 May 1868
.... +John Jr Wise b: 1798 in Maryland m: Abt. 1824 d: 18 Nov 1856
.... 3 John V Hunter b: 1804 d: 25 Oct 1879
.... +Elizabeth Johnson b: 1820 d: 1896
.... 3 Thomas Vaughan Hunter b: 18 Jul 1807 in White Hall, Maryland d: 05 Mar 1889 in White Hall, Maryland, Vernon Cm.
.... +Mary Cameron b: 1822 in Maryland d: 17 Dec 1904 in White Hall, Maryland
.... 3 Pleasant Hunter b: 23 Sep 1809 in White Hall, Maryland d: 02 May 1894 in Wiseburg Inn, Wiseburg, Maryland
.... +Margaret Smyser b: 03 Mar 1819 d: 25 Feb 1893
.... 3 Peter Grubb Hunter b: 1812 in Balt,Co. d: 11 Oct 1861 in Balt,Co.
.... +Mary Jane Elliott b: 25 Aug 1813 in Balt,Co. d: 03 Mar 1884 in Balt,Co.
.... 3 Elizabeth Hunter b: 1816 in White Hall d: in MLM
.... +William Henry Slade b: 1807 in MLM d: 04 Aug 1866 in MLM
.... 3 Frances Hunter b: 1818 d: 01 Dec 1879
.... +John George Belt b: 26 Aug 1822
...... 2 Gist Vaughan b: 07 Sep 1780
.... +Rebecca Unknown b: 1810
.... 3 Rachel Vaughan b: 1842
.... 3 Cathrine Vaughan b: 1844
.... 3 John Vaughan b: 1846
.... 3 Francis Vaughan b: 1847
.... 3 Pleasant Vaughn b: 1850

Descendants of Moses Collett

1 Moses Collett b: 1750 in Collett's Habitation d: 1836
. +Rachel Cross b: Abt. 1755
...... 2 Elizabeth Collett b: Abt. 1785
.... +William Sullivan b: Abt. 1785 m: 1802 in Baltimore Co., MD
.... 3 [2] Benson C. Sullivan b: 1810 in Ohio
.... +[1] Rebecca Ann Royston b: 1818 in Maryland
...... 2 Poly Collett b: 30 Nov 1783 in St James
...... 2 [3] Matilda Ann Collett b: 15 Nov 1785 in White Hall, Md. d: 29 Nov 1867 in Long Valley, Maryland Line
.... +[4] David Sampson b: 31 May 1784 in New Market, Md. m: 11 Feb 1841 d: 24 Aug 1862 in Long Valley, Maryland Line
...... 2 Jemima Collett b: 03 Nov 1787
...... 2 Rachel Collett b: 03 Sep 1789
.... +John Royston b: 1790 in Baltimore Co. m: 01 Oct 1816 d: in 6 TH District
.... 3 Thomas E. Royston b: Abt. 1819
.... 3 Moses Royston b: Abt. 1817 d: in Carroll Co., Md.
.... 3 [1] Rebecca Ann Royston b: 1818 in Maryland
.... +[2] Benson C. Sullivan b: 1810 in Ohio
.... 3 Caleb W. Royston b: 1821 in Maryland d: 06 Oct 1896 in Stiltz
.... +Sarah Ann Royston b: 1827 in Maryland m: 11 Jan 1848 d: 02 Oct 1876
.... 3 Rachel E. Royston b: Abt. 1824
.... 3 Edward C. Royston b: 1825 in Maryland d: in Buckeysville, Md.
.... +Mary E. Unknown b: 1833 in Maryland
.... 3 Priscilla Royston b: 1829
.... +Michael Baublitz b: Abt. 1828 d: in 7th District
...... 2 John Collett b: 05 Aug 1791
.... +Keziah b: 1800
.... 3 Cathrine Collett b: 1843
.... 3 Jemima Collett b: 1845
...... 2 Ann Collett b: 06 Sep 1792
...... 2 Susanna Collett b: 16 May 1794 in 7th District, Baltimore Co. d: 10 Jun 1856 in Stablersville
.... +George Stabler b: 26 Jun 1794 in Stablersville m: 1831 in Stablersville d: 03 Feb 1864 in Stablersville
.... 3 Henry Stabler b: 05 Jun 1823 in Stablersville d: 13 Oct 1904 in Stablersville
.... +Caroline Matilda Buck b: 1825 in Maryland m: 10 May 1849 d: 05 Dec 1894
.... 3 Sarah Elizabeth Stabler b: 25 Aug 1824 in Stablersville d: 16 Dec 1897 in Gorsuch Mills
.... +Samuel McClung Billingslea b: 26 Dec 1814 in Maryland m: 1841 d: 08 Jun 1892 in Gorsuch Mills
.... 3 Moses C Stabler b: 27 Dec 1828 in Stablersville d: 09 Apr 1835
.... 3 Rachel Ann Stabler b: 21 Jun 1831 in Stablersville, Maryland d: 14 Feb 1882
.... +Westley Billingslea b: Abt. 1809
.... *2nd Husband of Rachel Ann Stabler:
.... +Westley Royston Cuddy b: 21 Jan 1828 in Baltimore Co. m: 24 Jun 1849 d: 10 Oct 1905
.... 3 Rebecca Ruth Stabler b: 1836 d: 31 Dec 1836
.... 3 George Washington Stabler b: 04 Jul 1841 d: 12 May 1911 in Huron, Atchison, Kansas
...... 2 Moses Collett b: 03 Jul 1796
.... +Cathrine Stiltz b: 1807
.... 3 Margaret Collett b: 1843
.... 3 Ann Collett b: 1852
.... 3 Rachel Ann Collett b: Abt. 1854
.... 3 Moses Collett b: 06 Feb 1842 in Baltimore , Co. Md. d: 11 Oct 1911 in Baltimore , Co. Md.
.... +Mary Jane Collett b: 1842 in Baltimore , Co. Md. d: 1882 in Baltimore , Co. Md., Wiseburg UM
.... 3 Nicholas Collett b: Abt. 1840
.... 3 Thomas Collett
...... 2 [3] Matilda Ann Collett b: 15 Nov 1785 in White Hall, Md. d: 29 Nov 1867 in Long Valley, Maryland Line
.... +[4] David Sampson b: 31 May 1784 in New Market, Md. m: 11 Feb 1841 d: 24 Aug 1862 in Long Valley, Maryland Line

Descendants of William Hunter

1 William Hunter b: Abt. 1730 in Pa. d: 1785 in Balt Co
. +Frances Grubb b: Abt. 1730 in Chester Co., Pa.
...... 2 Ann Rachel Hunter b: Abt. 1760
.... +Darby Ensor b: Abt. 1760 m: 30 Nov 1792 d: 26 Jan 1825
.... 3 Sarah Hunter Ensor b: 1795 in Maryland d: 1841
.... +Luke Gorsuch Ensor b: 1776 in Ensor, Manor m: 04 Apr 1820 d: 1851 in Ensor Manor
...... 2 John Hunter b: Abt. 1762
...... 2 George Hunter b: Abt. 1764
...... 2 William Hunter b: 1765 d: 1835 in Reisterstown, MD
.... +Ann Unknown
.... 3 John Hunter b: Abt. 1790
.... 3 Peter Hunter b: Abt. 1792
.... 3 Horace William Hunter b: Abt. 1794
.... 3 Frances Hunter b: Abt. 1796
.... +Lewis Butler
...... 2 Thomas Hunter b: Abt. 1766
.... +Ann Gwyn
...... 2 Nathaniel Hunter b: 17 May 1767 in Baltimore , Md.
.... +Rachel Bosley b: Abt. 1765 in Baltimore , Md. m: 01 Feb 1804
...... 2 Peter Grubb Hunter b: 1775 d: 04 Nov 1838 in Wiseburg Cm.
.... +Esther Scott m: 30 Nov 1792
.... 3 Curtis Grubb Hunter b: 1793 d: 1822
...... *2nd Wife of Peter Grubb Hunter:
.... +Elizabeth Vaughan b: 07 Mar 1777 in Harford Co. m: 24 Feb 1796 d: 05 Jul 1850 in White Hall, Maryland
.... 3 William Hunter b: 22 May 1797 in White Hall, Maryland d: 1850 in Baltimore County, Maryland
.... +Rachel Perdue b: Abt. 1798 d: in Baltimore County, Maryland
.... 3 Rachel Hunter b: 1799 in White Hall, Maryland d: in MLM lot 58
.... +Labon Perdue b: 12 Jul 1791 in MLM lot 90, 91, 92 d: in MLM lot 58
.... 3 Ann Hunter b: 1801 in Baltimore Co. d: 10 May 1868
.... +John Jr Wise b: 1798 in Maryland m: Abt. 1824 d: 18 Nov 1856
.... 3 John V Hunter b: 1804 d: 25 Oct 1879
.... +Elizabeth Johnson b: 1820 d: 1896
.... 3 Thomas Vaughan Hunter b: 18 Jul 1807 in White Hall, Maryland d: 05 Mar 1889 in White Hall, Maryland, Vernon Cm.
.... +Mary Cameron b: 1822 in Maryland d: 17 Dec 1904 in White Hall, Maryland
.... 3 Pleasant Hunter b: 23 Sep 1809 in White Hall, Maryland d: 02 May 1894 in Wiseburg Inn, Wiseburg, Maryland
.... +Margaret Smyser b: 03 Mar 1819 d: 25 Feb 1893
.... 3 Peter Grubb Hunter b: 1812 in Balt,Co. d: 11 Oct 1861 in Balt,Co.
.... +Mary Jane Elliott b: 25 Aug 1813 in Balt,Co. d: 03 Mar 1884 in Balt,Co.
.... 3 Elizabeth Hunter b: 1816 in White Hall d: in MLM
.... +William Henry Slade b: 1807 in MLM d: 04 Aug 1866 in MLM
.... 3 Frances Hunter b: 1818 d: 01 Dec 1879
.... +John George Belt b: 26 Aug 1822

HEREFORD FARM HOUSE

The Historic Merryman Farm is located just south of the town of Hereford between the York road and I -83.. The original 1714 deed covered about 1,000 acres including most of the present town of Hereford. The main house was built in several sections over the years and the Merryman graveyard is located on a knoll just north of the buildings. Outlines of original slave quarters could still be seen in the yard to the west of the main house. **John Merryman** was a Magistrate and Justis of the Peace in1778. He was an Ensign in the Baltimore Town Battalion in and became Captain June 4, 1779. John was Judge of the Orphans Court of Baltimore County in 1784.
During the 1950s, George Roach's family operated a dairy farm on the property. Later the original house was damaged by fire and the new owner replaced the structure with the present house. Well known attorney Peter Angaols, now operates a horse breeding operation on the farm.
Benjamin Merryman also owned several large partials East of Hereford.
Abraham Hicks was a 1st Lt. in Capt. Cummins' Company Upper Battalion Aug.1777.

Elizabeth Miller and **John Miller** were large land owners North of Hereford in the 1798 Particular Assessments. She also was involved in the evaluation of confiscated proprietary reserve lands. **John Mays** descendants were very influential in the Hereford area. John Mays owner of Kingdeen Nursery, continues the Mays presence in the area. **John Foster** was an early settler to Baltimore Co., first settling on land near the Chesapeake. His descendant **Vernon Foster,** a well known farmer near Hereford, still owns a part of the original Foster lands. Vernon served in World War 11 as a Tank Commander, in France and Germany, under Gen. George Patton

Baltimore County Pioneers- 7th District

Descendants of John Merryman

```
1 John Merryman  b: 1703 in Balt Co  d: 13 Aug 1777 in Piney Hill, Hereford, Clover Hill
.  +Sarah Rogers  b: 1708 in Balt Co  m: 30 Dec 1725 in St. Pauls Parrish  d: 03 Mar 1775 in Piney Hill, Merryman Cm.
...... 2 Nicholas Merryman  b: 11 Dec 1726 in Balt,Co.  d: 14 Jul 1801
.........  +Elizabeth Jane Ensor  b: 29 Jan 1724/25 in Baltimore County, Maryland  d: 28 Aug 1802
............. 3 Jane Merryman  b: Abt. 1754  d: 1819
............. 3 Mary Merryman  b: Abt. 1756
.................  +Dennis Bond  b: Abt. 1752
............. 3 Sarah Merryman  b: Abt. 1757
.................  +John Orrick  b: Abt. 1755
............. 3 Ann Merryman  b: 08 Nov 1782
............. 3 Elijah Merryman  b: Abt. 1750  d: 1799
.................  +Frances Ensor  b: 14 Dec 1757
............. 3 Micajah Merryman  b: Abt. 1752  d: 07 Jun 1842
.................  +Mary Ensor  b: 20 Nov 1759  m: 1780
............. 3 Nicholas Merryman  b: 1751  d: 1832
.................  +Nancy Ann Merryman
............. *2nd Wife of Nicholas Merryman:
.................  +Deborah Ensor  b: Abt. 1761  m: 1778
............. 3 Elizabeth Merryman  b: 28 Aug 1750  d: 23 Sep 1784
.................  +[1] Elijah Bosley  b: 28 Mar 1740  m: 29 Jun 1769  d: 29 Aug 1841 in St. James
...... 2 Sarah Merryman  b: 12 May 1729 in Baltimore Co., MD.  d: in Kentucky
..........  +Robert Wilmont  b: Abt. 1726  m: 15 Dec 1748 in St. Paul's Parrish  d: 1773 in Maryland
............. 3 John Wilmont
............. 3 William Wilmont
............. 3 Robert Wilmont
............. 3 Richard Wilmont
............. 3 Benjamin Wilmont
............. 3 Sarah Wilmont
.................  +Benjamin Talbott  b: 11 Feb 1749/50  m: 24 Aug 1777  d: 05 Jan 1816
............. 3 Eleanor Wilmont
............. 3 Mary Wilmont
............. 3 Ruth Wilmont
...... 2 Mary Merryman  b: 1732 in Balt Co  d: 04 Feb 1774
..........  +Abraham Ensor  b: 05 Feb 1726/27 in Baltimore Co., Md., St. Paul's  m: 30 Jan 1749/50 in St. Pauls  d: 08 Jul 1797 in Sparks
............. 3 John Ensor  b: 1752 in Baltimore, Co. Md.  d: 01 Apr 1831 in Balt Co
.................  +Dorcas Gorsuch  b: 05 Jun 1752 in Coles Search, Western Run  m: 02 Jul 1772 in ST. JOHNS  d: 1794 in Balt Co
............. *2nd Wife of John Ensor:
.................  +Naomi Ensor  b: Abt. 1778  m: 08 Apr 1812
............. 3 Abraham Ensor  b: 1757 in Maryland  d: 23 Jun 1835
.................  +Bethier Brooks  b: Mar 1772 in Maryland  m: 20 Dec 1787  d: 01 Aug 1815
............. *2nd Wife of Abraham Ensor:
.................  +Jemima Ensor  b: Abt. 1765  m: Abt. 1820  d: 20 Apr 1837
............. 3 Luke Ensor  b: Abt. 1760 in Maryland  d: Bef. 04 May 1876
.................  +Eleanor Lemmon  b: 09 Aug 1777 in Baltimore Co.  m: 03 Feb 1824  d: Abt. 1837
............. 3 William Ensor  b: Abt. 1762  d: Bef. 21 Oct 1834
.................  +Nancy Headington  m: 02 Mar 1800
............. 3 Sarah Ensor  b: Abt. 1773  d: 23 Apr 1835
.................  +Jonathon Plowman Ensor  b: Abt. 1765  m: Feb 1785
............. 3 Ann Ensor  b: Bef. 1769  d: 31 Jul 1830
.................  +Darius Stansbury  b: Abt. 1766
............. *2nd Husband of Ann Ensor:
.................  +John Thomas Holland  b: Abt. 1760  m: 26 Feb 1783
...... 2 Elizabeth Merryman  b: 04 Jun 1734 in Hereford, Maryland  d: 02 Sep 1795 in Baltimore
..........  +John Gorsuch  b: 1730 in Baltimore Co., Md.  m: 11 Mar 1755  d: 02 Aug 1808 in Maryland
............. 3 Deborah Gorsuch
```

.... 3 Robert Gorsuch b: 07 Aug 1757 in Baltimore , Md. d: 18 Jan 1828 in Homestead, Baltimore
.... +Sarah Donovan m: 08 Aug 1782 in Baltimore , Md.
.... 3 Nicholas Gorsuch b: Abt. 1764 d: May 1796 in Baltimore
.... +Mary Lavely
.... 3 Richard Gorsuch b: Abt. 1765 d: 1834 in Balt Co
.... 3 John Merryman Gorsuch b: Abt. 1767 in Baltimore Co. d: 17 Nov 1840 in Gorsuch's Retirement, Glenco
.... +Sarah Stansbury Bowen m: 26 Sep 1804
.... *2nd Wife of John Merryman Gorsuch:
.... +Arienna Sollers Stansbury b: 07 Dec 1780 m: 28 Nov 1811
.... 3 Dickinson Gorsuch b: 1769 in BALT d: 12 Jan 1815 in Glenco
.... +Mary Talbott b: 1765 in MLM lot 39, 48 m: 27 Mar 1794 d: 22 May 1821 in GLENCOE
.... 3 Joshua Gorsuch b: Abt. 1770 in BALT d: 09 Aug 1844 in Verona, MD
.... +Ann Smith m: 24 Jun 1795 in Maryland
.... *2nd Wife of Joshua Gorsuch:
.... +Eleanor Lynch b: 1787 m: 23 Oct 1806 in Maryland d: 27 Feb 1863 in Verona
.... 3 Eleanor Gorsuch b: 1774 d: 1858
.... 3 Deborah Gorsuch b: Abt. 1776
.... +Unknown Bryan b: Abt. 1772
...... 2 John Merryman b: 16 Feb 1736/37 in Hereford, Maryland d: 14 Feb 1814 in Calvert St., Baltimore, buried Loudon Park
.... +Sarah Rogers b: 22 Mar 1743/44 in Maryland m: 08 Dec 1777 d: 20 Aug 1816 in Baltimore, Buried loudon Park
.... 3 Benjamin Rogers Merryman b: 22 Oct 1780 in Balt,Co. d: 1801
.... 3 Ann Merryman b: 08 Nov 1782 in Balt,Co. d: 08 Mar 1885 in St. James
.... +[1] Elijah Bosley b: 28 Mar 1740 d: 29 Aug 1841 in St. James
.... 3 Sarah Rogers Merryman b: 22 Mar 1784 in Balt,Co. d: 1856 in Balt,Co.
.... +Dr Ashton Alexander b: Abt. 1782 m: 01 May 1828
.... 3 John Merryman b: 03 Nov 1785 in Balt,Co. d: 24 Jan 1854
.... 3 Elizabeth Merryman b: 04 Mar 1786 in Balt,Co. d: 1860
.... 3 Nicholas Rogers Merryman b: 26 Apr 1788 in Balt,Co. d: 21 Jan 1864 in Piney Hill, Merryman Cm, Hereford
.... +Anna Maria Gott b: 09 Jan 1797 m: 15 Sep 1822 d: 25 Jan 1829 in Balt,Co.
.... *2nd Wife of Nicholas Rogers Merryman:
.... +Clarissa Philpot b: Abt. 1806 m: 19 Jun 1832 d: 05 Nov 1877 in Balt,Co.
...... 2 Benjamin Merryman b: 29 Aug 1739 in Hereford d: 30 May 1814 in Monkton
.... +Mary Bell b: Abt. 1740 m: 02 Feb 1762 in St. John's, Joppa, MD d: 06 Nov 1822
.... 3 Benjamin Merryman b: Abt. 1765 d: 1796
.... 3 John Merryman b: 03 Nov 1775 d: 31 Jan 1851
.... +Sarah Johnson b: Abt. 1770
.... 3 Joshua Merryman b: Abt. 1770 d: 1801
.... 3 Nicholas Merryman b: Abt. 1772 d: 1816
.... 3 William Merryman b: Abt. 1774
.... +Ann Presbury b: Abt. 1775
.... 3 Philemon Merryman b: Abt. 1776
.... +Elizabeth Norwood b: Abt. 1780
.... 3 Sarah Merryman b: Abt. 1777
.... 3 Catherine Merryman b: Abt. 1778
.... +John Buck b: Abt. 1776
.... 3 Mary Merryman b: Abt. 1779
.... +William Neill
.... *2nd Husband of Mary Merryman:
.... +Thomas Talbott b: Abt. 1777
.... 3 Eleanor Merryman b: Abt. 1780
.... +Thomas R. Harland b: Abt. 1780
.... 3 Elizabeth Merryman b: Abt. 1781
.... 3 Martha Merryman b: Abt. 1782
.... 3 Ann Merryman b: Abt. 1784
.... +Nicholas Merryman b: Abt. 1778
.... 3 Milcah Merryman b: Abt. 1785
.... +Thomas Carr b: Abt. 1784

.... 3 Rebecca Merryman b: Abt. 1786
.... +Lee Tipton b: Abt. 1785

Descendants of John Foster

```
1 John Foster  b: 03 Nov 1737  d: 20 Jan 1826 in Hereford, Md.
. +Eleanor Barney  d: 22 Apr 1817 in Hereford, Md.
...... 2 George Foster  b: 29 Sep 1759 in Baltimore Co., Md.  d: in Carroll Co. Md.
......... +Elizabeth Meyers
...... 2 John B. Foster  b: Abt. 1761  d: 1787
......... +Elizabeth Liddel  m: 07 Dec 1782
............ 3 Ellen Foster
............ 3 Sarah Ann Foster
...... 2 Patience Foster  b: 02 Jun 1764
......... +Christopher Walker  b: 1757 in Baltimore Co., Md.  m: 08 Jun 1782  d: 06 May 1841 in Cincinnati, Ohio
............ 3 John Walker  b: 1784  d: 1830
............... +Elizabeth  m: 29 Dec 1808
............ 3 [2] Edward B. Walker  b: 01 Nov 1799 in Baltimore Co.  d: 25 Feb 1875 in Hamilton Co. Ohio
............... +[1] Nancy Ann Foster  b: 08 Jun 1810 in Baltimore Co.
...... 2 Absalom Foster  b: 18 Dec 1766 in Baltimore Co., Md.  d: 31 Jul 1849 in Hamilton Co. Ohio
......... +Agness Meredith  b: 1774 in Maryland  d: 1837
............ 3 Samuel Foster  b: 1793 in Baltimore Co.  d: 1881 in Hamilton Co. Ohio
............... +Mary Shoe  b: 1808 in Indianna
............ 3 Eli Foster  b: 09 Feb 1796 in Baltimore Co.  d: 24 Apr 1873 in Adams Co. ill.
............... +Miriam Lemmon  b: 28 Oct 1807 in Maryland  d: 09 Nov 1883 in Adams Co. ill.
............ 3 John W. Foster  b: 25 May 1799 in Baltimore Co.  d: 18 Jun 1865 in Hamilton Co. Ohio
............... +Hannah Kilburn  b: 07 Nov 1803 in Vermont  d: 04 Nov 1875 in Hamilton Co. Ohio
............ 3 Jemima Foster  b: Abt. 1800 in Baltimore Co.  d: 1863 in Lee Co. Iowa
............... +David Richardson  b: 10 May 1793 in New Jersey  d: 07 Jul 1862 in Lee Co. Iowa
............ 3 Joshua Foster  b: Abt. 1800 in Baltimore Co.  d: 06 Dec 1899
............ 3 Mileson Foster  b: 1803 in Baltimore Co.
............ 3 Patience Foster  b: 1803 in Baltimore Co.  d: 1849
............... +Alex Lemmon  m: 02 Oct 1823
............ 3 [1] Nancy Ann Foster  b: 08 Jun 1810 in Baltimore Co.
............... +[2] Edward B. Walker  b: 01 Nov 1799 in Baltimore Co.  d: 25 Feb 1875 in Hamilton Co. Ohio
............ 3 Mary Foster  b: 11 Apr 1813 in Baltimore Co.  d: in Hamilton Co. Ohio
............... +John Jacob Haisch  b: 1798 in Germany
...... 2 Nicholas Foster  b: 03 Jan 1770 in Baltimore Co., Md.  d: 27 Apr 1839 in Hereford Med Cm.
......... +Sarah Cross  b: 16 Aug 1779  m: 07 Mar 1797  d: 05 Jan 1851
............ 3 Nicholas Foster  b: 1810 in Baltimore County  d: 1859 in Mt. Carmel
............... +Jemima Ensor  b: 1811 in Baltimore County  m: 02 Apr 1830  d: 15 Oct 1871
............ 3 Patience Foster  b: Abt. 1800
............... +Joseph Cole
............ 3 Harriet Foster  b: 1800 in Baltimore Co., Md.  d: 03 Dec 1884 in Hereford Med Cm.
............... +John C. Mays  b: 1808  m: 11 Mar 1834  d: 30 Oct 1887 in Hereford Med Cm.
............ 3 Grace Elizabeth Foster  b: 1800  d: 31 Jul 1898 in Wiseburg
............... +Thomas Melchor Armacost  b: 31 Jan 1803 in Maryland  m: 25 Dec 1825  d: 20 Feb 1881 in Wiseburg
............ 3 Maria Foster  b: Abt. 1805  d: 01 Nov 1861 in Hereford Med Cm.
............... +Ephriam Cox  b: 1797  d: 1857
............ 3 John Cross Foster  b: Abt. 1810 in Baltimore County, Maryland  d: in Delaware Co. Ohio
............... +Mary Ann Cooper  b: 1819 in Baltimore County, Maryland  d: 20 Mar 1876 in Delaware Co. Ohio
............ 3 David Foster  b: 1823  d: 1863
............... +Hannah Teresa Diven  b: 1823  d: 1862
...... 2 Comfort Foster  b: 30 Sep 1772 in Baltimore Co.
......... +Thomas Lemmon  b: 13 Apr 1770 in Baltimore Co.  m: 15 Oct 1793 in Baltimore , Md.  d: 29 Dec 1854 in New Albany, IN.
............ 3 Sarah Ann Lemmon
............ 3 Eleanor Lemmon
............ 3 Miriam Lemmon
...... 2 Elijiah Foster  b: 05 Jul 1775  d: 30 Sep 1856 in Indianna
......... +Anne Singrey
```

...... 2 Millison Foster b: 14 Apr 1778
...... 2 Solomon Foster b: 01 Feb 1780 d: 1873
.... +Mary Norwood
.... 3 John Tye Foster b: 19 Jan 1812
.... 3 William Foster b: Abt. 1814
.... 3 Nicholas Foster b: Abt. 1816
.... 3 Eleanor Foster b: Abt. 1818
...... 2 Mary Foster b: Abt. 1782

Descendants of John Mays

1 John Mays b: Abt. 1750 d: in Baltimore Co.
..... 2 Robert Mays b: 1775 in Maryland d: Mar 1859 in Middletown, Baltimore Co.
.... +Sarah Passonham b: 1787 in Maryland m: 02 Mar 1814 in First Methodist, Baltimore , Md. d: Jun 1884 in Middletown, Baltimore Co.
.... 3 Rachel Mays b: Abt. 1815 in Maryland
.... 3 Hannah Mays b: Abt. 1816 in Maryland
.... +Nicholas W. Bull b: Apr 1816
.... 4 George Augustus Bull b: 01 Jan 1843 in Baltimore Co. d: 19 Nov 1916 in Baltimore Co.
.... +Cathrine Unknown b: Abt. 1846 d: Aft. Oct 1816
.... 4 William A. Bull b: Abt. 1845 in Baltimore Co. d: 31 Jul 1905 in Baltimore Co.
.... 4 John Albert Bull b: 02 Oct 1848 in Baltimore Co. d: 04 Oct 1921 in Baltimore Co.
.... 4 Henry Bull b: Abt. 1853 in Baltimore Co. d: Aft. 1921
.... 4 Eli F. Bull b: 14 Aug 1853 d: 01 Jul 1922
.... +Lottie C. Unknown b: Feb 1859
.... 4 Margaret Bull b: Abt. 1856
.... 4 James A. Bull b: Abt. 1856
.... +Sarah B. Bull
.... 3 Abraham Mays b: 25 Feb 1819 in Baltimore Co. d: 15 Sep 1887 in Baltimore Co.
.... +Lydia S. Wilhelm b: 16 Mar 1826 in Maryland m: Abt. 1846 d: 18 Mar 1896 in Baltimore Co.
.... 4 John Mays b: 1846 d: 1908
.... 4 Robert Harrison Mays b: Oct 1847 in Baltimore Co. d: 14 Jun 1926
.... +Carie Ann Thompson b: Jul 1845 d: 20 Dec 1929
.... 4 Emory Mays b: Abt. 1849
.... +Fowble
.... 4 William Mays b: Abt. 1850
.... 4 Samuel George W. Mays b: 25 Oct 1855 in Baltimore Co. d: 04 Nov 1918
.... +Rose W. Tracey b: 16 Jun 1870 d: 06 Sep 1958 in Mt. Carmel
.... 4 Howard Mays b: Abt. 1856
.... 4 Daniel Mays b: Abt. 1858
.... 4 Frank Mays b: Abt. 1860
.... 4 Sarah Mays b: Abt. 1862
.... 4 Joshua Grant Mays b: 24 Sep 1862 in Baltimore Co. d: 07 Apr 1950
.... +Sara Elizabeth Tracey b: 13 Jul 1865 in Baltimore Co. m: Abt. 1887 d: 29 Sep 1957 in Hampstead, Mt. Carmel
.... 4 Rachel Mays b: Abt. 1864
.... 4 Lydia Mays b: Abt. 1866
.... 3 Mary Mays b: Abt. 1822 in Maryland
.... 3 Jehu Mays b: 1824 in Maryland
.... 3 Thomas B. Mays b: 1827 in Maryland
.... +Julia A. Unknown b: Abt. 1826
.... 4 Abraham Mays b: Abt. 1852
.... +Martha Shearer
..... 2 John Pitt Mays b: 12 Jul 1779 in Maryland d: 20 Sep 1868
.... +Temperance Green b: 10 Sep 1783 in Baltimore Co., Maryland m: 10 Mar 1807 in Baltimore , Md. d: 1835
.... 3 Elizabeth Ann Mays b: 1808 d: Mar 1892 in Mt. Carmel Cm.
.... +Robert Miller b: 1797 m: 1830 d: 1869 in Mt. Carmel Cm.
.... 4 John Grafton Miller b: 29 Aug 1835 d: 18 Apr 1911 in Mt. Carmel
.... +Hester Gorsuch b: 23 May 1844 in Mt. Carmel d: 01 Dec 1872
.... 4 Thomas Miller b: Abt. 1835
.... +Margaret A. Benson b: Jul 1836
.... 4 Hannah Ann Miller b: 1837
.... +Joshua Fowble Benson b: 14 Dec 1821 in Near Mt. Carmel 5th District m: 1856
.... 4 Rachel Jane Miller b: 1832
.... +Rev. Joshua Lemmon Benson b: 26 Jan 1831
.... 4 Laura Miller b: 1841
.... 4 Emma Miller b: 1843

```
..................... 4 Milton Miller  b: 1849
..................... 4 Silas Miller  b: Jun 1853  d: in 5th District, Baltimore County
........................ +Ida F. Markland  b: Mar 1856
............. 3 John C. Mays  b: 1808  d: 30 Oct 1887 in Hereford Med Cm.
................. +Harriet Foster  b: 1800 in Baltimore Co., Md.  m: 11 Mar 1834  d: 03 Dec 1884 in Hereford Med Cm.
..................... 4 Maranda Mays  b: 1837
..................... 4 Nicholas Foster Mays  b: 13 Nov 1838 in Baltimore Co., Md.  d: 07 Jul 1914 in Hereford Med Cm.
........................ +Margaret Ann Wilhelm  b: 18 Mar 1850 in Baltimore Co., Md.  d: 20 Mar 1920 in Hereford Med Cm.
..................... 4 George H. Mays  b: 31 Mar 1840 in Baltimore, Md.  d: 03 Mar 1915 in Hereford Methodist
........................ +Emily  b: Apr 1845  d: 1920 in Hereford Methodist
..................... 4 John T. Mays  b: 04 Jan 1842  d: 20 Feb 1910 in Hereford Med Cm.
........................ +Fannie A. Unknown  b: 21 Jul 1851  d: 17 Dec 1898
..................... 4 Sopharine Mays  b: 1846
............. 3 Thomas Mays  b: 1813 in Baltimore Co.
................. +Barbara Unknown  b: 1820
..................... 4 James Mays  b: 1846 in Baltimore Co.
..................... 4 John Mays  b: 1848 in Baltimore Co.
............. 3 John Pitt Mays  b: 02 Mar 1817 in Baltimore Co.  d: 02 Jun 1896 in Baltimore Co.
................. +Martha E. Mellor  b: 1825 in Baltimore Co.  m: Abt. 1846
..................... 4 Sarah Temperance Mays  b: 1848 in Baltimore Co.  d: 18 Aug 1900 in Glencoe
........................ +Thomas Talbott Gorsuch  b: 17 Sep 1845 in Gorsuch's Retirement, Balt Co  m: 20 Feb 1866  d: 12 Apr 1923 in Balt Co
..................... 4 Rachel Emma Mays  b: Sep 1849 in Baltimore Co.  d: 18 Apr 1918
........................ +William Hutchins Little  b: 16 May 1842  d: 1922 in Hill House, Parkton
..................... 4 George Albert Mays  b: 21 Sep 1852 in Baltimore Co.  d: Sep 1915
........................ +Elizabeth Ann Sterling  b: 1856 in Balt Co  d: 1919
..................... 4 John F. Mays  b: 13 Mar 1854 in Baltimore Co.  d: 27 Apr 1878
........................ +Harriet Unknown  b: 1856
..................... 4 William M. Mays  b: Feb 1855 in Baltimore Co.  d: 17 Feb 1873
........................ +Mary F. Unknown  b: Jun 1857 in Baltimore Co.
..................... 4 Charles H Mays  b: 06 Mar 1861 in Baltimore Co.  d: 31 Jul 1933 in Balt,Co.
........................ +Sarah Florence Elliott  b: Jan 1863 in Balt,Co.  d: 1934 in Balt,Co.
......... *2nd Wife of John Pitt Mays:
................. +Dorcas Hicks  b: 16 Aug 1825 in Baltimore Co.  m: Abt. 1860  d: 05 Mar 1862
...... *2nd Wife of John Pitt Mays:
.......... +Sarah E. Sparks  b: 1779  m: 04 Sep 1839  d: 14 May 1851
```

Descendants of Nehemiah Hicks

1 Nehemiah Hicks b: 1700 d: 02 Oct 1769
. +Philizanna Hitchcock b: 1708 m: 12 Jun 1725 d: 1769 in Baltimore Co.
...... 2 Mary Hicks b: 13 Dec 1727
...... 2 William Hicks b: 14 Jun 1728
...... 2 Isaac Hicks b: 05 Jan 1729/30
...... 2 Rebeckah Hicks b: 04 Apr 1731
...... 2 Elizabeth Hicks b: 20 Nov 1733
...... 2 Philizanna Hicks b: 23 May 1737
...... 2 John Hicks b: 08 Apr 1740
...... 2 Jacob Hicks b: 25 Jun 1742 in Balt,Co. d: 11 Nov 1816 in Balt,Co.
.... +Nancy Anne Hitchcock b: 12 Dec 1741 m: 02 Mar 1767 d: 1814
.... 3 Elizabeth Hicks b: Abt. 1772
.... +Robert Anderson b: Abt. 1770
.... 3 Amanda Hicks b: Abt. 1774
.... 3 Anne Nancy Hicks b: Abt. 1770 d: Abt. 1840
.... +Nicholas H. Bull b: Abt. 1775 m: 10 Mar 1803 d: 13 Jan 1846 in Baltimore Co.
.... 4 Jacob Hicks Bull b: 04 May 1801 d: Bef. 07 Mar 1865
.... +Sarah Ann Lowe b: 1805
.... 4 Ambrose Bull b: 11 Nov 1806
.... +Maria b: 1809
.... 4 Harriet T. Bull b: 18 Aug 1808
.... +Unknown Bull
.... 4 Nicholas H. Bull b: 30 Oct 1810
.... +Sarah Bull b: 1812
.... 4 John Wesley Bull b: 01 Jun 1805 d: 01 Oct 1871 in Mt. Carmel
.... +Sarah Ann Johnson b: 31 Aug 1806 m: 22 Feb 1828 d: 09 May 1892
.... 3 Mary Polly Hicks b: Abt. 1775
.... +William Bull b: 1773 d: Bef. 1828
.... 4 Asahel Bull b: 22 May 1806
.... 4 Nicholas Bull b: May 1807
.... 4 Milison Bull b: Abt. 1815
.... 4 Rebecca Bull b: Abt. 1816
.... 4 Mary Ann Bull b: Abt. 1822
.... 4 Eliza Bull b: Abt. 1824
.... 3 Asael Hicks b: Abt. 1780
...... 2 Margaret Hicks b: 22 Jul 1743
...... 2 Sarah Hicks b: 08 Jun 1744
...... 2 Abraham Hicks b: Abt. 1746 d: 01 Feb 1822 in Baltimore Co.
.... +Sarah Gorsuch b: Abt. 1764 d: 1794
.... 3 Charles G. Hicks d: 1845 in Baltimore Co.
.... +Sarah Cole b: Abt. 1789 m: 23 Feb 1814 d: 25 Apr 1867
.... 4 Elizabeth E. Hicks b: 14 Jan 1832 in Baltimore County, Maryland d: 21 Feb 1906
.... +George Washington Elliott b: 01 May 1828 in Balt,Co. m: 23 Oct 1858 d: 27 Mar 1905 in Balt,Co., Vernon
.... 4 Miranda Hicks b: 1823 d: 03 Sep 1898 in Wiseburg
.... +William H. Wise b: 08 Feb 1826 m: 12 Apr 1855 d: 14 Jun 1902
.... 4 Salathiel Hicks b: Abt. 1815
.... 4 Abraham C. Hicks b: Abt. 1817 in Baltimore Co. d: 18 Jun 1883
.... +Jane Tipton
.... 4 Mary Jane Hicks b: 23 Dec 1819 in Baltimore Co. d: 09 Feb 1892
.... 4 Sarah Ann Hicks b: Abt. 1820 in Baltimore Co.
.... 4 Dorcas Hicks b: 16 Aug 1825 in Baltimore Co. d: 05 Mar 1862
.... +John Pitt Mays b: 02 Mar 1817 in Baltimore Co. m: Abt. 1860 d: 02 Jun 1896 in Baltimore Co.
.... 3 Marys Hicks
.... 3 Elijah Hicks b: Abt. 1789 d: 07 Mar 1850
.... +Sarah Watts b: Abt. 1799

.... 3 Dorcas Hicks
.... 3 John Hicks
.... 3 Rebecca Hicks b: 29 Aug 1800
...... 2 Neamiah Hicks b: Abt. 1750

Descendants of John Miller

1 John Miller b: 20 Jun 1790 d: 11 Nov 1866 in Wiseburg
. +Mary Anderson b: 12 Feb 1801 d: 13 Apr 1867
...... 2 Thomas Miller b: 1822 in Maryland
.... +Sarah Unknown b: 1814 in Maryland
.... 3 William E. Miller b: May 1847 in Balt,Co.
.... +Sarepta Unknown b: Jun 1848
.... 4 Alverta Miller b: 1871 in Balt,Co.
.... 4 Mary Miller b: 04 Sep 1874 d: 10 Oct 1947
.... +Eli Emory Martin b: 25 Sep 1862 d: 01 Dec 1953
.... 4 Clarence Miller b: 1876 in Balt,Co.
.... 4 Garsfilia Miller b: Aug 1878 in Balt,Co.
.... 4 William T. Miller b: Nov 1882 in Balt,Co.
.... 4 Milton Albert Miller b: Apr 1887 in Balt,Co.
.... +Daisy V. Wisner b: 1892 in Balt,Co.
.... 4 Harry K. Miller b: Jun 1890 in Balt,Co.
.... +Martha E. Wisner b: 1895 in Balt,Co.
.... 3 John Miller b: 1850 in Maryland
.... 3 Jesse Miller b: 1851 in Maryland
.... 3 Elizabeth Miller b: 1854 in Maryland
...... 2 William H. Miller b: 1825
...... 2 Robert W. Miller b: 1827
...... 2 John R. Miller b: 1829
...... 2 Mary E. Miller b: 1831
...... 2 Stephen Miller b: 1833
...... 2 Hezaciah Best Miller b: Sep 1838 in Parktin d: 1913 in Parktin
.... +Margaret Ellen Cooper b: 29 Feb 1840
.... 3 Frederick Steven Miller b: 09 Sep 1883 d: 27 Oct 1970
.... +Hester Isabell Baker b: 17 Dec 1887 d: 1906
.... 4 Russell Norris Miller b: 1910
.... +Helen Virginia Rosier b: 1910
.... 3 Horace M. Miller b: 1867
.... 3 Lydia Miller b: 1870
.... 3 Edgar G. Miller b: Apr 1873
.... 3 Lula Miller b: Jun 1878
.... 3 Alice M. Miller b: Jul 1879
.... 3 Upton Miller b: Nov 1881
...... 2 Elizabeth Miller b: 1844

Baltimore County Pioneers- 7th District

RESEARCH SOURCES

There are many areas for the researcher to explore in finding land and family history records.

Baltimore County Genealogy Society

Located on Bel Air Road, the Society meets once a month and maintains numerous family histories and related materials.

Baltimore County Historical Society

Located in Cockeysville behind the Cockeysville Library, family books and other historical records are kept there.

Bible Records

Bible records are a very important resource. Relatives may also have recorded events about your family in their bibles. Sometimes the dates or even first and middle names may differ; so additional record sources always will help determine accuracy.

Cemeteries

Tombstones inscriptions and cemetery records provide valuable information. The location of the graves in relationship to others sometimes may show a close relationship or a child that died young.

Census Records

Federal Census records for Northern Baltimore County are available for the years 1773, 1783, 1790, 1800, 1810-1880, 1900, 1910, 1920 and 1930. Before 1850, only the head of the household was listed. Others were counted by different methods, often by age groups. 1850 and later census records listed all members of the household and their age. Other information may include relationship to head of house, occupation, place of birth, ability to read and length of time at present address.

Church Records

The Episcopal Church was the official record keeper of births, deaths and Marriages for Baltimore County before the revolutionary war. Several books have copied many of these records. St. John's and St. Georges Parrish Registers 1696-1851 by Henry Peden Jr. was transcribed from microfilm in the Maryland Historical Society Library in Baltimore, Maryland. St. George's Parish Registers 1689-1793 by Bill and Martha Reamy also contain valuable information. St. James, of Monkton also recorded many valuable records from the colonial period.
Bethel Presbyterian Church in Madonna, as well as the many other churches in the area, has maintained additional records. The Church of Latter Day Saints has the worlds largest collection

of genealogy records. These are available at the main library in Salt Lake City, Utah and can be accessed from local churches also.

Estate Records

Recorded in the County Court Houses, records of estate settlements should never be overlooked for important information about your family.

Family Books

Many family books are available at Genealogy bookstores, as well as in libraries and historical societies. Baltimore County, York County, Harford County and Carroll County Historical Societies all carry many books pertaining to this area. Sometimes, family books have been written for family members and not distributed in stores.

Historical Books

Books of a historical content can often have information on offices held, occupations and many facts of importance to your research. *"Harford Heritage"* by C. Milton Wright, contains much information of value to research in the Seventh District. *"Baltimore County Families"* 1759-1759 by Robert Barns is a very valuable book for family research. "*From Marble Hill to Maryland Line*", by S.B. Clemens and C. E. Clemens is an excellent history of Northern Baltimore County. "*A History of Baltimore County*", By Neal Brooks and Eric G. Rockel provides a great overall look at Baltimore county.

Baltimore County Genealogical Society, *Abstracts of the Baltimore County Land Commissions 1727-1762*, Westminster, Maryland, Family Line Publications, Jan 1989

Barns, Robert, *Baltimore County Families, 1659-1759, Baltimore, Maryland*, Genealogical Publishing Company, 1989

Barns, Robert, *Maryland Marriages, 1634-1777, Baltimore, Maryland*, Genealogical Publishing Company, 1975

Barns, Robert, *Maryland Marriages, 1778-1800, Baltimore, Maryland*, Genealogical Publishing Company, 1978

Brooks, Neal A. and Eric G. Rockel, *A History of Baltimore County, Towson*, Maryland, Friends of Towson Library, Inc., 1979

Clemens, S. B. and C.E. Clemens, *From Marble Hill to Maryland Line - an Informal history of Northern Baltimore County*, Baltimore, Maryland, Professional printing Services Inc.,1983

Clements, S. Eugene, and F. Edward Wright, *The Maryland Militia in the Revolutionary War*, Westminster, Maryland, Family line Publishing company, 1987

Horvath, George, *The Particular Assessment Lists for Baltimore and Carroll Counties, 1798*, Westminster, Maryland, Family Line Publications, 1986

Peden, Henry C. Jr., *Inhabitants of Baltimore county 1763-1774*, Westminster, Maryland, Family Line Publications, 1989

Peden, Henry C. Jr., *Revolutionary Patriots of Baltimore Town and Baltimore County, Maryland 1775-83*, Silver Spring, Maryland, Family Line Publications, 1988

Peden, Henry C. Jr., *Quaker Records of Northern Maryland 1716-1800*, Westminster, Maryland, Willow Bend Books, 1993

Peden, Henry C. Jr., *St. John's & St. George's Parish Registers 1696-1851*, Silver Spring, Maryland, Family Line Publications, 1987

Reamy, Bill and Martha, *St. George's Parrish Registers 1689-1793*, Silver Spring, Maryland, Family Line Publications, 1988

Reamy, Bill and Martha, *St. James Parish Register 1787-1815*, Westminster, Maryland, Family Line Publications, 1987

Richardson, Hester Dorsey, *Side-Lights on Maryland History with Sketches of Early Families*, Baltimore, Genealogical Publishing Company, 1967

Seitz, R. Carlton, Maps of Land Parents in Baltimore and Carroll Counties, Westminster, Maryland, Family Line Publications, 1995

Wright, C. Milton, *Our Harford Heritage A History of Harford County, Maryland*, Glen Burnie, Maryland, French-Bray Printing Company, 1967

Wright, F. Edward, *Inhabitants of Baltimore County, 1692-1763*, Westminster, Maryland, Family Line Publications, 1987

Land Records

Since Baltimore County was separated from Baltimore City around 1852, records from 1852 to present can be found in the Towson, Maryland Court House. Land records are found on the second floor of the New Courts Building.
Land records and wills before this time can be found in the Hall of Records in Annapolis. This building is located on Rowe Boulevard between Route 50 and Annapolis. Deeds can contain valuable information on family members.

Maps

The 1850 Map of Baltimore County, J. Sidney
The 1877 Atlas of Baltimore county, G. M. Hopkins
The 1898 and 1915 Atlases of Baltimore county, G. W. & W. S. Bromley

Maryland Historical Society

Located in Baltimore City, the Society maintains many records and manuscripts relating to Baltimore County.

Newspapers

Newspapers often contain news of weddings, births, deaths, and funerals. Larger libraries and historical societies may have a valuable collection of old newspapers.

Wills

See Land Records

Family Records

Interviews with older family members are a necessary and valuable source of information.

MCGINNIS FAMILY and TALBOTT HALL HOME SITE

Jay, Anne, Wayne, Harriet and Brett

Wayne McGinnis is the fourth generation of his family to live here and farm this land. The family of his mother, Marian Richardson McGinnis, came from England to Maryland in 1649 and settled on the Severn River, near Annapolis. Lawrence Richardson's son Lawrence Jr., came to Baltimore County about 1680 and bought land near the Gunpowder River. Descendants of these early families include many familiar Baltimore County names, such as Dorsey, Howard, Towson, Todd, Lenox, Cockey and Cromwell. As the descendants moved North into My Lady's Manor and East into Harford County, the family ties grew even larger. In Harford and on the "Manor", we find the names; Andrews, Bond, Wiley, Wright, Norris, Caldwell, Kirkwood, Amos, Street, Hall, Heaps, Hope, Price, Scarborough, Royston and Standiford.

Samuel McGinnis came from Ireland in 1755 and landed in New Castle, Delaware. After the Revolutionary War, he settled in Chester County, Pennsylvania. His Grandson Morris, came to York County in the early 1850's and settled near Stewartstown. After several years, he bought land East of Shane and in 1881 purchased the present farm on Graystone Road.

Great Great Grandfather, **Joseph McClung** also came from Ireland and in 1763 bought a farm on the present Shepperd Road near Monkton. His descendants include the names of Royston, Edie, Wiley, Jackson, Nelson, Strawbridge, McDonald,

Lt. Richard Hutchins, a GGGG Grandfather, settled on the "Manor" in the early 1700's. His descendants include the names of Perdue, Sparks, Bosley, Shaw, Almony, Ayres, Slade, Hope, Nelson, Rampley, Holmes, Pearce, Pocock, Rutledge and Gilbert.

This list of names are an illustration on the number of ways our families have become related over the generations since the the Pioneers first settled here.

Tydings McGinnis Family

Tydings Miller McGinnis, Beulah Elizabeth McGinnis, Carroll Milton McGinnis, Amanda Zana McClung McGinnis, John Tydings McGinnis

This 1927 Photograph was taken in front of their 1811 farm house.

The ancestors of this family represent the four cultures that merged to form the Northeastern Baltimore County Community. These cultures were English, Scotch, Irish and German. Tydings is descendant from Samuel McGinness, a Revolutionary War soldier and immigrant from Ireland. His mother's Swinehart family came from Germany in the early 1700s. Amanda McClung McGinnis' English ancestor was Nicholas Hutchins from England and her McClung family was of Scottish descent.

Descendants of Tydings Miller McGinnis

1 Tydings Miller McGinnis b: 02 Aug 1871 in Shane, Maryland d: 15 Dec 1963 in Shane, WhiteHall, Maryland
. +Amanda Zana McClung b: 07 Dec 1868 in Norrisville, Maryland, Harford Co d: 08 Jan 1957 in WhiteHall, Maryland, Centre Pres. Cem.
...... 2 Beulah Elizabeth McGinnis b: 23 Dec 1897 in Graystone RD, WhiteHall MD d: 21 Jul 1977 in Shane, WhiteHall MD
...... 2 John Tydings McGinnis b: 09 Mar 1902 in Graystone RD, White Hall , MD d: 11 Aug 1963 in WhiteHall MD
.... +Laura Elizabeth Almony b: 01 Nov 1902 in Fawn Grove, Pylesville, MD d: 08 Dec 1927 in WhiteHall, MD
.... 3 Tydings Owen McGinnis b: 08 Nov 1927 in WhiteHall, MD d: in Easton, Maryland
.... +Joyce Louise Fulton b: 20 Feb 1930
.... 4 Tydings Owen McGinnis b: 22 Feb 1949 in White Hall , MD
.... *2nd Wife of Tydings Owen McGinnis:
.... +Cathrine Elizabeth Yealdhall b: 17 Sep 1930
.... 4 Stephen Tydings McGinnis b: 20 Jan 1956 in Easton, Maryland
.... +Nancy Gail Stiff b: 25 Mar 1955 in White Hall, Maryland
.... 5 William Tydings McGinnis b: 02 Jan 1980 in White Hall, Maryland
.... 5 Brian Donald McGinnis b: 12 Feb 1986 in York, PA.
.... 4 Elizabeth Lynn McGinnis b: 10 Apr 1958
.... +James Kenneth Dillon
.... 5 Michael Lance Dillon
...... *2nd Wife of John Tydings McGinnis:
.... +Beulah Annetta Wallace b: 14 Jan 1908 in Peach Bottom, York Co., PA. d: 12 Oct 2002 in White Hall
.... 3 David Lee McGinnis b: 13 Aug 1931 in WhiteHall MD d: 14 Aug 1931
.... 3 Margaret Louise McGinnis b: 14 Aug 1932 in WhiteHall, MD
.... +Robert Henry Shaub b: 31 Dec 1929 in Railroad, York Co.
.... 4 Kevin Henry Shaub b: 23 Jun 1954 in Shrewsbury, Pa
.... 4 Kieth Daniel Shaub b: 24 Sep 1955
.... 4 Megan Jane Shaub b: 15 Aug 1960 in York, Pa
.... 3 John Wallace McGinnis b: 16 Sep 1939 in WhiteHall, MD
.... +Mary Catherine Norton b: 24 Apr 1942 in Baltimore City
.... 4 Mary Susan McGinnis b: 30 Mar 1963
.... 4 John Michael McGinnis b: 12 Mar 1965
...... 2 Carroll Milton McGinnis b: 15 Sep 1907 in Shane, Maryland d: 11 Apr 2000 in White Hall, Maryland,
.... +Marian Estelle Richardson b: 25 Oct 1908 in Fawn Grove, Pennsylvania d: 08 Jun 1999 in White Hall, Maryland
.... 3 Eleanor Elizabeth McGinnis b: 16 Feb 1935 in WhiteHall MD, Balt Co
.... +Carl John Yarema b: 25 Oct 1935 in Detroit, Mi.
.... 4 Carl John Jr Yarema b: 24 Aug 1958 in Maryland Line,Maryland
.... +Alma Warren Hoffecker b: Oct 1958 in Monkton, Maryland
.... 5 Christopher Thomas John Yarema b: 14 Jun 1976 in Baltimore Co.
.... +Shannan Whitaker
.... *2nd Wife of Carl John Jr Yarema:
.... +Sarah Little Howard b: 01 Sep 1958
.... 5 Carah Elizabeth Yarema b: 30 Mar 1989 in Melbourne, Fl.
.... 4 Elizabeth Carol Yarema b: 17 Jun 1969 in Sparks, Maryland d: 2008 in White Hall, Maryland
.... 3 Wayne Carroll McGinnis b: 20 Dec 1936 in 19524, Graystone RD, WhiteHall, Maryland 410-357-5969
.... +Harriet Ann Husted b: 11 Apr 1939 in 94 New St, Bridgeton, New Jersey
.... 4 Anne Husted McGinnis b: 14 Apr 1964 in White Hall, Maryland
.... +Kirk Dean Jones b: 15 Jul 1965 in Elmwood Rd. , Baltimore, Maryland
.... 5 Noah Derrick Jones b: 27 Jan 1999 in Forest Hill, Maryland d: 27 Jan 1999 in Centre Presbyterian Cem.
.... 5 Dawson Alexander Jones b: 15 Jun 2000 in Forest Hill, Maryland
.... 5 Shelby Anne Jones b: 20 Feb 2002 in Forest Hill, Maryland
.... 4 Jay Carroll McGinnis b: 12 Sep 1967 in White Hall, Maryland
.... +Nicole Lynn Branaman
.... 4 Brett Wayne McGinnis b: 27 Jun 1969 in White Hall, Maryland

CONCLUSION

This project started in 1975 with an interview of my Aunt, Miss Beulah Elizabeth McGinnis, about her knowledge of our relatives and neighbors. She had a keen interest in her ancestors and was a source of many stories of those who lived and worked on and near our farm. She kept numerous letters, cards and newspaper clippings about events from a period starting around 1900. After her death in 1977, I purchased a Family Tree Maker Program, for my computer to help record and straighten out our connections to many cousins named in these records. The total data base has grown close to 50,000 individuals that are mostly found in Baltimore, Harford or York Counties. The ability to connect families and communities through this program is amazing. Some families have been included in this book, that had held leases and patents outside the Seventh District, but maintained strong ties with our first families. Other families may have stronger ties to adjoining districts or there may be incomplete information available at this time. I am sure there are many interesting facts about each family that could be included in any future publications. Research for the area is never completed and corrections and additions are always welcomed. Different spellings of names and dates are sometimes found in family bibles and other family records. Often, names were spelled as they sounded to the census taker. Many early settlers had limited educational opportunities and changed the spellings of their names over the generations. Birth dates often are inaccurate, depending on the person giving the information to the census taker. Occasionally, even grave markers can be incorrect. If information seems to be in question, sometimes the abbreviation "abt." is used. While this project generally only covered three generations, many additional generations are available and can be printed out upon request. I hope you enjoy the project.

Wayne C. McGinnis
White Hall, Maryland
2005

Index of Individuals

Abram Gorsuch Ensor: 56
ADAMS -
  Jane: 31
  Mary: 24
  Ruth: 29
Ady -
  Samuel: 24
Alban -
  Mordecai: 33
Alexander -
  Dr Ashton: 171
Allen -
  Anthony J.: 69
  John: 49
  Robert: 53, 69, 82
Alloway -
  Laura: 125
Almony -
  A. Lucille: 37
  Abraham: 25
  Abraham: 25
  Agustus Caesar: 26, 63, 99
  Amor: 37
  Amor Davis: 37
  Ann: 25
  Ann: 24
  Ann Whitaker: 25
  Anna Margaret: 37
  Annie Maria: 93, 99, 112
  Benjamin: 25
  Benjamin: 24, 41
  Benjamin: 25
  Benjamin Franklin: 26
  Benjamin Franklin: 111
  Benjamin P.: 37
  Bettie: 37
  C. Albert James Bell: 47
  Capt James: 25
  Cathrine: 37
  Cathrine: 37
  Charles Linthicum: 47
  COL Col James: 25, 45, 48
  Daughter: 37
  Dorcas Ann: 25
  Dorothy: 37
  Elijah: 25
  Elizabeth: 24, 143
  Elizabeth: 24, 143
  Elizabeth: 25
  Elizabeth Ann: 25, 143
  Ella Leota: 37
  Ella M.: 37
  Ella May: 57
  Ephriam: 47
  Franklin T.: 47, 73
  Grandison: 25
  Grover Cleveland: 37
  Harriet: 25
  Harrison Ross: 37
  Henry Dunnuck: 25, 47

  James: 24
  James: 25
  James Franklin: 96, 99
  James Thomas: 55, 98
  James Walter: 37
  Jane: 25
  Jarrett: 25
  Jefferson S.: 25
  John: 24, 25
  John: 24
  John: 25
  John S.: 25
  John Thomas: 37, 125
  John Westley: 47
  Keziah: 96, 99
  Keziah Jane: 47
  Aunt Laura Elizabeth: 186
  Lida Adele: 37
  Mary Ann: 29, 35
  Mary Ann: 25
  Mary Cathrine: 47
  Mary Jane: 25
  Mordecai Azariah: 26
  Pearce: 37
  Rachel: 24
  Ruth: 26
  Ruth Ella: 37
  Sarah: 25
  Sarah: 25
  Stanley Pearce: 37
  Thomas E W: 99
  Unknown: 42
  Unknown: 111
  Virginia: 37
  William: 25, 29
  William: 26
  William H: 47
  William Harrison: 25, 143
Amanda -
  Unnamed: 42
Amos -
  Hannah: 88
  Hannah: 88
  Ida: 153
  John Streett: 143
  Mary Polly: 45
Anderson -
  Andrew Lemmon: 45
  Annie: 79
  Aquilla Brown: 80
  Benjamin Franklin: 45
  Delia: 152
  Elijah: 80
  Elizabeth: 80
  Elizabeth: 40
  Elizabeth: 80
  Francis Marion: 45
  George Lemmon: 45
  James: 45
  John: 80

  John James: 55, 98
  John Thomas: 45
  John Westley: 45
  John Westley: 31, 45, 48
  Joshua: 45
  Joshua: 45, 47
  Joshua James: 45, 47
  Josias: 80
  Juliet Elizabeth: 45
  Juliet Elizabeth: 45
  Juliet Elizabeth: 25, 45, 48
  Keziah Theresa: 145
  Leonard: 80
  Mararetta: 45
  Margaret: 88
  Mary: 49
  Mary: 179
  Mary Ann: 45
  Mary Sophronia: 31, 35, 45, 48
  Nancy: 80
  Penelope: 80
  Robert: 177
  Ruth: 80
  Sarah: 45, 48
  Sarah Ann: 80, 157
  Sarah Cooper: 77
  Son: 45
  Son: 45
  Sophrona: 45
  Sophronia: 45
  Thomas: 80
  Thomas: 80
  William: 45
  William: 45
  William: 45, 48
  William Franklin: 45
  William Franklin: 45
  William T.: 135
Anstine -
  Jemima: 59, 61, 64
  John C.: 128
  Mary Eva: 81
  Rebecca Jane: 100
Armacost -
  Thomas Melchor: 173
Arnold -
  Rebecca: 165
Arthurs -
  William H: 54
Ayres -
  Ann: 144
  Benjamin A: 144
  Dorcas: 24, 143
  Dorcas: 143
  Eliza: 143
  Elizabeth: 24, 143
  Elizabeth: 24
  Elizabeth: 87
  Elizabeth: 25, 143
  Elizabeth C: 88, 143

Capt James: 24, 143
James W: 74, 153
John: 24, 29, 143
John: 116, 143
Joshua: 24, 143
Lorenza: 29, 35
Margaret: 143
Mary: 24
Mary: 24, 143
Mary Cathrine: 151
Mary S: 144
Mary Susan: 143
Matilda: 24
Nancy Ann: 24, 143
Nancy Ann: 143
Rachel Ann: 143
Ruth Ellen: 143
Susanna: 24, 143
Thomas: 24, 143
Thomas Jefferson: 24, 143
Thomas Jefferson: 144, 151
Thomas Jefferson: 154
Thomas W: 24
Thomas W: 24
William Hitchcock: 143

Bacon -
Elizabeth: 147
Mary Virginia: 148
Olevia R: 148

Bagnel -
Margaret: 103

Bailey -
Unknown: 115

Baird -
Margaret A.: 55, 98

Baker -
Hester Isabell: 179

Baldwin -
Dr Thomas C.: 78

Ballard -
Edward: 165
Henry: 165
John: 165
COL Robert: 165
William: 165

Bankhead -
Jane: 42

Barney -
Eleanor: 173

Barringer -
Henrietta F.: 146

Barrow -
Alice: 148

Bartlow -
Nancy Jane: 80, 86

Bartol -
Aquilla: 77
Margaret: 77
Nathaniel B.: 77
Rosanna: 77
Sarah: 77

Barton -
Annie E: 25

James: 71
Baublitz -
Michael: 167
Bayne -
Thomas: 87
Beall -
Martha Ann: 72, 89
Beazell -
Phebe: 139
Beel -
John B.: 73
Bell -
Agnes: 48, 137, 138
Agnes: 48
Ann Elizabeth: 25, 47
David: 48
Dr Dr Ephriam: 48
Eleanor: 48
Elizabeth: 48
Elizabeth Mary: 48, 137, 138
James: 47
James: 48
Jane: 47
Lt John: 47
Jr John: 48
John: 48
John: 47
Joshua M: 47, 83
Kesiah: 48
Lovica: 48
Lovica Jane: 48
Mary: 171
Mary: 48
Mary: 48
Mary: 161
Mary Jane: 45, 47
Mary R. S.: 48
Rebecca: 47
Rebecca Ann: 48
Sarah: 48
William: 47
William: 48
William: 47, 83

Belt -
John George: 166, 168
Bennett -
Josiah: 148
Louise: 148
Benson -
Joshua Fowble: 83, 175
Lillian: 85
Margaret A.: 83, 175
Rev. Joshua Lemmon: 83, 175
Robert: 95
Samuel: 138
Bessler -
Sarah Ann: 72
-
Bettie Anstine: 128
Bickerstaff -
Mary: 24
Billet -
Unnamed: 104

Billingslea -
James: 137, 138
Samuel McClung: 108, 167
Sarah E: 71
Westley: 108, 167
Billingsley -
Walter Norris: 161
Birmingham -
James: 139
James: 139
Margaret: 40
Margret: 139
Mary: 139
Matthew: 139
Rebecca: 139
Robert: 139
Samuel: 139
Black -
Millard: 135
Blackburn -
Dr James: 80, 86
Blinn -
George Duckworth: 146
Bock -
Alice: 47
Bogue -
Henry: 114
Bond -
Alfred: 59, 61
Ann: 55, 98
Ann R.: 60, 62
Annie Louise: 60, 62
Charles: 55
Clara Howard: 60
Daniel S.: 60, 62
Dave: 126
David Keller: 59, 61
Dennis: 170
Edward: 55
Edward: 55
Edwin R.: 59, 61
Eleanor: 55
Eli Sampson: 60, 61
Elisha: 55, 98, 99
Eliza Jane: 59, 61
Elizabeth: 60, 62
Elizabeth: 55, 98
Elizabeth Ann: 55, 98, 99
Elizabeth Matilda: 60, 62
Ellen: 55, 98, 108
Francis Westley: 60, 61
Frank Smith: 59, 61
George: 59, 61
George Emory: 60, 62
George Sampson: 55, 98
George W.: 59, 61
Harriet S.: 55, 98
James: 53, 59, 61, 63, 82
James: 60, 62
James Hamilton: 59, 61
Jane Elizabeth: 55, 98, 165
Jesse Hinkle: 59, 61
Jessie Ross: 55, 98, 99

    John C.: 60
    John David: 60, 62
    John Ross: 55, 98
    John Westley: 60, 62
    Joshua: 60, 62
    Laura Agnes: 55, 98
    Lucy M. A.: 55, 98
    Luella Harriet: 55, 98
    Martha Ellen: 55, 98, 99
    Mary: 132
    Mary: 55
    Mary Cathrine Rebecca: 55, 98
    Mary Celestia: 60, 62
    Mary Jane: 60, 62
    Nancy Ann: 59, 61, 64
    Rebecca Jane: 55, 98, 99
    Rosa Eve: 55, 98
    Ross: 55, 77, 98
    Sallie: 60
    Sally E. G.: 55, 98
    Samuel: 60, 62
    Samuel James: 59
    Samuel John: 59
    Smith Daniel: 55, 98
    Thomas: 55, 98, 99
    Thomas Gorsuch: 59, 61
    Varena Julia: 55, 98
    William B.: 60
    William Henry: 59, 61
    William Moses: 59, 61
    William T.: 60, 62

Borneman -
    Philip: 72

Bosley -
    Unnamed: 132
    Abraham Elliott: 147
    Anna Pricilla: 72
    Belinda: 83
    Benjamin: 147
    Benniah: 132
    Clarinda: 75
    Daniel Webster: 84
    Edward: 75
    Edward Denmead: 147
    Elijah: 170, 171
    Elizabeth: 75, 116, 132
    Elizabeth: 75
    Elizabeth: 75
    Elizabeth: 76
    Elizabeth Green: 147
    Ezekiel: 75, 132
    Hannah: 75, 132
    Hannah: 75, 134
    Henry Smith: 147
    Isaac: 75
    Issac: 75, 132
    James: 75, 132
    James: 132
    James: 75
    James: 83
    James Chamers: 147
    John: 75
    Joseph: 75, 132
    Joseph Vincent: 133

    Joshua: 83
    Joshua: 83
    Kesiah: 83
    Letitia: 75
    Lucretia V.: 75
    Margaret Elizabeth: 147
    Mary: 75, 132
    Mary: 132
    Mary: 75
    Mary: 76
    Mary: 138
    Mary Agnes: 77
    Mary Ella: 75
    Mary Virginia: 147
    Nancy Ann: 75
    Nicholas: 76
    Norris: 75
    Prudence: 151
    Rachel: 75, 132, 166
    Rachel: 168
    Rachel: 83
    Samuel: 147
    Sarah Ellen: 147
    Shadrach: 83
    Susanna: 76, 132
    Susanna: 76
    Thomas: 83
    Vincent: 132
    William Talbott: 147

Bowen -
    Sarah M: 138
    Sarah Stansbury: 171

Bowman -
    Anstine George: 73

Boyd -
    Amy: 127
    Andrew: 48
    Andrew W Jr: 48
    David: 48
    David: 48
    Elsisa: 48
    James: 48
    Jane: 47
    Margaret: 48

Boyer -
    Joshua H. L.: 96

Boyle -
    Cathrine: 116

Boyles -
    Carrie Bell: 146

Bradenbaugh -
    Brown: 148
    Caroline: 148
    Eliza: 148
    Jacob: 24, 143
    Jacob: 25, 143
    Jacob: 148
    Margaret: 148
    Mary Susan: 143, 159
    Nancy Ann: 143, 148
    Oliver: 148
    Thomas: 143, 148
    Thomas: 148

Bradford -
    John: 159

Brady -
    Eliza Ann: 53
    Eliza Ann: 54

Branaman -
    Nicole Lynn: 186

Brian -
    Hannah: 156

BRIGGS -
    George: 89

Brooks -
    Bethier: 170
    Ruth L.: 125

Brown -
    Annie Waters: 60
    Frank: 126
    George: 135
    P. Bazel: 60
    Penelope: 79

Bruehl -
    Katherine F.: 110

Brundige -
    Annie Rebecca: 148

Bryan -
    Unknown: 171

Buck -
    Caroline Matilda: 108, 167
    John: 171

Buford -
    Desie: 148

Bull -
    Ambrose: 177
    Ann: 120
    Asahel: 177
    Belender: 120
    Belinda Jane: 120
    Betsey A: 120
    Edward Parish: 120
    Eli F.: 175
    Elisha: 120
    Eliza: 177
    George Augustus: 175
    Hannah: 120, 121
    Harriet T.: 177
    Henry: 175
    Isaac: 120
    Isaac: 120
    Jacob: 40
    Jacob: 40
    Jacob Hicks: 177
    James A.: 175
    John: 120
    John Albert: 175
    John Wesley: 177
    Josias Slade: 120, 132
    Josias Slade: 120
    Lucy Smith: 120
    Margaret: 93
    Margaret: 175
    Mary: 120, 121
    Mary Ann: 177
    Milison: 177
    Nicholas: 177

Nicholas H.: 177
Nicholas H.: 177
Nicholas W.: 175
Rachael: 120
Rebecca: 120
Rebecca: 177
Sarah: 177
Sarah B.: 175
Susanna: 120
Thomas Mitchell: 112
Unknown: 177
William: 177
William: 120
William A.: 175

Burditt -
Jane: 146
Sarah: 146

Burgee -
Welty F.: 128

Burgess -
Joseph: 145

Buris -
Harry M.: 128

Burk -
Mary A: 25

Burns -
Adam: 120, 121
Adam: 121
Amanda Jane: 121
Annie Estella: 128
Annie M.: 153
Annie M.: 152
Balinda Bull: 120, 121
Belinda Ann: 121
Benjamin: 120, 121
Benjamin France: 121
Betsy Ann: 120, 121
Betsy Morre: 121
Carl: 57
Charles J.: 149
Clarence Mitchell: 57
Edgar: 57
Elsie: 57
Georgia Frances: 57
Gladys May: 57
Henry Polk: 121
Henry Polk: 57
J. Howard: 57
James Jarrett: 121
James Thomas: 57, 121
John: 149
John: 120, 121
John B.: 149
John Moore: 121
John Thomas: 121
John Wesley: 121
Kenneth: 57
Mabe V.: 57
Mary Belinda: 121
Mary E.: 149
Mary Elizabeth Ann: 121
Mary Elsie: 57
Mary Jane: 121, 122
May V.: 57

Mortimer: 149
Rachel Ann: 121
Rachel Ann: 121
Rachel Belinda: 121
Richard Nicholas: 121
Ruth Adelaide: 57
Sarah Jane: 149
William: 121
William Bull: 120, 121
William Bull: 121

Burroughs -
John: 100

Burton -
Eugene: 110
Howard C.: 110

Butler -
Hennrietta: 30, 35
Lewis: 168

Cable -
Dorthy: 24

Cairnes -
Isabelle Rebecca: 31
Margaret: 31
Rebecca: 32

Calder -
Capt Capt James: 103
Charlotte: 103
Lt George E: 103
Margaret: 103
Mary: 103
Rebecca: 103
Sarah: 103

Cameron -
Adeline: 105, 106
Alice: 105
Ann: 105
Annie: 104
Benjamin Franklin: 104
Cathrine: 105, 106
Daniel W: 104, 106
Daniel Walker: 104
Daniel Webster: 104
Elizabeth: 104, 106
Elizabeth A.: 104
Eveline: 104, 106
F. Horace: 104
Frank: 105
George Hugh: 104
Gertrude: 105
Harry: 105
Hugh: 104, 106
James P.: 104
James W.: 104, 106
Jane: 104, 106
John M.: 104
Joseph: 105, 106
Lucinda Amelia: 105, 106
Mamie Margaret: 104
Margaret: 105, 106
Mary: 104, 106, 166, 168
Mary: 104
Mary: 104
Robert Norris: 104, 115
Stuart John: 37

William: 104, 106
William J.: 104

CAMPBELL -
Josiah: 31

Canoles -
Elizabeth: 125
Emeline: 125
John A.: 125
Mary J.: 126
Unknown: 125, 162
William: 125

Carl -
Lydia: 83

Carlin -
Aaron: 156
Aaron: 156
Arron: 40
Daniel Hughes: 156
Elijah: 156
Elizabeth Ellen: 154
Ellen Virginia: 156
Franklin: 156
James: 156
James A: 156
James Thomas: 156
John Oliver: 156
Josiah: 156
Josiah: 153, 156
Josiah: 156
Laura Frances: 153
Maria Elizabeth: 156
Mary Susan: 156
Rachel: 156
Rachel E: 156
Ruth: 156
Sarah Elizabeth: 156
Sarah Mae: 153
Thomas: 156
William: 79, 156
William: 156
William: 156

Carr -
Cassandra: 162
George W.: 77
Thomas: 171

Carrolis -
William: 73

Carroll -
William H.: 124

Carter -
Sarah Caldwallader: 96

Casey -
Sarah Marissa: 96

Cathcart -
Charles M.: 152
Joseph: 43, 73
Mary: 133

Cathrine -
Unnamed: 145
Unnamed: 89, 108
Unnamed: 78

Chenoweth -
Unknown: 104

Chilcoat -
    Elijah: 125, 162
    Elijah F.: 125
    Florence: 125
    George Rufus: 125
    Howard Greenberry: 125
    John Pearce: 125
    Lewis Edward: 125
    Ozella C.: 125

Chuffey -
    Unknown: 94

Clark -
    Caleb: 140
    Ida J.: 146

Clarke -
    Elizabeth: 59, 61

Clements -
    Melvina: 40

-
    Clinton R. Kirkwood: 37, 125

Coale -
    Charles: 161

Coe -
    Elizabeth: 42

Cole -
    Abraham: 85
    Charlotte Ophelia: 56
    Clarence Gorsuch: 84
    Delilah: 120
    Elizabeth: 132
    Joseph: 173
    Mary Elizabeth: 84
    Samuel Parkin: 84
    Sarah: 177
    Sophia: 138

Collett -
    Ann: 167
    Ann: 167
    Cathrine: 167
    Elizabeth: 167
    James Thomas: 120, 121
    Jemima: 167
    Jemima: 100
    Jemima: 167
    John: 63
    John: 167
    Margaret: 167
    Mary Jane: 167
    Matilda Ann: 63, 167
    Moses: 167
    Moses: 167
    Moses: 167
    Nicholas: 167
    Poly: 167
    Rachel: 79
    Rachel: 138, 167
    Rachel Ann: 156
    Rachel Ann: 167
    Susanna: 108, 167
    Thomas: 167

Collins -
    Elizabeth G.: 77

Coltrider -
    Joshua: 83

Combs -
    Sarah F.: 146

Conway -
    Dorcas: 79

Coole -
    Alice: 139

Cooper -
    Elizabeth: 95
    Elizabeth A.: 121
    Margaret Ellen: 179
    Mary Ann: 173
    Samuel Shaver: 96
    Susan Margaret: 40

Corbett -
    Unnamed: 150

Corbin -
    Elizabeth Ann: 126
    Georgette: 126
    John Putnam: 126
    Mary Lenora: 126
    William Parlett: 126, 162
    William Parlett: 126

Cornelius -
    Mary Jane: 69

Cotter -
    Ida: 100

Coulson -
    Francis: 82
    Jane: 48

Cox -
    Daniel: 106
    Ephriam: 173
    John Sellman: 106
    Miranda M.: 126, 162
    Selman: 106

Creighton -
    Delilah: 41

Croddy -
    Arnold J: 57

Cross -
    Rachel: 167
    Sadie: 65
    Sarah: 173
    Sarah: 113

Cuddy -
    Capt Capt Lawson: 137, 138
    Lawrence: 80
    Rebecca Ann: 109
    Susan: 87
    Westley Royston: 108, 167

Cumming -
    Daisy: 145

Cummings -
    Elizabeth: 71

Cunningham -
    Margaret: 147

Curfman -
    Mary: 89
    Mary E.: 113

Curry -
    Adam: 100

    Bettie R.: 127
    Carl Leroy: 127
    Elizabeth: 64
    James Irving: 127
    James Thomas: 127
    Lillian: 127
    Patrick Kean: 82
    Unknown: 100

Curtis -
    Amanda Young: 157
    Ann: 158
    Ann Eliza: 157
    Annie Elizabeth: 157
    Arabella Stansbury: 157
    Cathrine Jane: 157
    Charles E: 70
    Charles Henry Clay: 157
    Charles Merryman: 158
    Eleanor: 70
    Eli: 157
    Eliza: 158
    Elizabeth: 69
    Elizabeth: 157
    Frances Silizabeth: 59, 61
    George Worthington: 158
    John: 157
    John Sheppard: 80, 157
    Joseph: 69
    LEVI: 70
    Levi: 70
    Levi: 157
    Jr LEVI: 157
    Marion Manilla: 157
    Martha Garrison: 157
    Martha Jane: 53, 69, 82
    Mary: 157
    Mary Ann Shepard: 158
    Mary E: 157
    Mary Jane: 70
    Matilda S: 157
    Nicholas: 69
    Nicholas James Merryman: 157
    Rachel: 79, 157
    Rachel: 157
    Rebecca: 70
    Sarah: 157, 162
    Sarah Elizabeth: 70
    Susan Worthington: 157
    Thomas: 157
    William: 157
    William: 157
    William: 158
    William Harrison: 157
    William Thomas: 157

Dailey -
    Carrie M.: 110
    Christopher: 33
    Elizabeth: 33
    Harriet Lavinia: 112
    Jacob: 33
    Jacob: 33
    Jacob: 33
    Jehu: 33
    Jesse: 33

John: 33
Keziah: 33
Martha: 33
Miriam: 33
Ruth: 33
Sarah: 33
Thomas: 33
Thomas: 33

Davidson -
Capt Samuel: 122
Col Robert G.: 122
Daughter: 122
James John: 122
John G.: 122
Levinah Rebecca: 122
Martha: 122
Polly: 122
Rebecca: 122
Sarah: 122
Sarah Elizabeth: 122
Son: 122
Thomas J.: 146
William Thomas: 122

Davis -
Benjamin: 139
Bertha: 110
Elizabeth: 59, 61
Hannah Alice: 31
Harmon: 128
James Benjamin: 150
James Buchannan: 150
Maria Augusta: 146
Rachel: 57
Son: 128

Dawkins -
Joshua P.: 122

Deagon -
Julia Ann: 48

Dean -
Edson Benjamin Oles: 153
George Cassius: 153

Debois -
Leon: 128

Decker -
Ethel: 127
Isaac: 79, 86
Mary: 137, 139

Deford -
Robert Bell: 48
Thomas: 48

Delgar -
Robert: 153

Demoss -
Mary Susan: 143

Denmead -
Benjamin: 117

Dety -
William: 65

Devine -
11 Edward: 24

Dichter -
Samuel J.: 127

Dicken -

Amos: 81

Diffenderffer -
Harriet Minerva: 72

Dillon -
James Kenneth: 186
Michael Lance: 186

Disney -
Florence: 161

Diven -
Hannah Teresa: 173

Dixon -
William Edward: 37

Donovan -
Sarah: 171

Doran -
Mary Ann: 30, 35

DorseyD'Arcy -
Ann: 49

Downs -
Abraham Wilson: 53
Eli K.: 53
G. S.: 53
John Keller: 53
Louisa: 53
Thomas Rutledge: 53
Unknown: 94

Drake -
Matthew: 79

Dreisbach -
Sarah Cathrine: 65

Duncan -
Sarah: 139
Sarah Adelaide: 78

Dunnick -
Elizabeth: 29, 41

Dunnuck -
Cathrine: 29
Dorcas: 25, 29
John: 29
Jr John W: 29, 163
Joseph: 29
Joseph Sutton: 163
Joshua: 29
Kiturah: 29
Luke Wyle: 163
Rachel: 24, 29, 143
Ruth: 29
Sarah: 29, 163
Thomas: 29, 69

Dye -
Bernard: 72

Dykes -
Alexander: 69

Echtol -
Anna Elizabeth: 94, 112

Edie -
George Perry: 65

Edwards -
Sterling: 135

Eigelberger -
Rev Thomas: 125

Elder -

Margaret: 59, 61
Eleanor -
Unnamed: 143
-
Elizabeth: 48
-
Elizabeth: 26
Unnamed: 145
Unnamed: 173
Unnamed: 150
Unnamed: 111
-
Elizabeth: 134
Unnamed: 116
Unnamed: 77
Ellen -
Unnamed: 74
Elliot -
Elizabeth M.: 146
Female: 146
John Burditt: 146
Sarah Maria: 146
William Taylor: 146
Elliott -
Abraham: 147
Abraham: 145
Abraham James: 149
Abraham James: 148
Abraham Oliver: 148
Alice M.: 145
Almon D.: 146
Amelia Sterrett: 145
Ann Augusta: 146
Ann Elizabeth: 145
Ariel: 145
Benjamin: 145
Benjamin A.: 145
Benjamin Ezra: 145
Bernice: 71
Caroline Augusta: 145
Carrie Viola: 148
Charles Acton: 145
Charles Meredith: 148
Charles Westly: 71
Clarence Elmer: 148
Delilah Crayton: 145
Dorcas Cecelia: 148
Edward Thomas: 71
Edwin Dorsey: 148
Elizabeth: 145
Elizabeth: 146
Elizabeth Ann: 148
Emmaline: 146
Ezra Taylor: 145
Frank Boyd: 146
Frank P.: 148
George: 145
George: 71
George: 145
George: 146
George Washington: 148, 177
Grason: 71
Ida: 148
Irwin O.: 147

Jacob: 148
James Ramley: 145
James Rampley: 146
Jemima: 146
John C.: 146
John E.: 149
John H.: 146
John William: 71
Joseph M.: 145
Keziah: 145
Keziah Anderson: 148
Leonard: 145, 146
Leonard Taylor: 146, 147
Lilly: 147
Luella Jane: 148
Margaret A: 143, 148
Margaret Belinda: 148
Maria: 147
Mariah H.: 147
Martha: 145
Mary: 145
Mary Ann: 71
Mary Elizabeth: 145
Mary Elizabeth: 148
Mary Francis: 148
Mary Jane: 147, 166, 168
Mary Jane: 145
Nancy S.: 146
Orlando Bush: 146
Rachel: 149
Robert: 36, 148
Robert Vinton: 148
Samuel Meredith: 148, 152
Sarah Florence: 84, 149, 176
Sarah Gibson: 145
Sarah Henderson: 148
Sarah White: 147
Serena: 146
Serena W: 147
Temperance: 40
Thomas: 148
Thomas Andrew: 143, 148
Walter H.: 149
Wilbur Micajah: 148
William: 71
William: 146
William: 148
William Riley: 146
William Woodnut: 145

Ellison -
   Victoria W.: 145

Elwood -
   Cathrine Elizabeth: 37
   Margaret: 37

Emack -
   Elbert Grandison: 103

Emily -
   Unnamed: 48
   Unnamed: 83, 176

Emma -
   Unnamed: 121

Ensor -
   Abraham: 170
   Abraham: 170

Alexander R: 56
Ann: 170
Anna R.: 115
Anne Nancy: 56
Ariel Menta: 115
Bettie Florence: 56
Clarence D.: 115
Darby: 168
Darby: 56
Deborah: 170
Delilah: 56
Edward T.: 56
Elijah M.: 56
Elijah S.: 56
Elizabeth A: 56
Elizabeth C.: 56
Elizabeth Chilcoat: 56
Elizabeth Jane: 170
Ellen S.: 162
Emma R.: 104, 115
Eureka Philpot: 56
Frances: 170
George C.: 56
George Frank: 112
George Honor: 57
George W.: 56
George W.: 56
Georgia Honor: 57, 121
Harry: 115
Harry F.: 115
Hazel: 115
Isabell: 115
Isabelle Thelma: 128
James Victor: 56
Jemima: 170
Jemima: 173
John: 170
John Albert: 56
John B.: 56
John Edward: 56
John H: 56
John Hunter: 56
John Lewis: 37
Jonathon Plowman: 170
Julia Ann: 115
Laura Eugnia: 56
Lawerence E: 56
Leroy J.: 56
Luke: 170
Luke: 115
Luke Chilcoat: 56
Luke E: 115
Luke E.: 115
Luke Gorsuch: 56, 57, 168
Lydia: 56
Maggie Ruply: 56
Mary: 170
Mary Beulah: 56
Mary Francis: 56
Mary K.: 56
Naomi: 170
Noah F: 115
Peter William: 115
Rachel: 115

Rachel J.: 56
Robert: 56
Roy C.: 115
Ruth Ann: 56
Sallie: 56
Samuel Edward: 56
Samuel S.: 56
Samuel T.: 56
Sarah: 170
Sarah Ann: 157
Sarah Ann: 56
Sarah Hunter: 56, 168
Sarah J.: 56
Thomas E.: 57
Thomas Reverty: 56
William: 170
William: 115
William G.: 115
William Lewis: 56
William Pinkney: 56

Eton -
   Unknown: 98

Etz -
   Amelia: 135
   Annetta: 135

-
   Euhla Cameron: 104

Evins -
   Unknown: 94

Farlow -
   Elianor: 137

Farnum -
   Unknown: 127

Farrell -
   James: 98

Ferris -
   Jennifer: 96

Fields -
   William: 72

Fife -
   Rebecca Jane: 54

Fisher -
   Henry Boyd: 128

Fitzpatrick -
   Mary: 96

Flagg -
   Drucilla: 60, 62

Flayhart -
   John E.: 66

Fogal -
   Frank: 126
   John J.: 126, 162
   Oscar L.: 126
   Streett Baldwin: 161

Foght -
   Amelia: 111

Forrester -
   Jane: 87

Forwood -
   Jacob Edmund: 127

Foster -
   Absalom: 173

Comfort: 173
David: 173
Eleanor: 174
Eli: 173
Elijiah: 173
Ellen: 173
Francis Rebecca Diven: 110
George: 173
Grace Elizabeth: 173
Harriet: 83, 173, 176
Jemima: 173
John: 173
John B.: 173
John Cross: 173
John Tye: 174
John W.: 173
Joshua: 173
Maria: 173
Mary: 174
Mary: 173
Mileson: 173
Millison: 174
Nancy Ann: 173
Sr Nicholas: 173
Nicholas: 173
Nicholas: 174
Patience: 173
Patience: 173
Patience: 173
Samuel: 173
Sarah Ann: 173
Solomon: 174
William: 174

Fowble -
Unnamed: 175

Frances -
M.: 121

Francies -
Priscillia A.: 125

-
Francis Folsom Cameron: 104
Sarah Elizabeth: 126, 162

-
Frank Cameron: 104

Franklin -
George E.: 165

Frederick -
James N.: 147

Free -
Mary: 59, 61, 64

Freeland -
Abraham: 55
Child: 55
Child: 55
Child: 55
Mary: 82

Friend -
Mary: 45, 48

Fries -
Emily Gertrude: 145

Fugate -
Charlotte: 139

Fuller -
Elizabeth: 138
Elizabeth Ann: 40
Mary Ellen: 138

Fullerton -
Mary A.: 36

Fulton -
Joyce Louise: 186
Thomas B.: 45

Fussell -
Ruthanna: 36

Gaines -
Gladys Lucia: 161

Gallion -
Rachel: 163

Gardner -
Cathrine Ann: 25

Garman -
Ella: 125

Garrett -
Ann: 87
Ann: 150
Benjamin: 150
Benjamin A.: 150
Benjamin Howard: 150
Benjamin Howard: 150
Caroline: 150
Charles Howard: 150
Clara May: 150, 153
Elizabeth: 87
Elizabeth A.: 150
Hester A.: 150
Isaac: 120
Jehu: 150
Joanna L.: 150
John: 150
John: 150
John Amos: 150
John R.: 150
Margaret Ann: 150
Margaret E.: 150
Martha E.: 150
Martha Ellen: 150
Mary: 150
Mary Emma: 150
Mary Patterson: 150
Nancy: 150
Susanna Lavinia: 150

Garretty -
Lucy Kathrine: 35

Garrison -
Alfred Selman: 159
John: 139
Mary Elizabeth: 36

Gatch -
Annie T.: 36

Gemmill -
Ida Ellen: 72
Jennett: 25
John Smith: 47
Martha A: 78
Sarah: 31
Sarah Elizabeth: 78

Gendy -
Unknown: 94

Gent -
Mattie: 47

Gibbs -
McClellan: 78

Gilbert -
Abraham A: 123
Ann Elizabeth: 87
Elizabeth RUTLEDGE: 87
Laura J.: 60, 62
Shadrack Rutledge: 123
Susan Hannah: 60, 62

Gillespie -
Henrietta: 109

Gillis -
David: 122
Elizabeth: 122
Elizabeth: 122
Hannah: 122
James: 122
John: 122
Levinah Sharp: 122
Rebecca: 122
Robert: 122
Sarah: 122
Thomas: 122
William: 122
William Robert: 122

Gillispie -
Jane: 86
Westley: 109

Gilmore -
Anna: 140

Given -
James: 83

Glass -
Mary: 143

Glenn -
William: 123, 159

Gordon -
Agnes: 87
Alexander: 29

Gore -
James: 59, 61
Nancy: 33

Gorsuch -
Ann: 70
Belinda: 36
Belinda: 69
Charles: 36
Charles: 139
Charles: 53, 69, 82
Charles: 70
Charles Thomas: 69
David: 69
David: 70
David: 140
David: 69
Deborah: 170
Deborah: 171
Dickinson: 171
Dorcas: 170
Eleanor: 171

Eleanor: 29, 69
Eleanor: 69
Eleanor: 36
Eleanor: 69
Elisha: 69
Elisha: 53, 63, 82
Elisha: 69
Elisha: 69, 108
Elizabeth: 53, 69, 82
Elizabeth: 69
Frances Amelia: 70
Hannah: 69
Hannah: 69
Hester: 83, 175
John: 170
John: 139
John: 139
John Merryman: 171
John Thomas: 70
John Westley: 53, 69, 82
Joseph: 69
Joseph: 36
Capt Joshua: 171
Laura: 70
Luther Meredith: 36
Martha Jane: 70
Mary: 139
Mary: 69
Mary: 69
Mary Elizabeth: 36
Mary Ellen: 56
Nicholas: 171
Nicholas: 69
Nicholas: 36
Nicholas: 69
Rachel: 69
Rachel: 53, 69, 82
Rachel: 69
Rebecca: 69
Rebecca: 70
Rebecca: 140
Rebecca Ann: 69
Rebecca Ann: 69
Rebecca Ann: 70
Rev REV Thomas: 36
Richard: 171
Robert: 171
Ruth: 70
Ruth: 98
Samuel: 36
Sarah: 177
Sarah: 53
Sarah: 69
Sarah: 109
Sarah: 53, 69, 82
Sarah Ann: 36, 70
Sarah Jane: 69
Stephen: 69
Susannah: 36
Thomas: 139
Thomas: 139
Thomas: 53, 69, 82
Thomas Talbott: 84, 176
Unknown: 71

Wesley M: 36
William: 36
William: 36, 70
William: 69

Gosnell -
Charity C.: 96
Richard: 79, 86

Gott -
Anna Maria: 171
John: 29

Graham -
Nancy: 138

Grant -
James Franklin: 122
Levinah Ellen: 122

Green -
Ariann: 85
Benjamin: 84
Elisha: 138
Elizabeth: 83
Joshua: 82, 83
Matilda: 84
Nancy Ann: 83
Rachael: 47, 83
Rachel: 85
Sarah: 80, 85
Shadrach: 83
Susan: 85
Temperance: 83, 175
Thomas: 84
Thomas: 31
Westley: 83
William: 85

Gross -
Gertrude: 147

Grove -
Alexander Gordon: 31
Cathrine T: 77
Elizabeth: 31
J. Ralph: 128
John: 31
Mary: 31
Minerva: 78
Sarah A.: 54

-
Grover Cleveland Cameron: 104
Abraham: 49
Benjamin: 49
Drusilla: 49
Elizabeth: 49
Jemima: 49
Josiah: 49
Josias: 49
Mary: 49
Sarah: 49

Grubb -
Frances: 168

Gulius -
Lincinda: 59, 61

Gunter -
Anna Barbara: 157

Gwyn -
Ann: 168

Hair -
Charity: 137, 139
Susanna: 137, 139

Haisch -
John Jacob: 173

Hale -
George M.: 110
Thomas: 48

Hall -
Dennille: 45

Hamilton -
Jane S.: 122
Roland: 135

Hammond -
George: 76
Matthew Gilbert: 65

Hampshire -
Cassander: 113
Cathrine: 97

Hamptman -
John: 89

Hampton -
J. Dunham: 70

Hanlin -
Sarah: 140

Hannah -
Unnamed: 64

Hannigan -
Lavina: 96

Hardwick -
Unknown: 126

Hare -
Unnamed: 150
Claude: 100
Jennie: 128
William: 33
William Franklin: 95

Harkness -
Sarah: 71

Harland -
Thomas R.: 171

Harriet -
Unnamed: 112

Harris -
David: 100
James C: 103
Thomas Leonard: 96

Harrison -
Mary Jane: 53

-
Harry Elmer Lytle: 152

-
Harry Gladfelter Cameron: 104

Hartford -
Rachel: 139

Hartman -
Elizabeth: 74

Harvey -
Henry: 72

Harwood -
Jennie: 79, 86

Hawkins -

Mary Jane: 159
Hazeltine -
    Dr Dr Silas Wood: 54
Headington -
    Nancy: 170
Heaton -
    William: 75
Hedrick -
    Unknown: 111
Heffner -
    Edward Jr: 147
Henderson -
    Archibald: 36
    Edgar: 153
    Elinor: 87
    John B.: 147
    John Wesley: 147
    Laura Frances: 135, 152
    Rev Thomas: 36
    Sabra Ellen: 135, 152
    Sarah Ellen: 36
    Susan Elizabeth: 161
    Upton B.: 147
Hendrix -
    Abraham: 81
    Adam: 81
    Adam: 81
    Adam: 81
    Adam Miller: 81, 82
    Agustus: 81
    Assenth: 81
    Daniel: 81
    Darcus: 81
    Dorcus: 81
    Dr Isaac: 82
    Elizabeth: 82
    Elizabeth: 81
    Emma F.: 81
    Hannah: 81
    Hester A.: 81
    Ida L.: 81
    Isaac: 81
    Isaac: 81
    Isaac: 81
    Isabella H.: 81
    Jacob Frank: 81
    John: 81
    John M.: 81
    John W.: 81
    Joseph: 81
    Joseph: 81
    Joseph W.: 81
    Joshua: 81, 89
    Julia: 82
    Laura v.: 81
    Lucretia: 81
    Margaret Maggie: 81
    Margaritta: 81
    Mary Ann: 81
    Mary R.: 81
    Rachel: 82, 83
    Ruth: 53, 82
    Ruth: 82
    Ruth: 81

Sarah A.: 81
Tamer: 82
Thomas: 82
Thomas: 81
Walter: 81
Washington: 81
William H.: 81
Herbert -
    John: 42
    Mary Elizabeth: 88
    Mary Gertrude: 152
Herschner -
    Elizabeth: 108
Hersey -
    Lida E.: 42
    Minnie F.: 73
Hershner -
    William: 69
Hester -
    Eva: 156
    Martha: 156
Hetrick -
    Elizabeth: 59, 61
    Maria Elizabeth: 64
Hey -
    Malinda: 65
Hicks -
    Abraham: 177
    Abraham C.: 177
    Amanda: 177
    Anne Nancy: 177
    Asael: 177
    Charles G.: 177
    Dorcas: 178
    Dorcas: 84, 176, 177
    Elijah: 177
    Elizabeth: 177
    Elizabeth: 177
    Elizabeth E.: 148, 177
    Isaac: 177
    Jacob: 177
    John: 178
    John: 177
    Margaret: 177
    Mary: 177
    Mary Jane: 177
    Mary Polly: 177
    Marys: 177
    Miranda: 177
    Neamiah: 178
    Nehemiah: 177
    Philizanna: 177
    Rebecca: 178
    Rebeckah: 177
    Salathiel: 177
    Sarah: 177
    Sarah Ann: 177
    William: 177
Hill -
    Mary: 128
    William: 137, 139
Hinds -
    Mary Jane: 108

Sarah E: 108
Hitchcock -
    Amelia: 24, 143
    Nancy Anne: 177
    Philizanna: 177
Hobblen -
    Unnamed: 150
Hodgskin -
    Mary: 40
Hoffecker -
    Alma Warren: 186
Holden -
    John: 145
    Joseph: 145
    Melinda: 146
    Sarah L.: 145
Holland -
    John Thomas: 170
    Mary: 137
Hollingshead -
    John S.: 55, 98, 99
    Minnie E.: 115
Holmes -
    Anna: 116
    Charles Clinton: 60
    John Bacon: 159
Hoover -
    Christian G.: 110
    David: 158
    Louise: 111
    Susanna: 157
Hope -
    Ellen: 123
    Hannah Ann: 123, 160
    James D: 123
    Jennett: 31
    Lovisah: 159
    Mary E: 57
    Rachel: 75
Hoshall -
    Eleanor Ann: 33
    Johanna Hampshire: 47
    Lida: 127
Howard -
    Elizabeth: 54
    Maj Charles William: 41, 159
    Richard McGaw: 116
    Sarah Little: 186
Hoy -
    Jacob: 59, 61, 64
Hudson -
    William: 133
Hughes -
    Clemency: 135
    Elizabeth: 133, 134
    Elizabeth Ann: 156
    Hannah: 75, 132
    Sarah Amanda: 152
    Susanna: 137
    William Nelson: 159
Hunt -
    Annie B.: 93
    Cassander: 94

Charles: 93
Charlotte: 94
Elizabeth: 94
Enock: 94
George: 93
Grace: 93
Hannah: 94
Hannah: 93, 112
Henry: 93
Hugh Wilson: 93
John: 94
John Noah: 93
John T.: 93
John W.: 93
Joshua: 93
Julia A.: 93
Levinia: 93, 96
Lizzy: 93
Margaret: 93, 96
Mary: 94
Mary: 93, 96
Matthew: 93
Nancy: 93
Noah: 93
Penelope: 94
Rosie: 93
Ruth: 93
Sarah: 94
Sarah: 93
Susan: 93, 96
Susan: 93
Temperance: 93
Thomas: 93
Thomas: 93
Thomas: 93
Thomas: 93, 96
Tillie A.: 93
Wiley: 94
William: 93
William: 93
William Wiley: 93
Willie: 93, 96

Hunter -
Abraham Curtis: 147
Ann: 166, 168
Ann Rachel: 168
Anna L Marion: 104
Bette: 147
Curtis: 116
Curtis Grubb: 168
Elizabeth: 166, 168
Elizabeth: 53, 63, 82
Ellen: 147
Frances: 168
Frances: 166, 168
Frances Lytle: 104
George: 168
Horace William: 168
Ida Elizabeth: 104
John: 168
John: 168
John Brown: 147
John V: 166, 168
Josephine: 116

Margaret: 124
Margaret: 147
Nathaniel: 168
Peter: 168
Peter Grubb: 132, 166, 168
Peter Grubb: 147, 166, 168
Peter S.: 134
Pleasant: 166, 168
Pleasant C: 147
Rachel: 75, 116, 166, 168
Rebecca Jane: 147
Thomas: 168
Thomas Cameron: 104, 153
Thomas Vaughan: 104, 106, 166, 168
William: 168
William: 168
William: 75, 116, 166, 168

Hurst -
John E: 48

Husted -
Harriet Ann: 186

Hutchins -
Alice: 151
Amanda Zana: 159
Anna: 159
Dewitt Clinton: 143
Elizabeth: 75, 132
Elizabeth: 159
Elizabeth Ann: 41, 159
Elizabeth Ann: 159
Elizabeth E.: 143
Emily Elizabeth: 116
Hannah: 123, 159
Hannah: 123
Hannah: 159
Helen A.: 157
Jacob: 80
Jemima: 128, 159
John Standiford: 159
John Stansbury: 123
Letitia: 75, 132
Lovisia: 159
Lt Richard: 159
Margaret Ellen: 116
Martha Jane: 116
Mary Ann: 159
Mary Hope: 123, 159
Miranda: 103
Nicholas: 159
Nicholas: 24, 143
Nicholas: 159
Richard: 143, 159
Sarah: 159
Sarah: 75, 116, 159
Sarah McGaw: 159
GGGgf Thomas: 159
Thomas: 33
Thomas Ayres: 143
William: 159
William: 117
William: 116
COL William Given: 75, 116
William James: 143

Zana Ann: 159

Hyster -
Jarris: 89, 108

Idel -
Henry: 147
Martha B.: 147
Oro May: 147

Jackson -
Abendago: 83
John Robert: 116
Luella: 45
Rebecca: 45
Sarah: 25

Jameson -
Joseph: 122

Jane -
Unnamed: 72, 89

Jenners -
Mary Amanda: 148

Jennings -
John D.: 145

-
John Gillifillan Bryant: 53

Johns -
Rudolph: 87

Johnson -
Abraham: 24
Edward: 165
Edward Jr: 165
Eleanor: 162
Elizabeth: 24
Elizabeth: 166, 168
Elizabeth A.: 110
Isaac: 24
John: 24
Marie Caroline: 165
Mary Ann: 79
Nehemiah: 24
Rachel: 24
Richard: 24
Sarah: 123
Sarah: 171
Sarah Ann: 177
Thomas: 24
Unknown: 33
Viola: 128
Walter Elmer: 84
William: 24
William: 165

Johnston -
John: 24

Jones -
Dawson Alexander: 186
Jasper: 104
Kirk Dean: 186
Laura V.: 94, 111, 112
Luly M.: 111
Noah Derrick: 186
Shelby Anne: 186
William: 139

Jordan -
Archibald Steele: 45
Benjamin Franklin: 45

Benjamin Franklin: 45
Harriet: 45
James P: 46
John Lawrence: 45
Mary Sophronia: 45
Otho: 46
Rachel Alexander: 46
Rebecca: 45
-
   Joseph S. Cameron: 104
Kaufman -
   Frederick: 79, 86
   Unknown: 87
Kearns -
   Rachel H: 55, 98
-
   Kedelia: 71
Keller -
   Benjamin F.: 45
   Juliet S.: 45
   Mary: 45
   William: 45
   William G: 45
Kemp -
   Elizabeth: 146
   Joseph L.: 147
   Joseph O.: 147
   Margaret V.: 147
   Martha E.: 147
   Mary M.: 147
Kerns -
   Cyrus: 146
   Jacob: 146
   Joseph L.: 146
   Serena: 146
   Stephen Woodruff: 146
Kerr -
   Charles: 126
   Mary: 47
   Mary C.: 103
Keys -
   Martha: 93, 96
Keziah -
   Unnamed: 167
Kidd -
   John: 138
   Julia A.: 93
Kilburn -
   Hannah: 173
Kinstrick -
   Cathrine: 98
Kirkwood -
   Archibald T: 31, 35
   Benjamin: 31, 35
   Dorcas: 31, 35
   George Cairnes: 31
   Hannah: 32
   Hannah: 31
   Hannah: 31, 35
   Isaac Thomas: 31
   James: 31
   James Hope: 31
   Jane: 31

Jane: 31
Jane Ann: 47
Jennett: 31
John Bell: 47
John Henderson: 32, 36
John Henderson: 31
Joseph: 31, 35
Mary Bell: 47
Mary Dorcas: 55, 98
Mary Jane: 31, 35
Nathaniel Calvin: 47
Rebecca: 31
Richard Hope: 31
Robert: 47
Robert: 31
Robert: 47
Robert: 31, 35
Robert: 31, 47
Sally: 31
Samuel Miskimmons: 153
Sarah Ann: 80
Sarah Ann: 31, 45, 48
Sarah E: 31, 35
Thomas S: 31, 35
William: 31
William: 30, 31, 35
William: 31
William: 31, 35, 45, 48
William Henderson: 47
Kirschuer -
   Amilia: 72, 89
Klinefelter -
   Eva: 82
   Mary: 26
Koffett -
   George: 29
Koller -
   Daniel: 77
   Elizabeth: 82
   Isaac: 82
   Peter: 82
Krammer -
   Unknown: 94
Kroh -
   Blanche O.: 81
Krout -
   Adam: 65
   Adam: 64
   Adam Henry: 65
   Alice: 64
   Alice: 64
   Angeline: 65
   Ann: 64
   Ann: 59, 61, 64
   Anna: 64
   Benjamin: 64
   Benjamin F.: 64
   Charles: 64
   Clara Bell: 100
   Colwell: 66
   Dr. Adam Nelson: 59, 61, 64
   Elizabeth: 59, 61, 64, 78
   Elizabeth: 64
   Elizabeth: 64

Elizabeth: 64
Elizabeth: 65
Elizabeth: 65
Ella: 65
Emma: 66
Eve: 66
George W.: 64
George W.: 65
George Wesley: 59, 61, 64, 65
Henry: 64
Henry: 65
Henry: 59, 61, 64
Jacob: 64
Jacob: 64
James: 65
John: 59, 61, 64
John H.: 65
John L.: 59, 61, 64
John Michael: 64
John N.: 64
Joseph: 64
Joseph: 64
Joseph: 64
Keziah: 64
Margaret: 64
Margaret Ann: 53, 63, 65, 82
Maria Elizabeth: 65
Mary: 64
Mary: 59, 61, 64
Mary A.: 64
Mary A.: 65
Mary Ann: 65
Mary Jane: 65
Michael: 64
Michael: 65
Michael: 65
Milton Kelly: 59, 61, 64
Nancy J.: 65
Noah: 65
Noah: 64
Noah: 65
Rachel: 65
Rebecca: 65
Samuel: 64
Sarah Ann: 65
Susan: 64
William: 64
William B.: 65
William D.: 65
Kunkel -
   Julia: 74
   Walter: 37
Kurtz -
   Elizabeth: 77
Lamb -
   Margarette: 56
Lanius -
   Edward Weist: 77
Lattin -
   William: 126
Lavely -
   Mary: 171
Lawless -
   Charles Clarence: 127

    David Oliver: 127
    Elizabeth Margaret: 127
    James Albert: 127
    John Quincy: 109, 127
    John Thomas: 127
    Margaret Elizabeth: 152
    Mary Ann: 127
    Orville Henry: 127
    William Conrad: 109, 127
    William Wilbur: 127

Leaf -
    John: 113

League -
    Joseph L.: 65

Leahy -
    Lydia Ann: 72

Leddy -
    Rebecca: 30, 35

Lee -
    Elizabeth: 24
    Frances Asbury: 71
    John Webster: 71
    John Westley: 71
    Josiah Pearce: 71
    Rachel: 71
    Richard: 77
    Thomas Pearce: 71

Lemmon -
    Alex: 173
    Eleanor: 173
    Eleanor: 170
    Elizabeth Ann: 45
    Miriam: 173
    Miriam: 173
    Sarah Ann: 173
    Thomas: 173

Lentz -
    Reba Vivian: 95

LeSourd -
    Anna Provost: 122
    Benjamin: 70
    Benjamin Jr: 70
    David Gorsuch: 70
    Francis Asbury: 70
    Hannah: 108
    Hannah: 108
    Hannah: 70
    John: 137
    John Westley: 70
    Joseph: 53, 69, 82
    Levi Curtis: 70
    Martha: 70
    Mary Elizabeth: 70
    Nicholas: 69
    Rachel Eleanor: 70
    Samantha Jane: 70
    Sarah: 40
    Sarah: 70
    Stephen: 69
    Susannah: 69

Liddel -
    Elizabeth: 173

Liggett -
    Janett: 45

Limb -
    James: 153

Little -
    Charles: 103
    George: 103
    Thomas: 103
    William G.: 105
    William Hutchins: 84, 176

Lloyd -
    Dr Oliver S.: 128
    Paul: 59, 61
    Sarah: 25

Lochard -
    E C: 148

Long -
    David: 82

Loveall -
    Hannah: 165

Low -
    Maacha: 87

Lowe -
    Catherine: 106
    John Clark: 59, 61, 64
    Joshua: 108
    Julia A.: 64
    Sarah Ann: 177

Luckey -
    Bessie: 153
    Charity Luella: 153
    Clara M.: 104, 153
    Edward T: 153
    Ella: 153
    James B: 153
    ESQ Joshua Guyton: 153
    Laura: 153
    Octavia A: 153
    Virginia: 153

Lummis -
    Frank: 152

Lynch -
    Eleanor: 171

Lyon -
    Matilda: 156

Lytle -
    Amanda Mary: 153
    Amanda Victoria: 152
    Ann Hughes: 152
    Asenath Charity: 153, 156
    Charles: 152
    Charles R: 152
    D Owen: 153
    Edgar Hughes: 152
    Elizabeth M: 152
    Elizabeth O.: 135, 152
    Emma: 152
    Frances Ellen: 73, 153
    J Marche: 150, 153
    James Onion: 152
    Jennie: 152
    Julia P: 152
    Mary Frances: 127, 152
    Mary Francis: 148, 152
    Mary Susan: 153
    May Charlotta: 128
    Nathan: 152
    Nicholas Day: 152
    Nicholas McComas: 152
    Rachel Hannah: 74
    Thomas: 152
    Thomas: 152
    Thomas Grant: 152
    Thomas Winfield: 152
    Wilbur B: 152
    William: 152
    William: 152
    William Clayton: 152

Macabee -
    John W.: 93

Mackey -
    Serena: 104

MaGaw -
    Richard: 41, 159

Magness -
    Georgianna: 122

Magnus -
    Nancy: 79, 86

Margaret -
    Unnamed: 89, 108
    Unnamed: 90
    Unnamed: 94, 112

-
    Margaret Elizabeth Wilgis: 87

Maria -
    Unnamed: 177

Markey -
    Jane: 77

Markland -
    Ida F.: 83, 176

Marsteller -
    Mertyle E.: 128

Martin -
    Eli Emory: 179

-
    Mary: 29

-
    Mary Jane: 72
    Viola: 113

Masemore -
    Charles V.: 104
    William Harrison: 95

Masters -
    Ezekiel: 139

Matthews -
    Agnes Frances: 89
    Cathrine Beall: 72
    Cathrine Hinkle: 73, 89
    Charles: 72
    Charles Lee: 72
    Charlotte: 90
    Comfort Elizabeth: 89
    Davie: 89
    Deborah Ann: 89, 108
    Edward: 89
    Edward: 72, 89
    Edward: 72, 89

Edward Clarke: 89
Eli Free: 89
Elizabeth: 73
Elizabeth: 89
Elizabeth Hinkle: 72, 89
Ezekiel: 72, 89
Fannie Elizabeth: 72
Franklin: 72
George W: 73, 89
Henry: 72
Jarrett: 72
John: 72
John Curfman: 90
John T.: 72
Laura Virginia: 72
Louisa: 72
Mary: 53
Mary E.: 72
Mary Elizabeth: 89
Minnie: 72
Naomi Francis: 90
Rachel: 89
Rachel: 73, 89
Rachel Ann: 89
Rosana: 89
Sarah Jane: 89
Sarah W: 89
Scott P: 72
Silas P: 73
Vanard Osinnern: 72, 89
Westley: 73, 89
William H.: 72
William K.: 72
William P: 72, 89
William T: 89
William Westley: 89

Mattingly -
Anastaqsia: 35

Maul -
Frances R.: 123

Mayes -
Cecelia Lavinia: 84

Mays -
Abraham: 175
Abraham: 175
Charles H: 84, 149, 176
Daniel: 175
Elizabeth Ann: 83, 175
Emory: 175
Fannie G.: 110
Frank: 175
George Albert: 84, 176
George H.: 83, 176
Hannah: 175
Hester J.: 56
Hobart: 110
Howard: 175
Irene Morford: 110
James: 84, 176
Jehu: 175
John: 175
John: 175
John: 84, 176
John C.: 83, 173, 176

John F.: 84, 176
John Pitt: 79, 83, 175, 176
John Pitt: 84, 176, 177
John T.: 83, 176
Joshua Grant: 175
Laura Emma: 110
Lydia: 175
Maranda: 83, 176
Mary: 175
Nicholas Foster: 83, 176
Rachel: 175
Rachel: 175
Rachel Emma: 84, 176
Robert: 175
Robert Harrison: 175
Samuel George W.: 175
Sarah: 175
Sarah Temperance: 84, 176
Sopharine: 83, 176
Thomas: 83, 176
Thomas B.: 175
William: 175
William Henry: 110
William M.: 84, 176

McCann -
Elizabeth Jane: 37, 125

McClung -
Adam: 139
Alice: 145
Grandmother Amanda Zana: 186
Baby: 48
Caleb: 139
Charlotte A.: 87
Elizabeth: 139
Elizabeth: 137, 139
Isaac: 138
GGGgf Joseph: 137, 138
Joseph: 137, 138
Joseph: 137, 139
Margaret: 137, 139
Mary: 139
Mary: 137, 139
Mary Polly: 139
Mordecai: 139
Nancy Ann: 139
Rachel: 139
Rachel: 137, 138
Rebecca: 139
Rebecca: 137, 138
GGGGgf Robert: 138
Robert: 138
Robert: 48, 137, 138
Ruth: 138
Samuel: 139
Samuel Francis: 137, 139
Thomas: 138
Thomas: 138
Thomas R: 137, 139
William: 138

McClure -
Unnamed: 145
Martha: 49

McComas -
Charity: 152

Hannah: 40
John Marche: 75
Nicholas: 75
Priscilla: 40
Unknown: 33
William Glenn: 87

McConnell -
Thomas: 95

McCord -
Mary Ann: 24

McCray -
Rachel: 79

McCubbin -
Elnora: 81

McCullough -
Anne: 33
Charles: 33
Clara: 33
Clara: 33
Dorcas: 33
Franklin: 33
George: 33
Henry C.: 100
James: 33
James H.: 33
James W.: 33
Jane: 33
Lysander: 33
Maria: 33
Martha: 33
Martha: 33
Mary: 33
Mary Ann: 33
Nellie: 33
Sallie: 33
Sarah: 33
Susan: 33
Thomas: 33
Tufair: 33
Vincent: 33
William: 33
William: 33
William: 33

McDonald -
Unnamed: 78
Abraham: 77
Agnes: 81
Amanda Roseela: 78
Anna Ettaworth: 78
Annie H.: 78
Aquilla: 77
Jr Aquilla: 78
Aquilla: 78
Aquilla W.: 77
Barbara A.: 77
Benjamin Gemmill: 78
Carrie Victoria: 78
Elizabeth Jane: 77
Emma G.: 78
Eva: 77
Eva: 77
Grizella Ann: 77
Grizzella A.: 77
Ida Elizabeth: 78

Irene: 78
Jacob M.: 77
James Franklin: 78
John Ross: 59, 61, 64, 77
Julia A.: 77
Laura Mary: 78
Lydia A.: 78
Margaret: 77
Margaret Lillie: 78
Mary: 78
Mary E.: 78
Mary Jane: 55, 77, 98
Nancy R.: 77
Nelson: 78
Priscilla E.: 77
Rachel E.: 77
Richard: 78
Richard: 77
Richard W.: 78
Robert: 78
Robert: 77
Robert Harvey: 78
Samuel M.: 78
William Garretson: 78
William Thomas: 78
Willis R.: 78

MCGAW -
John: 159

McGinnis -
Anne Husted: 186
Beulah Elizabeth: 186
Brett Wayne: 186
Brian Donald: 186
Carroll Milton: 186
David Lee: 186
SISTER Eleanor Elizabeth: 186
Elizabeth Lynn: 186
Jay Carroll: 186
John Michael: 186
Uncle John Tydings: 186
John Wallace: 186
Margaret Louise: 186
Mary Susan: 186
Sarah Luella: 152
Stephen Tydings: 186
Grandfather Tydings Miller: 186
Tydings Owen: 186
Jr Tydings Owen: 186
Wayne Carroll: 186
William Tydings: 186

McGuire -
John: 145

McKeon -
Patrick H.: 55, 98

McLaughlin -
William: 165

McLeod -
Jane Mary: 103

Mcnabb -
Unknown: 151

McPhail -
Louisa: 123

Meads -
Thomas J: 54

Mellor -
Martha E.: 84, 176

Meredith -
Agness: 173
Anne Olivia: 161
Charles Gorsuch: 36
Cora Mildred: 128
Eleanor Nellie: 36
Elizabeth: 36
Elizabeth Bell: 47
Hannah Gorsuch: 32, 36
James Samuel: 42
Macajah: 36
Mary Ann: 36
Micajaha: 36
Nancy Ann: 36
Samuel: 36
Samuel Whitfield: 36
Sarah: 47
Sarah: 83
Sarah Jane: 36, 148
Susan Tipton: 36
Susannah: 36
Thomas: 36
Thomas Coke: 36

Merryman -
Ann: 170
Ann: 171
Ann: 171
Benjamin: 171
Benjamin: 171
Benjamin Rogers: 171
Catherine: 171
Cathrine Jane: 157
Eleanor: 171
Elijah: 170
Elizabeth: 170
Elizabeth: 170
Elizabeth: 171
Elizabeth: 171
Frances: 158
Jane: 170
John: 170
John: 171
John: 171
John: 171
Joshua: 171
Martha: 171
Mary: 170
Mary: 170
Mary: 171
Micajah: 170
Milcah: 171
Nancy Ann: 170
Nicholas: 170
Nicholas: 170
Nicholas: 171
Nicholas: 171
Nicholas Rogers: 171
Philemon: 171
Rebecca: 172
Sarah: 170
Sarah: 170

Sarah: 171
Sarah Rogers: 171
William: 171

Meyers -
Elizabeth: 173

Michael -
Lydia: 89

Middleton -
George M.: 145

Miles -
Abraham: 84
April: 84
Cathrine: 84
Cecilia Lavinia: 84
Clarence D.: 85
Clinton: 84
Dora I.: 85
Elizabeth: 84
Ella M.: 84
Eugene: 84
Florence: 84
Harry: 84
Harry: 84
Herbert: 84
Howard: 84
John: 84
John W.: 84
Joshua: 84
Nelson: 84
Nelson: 84
Otis T.: 84
Rev Nelson Reed: 84
Sarah: 84
Sarah Elizabeth: 84
Tabitta: 84
William T.: 84
Winefred F.: 84

Miller -
Alice: 59, 61
Alice M.: 179
Alverta: 179
Clarence: 179
Courtland L.: 42
Edgar G.: 179
Elizabeth: 108
Elizabeth: 179
Elizabeth: 179
Elizabeth E.: 115
Emma: 83, 175
Frederick Steven: 179
Garsfilia: 179
Hannah Ann: 83, 175
Harry K.: 179
Hezaciah Best: 179
Horace M.: 179
Jesse: 179
John: 179
John: 179
John Grafton: 83, 175
John K.: 55, 98
John R.: 179
Josephine: 161
Laura: 83, 175
Lula: 179

Lydia: 179
Mary: 77
Mary: 179
Mary E.: 179
Milton: 83, 176
Milton Albert: 179
Rachel A: 77
Rachel Jane: 83, 175
Robert: 83, 175
Robert M.: 42
Robert W.: 179
Russell Norris: 179
Sarah: 97
Silas: 83, 176
Stephen: 151
Stephen: 179
Thomas: 179
Thomas: 83, 175
Upton: 179
William E.: 179
William H.: 179
William T.: 179
Zeca A.: 110

MILLS -
Margaret Ruth: 123
Rachel: 79
William P.: 138

Mockbee -
William: 49

Molesworth -
Betti Dawes: 150

Montgomery -
John: 25

Moore -
Bazil: 145
Dr James Reed: 122
Elizabeth: 123
Elizabeth Caroline: 122
James Oscar: 122
James Thomas: 121, 122
Jane: 147
John James: 122
John Thomas: 122
Mary Emma: 122

Morris -
Ada: 95
Alexius: 71
Charles Henry: 95
Charlotte Owings: 41
Clarence Upton: 95
Edwin: 95
Ellenora: 95
Emma: 95
Emma Jane: 71
Ernest A.: 95
Florence V.: 95
George: 95
George Palmer: 95
Harvey: 95
Hattie: 95
Herbert Clinton: 95
Howard K.: 95
John Samuel: 95
John Samuel: 95

John Samuel: 95
Lawrence: 93
Lettie: 95
Lewis: 71
Margaret: 64
Mary: 111
Myrtle Gertrude: 95
Nathan: 71
Oscar: 95
Sarah: 95
Sarah A: 73
Sarah C.: 95
Serina: 95
Sophrona: 71
Stella: 95
1852 Thomas A.: 71
Unknown: 55, 98
Wilbur Oscar: 95

Mortin -
Clarissa: 156

Mossman -
William: 122

Mullally -
Cathrine R.: 145

Muller -
Narcissa Ann: 109

Mundis -
Unknown: 128

Murphy -
Abigail: 47
Charity: 146
Harriet: 146

Murray -
Isabelle: 81
Rebecca: 81

Mutchner -
Ann: 41
Elizabeth: 145
Jarrett: 145
Philip Mckandree: 145
Rachel: 40
Rachel Ann: 145

Nace -
Cathrine: 114
Mary Polly: 114

-
Nancy: 48

-
Nancy: 29
Unnamed: 71

Neal -
Unnamed: 77

Neely -
Mary: 122

Neill -
William: 171

Nelson -
Amanda C.: 150
Amanda Zana: 123
Betaye: 123
Betty: 45
Charles: 124
Elizabeth: 123

Elizabeth: 123
Elizabeth Bowen: 123, 159
Hannah: 123
Hannah Elizabeth: 153
SEN James: 123
James: 123
James H: 124
Jarrett: 123, 165
John: 123
John Hutchins: 123, 165
John Thomas: 153
Joshua: 123
Dr Joshua Nelson: 123
Lovisah Hope: 116
Martha E: 159
Mary: 124
Mary Jane: 123
Nathan: 123
Nathan: 123, 159
Jr NATHAN: 159
Nicholas: 153
Nicholas Hutchins: 123, 159
Richard Hutchins: 123
Robert: 123
Robert: 123, 159
Robert: 124
Robert: 147
Sallie E.: 115
Sarah: 123, 159
Sarah: 123
Sarah: 124
Sarah Elizabeth: 121
Thomas: 123
William: 123, 159
William H: 123

Noland -
Margaret Jane: 161, 162

Norris -
Unnamed: 151
Alice Ann: 144, 151
Althelia: 133
Andrew: 134
Anna Mary: 135
Benjamin: 133
Benjamin: 134
Benjamin P.: 76
Charlotte: 132
Clarence Emory: 128
Clarinda: 134
Daniel: 134
Daniel Treadway: 134
Delia: 132, 135
Dr George: 134
Dr John: 134
Edward: 133
Edward: 134
Edward: 134
Edward Wiley: 128
Eliza: 134
Elizabeth: 75, 132
Elizabeth: 133
Elizabeth: 151
Elizabeth J: 134
Esron Hughes: 134

George Chalk: 133, 134
George Washington: 75, 134
George Washington: 134
Greenberry Wiley: 134
Hannah: 132
James: 133
James W: 134
John: 132
John Stevenson: 159
John Vincent: 133
Jonathan: 133
Jonathan: 134
Joseph: 132
Joseph: 132
Joseph Smith: 132
Mary: 132
Mary: 132
Mary: 133
Mary: 134
Mary A: 134
Mary Miranda: 151
Milford C.: 128
Molly: 151
Nicholas: 134
Nicholas J: 151
Rachel: 132, 166
Rachel Ann: 151
Rebecca: 120, 132
Sophia Charlotte: 133
Susanna: 132
Susanna: 132
Temperance: 133
Thomas: 151
Thomas J Jr: 151
Unknown: 135
Wilbur Paul: 128
William: 75, 132
William: 134
William Henry: 134
William Payne: 78
Willimina: 132

Norton -
Mary Catherine: 186

Norwood -
Elizabeth: 171
Mary: 174

Noswanger -
Unnamed: 146

Nye -
Luxima Chloe: 70

Obitz -
Annie Florence: 126

Olmstead -
Frank: 148

Orrick -
John: 170

Orwick -
Rachel Ann: 59, 61, 64

Orwig -
John: 64

Palmer -
Charlotte: 42
Flora J.: 42

Jemima: 95
Johnsey S.: 53, 63, 82
Sarah A.: 42

Parke -
Davis B.: 103
Mararetta: 103

Parker -
John: 157

Parks -
Sarah M.: 46

Parrish -
Caldwell Henderson: 135
Charles Norris: 135
Clarence Miller: 135
David Edward: 135
Edward: 132, 135
Edward: 136
Edward Moore: 135, 152
Rev Edward N: 135
Eliza Susan: 135
Elizabeth: 137
Elizabeth: 135, 138
Elizabeth: 135, 152
Elizabeth Ireland: 135
Leland: 135
Lillian Edna: 135
Margaret Elizabeth Onion: 135
Mary: 135
Mary Elizabeth: 135
Nicholas Morgan: 135, 152
Norris Bosley: 135, 152
Sabra Ellen: 135
Samuel R Wallace: 135
Thomas L: 135, 152
Walter Henderson: 135
Rev William Caldwell: 135

PARSONS -
Joseph: 85

Passonham -
Sarah: 175

Patton -
John: 24

Paul -
John: 49

Paules -
Margaret: 111

Payne -
GGGgf Benjamin: 133
Dr. Josiah: 159
Elizabeth: 134
Fannie Elizabeth: 78
Jacob Wiest: 77
Mary: 137, 138
Mary Ann: 40
Sophia Charlotte: 135

Pearce -
Abraham: 74
Addie: 127
Alice Virgie: 128
Amanda Jane: 157, 163
Amon: 71
Ann Elizabeth: 157, 163
Annie: 125

Arthur: 74
Arthur: 126
Benjamin: 71
Bertha Eleanor: 128
Bettie: 128
Betty E: 128
Beulah Grace: 128
Blanche: 126
Carrie Estelle: 128
Cassandra: 128
Charles Henry: 157, 163
Charles Leroy: 127
Charles Wesley: 126
Clara Frances: 126
Clarence N.: 128
David: 109, 127
David: 74
David Johnson: 162
David Otho: 127
Dorcas: 71
E. Frank: 126
Eleanor E.: 126
Eleanor Ella: 126, 162
Eliza: 71
Eliza: 74
Eliza Jane: 71
Eliza Moore: 126, 162
Elizabeth: 41, 73
Elizabeth: 161, 162
Elizabeth: 125
Elizabeth: 125, 162
Elizabeth Stabler: 109, 127
Ella: 128
Ella Edith: 126
Elmer: 128
Elva M.: 128
Emaline: 74
Emma: 74
Emma Gertrude: 126
Ethel Lavina: 126
Fannie: 128
Florence: 126
Francis Marion: 157, 163
Frank S.: 74
Franklin S.: 74
George: 128
George T: 127
Gladys Minerva: 128
Goldie Lillian: 128
Grace: 127
Greenberry Wyle: 157, 162
Greenbury Arpheus: 126, 162
Harry Gladden: 127
Ida: 126
Isaac: 74
Isaiah: 71
Isaiah: 71
James S: 71
Jennie: 74
Jessie Viola: 127
John: 72
John A: 162
John Bosley: 152
John C: 71

John Christian: 109, 127
John Cole: 125, 162
John Cole: 125
John Cole: 126
John Crawford: 126
John Hutchins: 129
John Talbott: 127
John Westley: 157, 163
Joseph: 162
Joseph: 40
Joseph: 125, 162
Joseph: 126
Joseph L.: 126
Joseph Wright: 127, 152
Joshua: 128
Josiah: 73, 79, 86
Josiah: 71
Josiah Sparks: 87, 127
Josuha Francis: 116, 128
Laura: 128
Laura E.: 74
Laura Louise: 72
Lavinia: 126, 162
Levi: 72
Levi Nickolas: 72
Levi Wilson: 157, 163
Lieurena: 74
Loula: 129
Lucy A: 156
Luke Wiley: 162
Lydia Beulah: 127
Lydia Jennie: 72
Margaret E: 37, 125, 162
Margaret Ruth: 127
Martha Estella: 126
Mary: 129
Mary A.: 74
Mary Ann: 71
Mary Ann: 125, 162
Mary Ann: 75
Mary Ann: 109, 127
Mary C: 157, 162
Mary Elizabeth: 162
Mary Elizabeth: 127
Mary J: 72
Mary J.: 125, 162
Mary Jane: 126
Mary Virginia: 74
Maude Della: 72
Micajah: 72
Millard Wallace: 128
Minerva: 127
Nancy: 71
Nannie Cathrine Idalvet: 72
Nathan: 71
Nathan: 74
Nathan Hinkle: 71
Nathaniel: 74
Nicholas: 74
Olevia: 127
Peter: 74
Rachel: 163
Rachel: 125
Rachel: 125, 162

Rachel: 109, 127
Rachel Ann: 25
Rachel Elizabeth: 157, 163
Rachel O: 72, 89
Rachel Talbott: 161, 162
Rebecca: 109
Richard Wood: 125
Rufus T.: 126, 162
Ruth T.: 126, 162
Salem: 74
Sallie Ann Fenette: 72
Samuel D: 71
Samuel W: 72
Sarah: 71
Sarah Ann: 71
Sarah Ann: 72
Sarah Ann: 126
Sarah Elizabeth: 74
Sarah Johnson: 162
Sarah Ruth: 109, 127
Silas Wright: 42, 128
Thomas: 71
Thomas: 71
Thomas: 71
Thomas: 72
Thomas: 71
Thomas C.: 128, 159
Thomas Carroll: 128
Thomas Cole: 109
Thomas David: 109, 127
Thomas Emory: 128
Thomas Gott: 125
Thomas J: 129
Thomas Riley: 157, 163
Thomas Wesley: 72
Unknown: 115
Wilbur Scott: 72
William: 79, 125
William: 125, 161
William: 157
William: 74
William: 104
William: 128
William: 74
William Crawford: 162
William Crawford: 157, 162
William Crawford: 126
William H: 72
William H: 128
Capt William Hutchins: 129
William Silas: 126, 162
William Silas: 126
William Slade: 128
William Taggart: 125
Zany Amanda: 126, 162
Zany Amanda: 126

Peeling -
　Eleanor: 104
Perdue -
　Carvel Richard: 116
　Eleanor Ellen Sparks: 116
　Elizabeth: 75, 116
　Elizabeth: 116, 143
　Hannah: 116

　John: 75, 116, 159
　John: 116
　John: 116
　Laban: 116
　Labon: 75, 116, 166, 168
　Mary: 71
　Mary: 41, 75, 116
　Mary Elizabeth: 116
　Mary Slade: 116
　Prudence: 106
　Rachel: 80
　Rachel: 75, 116, 166, 168
　Thomas: 75, 117
　Walter: 75, 116, 132
　Walter: 75, 116
　Walter: 116
　William: 41, 75, 116
　William Thomas: 116
Peregoy -
　Carl: 110
　Silas M.: 110
-
　Peter Grubb Hunter: 147
Peters -
　Mary J: 88
　Robert W.: 146
Phillips -
　May: 37
Philpot -
　Clarissa: 171
Pierce -
　Mary Elizabeth: 79, 86
Piersol -
　Emma Elizabeth: 148
Plowman -
　Ann: 165
　Charles E.: 55, 98, 165
　Henry Ballard: 73, 165
　John: 109
　ESQ Jonathon: 165
　Jonathon: 165
　Jonathon: 165
　Martha: 165
　Mary: 165
　Mary Ann: 123, 165
　Rebecca: 165
　Susanna: 123, 165
Pocock -
　Ann: 98
　Asenath: 99
　Cathrine: 99
　Charity: 98
　Charles Francis: 99
　Daniel Beckley: 99
　Eleanor: 98
　Eli: 98
　Elisha Gorsuch: 99
　Eliza: 55, 98, 99
　Elizabeth Ann: 98
　Elizabeth Matilda: 99
　George W: 99
　Israel: 98
　Israel Putnam: 99

Isreal Beckley: 99
James Franklin: 99
Jr James Franklin: 99
Jemima: 55, 98
Jesse: 98
Jessie Price: 99
Juliet Elizabeth: 99
Keziah: 63, 99
Margaret: 137, 139
Mary: 99
Mary Ellen: 99
Mary Margaret: 99
Rebecca Jane: 99
Rebecca Jane: 99
Ruth Ann: 99

Porter -
Unknown: 143

Poteet -
Sarah: 156

Powell -
Ruell: 24
Sarah E: 109, 127

Presbury -
Ann: 171

Preston -
Lida: 124

Price -
Asbel: 161
Calvin D.: 85
Calvin D.: 85
Cathrine: 98
Eleanor Richardson: 161
Hannah: 127
John Moore: 103

Procter -
Laura: 43, 73

Quigley -
Adaline Frances: 47

Quinlan -
Charles: 116

-
Rachel Ann Lesourd: 108
-
Rachel Jane Elliott: 147

Ramley -
Jemima: 145

Rampley -
Dorcas: 143
Elizabeth: 143
James: 123
James: 103, 123
Mary: 159
Nelson: 123
Robert Nelson: 123
Sarah: 80
Sarah: 79
Thomas A: 143
William: 24, 143
William: 143
William Nelson: 123
William R: 127

Ratcliffe -
William W: 54

-
Rebecca: 80
-
Rebecca Ann: 25

Reed -
Dr Dr J. S.: 116
James: 36
John: 49
Samuel Ferquar: 78

-
Richard McGaw Hutchins: 159

Richardson -
Annie: 43, 73
Charlotte Howard: 60
Cynthia: 59
Cynthia: 59
David: 173
Emma Jamima: 134
Ezekiel J.: 143
Marian Estelle: 186
Mary Emma Taylor: 116

Ring -
Mary Ellen: 156

Riston -
Cassius: 135
Jacob K. P.: 135
John F.: 135
Syphonia: 135

-
Robert Lee Cameron: 104

Roberts -
Lawrence: 153
Marab: 120, 121
Silas: 80, 86

Robertson -
Hannah: 120

Robinson -
Charles: 80
Emma: 47
Florence: 95
Ida: 153
John Calvin: 47
Joseph: 47
Joshua S.: 74, 153
Margaret: 47
Mary Elizabeth: 31, 47
Rachel Blanche: 47
Rebecca Jane: 47
DR MAJ Robert Kirkwood: 47
William: 47
William Thomas: 47

Rockhold -
Elijah: 143
Susanna: 99

Rogers -
Sarah: 170
Sarah: 171
Sarah Elizabeth: 87
Susanna Jane: 36

Rosier -
Abijah: 111
Abijah: 111
Agnes: 112
Alice E.: 112
Amanda: 113
Aquilla W.: 112
Benson D.: 94, 112
Cathrine: 112
Cathrine Kate: 112
Daniel: 112
Dennis: 111
Dennis: 112
Dorcas Ann: 111
Edward: 112
Eliza Jane: 111
Elizabeth: 111
Elizabeth: 111
Elizabeth Ann: 112
Francis M.: 96
George: 111
George Albert: 112
George Washington: 111
Hannah: 112
Hannah Jane: 112
Hannah Jane: 111
Helen Virginia: 179
Hosea: 93, 112
Jacob Elmer: 111
James MacCord: 93, 112
James MacCord: 111
John: 111
John: 111
John: 111
John: 112
John W.: 111, 116
Joshua: 112
Julia Ann: 111
Laura L.: 112
Lewis: 111
Lucinda R.: 113
Margaret: 111
Mary: 111
Mary A.: 112
Mary Ann: 111
Mary Jane: 96, 112
May C.: 112
Moses: 111
Nancy J.: 112
Nicholas Westley: 111
Pleasant Hunter: 112
Sarah Cathrine: 111
Sarah Jane: 60, 62
Susanna: 111
Thomas: 127
Westley: 112
Wiliam: 112
William: 111
William S.: 93, 99, 112
William Thomas: 111

Ross -
Minnie: 146

Royston -
Abraham Riston: 137
Abraham Riston: 137
Caleb C.: 138
Caleb W.: 167
Chester: 104

Cloe Riston: 137, 138
Edward C.: 167
Elizabeth: 138
Jesse: 137
Jesse Riston: 137
Jesse Riston: 135
John: 138
John: 135, 138, 167
John: 137
John E. Riston: 135
John Riston: 137
Jonas: 137
Joshua: 137
Joshua: 137
Joshua: 138
Margaret: 138
Mariah: 137
Mary: 138
Mary Mollie: 104
Moses: 167
Priscilla: 167
Rachel E.: 167
Rebecca Ann: 167
Robert: 138
Ruth: 138
Sarah: 162
Sarah: 137
Sarah Ann: 167
Sarah Elizabeth: 104
Thomas: 138
Thomas E.: 167
Westley A.: 138
William: 138

Ruhl -
William: 93

Rutledge -
Unnamed: 63
Alexander Brady: 54
Alexander Brady: 53
Catherine: 99
Chariety: 99
Cornelia Jane: 54
Elizabeth: 63
Elizabeth: 123
Elizabeth: 99
Elizabeth Ann: 53, 63, 82
Elizabeth Ann: 54
Irene: 53, 54
Jane: 96
Jarrard: 99
Jesse: 99
John Cottrell: 120
John Fife: 54
John Joshua: 43, 73
Joshua E.: 165
Joshua Smiley: 53
Rev Joshua Wells: 53, 54
Julian: 99
Leah Susan: 53
Leah Susan: 54
Mary Frances: 54
Mary J.: 99
Mary L: 53
Mary Louisa: 54

Priscilla Elizabeth: 99
Rufus Franklin: 54
Ruth: 53, 69, 82
Sarah Ann: 53
Sarah Ann: 54
Sarah Grace: 54
Thomas Gorsuch: 53, 54, 82
JUDGE Thomas Gorsuch: 54
William H.: 99

Sager -
Rev A.: 65

Sampson -
Agnes Jane: 54
Anne A.: 96
Clara Ann: 65
David: 53, 63, 82, 167
David: 53, 63, 82
David Hinkle: 65
Deliliah: 120
Edwin Hindle: 53, 63, 82, 96
Eli A.: 96
Eli S.: 53, 63, 65, 82
Elizabeth: 65
Elizabeth: 59, 61, 64, 65
Elizabeth Ellen: 26, 63, 99
Elizabeth Jane: 53, 59, 61, 63, 82
Hinkle E.: 96
Isaac: 63
Isaac: 63, 99
Isaac: 65
Isabelle: 65
John: 65
Levi: 64
Lora F.: 96
Maggie Elizabeth: 65
Mary: 63
Mary: 53, 63, 82
Mary Ann: 65
Mary L.: 96
Michael W.: 65
Neomi: 65
Nicholas: 53, 63, 82
Ruth: 55
Ruth: 53, 63, 82
Ruth Gorsuch: 65
Sara Jane: 65
Sarah: 63
Stephen: 53, 63, 82
Susannah: 63
Unknown: 120

Sanderson -
Unknown: 138

Sarah -
Unnamed: 40
Unnamed: 138

Sater -
Sarepta: 83

Saxton -
Unknown: 139

Scarborough -
Nellie Beatrice: 127

Schrodes -
Julia: 144

Schuppert -
Mary Agnes: 100

Scott -
Cecelia: 147
Esther: 168

Seckrider -
Lenera: 65

Seitz -
Anna Maria: 109
Elizabeth: 134
William: 96

Sellers -
George: 83
Mary: 83

Shane -
Annie Elizabeth: 37, 125
Arthur: 37, 125, 162
Ella Dorcas: 37, 125
Emma Jane: 37, 125
Mary Susan: 37, 125
William F.: 37, 125

Shannon -
Maria: 139

Sharp -
Benjamin: 86
Elizabeth: 122
Hannah: 80, 86
John: 86
John: 86
John: 79, 86
Susan: 24

Shaub -
Kevin Henry: 186
Kieth Daniel: 186
Megan Jane: 186
Robert Henry: 186

Shauck -
Jarrett: 106
William: 106

Shaul -
J. Walter: 115
Julia Ann: 115

Shaver -
Elmer Ellsworth: 100
Susanna: 53, 111

Shaw -
Anne: 151
Daniel: 151
Daniel: 151
Edward P.: 151
Elizabeth: 151
Elizabeth: 151
Harrison: 159
James: 151
Jesse: 151
Joshua: 151
Mary: 151
Nathan: 48
Nicholas Hutchins: 151
T. F.: 147
William: 151
William: 151

Shean Shane -

Elizabeth A: 71
Shearer -
   Martha: 175
Shelley -
   Mary Ann: 138
Shepperd -
   Alice: 161
   Amelia Elizabeth: 161
   Ann: 157
   Ann Elizabeth: 161, 162
   Arthur Henderson: 161
   Catharine Virginia Mota: 161
   Charles Pearce: 161
   Dorothy: 161
   Eleanor Margaret: 161
   Elias: 161
   Elizabeth: 161
   Eva Leona: 161
   Francis: 161
   George: 145
   George Leon: 161
   Greenberry: 161
   Greenbury Pearce: 161
   James: 161, 162
   James Albert: 161, 162
   James Albert: 161
   James Matthew: 161
   John: 161, 162
   John Carroll: 161
   John W.: 161
   John William: 161, 162
   Josephine Millen: 161
   Josiah: 161
   Josias: 161
   Leonard Edward: 161
   Margaret: 161
   Margaret Olivia: 161
   Mary: 161
   Neal: 161
   Rachel Rebecca: 161, 162
   Sarah: 161
   Sarah A.: 125, 161
   Wilmer Daniel: 161
   Wilmer Thomas: 161
Sheridan -
   John E.: 126, 162
Shields -
   Daniel Clayton: 65
Shipley -
   Benjamin: 35
   Charles Edward: 126
   John R.: 29
   Mary Ann: 29, 35
Shock -
   Crawford: 125
   John: 125
   Josephine: 125
   Martha: 125
   Mary A.: 125
   Nicholas: 125, 162
   Nicholas: 125
Shoe -
   Mary: 173

Shrader -
   Elizabeth Ellen: 79
Shunk -
   Mary Jane: 104
Siddall -
   Alvira: 59, 61
Sillik -
   John A.: 65
Simmonds -
   Ed: 153
Simmons -
   Sarah Eliza: 36
Simms -
   Martha Jane: 126, 162
Simpson -
   Edith: 95
   Henry Wickersham: 111
Sinclair -
   William: 132
   Willimena: 132
Singer -
   Rachel: 139
Singrey -
   Anne: 173
Six -
   Alta: 153
   Jeramiah Jerry W.: 42
Skinner -
   Joseph: 104, 106
   Mary E.: 104
Slade -
   Abraham: 41
   Abraham: 40
   Abraham: 41, 73
   Abraham: 116
   Abraham: 153
   Abraham: 73
   Ada: 129
   Alice: 74
   Alice Ann: 73
   Amanda Zana: 41, 159
   Andrew: 40
   Ann: 40
   Ann: 40
   Ann: 41, 75, 116
   Ann: 152
   Ariel: 41, 106
   Bazeleel: 40
   Benjamin A: 116
   Carloline Sparks: 72
   Caroline: 40
   Charles: 153
   Christoper: 156
   Christopher: 41
   Cornelia Victoria: 73, 165
   Creighton: 129
   Delilah: 156
   Delilah Ann: 152
   Della: 153
   E. R.: 73
   Eliza: 40
   Elizabeth: 24, 41
   Elizabeth A.: 73

Elizabeth Ann: 120
Elizabeth Ann: 112, 116
Ella: 152
Ella May: 153
Emma: 153
Emma: 129
Ezekiel: 40
Jr Ezekiel: 40
Ezekiel: 40
Ezekiel: 40
Ezekiel: 40
Fannie L.: 74, 153
Franklin: 73
Franklin: 73
Harvey Milton: 73, 153
Isaac Whitaker: 40
James: 40
James Whitaker: 40
John: 41, 159
John: 41, 75, 116
John: 40
John: 112
John: 116
John Brandon: 162
John J: 73
John Vinton: 54
Josephine: 73
Josiah: 29, 41
Josias: 40
Julia: 153
Laura: 153
Laura Elizabeth: 73
Lemuel: 40
Levi Anderson: 40
Lida V: 153
Madison: 73, 153
Mary: 116, 128
Mary Alverta: 129
Mary F: 152
Micajah: 40
Micajah: 73
Nancy: 40
Nathan: 153
Penelope: 124
Rachel: 40
Rachel: 43, 73
Sallie L.: 73
Sally Ann: 41, 159
Samuel: 40
Seldon: 153
Silas: 73
Stephen: 40
Susanna: 40
Thomas: 40
Thomas: 41
Thomas Jefferson: 40
Van Rensalear: 73
William: 40
William: 80
William: 40
William: 40
William: 152
William: 129
William A.: 73

William Clayton: 153
William Henry: 166, 168
Zana Victoria: 47, 73
Zillah T.: 73
Zora May: 74, 153
Slater -
   Henry: 87
Sly -
   Annabella: 100
Smiley -
   Rachel Bell: 53
Smith -
   Adda E.: 55, 98
   Ann: 171
   Daniel B.: 55, 98
   George A.: 55, 98
   Rachel: 83
   Samuel Hume: 46
   W. W.: 126
Smithson -
   Amelia: 87
   Thomas Poteet: 75
Smyser -
   Margaret: 166, 168
Smyzer -
   Elizabeth: 77
Snoke -
   Mary: 65
Snyder -
   Elizabeth: 59, 61
   Mary Irene Virginia: 72
Souder -
   Daniel: 146
   Lucretia: 146
   Margaret: 146
   Sarah E.: 146
Sparks -
   Aaron: 80
   Aaron: 79
   Annie E: 85
   Aquilla: 79
   Aquilla: 80
   Cassandra: 80, 86
   Cecilia: 85
   Daniel Collett: 79, 157
   Edward A: 79
   Elijah: 79
   Elijah Brown: 80
   Elizabeth: 79, 86
   Elizabeth: 80, 86
   Elizabeth: 79, 80
   Francis: 79, 86
   Francis: 79
   James: 80, 86
   John Sheppard: 157
   John T: 79, 86
   Josiah: 79
   Josiah: 79, 86
   Josiah Alfred: 157
   Josias: 79
   Josias L: 79
   Laban: 80, 85
   Laban: 85

Lemuel: 80, 86
Leonard: 80, 86
Levi: 157
Levi: 80, 86
Mary: 79
Mary: 79, 86
Mary Elizabeth: 147
Mary Ellen: 147
Matilda: 85
Matthew: 80, 86
Matthew: 79
Penelope: 79, 86
Penelope: 80
Penelope: 80, 86
Prudence: 79, 86
Rachel: 85
Rachel: 80
Rachel Annie: 156
Rachel Elizabeth: 79, 156
Reverdy B: 85
Richard B: 85
Ruth: 80
Ruth: 79, 125
Ruth: 80, 86
Ruth: 73, 79, 86
Sarah: 80
Sarah E.: 79, 176
Shadrach Green: 85
Shadrack Green: 85
Thomas: 80
Thomas: 79
Thomas: 80
Thomas: 79, 86
Walter: 80
William Curtis: 157
Wright: 79, 86
St. Clair -
   Elizabeth Jane: 40
   James: 76, 132
Stabler -
   Adam: 108
   Adam Joseph: 109
   Alfred Griffith: 108
   Ann Elizabeth: 109
   Anna Mary: 109
   Benjamin L: 108
   Charles: 109
   Christian: 108
   Christian: 108, 109
   111 Christian: 108
   V1 Christian: 108
   Daniel: 108
   Daniel: 89, 108
   Daniel E: 109
   Daniel F: 108
   Edmund: 109
   Elisha: 109
   Elizabeth: 109, 127
   Elizabeth: 109
   Elizabeth Ann: 109
   George: 55, 98, 108, 167
   George Washington: 108, 167
   Henry: 108
   Henry: 108, 167

Hester Ann: 109
Jacob: 89, 108
Jarred: 89, 108
John: 108
John: 108
John: 109
John W: 108
Kathrine Maria: 128
Margretta: 109
Mary Ann: 108
Mary Ann: 108
Moses C: 108, 167
Rachel Ann: 108, 167
Rebecca: 108
Rebecca Ruth: 108, 167
Sarah: 89, 108
Sarah Elizabeth: 108, 167
Sarah Elizabeth: 69, 108
Sarah Jane: 109
Stephen G: 108
Susanna: 109
Thomas: 108
Thomas William: 109
William: 89, 108
Staley -
   Amanda D.: 145
Standiford -
   Annie Elizabeth: 96
   Benjamin: 96
   Charity Ann: 93, 96
   Charles Arthur: 96
   Charles Henry: 72
   Clement: 96
   Elizabeth Celesta: 96, 99
   Giles D. M.: 97
   Henry K.: 60, 62
   Howard T: 97
   J. Milton: 96
   James: 60, 62
   James A.: 96
   John: 96
   John C. B.: 96
   John C. R.: 96
   John R.: 96, 99
   John W.: 60, 62
   John William G.: 97
   Joshua: 96
   Joshua P.: 96
   Joshua P.: 96
   Joshua R.: 96, 112
   Kyantha Nancy: 96
   Marie: 96
   Mary: 96
   Mary Frances: 96
   Mary Jane: 53, 63, 82, 96
   Philiszana Standeford: 159
   Priscilla Elizabeth: 96
   Sarah Jane: 96
   Thomas E.: 60, 62
   Unknown: 65
   Vincent: 96
   Vincent: 97
   Vincent: 96
   William Bond: 60, 62

William F.: 96
William T.: 97
Stansbury -
    Arienna Sollers: 171
    Clara M: 128
    Darius: 170
    Martha Charlotte: 45
Starbuck -
    Esther H.: 70
Steckel -
    Ellen Jane: 146
Sterling -
    Elizabeth Ann: 84, 176
    Robert Henry: 29
    William: 25
Sterrett -
    John K.: 145
    Mary Creighton: 40
    Robert C: 156
Stevenson -
    John: 163
Stewart -
    George: 153
    Joseph: 85
    Susannah: 85
Stiff -
    Nancy Gail: 186
Stiffler -
    Isabelle: 104
    Peter: 139
Stiltz -
    Cathrine: 167
Stowers -
    Mary Emeline: 75
Stratton -
    Unknown: 45
Strawbridge -
    Aquilla McDonald: 77
    David: 70
    Eleanor: 70
    Franklin Pierce: 77
    Henry Manifold: 25
    John B.: 77
    John Clarkson: 77
    Joseph: 70
    Joseph B.: 70
    Joseph Ross Esq.: 77
    Louisa M.: 77
    Martha: 70
    Mary: 70
    Mary Ellen: 77
    Rachel Ann: 77
    Richard A: 77
    Sarah Jane: 77
    William: 70
Strayer -
    Cristina: 65
    Nicholas: 65
Streett -
    Martha: 137
    Martha Elizabeth: 123
    Oscar Vernon: 127
    Shadrach: 56
Strickler -
    Edgar: 148
    Lewis: 148
Stritehoff -
    Elizabeth Ann: 31, 35
Stromenger -
    Charles: 124
Stump -
    Anna Mary: 114
    Unknown: 111
Sullivan -
    Benson C.: 167
    William: 167
Sumerwalt -
    John: 80
Sumwalt -
    Jacob: 81
Sutton -
    Abram: 53, 69, 82
    Albritt: 156
    Ann: 29
    Ann: 29
    Benjamin: 29, 35
    Benjamin Doran: 35
    Cathrine: 29
    Christopher: 29
    David: 156
    Elizabeth: 29
    Francis Joshua: 35
    Henry Adams: 29
    James Alfred: 35
    John: 29
    John Bennet: 35
    John Liquori: 35
    Sr Joseph: 29
    Jr Joseph: 29
    Joseph: 29
    Joseph: 29, 35
    Joseph: 35
    Lawrence I.: 35
    Maria: 35
    Marianna B.: 35
    Mary: 25
    Mary Ann: 35
    Mary Dorcas: 30, 31, 35
    Mary E.: 35
    Mordecia: 29
    Nicholas: 29, 35
    Jr Nicholas: 35
    Queen Mary: 115
    Rachel Ann: 35
    Ruth: 29
    Ruth: 25
    Sarah: 29, 163
    Thomas: 29, 35
    Thomas: 30, 35
    Thomas: 35
    Thomas L.: 35
    Virginia H.: 35
    William: 29
T. Ensor -
    Joseph: 56
Talbert -
    Eliza: 71
Talbot -
    Mary: 132
Talbott -
    Anna Louise: 110
    Benjamin: 170
    Jeremiah: 49
    Mary: 86
    Mary: 171
    Penelope Rutledge: 123
    Richard Colgate: 49
    Thomas: 171
Talley -
    Kathrine: 145
Tandry -
    Safronia: 148
Tatham -
    Mary E.: 147
Thomas -
    Alverta Virginia: 57
    Mary Maudice: 115
Thompkins -
    Winnie: 152
Thompson -
    Aquillia: 137, 138
    Archibald Purdy: 31
    Archibald Purdy Jr: 31
    Carie Ann: 175
    Elizabeth: 31
    Hannah: 31
    James: 31
    Joseph: 31
    Margaret: 31
    Robert A: 31
    Sarah Anderson: 31
    William: 31
Thorne -
    Charles O.: 104
Through -
    Cathrine Jane: 111
Tipton -
    Clara E.: 73, 153
    Jane: 177
    Lee: 172
    Rosanna: 40
    Samuel Slicer: 147
    Sarah: 36
    Temperence: 40
Todd -
    Rosanna: 24
Tompkins -
    Mary Unknown: 25
Trabert -
    Bessie: 100
Tracey -
    Unnamed: 150
    Agnes: 113
    Alfred: 113
    Amanda: 113
    Amos: 113
    Anna Mary: 114
    Annie: 113
    Arthur: 114

Belinda: 113
Benjamin Preston: 114
Cathrine: 114
Crayton Salem: 113
Curtis: 114
Daniel: 114
Edward Amos: 114
Edward M.: 90
Eli: 113
Elias: 113
Eliza: 111
Elizabeth: 114
Elizabeth Betsy: 113
Ellen: 114
Ellen: 114
Emmanuel E.: 113
Geneva: 113
George: 114
George Washington: 113
Gilson: 114
Goldie C.: 114
Harry E: 113
Henry: 114
Herbert Clarence: 113
Jacob: 114
James: 114
James: 114
James Franklin: 113
James H.: 113
James Westley: 114
Jasper Newton: 114
Jesse: 113
John: 114
John: 114
John: 114
John: 113
John David: 113
John F.: 113
John M.: 90
John Taylor: 114
Justis Wilson: 114
Laura: 114
Mable V.: 114
Margaret E.: 114
Mary Elizabeth: 113
Mary Elizabeth: 114
Matha Ellen: 113
Micajah: 90
Michael: 114
Nelson: 114
Nora D.: 114
Oliver H.: 114
Peter: 114
Pleasant S.: 113
Rose W.: 175
Salem: 113
Salem N.: 114
Samuel Eaton: 113
Samuel S.: 114
Sara Elizabeth: 175
Sarah: 89
Sarah: 90
Sarah: 114
Sarah: 113

Sarah Jane: 114
Serena: 114
Susan: 33
Susan: 114
Susanna: 113
Thomas Edward: 114
Unknown: 82
Walter C.: 113
Walter H.: 114
William: 113
William Arthur: 114
William W.: 90
Treadway -
  Clarenda L.: 36
  Daniel T.: 75
  Eleanor H.: 152
  John H: 75
  Sarah Ann: 69
  Unknown: 75
Trone -
  Mary Louise: 59, 61
Trout -
  Cora Elizabeth: 42
Turnbaugh -
  Alice Virginia: 110
  Anna May: 110
  Annie M.: 110
  Annie Mable: 110
  C. Edna: 110
  Calvin: 110
  Charles Franklin: 110
  Clarence Walter: 110
  Cora M.: 110
  Edward Allen: 110
  Edward Grant: 110
  Elizabeth: 150
  Elmer: 110
  Emory P.: 110
  Ernest Johnson: 110
  George Westley: 110
  Gilbert: 110
  Harry Ned: 110
  Helen: 110
  Isaac: 110
  Isaac Newton: 110
  Jacob C.: 110
  James Stanley: 110
  James Walter: 110
  Leroy: 110
  Margaret: 110
  Marie: 110
  Mary Louise: 110
  Nancy Ann: 150
  Sara Mildred: 110
  Vesta Elizabeth: 110
Turner -
  Dr Dr Frank: 57
  Eleanor: 103, 123
  Eli: 57
  George Washington: 103
  Capt James: 103
  Maj James Calder: 103
  Margaret: 103
  Martha: 103

  Mary Ann: 103
  Miranda: 103
  Rachel: 103
  Samuel A.: 43, 73
  Sarah Ellen: 57
  Thomas Kurtz: 103
Tutwiller -
  Unnamed: 138
Tyrrell -
  James: 133
Uhler -
  Mary W.: 104, 106
Unkmown -
  Elizabeth: 89, 108
  Elizabeth: 73
Unknown -
  Unnamed: 71
  Unnamed: 96
  Unnamed: 36
  Unnamed: 81
  Amanda: 111
  Ann: 168
  Ann: 137
  Ann: 53
  Annie: 112
  Annie M.: 115
  Barbara: 84, 176
  Cathrine: 175
  Della: 59, 61
  Dorthea H.: 48
  Eizabeth A. B.: 87
  Eliza: 111
  Eliza Jane: 82
  Elizabeth: 35
  Elizabeth: 93
  Elizabeth: 33
  Elizabeth: 139
  Elizabeth: 60, 62
  Elizabeth: 33
  Elizabeth E.: 42
  Ellen V.: 93
  Fannie A.: 83, 176
  Frances A.: 147
  Hanna: 93
  Hannah: 165
  Hannah E.: 73
  Harriet: 84, 176
  Jane: 81
  Julia A.: 175
  Katie M.: 42
  Lena K.: 135
  Lottie C.: 175
  Maggie P.: 115
  Margaret R.: 93
  Maria: 81
  Martha: 33
  Martha E.: 84
  Mary: 138
  Mary: 29
  Mary: 33
  Mary Ann: 111
  Mary E.: 167
  Mary E.: 72
  Mary F.: 84, 176

Mary J.: 89
Mary J.: 114
Rachel: 111
Rachel A.: 78
Rachel A.: 60, 62
Rebecca: 132, 166
Rosanna: 42
Rose E.: 84
Sara E.: 115
Sarah: 179
Sarah: 36
Sarah E.: 111
Sarah J.: 78
Sarah L.: 113
Sarah V.: 147
Sarepta: 179
Sophia S.: 71
Tabitha: 137
Tilitha: 135
Tracey B.: 25
Tresa: 78
Virginia: 84

Varney -
   Asenath C.: 145

Vaughan -
   Abraham: 75, 132, 166
   Benjamin: 132, 166
   Cathrine: 166
   Elizabeth: 132, 166, 168
   Francis: 166
   Gist: 132, 166
   John: 132, 166
   John: 166
   Rachel: 132, 166
   Rachel: 166

Vaughn -
   Gist: 132, 166
   Pleasant: 166

Verry -
   Caroline: 103

Vogan -
   Ann: 40

Waddham -
   Elizabeth: 24

Wadlow -
   Elleanor: 93

Wadsworth -
   Unknown: 151

Waggner -
   Grace: 85

Wagner -
   Blanche Elinor: 110

Waldow -
   Nancy: 71

Walker -
   Catherine: 106
   Christopher: 173
   Christopher: 106
   Daniel: 106
   Daniel: 106
   Edward B.: 173
   Edward M.: 105, 106
   Elizabeth Jane: 100

Hannah: 100
John: 173
John: 106
Joseph: 106
Mary: 106
Rachel: 104, 106
Sarah: 104, 106
Thomas: 36
Walter Coleman: 41, 106

Wallace -
   Aunt Beulah Annetta: 186
   Margaret B: 135, 152

Wallingford -
   Bailey: 55, 98

Waltemire -
   Eliza Jane: 60, 61

Waltermire -
   Susan: 64

Walters -
   Charlotte D: 53

Wantland -
   Jane: 89
   Mary: 81, 89
   Rachel: 89
   Thomas: 89
   Thomas E.: 89
   Westley Joseph: 89

Ward -
   William: 153

Warhorn -
   Elizabeth: 25

Warner -
   Mary E: 26

Watkins -
   Eliza: 47

Watson -
   Mary: 25
   Mary Alice: 161

Watts -
   Sarah: 177

Weaver -
   Sarah H.: 35

Webb -
   Julian: 87

Wetzel -
   Annette Sophie: 126

Wheeler -
   Addie: 56
   Austin: 135
   H. Edward: 135
   James Austin: 135
   Mollie: 148
   Unknown: 135
   Unknown: 135

Whieley -
   Unnamed: 150

Whitaker -
   Ann: 40
   Shannan: 186

Wiers -
   Delilah: 123
   Squire Henry: 121

Wiley -
   Ann: 93
   Caroline Bradford: 45
   Caroline Missouri: 124
   Comford: 163
   James R.: 78
   Capt John: 159
   John: 144
   John Calvin: 77
   John Stephenson: 29, 163
   Joshua C: 163
   Malcolm Fields: 37
   Mary: 133
   Mary Elizabeth: 134
   Mathew William Nelson: 47
   Thomas Sutton: 29, 163
   Vincent: 29, 163
   William: 29, 163

Wilhelm -
   Louisa Jane: 95
   Lydia S.: 175
   Margaret Ann: 83, 176

Williams -
   Bessie Lillian: 37
   Cathrine: 113
   Dorothy Dorcas: 111
   Elizabeth: 113
   Frank: 113
   Gibson: 113
   Harry: 127
   Harry Benton: 60, 62
   Jacob: 113
   James: 113
   Laura: 113
   Lorena Jennie: 60, 61
   Nelson: 113
   Rachel: 113
   Richard: 113
   Sarah: 113
   Susan: 113
   Thomas: 113
   Thomas Jr.: 113
   Victor: 113

Williamson -
   Ann Elizabeth: 126
   Elizabeth J: 108
   Riley Seth: 126, 162
   Susie: 108

Wilmont -
   Benjamin: 170
   Eleanor: 170
   John: 170
   Mary: 170
   Richard: 170
   Robert: 170
   Robert: 170
   Ruth: 170
   Sarah: 170
   William: 170

Wilson -
   Abraham: 43, 73
   Abraham: 43, 73
   Alyce Irene: 113
   Annie F.: 42

Annie Mary: 43, 73
Benjamin Franklin: 42
Caroline M.: 36
Cornelius: 100
Daniel: 100
David: 42
David: 43, 73
David Bartene: 42
David Hutchins: 43, 73
David Hutchins: 43, 73
Delilah: 100
Dr Thomas M.: 60, 62
Ebenezer: 43
Edith: 43, 73
Edwin: 42
Eli: 100
Eli Daniel: 100
Elizabeth: 43
Elizabeth: 100
Elsie Norris: 113
Emanuel: 93
Emma Irene: 93
Ephriam: 42
Fannie: 42
Frank Lindsay: 100
Frank P: 43, 73
George: 42
George W.: 100
Grace Annie: 100
Hannah: 73, 89
Harvey Nelson: 42
Jackson: 157
James: 137, 139
James: 42
James A.: 42
James Standiford: 42
Jane: 114
Jane: 42
Jane: 42
Jane Alice: 42
Jean: 42
John: 42
John: 42
John T.: 100
John W.: 100
Josephine: 42
Katherine: 100
Laura Victoria: 42
Leah L.: 93
Margaret E.: 100
Margaret Jane: 100
Martha: 42
Martha E.: 42
Mary: 42
Mary: 100
Mary Ann: 100
Mary Frances: 42
Milton: 42
Minnie Ida: 42, 128
Nancy: 139
Nellie Pauline: 100
Robert G.: 42
Salie A.: 148
Samuel Young: 100
Sarah: 42
Sarah E.: 42
Silas: 100
Thomas: 100
Thomas: 42
Thomas W.: 100
William: 43
William: 90
William: 42
Young Owen: 116
Zane Ann: 43
Zora: 42
Zora: 43, 73

Wink -
Elmer: 148

Wise -
John Jr: 166, 168
William H.: 177

Wisner -
Daisy V.: 179
Martha E.: 179
Sarah: 157

Withers -
Charlotte: 103
Edwin: 103
Michael: 103
Susan: 103

Wolf -
Caroline V.: 146

Wolfgang -
Dora A.: 150
Solomon: 150

Wood -
Sarah Achia: 125, 162

Wright -
Blois: 86
Bloys: 86
Caleb: 87
Cassandra: 79, 86
Cassandra: 87
Charlotte Stevens: 125
Daniel S: 87
Elizabeth: 86
Elizabeth Ann: 87, 127
Elizabeth D: 87
Emily: 87
Emory P.: 87
Rev Henry Slicer: 87
Isaac: 86
James: 86
James Lawrence: 87
Jane: 86
Johanna: 87
Jr John: 87
John G: 86
John Talbott: 87
John W: 87
John Wesley: 88
Joshua Low: 87
Joshua Wells: 87, 88
Mary E: 87
Mary Farnandis: 87
Mary Talbott: 86
Matthew: 86
Nathan: 86
Prudence: 80, 86
Ruben T.: 42
Sarah: 86
Sarah Ann: 87
Susanna: 87
Thomas: 86
Thomas: 87
Thomas: 87
William: 87
William: 87
William: 87
William: 87
William: 87
William: 88, 143

Wyle -
Agnes: 79
Andrew: 29, 163
Comfort: 80
Comfort Rebecca: 162
Esther: 163
Greensbury: 163
Hannah: 163
John: 163
Joseph Dunnuck: 163
Joshua: 163
Luke: 162
Mary: 133
Mary: 163
Sarah: 29, 163
Walter: 132
Walter: 163
William Benjamin: 162

Yambert -
Caroline: 111

Yarema -
Carah Elizabeth: 186
Carl John: 186
Nef Carl John Jr: 186
Christopher Thomas John: 186
Niece Elizabeth Carol: 186

Yarison -
Raymond: 128

Yealdhall -
Cathrine Elizabeth: 186

Yeargain -
Edward A.: 109, 127

Yost -
Rachel Klingman: 81

Young -
Ariel: 100
Eliza Emma: 100
Randolf: 89

Zouck -
George: 127

Zubrowski -
Unknown: 126